Early Professional Baseball
in Hampton Roads

Early Professional Baseball in Hampton Roads

A History, 1884–1928

Peter C. Stewart

McFarland & Company, Inc., Publishers
Jefferson, North Carolina, and London

LIBRARY OF CONGRESS CATALOGUING-IN-PUBLICATION DATA

Stewart, Peter C.
Early professional baseball in Hampton Roads :
a history, 1884–1928 / Peter C. Stewart.
p.   cm.
Includes bibliographical references and index.

ISBN 978-0-7864-4808-1
softcover : 50# alkaline paper ∞

1. Baseball — Virginia — Hampton Roads (Region) — History.
2. Norfolk Mary Janes (Baseball team)   I. Title.
GV863.V82.S84   2010   796.357'64097555 — dc22   2010021401

British Library cataloguing data are available

©2010 Peter C. Stewart. All rights reserved

*No part of this book may be reproduced or transmitted in any form
or by any means, electronic or mechanical, including photocopying
or recording, or by any information storage and retrieval system,
without permission in writing from the publisher.*

On the cover: Team photograph of the 1900 Norfolk Mary Janes
(National Baseball Hall of Fame Library, Cooperstown, NY)

Manufactured in the United States of America

*McFarland & Company, Inc., Publishers
Box 611, Jefferson, North Carolina 28640
www.mcfarlandpub.com*

Table of Contents

Acknowledgments	vi
Preface	1
1. Early Sports in Hampton Roads	3
2. Professional Baseball Comes to the City by the Sea	7
3. The Virginia League, 1894–1896	20
4. Agony in the Atlantic League, 1897–1898	44
5. Hampton Roads at the Turn of the Century, 1900–1901	58
6. The Era of the Dead Ball, 1906–1910	72
7. "The Tide of Victory Ebbs and Flows," 1911–1914	100
8. Mary Jane at Low Tide, 1915–1918	123
9. Stormy Seas, 1919–1923	147
10. Final Voyages, 1924–1928	182
Epilogue	219
Appendix: Leagues and Standings	225
Chapter Notes	239
Bibliography	247
Index	249

Acknowledgments

All historians are indebted to a host of librarians, archivists, and fellow historians. In my case, Stuart Frazier at Old Dominion University secured microfilm from numerous places. The staff in the microform room at the university had to put up with my constant use of the readers and requests for help. The same may be said about the folks at Norfolk's downtown library, especially in the Sargeant Memorial Room. Troy Valos worked on the photographs from the library's collection and traced elusive information. Pat Kelly found several pertinent photos at the National Baseball Hall of Fame Library in Cooperstown, New York. Those who preserve and make available the documents of the past are very important, but I would be remiss not to mention the several hundred students I have taught over the years who have had to listen to me talk incessantly on sports in American life. Jim Ducibella, a retired sportswriter, helped to improve the writing and Elaine Dawson worked her magic with her computer to prepare the manuscript.

My friend Tom Garrett also should be mentioned, as he and I share a mutual love for the national game and its idiosyncrasies. Tom's ties with the Baseball Hall of Fame produced leads, as did his persuading me to join the Society for American Baseball Research. A committee of that society working on minor league baseball is gathering material for an existing website. It already contains some players' names that proved useful to me. I have turned over the individual statistics concerning the Norfolk club to that website (http://www.baseball-reference.com/minors). The existence of this site means everyone will have an ever-increasing supply of details at their fingertips and I don't need to include a 60-plus page appendix in this book. This tool should eventually allow researchers to trace the minor-league careers of nearly all players. My thanks go to Kevin McCann and his colleagues for creating the website and giving me permission to notify readers of its existence.

I owe the greatest debt to the hundreds of young men who played minor-league baseball for Norfolk and other Virginia and North Carolina cities, and the reporters who recounted their exploits.

Preface

This book relates the story of professional baseball in Hampton Roads, Virginia, between 1884 and 1928, the year the Virginia League disbanded. In ferreting out this story, I have relied mostly on information from local newspapers and, to a lesser degree, from national magazines. Citation notes have been mostly used for quoted material or for information that did not follow the natural course of each baseball season. As far as can be determined, few players left reminiscences, and business records apparently have not been preserved. Secondary sources noted in the bibliography provided background about the rise of baseball on both national and local levels. Others gave leads and supplementary material about the hundreds of players who passed through Virginia and North Carolina. A brief history of the Virginia League, written several years ago, contains some data.

Gathering accurate statistical material has proved quite troublesome. Although I originally did not plan to emphasize numbers, I soon became absorbed with trying to set straight the statistical record. In wading through the data, I often found that individual numbers were either transcribed or calculated inaccurately in both national magazines and local newspapers. Errors or discrepancies appear in season-ending statistical reports as well as reporters' accounts of particular games.

The real names of players also vary. For example, a player and manager of some prominence in local lore, Win Clark, had his name appear in print as "Winn Clarke," "Win Clarke," "Winn Clark," "Wyne Clark," in addition to the one that finally won out. At the time of his death in 1959, it turned out his full name, was William Winfield Clark, but his first name had never appeared in any account of his activities. Most reporters avoided using the first names of the majority of players, although they often employed a nickname. In addition, players gave false names in signing contracts or management gave out the wrong information. Lacking the official scorecards from each game and sufficient genealogical material, many questions remain.

Equally disconcerting was the lack of precise information on the scribes who produced accounts of games, as well as columns filled with gossip about the sport. If the reporters often did not bother to find out the first names of many of the players, they were even more secretive about disclosing their own names. Sometimes in engaging in a war of words with a reporter for another newspaper, they mentioned a rival's name, but the routine use of a byline did not occur locally until the 1920s.

These reporters doubtless had fun taking literary jabs at some of those they wrote about rather than seeking objectivity. Reporters certainly did not feel constrained in criticizing players, managers, umpires, fans, or even owners. Newspapers in those far off times did not adhere to today's political correctness. Yet, with an occasional major exception, criticisms were free of blatant ethnic and racial slurs.

Reporters turned out to be an essential element in this story. They reflected their cultural milieu in commenting on the games and the actions of individual players. In addition, newspapers hired cartoonists who also mirrored the culture of the time. Even poetry — if one is quite generous with that label — appears from time to time.

Stopping the story in 1928 may seem arbitrary, but reporters ceased referring to the *Mary Jane* in the 1920s. Even though the Virginia League resumed after its disbanding in 1928, it did not have representation from Norfolk or Portsmouth. In the not too distant future I hope to relate the story of the Norfolk Tars in the Eastern League (1931–1932) along with the record of Norfolk, Portsmouth and Newport News in the Piedmont League (1934–1955).

The book provides some details about controversies related to the business end of baseball, such as disputes among league teams or the relationship to major league clubs before the ascension of the official farm systems. This study delves into failed efforts to persuade Virginians to ease up on laws against playing professional baseball on Sunday.

1

Early Sports in Hampton Roads

In 1896, a reporter for a national magazine called *Sporting Life*, noticing how much fun local professional baseball players were having as they toured the waterways of the Norfolk area in a sloop, dubbed them the "Jolly Tars." The name originated in America's colonial past when sailors were often called "Jack Tars," because they often exhibited the coloration of the tar they worked with on sailing ships. In this case, the reporter also highlighted the name of the sloop, the *Mary Jane*. And so the sailors became the "Crew of the Mary Jane." Once the name caught on in the early years of the 20th century, reporters wrote about the start of several baseball seasons as if the players were about to embark on a voyage, with potential members of the crew greeted by the ship's captain as they came on deck. So far as is known, reporters failed to create an imaginary ship's log to report each voyage on a daily basis, but the nautical image reflects the essential nature of Hampton Roads or what some call the "Lower Tidewater."

This book focuses on Norfolk and four other Hampton Roads communities — Portsmouth, Hampton, Newport News, and Suffolk — all of which had teams in the Virginia League at various times. The area was the recipient of English culture, a trend starting in the early 17th century and continuing long after the end of the colonial era. Settlers in lower Virginia carved out a rural life based on farming, fishing, shipping and shipbuilding. By the middle of the 18th century, the small community of Hampton emerged on the north side of the roadstead of Hampton Roads, at the confluence of the Chesapeake Bay and the James River, while the much larger borough of Norfolk arose on the Elizabeth River, an estuary south of the Roads. A commercial center that relied heavily on trade with the West Indies and North Carolina, Norfolk eventually grew into the largest community in colonial Virginia, with smaller Portsmouth arising later, south of the Elizabeth, across the harbor from Norfolk. West of the Roads at the head of navigation of the Nansemond River emerged the town of Suffolk, a center for naval stores.

After the destruction of both Norfolk and Suffolk during the War for Independence, the area entered a prosperous but troubled time when Great Britain and France engaged in a protracted war. Then Norfolk, along with all the rest of the area, settled down for a long commercial snooze, when population growth stagnated despite the appearance of two railroads, two canals, a major federal fort, and a large naval shipyard.

Despite the lack of growth, residents participated in several sporting activities. Of these only horse racing was fully organized. In the years before the Revolution, wealthy Virginians adopted English thoroughbred racing. This form of long-distance racing could be found throughout much of Tidewater, although only one track surfaced in the immediate area, that being near Portsmouth. After the Revolution, organized thoroughbred races reappeared, attracting participants and spectators in some numbers. Excessive gambling marred these races, and probably caused their temporary closure, but they reappeared in the mid–1820s and continued for about 25 years, when sportsmen stopped offering them in the Norfolk area. A few harness races took place in coastal Virginia in the 1850s in conjunction with agricultural fairs.

Also in the 1850s mock jousting tournaments attained some popularity, especially for young men. Developed in the interior of Virginia at one of the resorts, this sport, requiring a horse rider to use a lance to spear rings from poles arrayed over a course, gained a considerable following in Tidewater. Its resemblance to life in the medieval world had great appeal, reminding people of the literary works of Sir Walter Scott.

Other than equestrian contests, locals carried out informal and decidedly amateur sports as a source of exercise and entertainment. Ninepins or other ball and pin contests appeared from time to time in Norfolk and surrounding communities. Cricket matches also occurred sporadically, with a minimum of newspaper coverage.

After the Civil War, the residents of Hampton Roads pursued material progress at a decidedly more rapid rate. Large volumes of cotton, timber and coal began to flow through the port. Peanuts, now a popular product for human consumption produced in nearby rural areas, added to the volume of business, especially in Suffolk. Expansion of existing railroads, along with the introduction of new shipping lines greatly increased the number of steamboats plying the area's harbors. Textile mills began operations before the end of the century and ship construction reached levels that experts had long predicted would happen. In the last two decades of the century, the entirely new city of Newport News emerged, dependent almost wholly on the production of ships by a company that came to be called the Newport News Shipbuilding and Drydock Company.

Hampton became an active center for canning crabs and processing tons of fish and oysters. Portsmouth still relied on work at the nearby federal shipyard, but residents pursued a wide variety of occupations. All the urban communities grew at rates that far exceeded anything experienced in earlier times

Like most urban areas in the country, Norfolk and Portsmouth contained a "sporting fraternity" in the late 19th century, a group of two or three hundred residents, many either Irish or of Irish descent, who followed prize fighting, an illegal activity in Virginia as in most of the nation. These young men, with a penchant for gambling and drinking, followed pugilists to obscure spots to watch matches.

In the 1870s, the most popular sport for spectators of southeastern Virginia was rowing, with tournaments also experiencing some popularity. Thousands of residents flocked to the waterways to watch sculling during that decade. In 1876, local residents were especially interested in a club called the Elizabeths (named for the river on which they rowed) composed of Irish-Americans, none of whom belonged to the "sporting fraternity." This team participated in the great Centennial Regatta (1876) in Philadelphia, but for unknown reasons this sport lost both its clientele and its fan base by the late 1880s. Tournaments also gradually faded. Football and basketball put in their appearance in the 1890s, but provided little direct competition to summer sports. Curiously, there was little crossover in these sports. Few rowers became baseball players or the reverse, even though, at least in Hampton Roads in the 1870s, both drew on the same spectrum of society — the sons of the commercial and professional classes.

With roots in games played in 18th-century England, baseball evolved in the early 19th century in several northern states as "town ball," a game involving striking a thrown ball with a stick and advancing counterclockwise around three bases (or poles) until one reached a fourth base to tally a score. In the 1840s, skilled tradesmen and young Manhattan professionals, often playing their games across the Hudson River in Hoboken, New Jersey, started a peculiar brand of the game, allowing each side three outs instead of the conventional one per half-inning and making the fourth base home plate. It was also no longer necessary or even permitted to hit the runner with the ball on purpose before he reached any base. In the 1850s, this new brand of ball caught on with increasing numbers of young men. New Englanders continued to play the older style for some time, but during the Civil War Era, they adopted the newer form.

Baseball arose among Virginians during the Reconstruction Era in the late 1860s, having been introduced to the sport during the Civil War by Union troops that played the game in military camps. Even though it is possible that a few Virginians played some version of "town ball" before this great struggle, the vast majority of Virginians never played the game that originated in New York or as played in New England before or even during the war. But during the autumn after the war ended, residents of the Old Dominion read rule books, took up bats and balls, and began throwing, hitting and running bases. In 1865, several Norfolk men, after organizing the Juniper Base Ball Club, lost, 44–30, to a team from an Illinois regiment then encamped near Norfolk's Cedar Grove Cemetery, which was adjacent to the site of their game. The local paper, edited by a former aide to military governor Ben Butler, praised the exhibition and urged the local lads to build up their muscles for more hitting and develop dexterity for catching and fielding.[1]

The fundamentals of the game were pretty much the same as now, but the size of the ball, rules for pitching, equipment of the players, tactics and strategies underwent considerable alteration over the years. In the beginning, pitchers tossed the ball on an arc, thus allowing easy contact with the bat. The completion of a nine-inning game in two hours, despite the scoring of 74 runs, meant that batters did not wait too long to hit the ball, but most of these early contests lasted a good bit longer. In those far off times participants used bare hands to field the ball. By the time the New York game reached this area, fielders had to catch the ball on the fly to make an out, not after one bounce, as had been the case before the war. As had already happened in some parts of the nation by the time baseball arrived in Virginia, local pitchers eventually began to throw the ball with some speed and deceptiveness, forcing batters to develop new techniques to make solid contact. Scores would drop even occasionally into single digits.

The experience for the Junipers held them in good stead, as they shortly thereafter defeated a new team known as the Creightons by 94–25, primarily because the Juniper pitcher "beguiled the hitters into flying out." That contest took place on Thanksgiving at the grounds near the cemetery. The Creightons, named for a famous deceased pitcher from New York, must have been fast learners, especially on defense. In a five-inning encounter in late December 1865, they scored 25 runs against but 16 for the Junipers. And a February box score (one wonders why they played in the winter) shows the Creightons victorious once again by a 38–29 count over a team known as "Virginia," probably from Portsmouth.[2]

In 1867, baseball suddenly took off in popularity, with the formation of several clubs. The Creightons dominated play for a time in the southern part of Hampton Roads while a club from Old Point carried the laurels for the Peninsula. Following one of these contests between the two, a local news editor, a hard-core Confederate, thought that Northerners would make greater headway in reconstructing Southerners if they relied more on the baseball players at Fort Monroe than on Radical Republican politicians. Another Norfolk reporter thought, "Our people seem to be going base ball mad," as an obsession for the game dominated lives.

That year, the Creightons even played a club from Petersburg for what some said was a state championship, winning two of the three contests. The rubber game was played in Suffolk before a crowd that contained many young ladies, whose applause encouraged the players, especially those from Norfolk, to high levels of exertion.[3]

At first, gentlemanly behavior dominated such contests, but all too soon teams resorted to underhanded tactics. After initially enjoying positive relations with teams from Old Point, a Norfolk club complained about the stalling tactics, such as using darkness to force the umpire to end a game before the completion of an inning when visitors had pulled in front. The home team, in the unwritten code, was obligated to greet the visiting team and escort them to pleasant quarters and provide sumptuous repasts. Accounts of these early games rarely fail to mention these amenities. But in this case, the Old Points failed to perform the most basic services; even worse, after the game a mob of 250 blacks attacked the Norfolk players. Only the timely intervention of soldiers from Fort Monroe averted disaster. Times, from the perspective of gentlemanly play, were clearly changing for the worse, but at least Reconstruction ended in 1870.[4]

Precisely when these clubs began to pay a few of their players will likely never be ascertained. For the most part these teams remained amateurs, as the game picked up interest mostly with white-collar workers such as bank or grocery clerks or professionals like doctors and lawyers. Within a few years the game became popular with a broader spectrum of the population and included teams of cigar makers, typographers, policemen, and firemen, among many lines of work. By the early 1880s, black residents of the area also formed clubs. And most public elementary schools and private academies played the game in an organized fashion.

2

Professional Baseball Comes to the City by the Sea

Full-fledged professional baseball showed up in Norfolk in 1884, when residents organized the Norfolk Gymnasium Baseball Club, leased some land for four years, and built Gymnasium Park. The park was located a couple of blocks east of Church Street on Princess Anne Road within the city limits, a few blocks south of the old fair grounds, then the terminus of the mule-propelled cars of the street railway. The president of the street railway corporation, seeing possibilities for extra passengers, offered to assist in making the enterprise a success. The grounds were enclosed, allowing management to charge 25 cents admission for adults, 15 cents for children, with girls and ladies usually admitted free. A roof over the stands shaded some 500 customers from the summer sun. This gymnasium club pioneered in organized physical activity a year or two earlier than the Young Men's Christian Association, and equipped its downtown quarters with everything gymnasts needed at the time, before casting about for other sports-related activities. Among other activities, it sponsored a rowing regatta. Its baseball committee soon convinced the best baseball club in Norfolk, the Athletics, to join the new association as individuals.

In late April 1884, the association negotiated for some professional players to come to Norfolk, especially pitchers and catchers, with the rest of the team being composed of local players. Reporters never provide a detailed list of the professionals, but the pitchers and catchers must have been paid, along with three or four others who played regularly in the field. Personnel changed quite a bit, as several individuals who played for visiting clubs sometimes ended up on the local roster. When the club upgraded its schedule to play major league clubs in September and October, it pursued even higher quality pitchers and catchers.[1]

The 1884 season demonstrated an awakening of interest in professional baseball. Possibly helped along by a booming economy, people in both Norfolk and Portsmouth took baseball to a new level. Instead of learning about a game once every two or three weeks from a snippet in the newspaper — unless some controversy arose — more frequent and fuller reports now surfaced. In the same year, people in Portsmouth created a club also known as the Athletics that, although theoretically amateur, likely included a few players paid for each contest. The Norfolk newspapers also covered their contests, oddly enough, in more detail than they did the Norfolk club, probably because the Portsmouth correspondent had the most interest in the sport.

Although the season did not start until almost mid–June under manager Wesley Blogg, a one-time American Association (one of the major leagues at the time) player, the Norfolk club Athletics (later the Gymnastics) played on a fairly regular basis. Visiting clubs sometimes engaged the locals in a series. On June 12, "streams of people" made their way out of downtown to watch the first professional game of the season. On that same day, Long Island and D.C. roosters were competing in the second day of a cocking main held at the Driving Park (race course) a mile or two east of the ball yard on Princess Anne. A big crowd was also expected to watch a sparring match between professional pugilists at the same location. Despite competition for the entertainment dollar, the ballgame attracted several hundred, but the locals lost, 4–1, to the Nationals, a club that represented the Soldiers Home near Hampton, whose governor subsidized games to entertain the Union veterans. A few days later, some 1,200 at Gymnasium Park watched Norfolk subdue the reserve team of the Virginias, the professional team from Richmond, 16–2. The next day, Norfolk won again, 19–5, over the same adversary. Toward the end of June, Norfolk turned on the Nationals of the Soldiers Home, winning 14–4, Robert Cleland being the winning pitcher. Sometime-pitcher Ben Underwood made a magnificent one-hand catch in center garden. He had come to Norfolk by way of Alexandria, for whose team he played against Norfolk and Portsmouth earlier in the season.[2]

The team then ran into a rough spell. The Monumentals from Baltimore, then a member of the Eastern League, took two, 6–5 and 9–7. Cleland lost the first game, allowing seven walks and throwing three wild pitches, while he and his team made 10 errors. In early July the Athletics lost to the Waverlys of D.C. and succumbed to the first nine of the Virginians out of Richmond, 13–4. The Mutuals of Danville then edged out Norfolk, 3–2.

The battle against the Waverlys typified games of that era. Norfolk pitchers, Underwood and Cleland, gave up no earned runs, while the home team managed only one earned run. The Norfolk Athletics made 13 errors plus four passed balls to go along with five wild pitches. Their rivals made nine errors but suffered no passed balls and only two wild pitches, which likely explains Norfolk's 7–5 loss, despite outhitting the winners, 8–3.

Changes and interpretations of the various rules make it very difficult to discern the quality of the pitching. Overhand pitching would be permitted as early as 1884, but in many cases that form of throwing did not take root until the following year. The thrower had to release the ball from at least 50 feet away from the plate with one or possibly both feet planted on a slab as the ball was released. Not until the late 1880s did baseball officials settle on four balls for a walk and three strikes for an out. Until 1887 the pitcher had to offer a high or a low pitch, depending on the hitter's preference, thus creating a changing strike zone.

In the game noted above, 19 batters (one more for the Waverlys than for Norfolk) struck out. Reading between the lines, at least 12 Norfolk players popped up to the catcher or struck out, with credit given to the catcher for the putout, while six at most flied out to the fielders. On the defensive side, the Norfolk pitcher handled an unusually large number of ground balls. Clearly, different styles of pitching prevailed for each side.

Norfolk later lost twice more to the first team of the Virginians, the first team of the professionals from Richmond, 5–1 and 13–0. That year Richmond started play in the Eastern League but moved up to the American Association, one of three major leagues at the time. In so doing, they also upgraded their talent, but not enough to compete successfully in the majors. In the July game, neither team had an earned run, but Norfolk had 12 errors to eight for the better team.[3]

In late July, the Athletics bested the Monumentals, making "only" eight errors, and holding their rivals to just two runs in a game that took but an hour and thirty minutes and was considered "one of the best and most spirited games ever witnessed in this city." In the last inning, Underwood called for a low ball with two strikes on him and the crowd yelling for him to "hit a daisy." He then drove in two runs and scored himself to seal the verdict. The day before, when the two teams played to a 1–1 tie, catcher Jessie Price went to St. Vincent's Hospital when he sustained a broken jaw after a ball struck a rock while he was warming up.[4]

Norfolk came back for an easy win over the Portsmouth Cardinals, an amateur club. A few days later, Norfolk's second nine bowed to the Cardinals. The main club supposedly "cooked" the Monumentals out of Baltimore, in a game that ended after five innings in a 5–5 tie, when rain and wind broke the 94-degree heat. They beat the Stonewalls of Richmond, 6–4, in late July, with new pitcher Paul Latouche getting the win, and then defeated the same team the next day, 11–6. In that game, Henry Boschen, who had introduced baseball in the capital city but had been deprived of participating with the capital's professional club, pitched for the Stonewalls in a game that lasted 1 hour and 44 minutes. Underwood made six of his team's 15 errors that day, but Norfolk rattled Boschen for 15 hits, while the Athletics' pitcher held the Stonewalls to just six.[5]

After Latouche lost to the Nationals on the Soldiers Home field, 7–3, Norfolk played Allentown, a fixture in the Eastern League that season. Norfolk gave up three runs in the first, mostly due to three errors, but then held the visitors to one more run the rest of the game, incurring only three more errors. The Pennsylvanians, however, made but three errors overall, and although Norfolk out-hit their opponents, 9–7, they lost 4–1. Pitcher Latouche had 10 assists, while new catcher Tate had 11 putouts.

The battery of Latouche and Tate came from Richmond. In 1884, Latouche started the season as a backup player for the Virginians. Since Latouche's name does not appear in the box scores for the Virginians for most of the 1884 season, he likely had been dropped from the main roster of the professional club. Edward Tate's name appears on the roster for Henry Boschen's club from Richmond when it played Portsmouth early in the 1884 season. In 1885, he played with the Virginians as a left-handed catcher and occasional outfielder, but he started his full professional career as a catcher/outfielder in Norfolk the year before. In 1886, he joined Boston in the National League. After "Pop" Tate's tenure with Boston in the majors, he returned to the Virginia League for several teams, playing for Portsmouth and later for Norfolk in 1895.

As the 1884 season continued, Norfolk renewed its series against the Monumentals, winning 6–0, with Latouche again in the box, in a game that lasted just over an hour and a half. No errors were recorded, a remarkable feat given the absence of gloves for the fielders. Underwood, playing center field, drove in several runners with a double. With a stronger battery, the Monumentals recovered to win the next day when Norfolk, behind Underwood, gave up nine hits and the team made 12 errors (some by Underwood), in a game that took less than an hour and a half and the home club lost by only 5–4, with no runs earned for either team.

In the middle of August, as many as possibly nine teams formed the Virginia and North Carolina Baseball Association. The Norfolk Athletics then went on a tour, where they prevailed over Raleigh, 18–10, one day before 500 fans, and 9–7 the next day. They later crushed teams from Oxford and Henderson (both in North Carolina) and eased by the Danville Mutuals, 9–5 (with 15 base hits), after Danville whipped them, 10–8, their only loss on the tour against seven wins. Local newspapers gave only brief accounts of these games, with no box scores.

In the 9–7 win at Raleigh, the home Swiftfoots treated the visitors unusually well. Right after the game, the home club presented their guests with a gold-lined silver cup donated by a local lawyer. The recipient of the cup, representing the players, profusely thanked the club and the North Carolina city's citizens for their generosity and courtesy. The cup would provide a constant reminder of the cordiality received that day. The Norfolk players followed with three cheers to their hosts. The press praised all involved, including the Norfolk club as "skillful players and ... as gentlemen worthy the association of the best of men." The treatment contrasted sharply with that received by the supposed amateurs from Portsmouth in the same city. Swiftfoot officials failed to meet the visitors at the rail station, and an abusive crowd, yelling all sorts of epithets, almost led to a breakdown in relations between the cities of Raleigh and Portsmouth.[6]

After their pleasant excursion into North Carolina and Southside Virginia, the team returned home to defeat the Baltimore Actives, 18–0, with Latouche in the box in the first encounter. In the second game, Norfolk tried out its new battery of Ryan and Hardy. In that game, the visitors left the field after six innings, trailing 7–1, claiming a great need to catch the steamer to the Monumental City. The fans, howling in derision and noting they had plenty of time to catch the boat, demanded that the visitors receive no pay for their paltry efforts.

In early September, 2,000 fans showed up at Gymnasium Park to watch Norfolk take on the Baltimore Orioles, then running third in the major-league American Association. Against a Baltimore reliever named Bob Emslie, Tate hit into a triple play by the visitors in the ninth with the bases loaded. Tate smacked the ball to the Baltimore first baseman, who caught it, stepped on first, and then threw home to catch the runner on third at the plate. That sent the game into extra innings where it remained tied, 1–1, in the 12th.

Underwood managed to swipe home in the first half of the 12th. Excited Norfolk fans threw their hats in the air and ladies waved their handkerchiefs, but the game ended after the Orioles tied the contest in the last of the inning and had to catch a steamboat. Latouche, probably using a sinker, pitched an eight-hitter. He also yielded five walks while his mates committed seven errors behind him, four by center fielder Underwood. Baltimore pitchers walked no one, and their fielders made five errors. That Baltimore did not score until the 12th inning seems remarkable and attests to Latouche's ability to pitch in the clutch and the team's infielders to handle the ball. The Norfolk first baseman made 18 putouts, while the shortstop and third basemen had 17 assists between them. In the eighth inning, Baltimore brought the supposed "finest pitcher in the United States" in as a relief pitcher to get out of a jam, and then inserted another reliever when the game went into extra innings. This contest was undoubtedly the most exciting contest played that year in Norfolk and may well have been one for the ages.[7]

In the middle of September, Norfolk beat the Clifton Club from Baltimore, 6–1, and then crushed the same visitors, 24–6, the next day. In the second game Tate, who had not hit well earlier in the season, came through with the supposed first home run over the fence by anyone at Gymnasium Park. Tate followed up this marvelous achievement by going 4 for 6 against the Swiftfoots, who again surrendered to the Athletics, 20–2, at Gymnasium Park. Latouche got credit for the win, with Tate doing the catching.

The next day the Carolinians crumbled again, 9–3, as Underwood beat them. Earlier in the month, Norfolk battered the Petersburg Red Sox, another Virginia and North Carolina League member, 13–2 and 12–2.

In mid–September, one Norfolk newspaper assessed the season for its professional team. Considering that no team existed as late as May and despite the disappointment over the failure to join the Eastern League, the writer thought the home record of 19 wins and 9 losses, plus two ties, quite acceptable. Winning 29 out of 40 games in the Virginia–North Carolina

Association also called for plaudits, even though the newspapers frequently failed even to give line scores, let alone box scores, for such contests. The association included the Nationals from Hampton, with whom the locals had quite a rivalry.[8]

At this point, the club had an intra-squad game in which the battery of Latouche and Tate triumphed. The winning battery got to share the awards of a ball and a bat, silver trophies offered by a Church Street merchandiser. A local politico gave the awards on behalf of the donor and *The Virginian* editor, with appropriate remarks, accepted them for the players.[9]

After losing to the Whartons from Philadelphia (a team of castoff professionals) and the Virginians (the 13–0 loss mentioned earlier), Norfolk rebounded, with the help of "Boston Reserves," in beating the Nationals of the Soldiers Home, 6–4. Norfolk surprised the visiting Nationals, who came to town pretty confident because they had two reserve players from the Providence Grays, the winners of the World Series that year. But the Providence pitcher gave up 12 hits.[10]

Despite the generally good showing, one of the players grumbled about "Norfolk people never being satisfied." Despite a rumor that the team planned to break up, the club won again over the Soldiers Home after losing to the same team at Hampton.[11]

Although it was well into October, Norfolk extended the season by playing more major league competitors. Armed with pitcher Horner and catcher Warner (first names unknown) and one other player secured from Fort Wayne by Blogg, Norfolk took on the Toledo team that had just beaten the Virginians in Richmond as well as the New York Mets, the winner of the American Association race. The Toledo contest ended scoreless when, in the ninth inning, the visitors took the boat to Baltimore. Amazingly, Norfolk made absolutely no errors and the game only lasted 1 hour and 28 minutes. Norfolk then twice defeated the Whartons from Philadelphia, 3–2 with Horner in the box in the first and 7–3 with Cleland relieved by Horner in the second game. Norfolk then walloped the Nationals from the Soldiers Home, 13–1. To make room for Horner, the club released Underwood, a mainstay of the club for most of the season.

The local club also shut out the Columbus contingent of the American Association, 5–0, with Horner yielding but three hits, catcher Warner not flubbing one ball, and the team making but one error. Nearly every seat in the stands was occupied, several by ladies, who for some of these games outnumbered men. In a return engagement Toledo, "back for blood" and armed with an ambidextrous pitcher, again lost to Norfolk's Horner, 8–1. The pitcher for Toledo, Tony Mullane, dubbed "the Count of Macaroni," had won 35 games for St. Louis the year before he jumped to the Union Association. Even before the season started, he reneged on his Union Association contract and signed on with Toledo. Norfolk had the only earned run in the contest. Toledo made 12 errors, five by the catcher. Norfolk made only two errors.[12]

But in the next encounter, the Ohioans beat Horner, 9–1, leading to speculation that the visitors did not do their best in the first contest in order to build up the crowd for the next game. Another explanation given at the time was that Toledo was worn out, having just played "a series of hard-fought championship games" on the road and also by the actions of "a refractory player." Whatever the case, Norfolk then lost three straight to the Baltimore Orioles, 8–3 and two low-scoring affairs, with Latouche in the box for two of these games.[13]

The season brought controversy between Norfolk and Portsmouth. James W. McCarrick, a steamboat company agent and president of the Norfolk Gymnastic Club, advised Isaac T. Van Patten, secretary of the Portsmouth Athletic Base Ball Club, whose team also went by the name "Athletics," to ignore an apparent challenge appearing in one of the area's newspapers, as it had come from the captain of the second nine. If any challenge were to be issued, it would come through manager Henry, and, moreover a game between the two clubs seemed unlikely.[14]

Late in August, Norman Cassell, president of the Portsmouth Gymnasium, made a two-edged offer in an open letter: to play "a nine composed of the local domiciled residents of the city of Norfolk" for a ball and bat and a silver cup donated by local citizens in a potential three-game set or "your regular paid professional nine" using the same scenario as for the amateurs but for one-half the gate. Although Norfolk management now seemed receptive to the challenge, a serious problem arose that delayed any such game. Van Patten complained when an official with the Star Baseball Club of D.C. turned down a chance to play Portsmouth on September 4 and 5. Norfolk representatives had told the visiting team that their club could not play them if they planned to play Portsmouth after their stay in Norfolk. Indeed, Norfolk could not play anyone who either had played or planned to play Portsmouth because it would be a violation of the National Agreement. In his note to Captain McCarrick, Van Patten wanted to know how it would be possible for Norfolk to honor the agreement if they played Portsmouth. He felt that the Norfolk team had insulted both the Portsmouth Athletic Association and the people of Portsmouth. He also wanted to know why the agreement had not prevented Norfolk from playing the Nationals of the Soldiers Home and the Raleighs after they played Portsmouth. Cassell, after consulting with his committee, decided not "to play you at all."[15]

The reason Norfolk and Portsmouth were embroiled in this controversy stemmed from the situation in major league baseball, although Portsmouth people may have also been upset with Norfolk's hiring Wesley Blogg, who started off the season helping out in Portsmouth. In late 1883, several teams organized the Union Association in opposition to the reserve clause of the National League and the American Association. Under this system, the major leagues signed players to single-year contracts but reserved several players on each team for the ensuing year, so that no other team could compete for their services. In 1884, the Unions recruited several reserved men from both the National League and American Associations and ran a season of about one hundred games. The existing major league teams responded to the challenge by blacklisting players and teams. Under a National Agreement, all part of a determined effort to destroy the Union Association, minor league teams and apparently even amateur teams like Portsmouth could not schedule games against Union Association clubs.

A few days after Portsmouth decided not to play any contest against Norfolk, general manager Henry reported that prominent baseball officials told him and the Nationals of Hampton that under terms of the National Agreement if they played Union clubs, or any clubs playing Unions, the two teams would be banned from contests with clubs such as the Virginians and teams from Allentown and Baltimore that "afforded our citizens so much pleasure." Playing Portsmouth would also mean they would have to cancel scheduled contests with teams like the Metropolitans, Toledo, or Columbus. As to a point raised by Van Patten that some American Association clubs had expressed interest in playing Portsmouth, it could only be that they did not know that all "your games with professionals have been with Union clubs." The arbitration committee that supervised the National Agreement could not let Portsmouth violate the rules and "penalize us for doing so." Henry had to tell managers of visiting teams that "we cannot play" those clubs that announced plans to play Portsmouth, but if Norfolk management had no knowledge of future plans, what clubs did "after playing us is none of our business, and we try not to be meddlesome."[16]

McCarrick earlier noted that Norfolk received permission to play the Nationals and

Raleighs after they played Portsmouth because they wanted to form an association. Norfolk had also received permission from the Eastern League president, who was also on the arbitration committee that supervised the National Agreement, to allow Norfolk to play Portsmouth because of the special relation of the two towns. McCarrick urged Van Patten to join with Norfolk and invite non–Union Association connected teams to come to play both teams on the Elizabeth River. As all this communication went on, the Actives of Baltimore came to Norfolk to lose 18–0 and then refused to honor a prior commitment to Portsmouth.[17]

Portsmouth had been playing Union Association clubs like the Washington Nationals, Kansas City Unions and Chicago Unions, losing by a big margin to the first club but only narrowly to the two latter powerhouses in exciting contests. Then Portsmouth entertained the Union team from Cincinnati, which had defeated the leading club in that league five times, ended second in the standings, and paid an impressive total annual salary of $18,000 to its players. A Portsmouth reporter noted that in April the team in question shut out the New York Mets, the future winners of the American Association race. Then Cincinnati defeated the Baltimore Orioles, 10–1, as well as Philadelphia, Chicago, Buffalo, and Detroit, all of the National League. They even defeated Providence, the current National League leader and eventual world champion. The writer never made the obvious point, implied throughout, that the National Agreement seemed not to have applied in these cases. Noting that young boys virtually idolized these visiting players, he hoped the locals worked hard to keep the score down. About 900 people gathered to see the slaughter, but it was not as bad as expected, only 15–4 for the vaunted visitors.[18]

Earlier in August, Portsmouth was celebrating a victory over the Union team from Baltimore, only to have the press disclose that the professionals were trying to keep the game interesting so attendance would be greater the next day. In so doing, they mistook the score, and ended up losing to the locals. In the next game they surreptitiously switched baseballs to avoid a mushy sphere they had not been able to hit well. A black ball boy discovered and reported the deceit. The juxtaposition of disclosures about the status of Union Association teams and the behavior of their representatives in Baltimore doubtless left Portsmouth supporters a bit befuddled.[19]

Finally, in the middle of October, after the Union Association folded and controversy about its existence subsided, Norfolk and Portsmouth faced each other in an anti-climatic contest. On a cold day, with few people at the park, Portsmouth succumbed to superior Norfolk talent, 16–3, making 15 errors to but four for Norfolk, with the latter scoring the only earned run in the game. Norfolk pitched Latouche, saving Horner for their game the next day against Toledo.

With the season technically over, Norfolk's sportsmen came up with funds to help the players pay for transportation home. Portsmouth players helped out by participating unofficially in another encounter, won by Norfolk, 10–6, to give the Norfolk players travel money. They split $152. The Norfolk Gymnasium Baseball Club then disbanded for the season.[20]

Thus ended Norfolk's first season with a team of professionals. Although professional personnel changed over the course of the season, fans had undoubtedly enjoyed the games, especially the close encounters with major league clubs. That Norfolk competed rather well against such clubs as Toledo and the Orioles (winning or tying about half these contests) strongly suggested that Norfolk might be ready to join one of the better leagues the next year.

Norfolk Joins the Eastern League (1885)

In February 1885, the situation looked promising for Norfolk baseball. The newspaper announced the addition of 125 more seats in the Gymnasium Park, giving the city the "prettiest grounds in the state," which even featured netting over the reserved seats. Season tickets cost $25, not a bad deal for a potential one hundred games against league and non-league teams. The press urged everyone to rally in support of Norfolk's first team to perform in a real professional league, encouraging every man, woman and child to attend a money-raising "grand entertainment" at the Academy of Music.[21]

According to reminiscences written nearly forty years later, some black residents watched the games from the belfry of the Mission College a block or two farther along Princess Anne or in a tall tree at the corner of Princess Anne Avenue and Wide Street. In a game against the Orioles either in 1884 or 1885, blacks were excited over the prospects of watching a black player for Baltimore, but so far as is known, no black ever played in such a contest. Blacks also organized a local club known as the Lancasters in honor of the city in Pennsylvania, whose baseball club had a following in Norfolk. Why that was so must have been attributed to something other than the success of the Lancaster club that lost seven of nine games played at Norfolk.[22]

However they viewed these contests, fans looked forward to a 112-game schedule with 56 home contests and cheering for pitcher Robert Cleland and right-fielder Edward Stratton from the previous year's team along with new manager Andy Swan and Jim Powell, who played for the Virginians the previous year. Jesse Hoofnagle, Portsmouth's best player the previous year, signed but did not make the club for regular-season play. Criticism from one of the other Eastern League cities that Swan moved too slow in securing players and that the best men had already been taken by other league clubs led the local press to remark that Swan did not want "Johnny-come quicklies," only those who could be "relied on, and who will stick out the season." But Richmond had two ace pitchers in harness, leading to a general belief that it would win the Eastern League race in a walk. Norfolk's newsmen wanted to know why the teams should bother to play if such were the case.[23]

Just before the start of the season, the financial problems that surfaced nationally finally reached Norfolk. The Exchange Bank, considered a "Rock of Gibraltar," suspended operations as its biggest customer, a Portsmouth finance company, collapsed. This "Black Thursday" sent shockwaves through the area, only partially offset by the news that the city's baseball team pummeled the Waverlys of D.C., 24–0, before a fair-sized crowd. This financial crisis took place just as the Gymnastics association assembled its membership and asked for $1,500 to cover salaries. Those who attended subscribed $650, but at this point the Gymnastics Club decided to release ownership to a private corporation, thus making the club more like those on a major league level.[24]

Norfolk started off the 1885 season by playing at home in a series against the world-champion Providence Grays, losing a close match, 5–4, and then two others by wider margins. Hoss Radbourne, who established a major league record in pitching almost every game for Providence the previous year, played first base the first day and pitched the next. The home club then lost to the visiting Brooklyn team, 12–7, not a poor showing since that club had one of the highest aggregate salaries ($35,000 annually). Most of their players had played for Cleveland the previous year, but when St. Louis put a team in the National League, the former franchise folded and its players joined the Brooklyn club of the American Association. Baltimore of the American Association forced the Eastern League to exclude the Monumentals. Norfolk also crushed Portsmouth, which had many players (mostly amateurs) returning from the previous year, 14–7 and 12–0. But at least Portsmouth looked good in its new uniforms — dark green trimmed with red, with white shoes and red caps. Earlier, the press praised Norfolk's players for their "gentlemanly, quiet, well behaved" demeanor.[25]

Norfolk's first season in a league of teams fully composed of professionals turned out to be less than a rousing success. After splitting eight road games, Norfolk lost its season opener to the Virginians of Richmond, 8–1, before some 1,400 at Gymnasium Park, a result that turned out to be pretty indicative of much of the season. The Norfolk reporter recorded 11 unfair umpire decisions against Norfolk, mostly relating to losing pitcher John Henry's motion in the box, but Norfolk's 11 errors could not have helped. Ten games into the season, manager Swan released Henry, who once supposedly pitched for Cleveland in the National League, noting that the latter admitted he could not pitch according to the new rules. Major league baseball allowed overhand pitching, but umpires were calling balks when pitchers failed to keep their feet on the slab or when an arm motion seemed irregular.[26]

These defects were so common that year that the major leagues altered the pitching rules after the season started. The new Eastern League rules, which copied those of the American Association, gave the "pitcher the entire freedom of the box and does away with the balk rule. The pitcher may now jump as much as he pleases, and can deliver the ball with his arm at any height above the shoulder, or as far below as he likes." Every club had to put a piece of "flagging or marble in front of the pitcher's box to prevent him from stepping outside of his position." A resident of Church Street gave the Norfolk Base Ball Association some marble to do the job. At the same Eastern League meeting where it was decided to change the balk rule, the president of the league, holding a proxy for Norfolk favoring the rule change, ordered Norfolk to take Henry back. At the meeting, George Pierce, released by Norfolk, received a fine of $25 "for conduct unbecoming of a gentleman and a ball player," and was returned to Norfolk for reinstatement.[27]

With dissatisfaction mounting over Andy Swan's treatment of Henry and the team's tendency to lose more than it won, the manager resigned and was replaced by first baseman Jim Powell, though Swan retained his position in the field. The team picked up some cast off pitchers and continued to play. Several easy wins over Wilmington, Delaware, and occasional victories over Lancaster, Newark, Trenton or Jersey City permitted the club to stay afloat. As Richmond amassed a record of 23–4 after a 3–1 victory at Norfolk, the capital city club returned home to a grand welcome. At that time Norfolk's record stood at 9–14 and about a week later at 9–20, as the club continued to lose to the top clubs in the league.

In mid–June, the Gymnasium and Athletic Association formally transferred ownership of the club to the Norfolk Base Ball Association, a joint stock company capitalized at no less than $5,000 or more than $50,000, much like the club that operated in Richmond. Prospective stock purchasers could apply to the treasurer. The more financially solvent new organization signed a new catcher that had played for Philadelphia the year before and Hughes, a pitcher/right fielder who had previously played in Dayton.[28]

Despite these changes, the team experienced a disastrous showing against Wilmington, losing 18–7, during which "the wild and fancy" pitching of Tom Healey contributed in no small measure to the margin of defeat. Dozens of fans yelled to the manager, "Take him out of the box," as one pitch after another eluded the strike zone and even the catcher. According to one account, if the work of the catcher in stopping numerous balls in the dirt had not been superior, the score would have even been worse. In early July, Norfolk lost a home game to Trenton, 12–11, in a contest that started at 5 P.M. and ended after the seventh inning because of darkness. But at least the home team was in the game the whole way even though the visitors pounded Henry. The press took the occasion to notify potential customers that a grandstand had been erected behind the catcher and even fitted up with cushions and comfortable backed seats. Gentlemen paid 35 cents for the privilege of sitting down and ladies only 15 cents.[29]

Norfolk struggled to a 17–28 record as Richmond and the Nationals (D.C.) soared far ahead of the rest of the league. On July 4, a large crowd saw Norfolk lose to Trenton, 5–4, in 10 innings, but Norfolk beat the Newarks the following Monday, 15–6. Chipping away, a revitalized Norfolk club improved its league record, largely because it avoided playing the two best teams in the league. At this point Eugene Derby, a catcher and right fielder, was batting .347 and Powell, who early in the season actually hit a home run over the fence, raised his average to .280. The returning Henry, no longer so concerned about the rule about balks, pitched well enough to win some games, but he also hit the ball pretty well for a time. Fred Carl led the team with a .362 mark. When Henry and new pitcher Hughes split pitching chores in July, Norfolk went 15–6. Its record now stood at 30–32. Management released both George McElroy, who had made 27 errors in eight games, and Tom Healy. When Henry took ill, Hughes pitched several games in a row quite satisfactorily.

In light of this improvement, a reporter thought the players would soon rise in league standings and certainly deserved "sustaining patronage" and local pride. "Give them a better attendance," which lately "had been discouragingly small." Without more spectators "it will be difficult to sustain their present good standing and good ball playing," the newsman warned.[30]

Whatever the case with attendance, the team went into a slump. Playing mostly the Washington Nationals and Richmond, teams that were in a red-hot race for the league lead, Norfolk lost game after game. Then on August 18, a day that must have resonated in infamy in Richmond, Norfolk finally defeated the Virginians at Richmond by a count of 10–3, its first victory over the league leaders after 10 losses. They pounded out 12 hits and played an "almost faultless game." Stunned by the outcome, the Virginians released the losing pitcher shortly after this game. As described in the Richmond press, the Richmond pitcher seemed angry at the start. As Norfolk players began to make contact with his drop pitch, the Richmond fans yelled at him, "which he did not take in good humor." Many in the audience believed that he was trying "to see how many hits the visitors could get 'off' him." The Virginia manager became so concerned about the crowd that he called for police protection. The Richmond writer thought the crowd had good reason to exhibit its disgust for "such a club as the Norfolks to get a game from our nine under such circumstances." He believed that except for hitting, "our boys outplayed, or equaled the performance of the visitors."[31]

Playing at home later in August, Norfolk whipped the state capital city club twice, 7–1 and 3–2, beating its ace, as Henry won both games. The Virginians recovered the next day to win, with Hughes the loser. Henry, not being permitted to pitch three days in a row, objected and received his release. It really did not matter, as fans had already pretty much lost interest. At least two league teams moved to other locales during the season due to weak support and the league looked suspect. The Norfolk team, lacking attendance, stopped playing soon after the Richmond series. By that point, club stockholders were $2,300 in the hole, not counting $350 needed to compensate the players.[32]

On the next-to-last day of play, the club released an outfielder "because of his conduct on the grounds." What he did was not disclosed, but one is struck by the relative absence of violent behavior by both the players and fans in Norfolk, given the future record in this regard. A fan in another Eastern League city struck an umpire in the face with a brick, but nothing of the sort happened in the City by the Sea. The local press generally refrained from making negative comments about the officials, as would be commonly the case just a few years later. In late July, one of the dailies did express the view that "as an umpire, Mr. Holland [William] is a miserable failure," and would do better to work on "some farm." The reporter quickly apologized to farmers for a gross insult to their profession. Such a comment would be standard fare a few years later, but in 1885 they were relatively rare.[33]

With a record of 64–24, but averaging about 500 fans per game, Richmond, the victim of thievery by the team treasurer, sold off its top players. With players ready to jump ship because they were not being paid, the season ended abruptly in mid–September with the Virginians in second place, the Nationals of D.C. having the best record.[34]

Quiet Interlude

In April 1886, a few hundred customers came out to the park to watch the Boston team in the National League win a match over Rochester of the New York State League. The reason the two teams played in Norfolk and later in Richmond was that several men from both organizations had previously played for or against Norfolk or Richmond, including Tate and Horner.[35]

In June 1886, various parties strove to create a Virginia state league, which included teams from Norfolk, Petersburg, Richmond, Lynchburg and Danville. Norfolk players paraded their new uniforms (gray with red stockings) as they rode the horse-drawn streetcars downtown to open the season against Petersburg at Gymnasium Park, which now contained an improved grandstand. Petersburg prevailed, 9–3, a loss that served as a barometer for the season. The season quickly deteriorated, as the professionals representing Norfolk appeared to be too well fed at one of the local hotels, as they lost several games in a row, leading a reporter to opine that they were "far below mediocrity."[36]

Norfolk's "people well up on the great American sport" expected better outings against Lynchburg, but the latter bettered pitcher Opdyke, although he did manage to knock out (literally) one of the opposing batters. Norfolk finally won its first game, 11–6, over visiting Lynchburg, but lost the rubber game of the series, 7–4. Norfolk traded victories against Richmond, then "sulked" through a loss in the Hill City, after which pitcher Driscoll lost an extra-inning affair. After one of the losses at Lynchburg by a close score, manager W.A. Young, a future Democratic Congressional candidate from Virginia's second district, telegraphed the press that the new players he had acquired were doing well and fans might expect improved performances when the lads returned to Norfolk. That turned out to be an oft-stated theme, as Norfolk constantly sought new players to replace those acquired earlier. After splitting with Petersburg, the team won once and lost twice to Lynchburg at home. Although the games started at 4 P.M. with ladies admitted free when accompanied by a male escort who paid the fare, attendance remained quite thin. Norfolk lost one of these games, 9–0, in a game that provided little interest. In the next loss to Lynchburg by 7–5, Pat Rollins, the visiting catcher, impressed folks by hitting a ball all the way over the fence. The visiting players were nice enough to praise the condition of the grounds.[37]

Norfolk won one contest against Danville, the new team in the loosely organized league, 8–4, at home in late July and then lost to the same team 4–3, allegedly because of the umpire. In the first contest, Ettinger made sensational catches in left field but needed to cover the area right in back third base more alertly.

At one point, the Hill Toppers ran off a record of 15–5 to 11–5 for Petersburg, 5–9 for Richmond, and 4–12 for Norfolk. Danville supposedly came in with one victory in six outings, that being the one over Norfolk. Norfolk also won two games against Lynchburg played at Hampton, which did not count in the standings. A reporter for the Soldiers Home thought the game that Norfolk won, 3–2, was the best ever seen on the grounds of the Soldiers Home.[38]

Late in July, Norfolk routed Richmond, 17–6, and then proceeded to win two contests against the men from the capital city by closer margins, 9–8 and 6–4. These games attracted unusually large crowds, despite which the team experienced a shakeup. Although the local newspapers reported that the team disbanded, a national magazine reported the club reorganized on the last day of July. An article written by someone calling himself "Princeton" claimed an infusion of new capital now backed the old management. With the exception of five men, the players were released and paid in full. Kilroy and Cullen formed a new battery, along with O'Rourke, who had been hitting solidly and playing a brilliant third base. Rosenthal, a local lad, was still doing well. Two of those released, John Firth and "Whitey" Gibson, would be missed. This reporter urged potential professionals to write manager Young right away. Despite this glimmer of hope for those who wanted to watch professionals play the game in Norfolk, no games seem to have taken place in August, as the league simply stopped functioning. In Richmond, Henry Boschen also broke up his team due to poor attendance.[39]

No one seems to have organized a league in 1889, but that year Bermuda Street news storeowner James Tierney had a team practicing at Gymnasium Park at the end of March. Tierney's boys beat back some visiting actors of the Dixie Adonis Company then performing at the Academy of Music, 13–7, with Montague receiving poor support in the field and the umpire allowing great latitude for the runners. Some of the gate went to the Retreat for the Sick and an orphan asylum. A few weeks later, with Trower and Hutchins serving as the battery and near flawless fielding, they beat a D.C. club 12–2. They planned to tour some northern states in May. They must have become lost somewhere on the way, for newspapers said little about them until the end of the month, except disclosing that they lost close encounters to the Hampton Y and the Roselands, a team that represented the Soldiers Home.[40]

On May 30, 1889, the Norfolk baseball team arrived on the 5 o'clock train at Roanoke and after registering at the Palace Hotel and eating supper, they walked around Magic City. "Each one looks like an athlete and every inch a base ball player," a Roanoke writer noted. The portending contest was the first between the two cities, but the local reporter pointed out that the previous year Norfolk defeated several teams that easily beat Roanoke's club. This statement provides evidence that Norfolk must have had a club in 1888, despite the absence of newspaper commentary. The Roanoke man claimed the 1889 contest would determine the state championship. The next day, when Roanoke won, one assumes the team from Magic City put in a claim as the best in Virginia.[41]

Also in 1889, a "picked nine" from the Norfolk club, with Montague pitching for an incapacitated regular thrower, lost to Portsmouth, 3–2, in June, with both sides doing well. Nearly a week later Norfolk emerged victorious over the Roselands from Hampton at Gymnasium Park, 14–1, with Montague getting credit for the win. A few days later the club again overcame the Roselands at the Soldiers Home, 7–5, with Montague the winning pitcher, following a loss to the Artillery School at Fort Monroe, with Trower at the point (pitching).

With the capital city having lost all interest in the game, Norfolk, Roanoke, Danville and Staunton were the best baseball cities in Virginia, a national magazine claimed. Given the absence of newspaper coverage in Norfolk, one has to wonder about the accuracy of this assertion.[42]

The next year brought even fewer comments about professional ball. After some talk about Norfolk and Portsmouth playing in Norfolk, with Montague to pitch, no account followed. The situation became so desperate for Tierney that when a team from Phoebus, a village near Fort Monroe, passed through Norfolk to entrain to Roanoke to play a three game series, Tierney considered borrowing the team to represent the city of Norfolk against the Portsmouth club. The touring club won at least one of its contests in Roanoke, with Ed Rosenthal, who once played for Norfolk and Portsmouth, hitting two home runs in the series. Opdyke, another former Norfolk player, also performed for Phoebus.[43]

In the late 1880s and early 1890s, baseball men kept changing the rules, especially those relating to pitching. In 1887, they allowed the batter an additional strike and ball before either being declared out or taking first base. But somehow the phrase "four strikes and you're out" did not resonate very well. The owners finally settled on four balls and three strikes as the preferred numbers. In 1893, rules makers, with the help of a mistaken measurement, placed a slab 60 feet, six inches from the front edge of home plate, where it has remained ever since. This change gave hitters a decided advantage. Pitchers later gained a significant advantage when they stood on a mound and the rules were changed again to the decided advantage of the defense.

All through the late 1880s and early 1890s the tide for professional baseball in Hampton Roads was at low ebb. In March 1890, promoter Ted Sullivan visited Norfolk after working on organizing teams for the Southern League. While in Norfolk, he urged the formation of a Virginia League, pointing out that census estimates for Virginia yielded at least eight cities with between 15,000 and 90,000 residents. With these numbers in mind he talked about the talent available locally and named players that might be enticed to come to Virginia, even though the salaries would be on the low side. No one acted on this advice at the time.[44]

From 1887 through 1893 baseball fans locally had to rely on amateur and semi-professionals for entertainment. A team composed of black residents, known as the Red Stockings, continued their play and likely received some pay for their efforts. Local writers considered them the "champion colored team of the South," once it was reorganized under manager George Wright in 1894. Collegians also represented the city. Most of these men either had attended college at some point or were currently enrolled at places like the University of Virginia. Undoubtedly some of them played a pretty fair brand of ball, but local baseball enthusiasts wanted real professional ball.[45]

3

The Virginia League, 1894–1896

In 1894, professional baseball returned to Norfolk, as the city joined the new Virginia League. Newport News entered the same competition later that same season, but only to complete the schedule. Portsmouth organized its first fully professional team the next year, and became a member of the association. In some of the most exciting and acrimonious seasons ever known in local sports annals, the Virginia League carried on for three years before disbanding.

The First Virginia League Race (1894)

As early as November 1893, despite a financial panic, preliminary steps were taken to organize a state baseball league. At a March meeting in Richmond, baseball promoter Ted Sullivan pushed for the alignment, which started after the Tri-City League (Richmond, Manchester, and champion Petersburg) ended its season. Manchester and Richmond merged teams; Richmond and Petersburg then sent representatives to meet with delegates from Staunton and Norfolk at the American Hotel in the capital city. The manager of the Charleston, West Virginia, team, acting on behalf of Camden Sommers, represented Norfolk at this session at which it was agreed to solicit two more clubs from among Lynchburg, Roanoke, Danville and Alexandria. The first two received the nod, and league moguls capped a team's total payroll at $600 a month at the same meeting.[1]

When organized, the league included cities that varied widely in population. Richmond contained some 80,000 residents; Norfolk had about half as many. Petersburg, Lynchburg and Roanoke had about half as many as Norfolk. Staunton, the sixth city and not included on the initial list of potential league towns, recorded about 7,000 in 1890 and 8,000 in 1900.

This particular year found the nation mired in a prolonged depression, thus belying the characterization "Gay Nineties." High levels of unemployment and labor violence characterized Grover Cleveland's second term as president. Although much of Virginia felt the shockwaves of this economic downturn, Norfolk (at least if its press can be trusted) was in relatively good shape, with sustained sales of residential properties in the suburbs and the start or expansion of several businesses. The National Brewing Company opened for business during the summer and one of Norfolk's numerous producers of peanuts substantially expanded operations. Despite the Depression, beer and peanuts, two items often associated with baseball, did quite well. Weakness in the economies of other Virginia cities, however, threatened the league. Low attendance remained a problem in Roanoke and Lynchburg, but the league survived, although Staunton proved entirely too small to support its team, forcing the club's removal to the Peninsula in the middle of the season.[2]

Over the winter, Camden "Doc" Sommers, who the previous year led Staunton to a Valley championship, arranged for a new League Park, constructed some four blocks north of the site of Gymnasium Park and just two blocks east of Lesner's Park, a restaurant-animal exhibit combination on Church Street. That principal north-south thoroughfare would be equipped with electrified streetcars later that year. In early April 1894, workmen finished rolling the new diamond in time for the second pre-season contest. A local reporter opined that residents of Norfolk "have always been fond of good, clean ball and if they are given a first class article, the enterprise ought to prove a great success."[3]

A little later, Lesner's became a brewery, which featured a rathskeller that baseball fans doubtless frequented before and after ball games. The Virginia League followed the National League rather than the American Association, known in some circles as the "Beer and Whiskey League," in neither selling nor permitting alcohol to be consumed on the premises. In 1894, Norfolk's voters picked a prohibitionist-minded Methodist minister as mayor over the formerly entrenched Democratic machine as part of a drive against so called "ring rule," an organization strongly influenced by saloonkeepers.

Just before the players showed up in Norfolk, Dwight Moody, the greatest evangelist of the time, came to Norfolk, along with his soloist Ira Sankey. They carried out a revival, held at Armory Hall, with 4,000 attending the opening session. Smaller crowds came to subsequent meetings. Professional baseball drew a similar number on opening day, and trailed off as the season continued. Baseball sometimes had double headers, as did the revivalists, except the latter had day and night performances.[4]

Norfolk's "cranks" waited anxiously as Sommers, the president of the new league and Norfolk's principal owner and manager, formed the club roster and arranged for housing the players. The Washington YMCA club was touring Virginia at the time, playing several of the new Virginia League teams — and usually beating them. Around the time they played in Norfolk, Sommers signed a host of players, foremost among them D.C. native Ernie A. Hodge, a favorite on the Washington Y and "as brilliant a little catcher as ever wore the mask and mitt." Others included Harry Colliflower, a "left handed cyclone twirler" (possibly ambidextrous), who had recently shut out the league team from Petersburg; third baseman Eddie Johnson; pitcher Joe Fry, fleet Harry Hauptman and one or two others from the YMCA club from the nation's capital.[5]

Preliminary play started with a game between the Norfolk Y and the D.C. counterpart in an open field in Ghent on the property of a real estate development company on a wintry day in April before a number of "incurable cranks" dressed in storm coats. Joe "Foxey" Fry, a West Virginian who had pitched for Staunton the previous year and was currently on tour with the D.C. club, threw for the local Y. "His curves froze at the elbow" and he lost, 12–6, in five innings. Those not affiliated with the D.C. team included Charles Elsey out of Cincinnati by way of West Virginia and Dennis Cleary from Trenton, New Jersey.

In the first fully professional game of the exhibition season, the new Norfolk club, with Fry in the box, eked out a 10–9 triumph over Altoona of the Pennsylvania League. "Handsome" Harry Hauptman of D.C. moved like a deer in left field. The mustachioed Eddie Johnson, a stalwart at third base and occasional pitcher, proved a favorite with the ladies. Norfolk tuned up for the season by playing Altoona five games, of which the home boys won four, along with a "burlesque" victory in the mud over the Baltimore All-Americans in front of just 200 fans.

With the regular season about to start, management clarified rules for the new park. No betting would be permitted in the grandstand. "Sporty boys" who wanted to enhance their excitement could exchange "the coin of the realm, only in the 'quarter-stretch' bleachers just east of the grandstand." "Objectionable characters" and "swearing and loud and boisterous language" would not be allowed in the grandstand, where women might be listening. Management wanted to attract "the very best class of our ladies and gentlemen with the least possible discomfort and unpleasant surroundings."[6]

A large blackboard in right field featured updated scores each inning, this done at the suggestion of a local fan who admitted that he previously pestered the official scorer and newspaper reporters for such information. Sometime during the season, the club installed another board that held the scores of other league contests as delivered by telegraph during the game.

As the regular season was about to start, Coxey's army of the unemployed moved into the District of Columbia to try to convince Congress to spend money on public works to help combat the Depression. Labor violence loomed in connection with the Pullman strike near Chicago. Sam Small, the revivalist and prohibitionist, thundered against alcohol and ring rule at the Academy of Music on Granby Street. Black preachers did the same at The People's Tabernacle on Queen Street. On a pleasant April day, the Second Regiment Band led three hacks filled with players, along with a the rest of a parade up Church Street to the new park as the locals took on the men from the Hill City of Lynchburg. Norfolk's players were dressed in blue with "NORFOLK" spelled out in large white letters across the breast. Colliflower then proceeded to shut out the visitors, 9–0, in front of a large crowd, with many viewers perched on the top stories of neighboring houses.

Based on Colliflower's winning effort and another walkover against Lynchburg, with Fry recording a win, one reporter predicted the City by the Sea would capture the pennant. Pennant hopes, however, took a sudden plunge the next day when visiting Staunton easily subdued the home club. The Valley of Virginia visitors included left fielder David Fultz. A resident of Staunton, a future major leaguer, still later a football star at Brown University and a prominent lawyer, Fultz organized the major league baseball players' association. Around 1900, he was reputed to be the greatest of all Virginia athletes. Win Clark, a future player and manager for Norfolk, also played for the visitors. Norfolk did manage to win the third game of the series, with Eddie Johnson doing the slab chores. The home team then swept three from Roanoke.

On the road, Norfolk lost to league-leading Petersburg, the experienced club that most knowledgeable folks thought the best in the league. Despite losing to the Appomattox club, the cranks in Norfolk were "baseball wild," with interest far exceeding that produced in 1885, according to Thomas Spaine, the local correspondent to a national magazine. Attendance usually ran around 1,000, but games occasionally attracted between two and three times that number. In the middle of June, a Petersburg paper noted that the "Lightning Bugs" from Norfolk only attracted between 800 and 1,000 fans in a 19–2 win over Roanoke, a crowd that fell well below the usual number. A reporter for the local newspaper named Myers became a favorite with the fans because he put "life in his articles by using some up-to-date base ball talk," thereby adding to the excitement.[7]

Although Lynchburg crushed visiting Norfolk in a May encounter, 18–10, Norfolk recuperated to win 16–14, scores that indicate that the increased distance from the pitcher's box to home plate took its toll on pitching. Later, facing Richmond, Fry hit three of the visitors in the back, whereupon he lost his nerve, losing the game, 13–7. William F. "Rube" Kissinger, recently purchased from Atlanta, lost to Roanoke in his first outing. The newcomer also proved to be "easy fruit" in another against Staunton, losing 13–4. But in a curious encounter at Roanoke in mid–June, he tossed a no-hitter through five innings, after which Sommers removed the lanky hurler for undisclosed reasons. Reliever Fry was totally ineffective in relief, the paper headline noting: "Fry Caused a Defeat." Soon Kissinger became the mainstay of the staff, and ended up in the National League the next year.

In an early season showdown with the Petersburg Farmers ("Hayseeds") the Norfolk Clams (also known as "Clam Diggers," "Crabeaters," "Oyster Tongers," or "Mariners") lost two close home matches against the league leaders. One game was so packed that the bleachers collapsed. No one was seriously injured, and the reporter was more concerned about management's perceived need to stop the cursing that invariably accompanied these contests. During one game, someone described only as "a huge black man" tossed a large stick into the stands, striking a woman of social standing in the temple. The miscreant escaped. Such incidents added to press urgings for Sommers to hire police. Because the park was located in Norfolk County, which had no regular police force, Sommers would have to pay for police protection.[8]

The problem of foul language was sometimes related to the amount of gambling that was taking place. After an 8–6 loss to Petersburg at home, the "Cockade City" daily newspaper asserted that although betting was not technically allowed on the grounds at Norfolk, somehow a "good deal of money changed hands all the same." And none of it was Petersburg money.[9]

The appearance of the professional Clams did not prevent other ball playing at the new park. In early June, two "crack colored clubs," the Red Stockings and the Manhattans (Richmond), battled before some 100 whites and 300 blacks at League Park. To say that the players and spectators enjoyed themselves, the reporter noted, "would be putting it mildly, for fun ran high." Comments from the sidelines like "kill him" amused the writer. When a hero for the home team drove in two runners with two out in the last of the ninth to produce an 8–7 win, the scene became "indescribable," with the player being "picked up bodily and carried around the field, the drum corps following."[10]

Portsmouth people joined the throngs at League Park, usually rooting for the visiting Virginia League teams. The sister city had one crank, weighing some 250 pounds (probably Captain John Brady), who constantly poked "jovial remarks" at the Norfolk players. When Norfolk easily won a contest, Brady allegedly took a back route away from the park to avoid confronting Norfolk fans. Portsmouth sent a group called the Independent Order of Knockers, whose principal purpose was to bring "hammers to knock Norfolk in anything she competes for."[11]

The team record in the league fell to 23–18, with Richmond one game ahead of Norfolk, while Petersburg amassed 32 wins against but 10 losses, placing the Farmers or "Goobers" well in front. But in late June, Norfolk won 12 straight, scoring almost 13 runs per game while allowing just over four. Kissinger won half of those games himself. Norfolk finally lost to Staunton 12-6, with Fry taking the loss. Norfolk reversed matters the next day, getting by the Mountaineers, 15–12, although Fultz battered Kissinger for five hits. Norfolk then won two of three at home against Lynchburg, splitting the July 4 twin bill. It then bested Petersburg, 10–2, before some 2,000 at home, roughing up Foreman and securing a win for Bill "Long Boy" Kissinger, who tossed a two-hitter. The next day the Farmers rallied to hold off Norfolk, 8–4, and even though Norfolk took the rubber game in the series, 12–4, in a rain-shortened affair, Petersburg still left with a sizeable lead.[12]

As would be the case in every season, management strove to field a better club. Veteran minor leaguer "Pop" Lanser came in May to cover several different positions in the field. Within a week or two after a national magazine praised the fielding and "eye" of shortstop Will Ransome, Sommers replaced him with Jack Corcoran. Charlie Elsey asked for and received his release, and after being reinstated was released again. He finally signed with Lynchburg. Outfielder Denny Cleary also disappeared from the lineup. Gus "Turkey" Land came on board to help with the catching and at first base, but mostly to serve as an emergency umpire. Another backup catcher and outfielder, Fred Hager, joined the club, but soon retired with a broken hand. The manager tried Jack Thornton at second, but his three errors led a reporter to describe his initial performance as "amateurish," and Sommers put him in the outfield.[13]

In the middle of July, with Norfolk still trailing Petersburg by a substantial margin, the newspaper grumbled that Sommers shifted players from one position to another too much. A couple of weeks earlier the newspaper argued that Colliflower should be pulled off first base. Sommers brought on board Ralph Joanes, a sometime resident of Newport News who came over from Macon of the defunct Southern League. Although a light hitter, he helped plug a major hole in the defense. The hard-hitting Colliflower then moved to the outfield when he was not pitching.

Bad luck forced Sommers to make more changes. In June, Eddie Johnson and Ed Herr went to St. Vincent's Hospital, both suffering from typhoid. Johnson died later that month, while Herr was out of commission for much of the rest of the season. The team attended Johnson's funeral in D.C. and wore mourning badges in his honor. Sommers tried Hauptman at third for a time, but the manager could not adequately fill the hot corner until deep in August.

Without Herr, management relied on Fry, Kissinger and Colliflower to handle the pitching. For a time Fry lost his touch, especially after beaning Harry O'Hagen of Roanoke, an injury which imperiled the third baseman's life. In several subsequent outings, whenever Fry hit an opposing batter, he fell completely to pieces. Reporter Spaine urged Fry not to let sympathy for fellow players make him a less aggressive pitcher. Presumably the advice worked, for Fry fortified his record. Although Richmond wracked him in his first appearance, Dick Cogan from Paterson, New Jersey, joined the team at the mid-point of the season and won some outings before eventually fading from the roster. He showed up in Norfolk a few years later as a player for the Paterson club.[14]

As the club endured a tough patch in late May, Sommers, "always ready to give his players a good innocent time," took his "family," along with members of the Roanoke team, to the Ariel Club on Princess Anne Road to a gloved match between boxers representing Norfolk and New Jersey in a "fine display of the manly art." Charles Elsey likely joined the crowd, with considerable interest, as at some point he helped train one of Norfolk's boxers. The fight, with no prize money offered, at least publicly, ended in a draw, stopped by the county sheriff after 24 rounds. The outing suggests Sommers treated his men well, but probably put him at odds with religious interests in the city like Sam Small, not to mention the governor of Virginia, both of whom wanted laws against pugilism rigidly enforced.[15]

In late July, Norfolk moved within one and one-half games of first place. A 20–2 triumph over Petersburg on the latter's field possibly reminded folks of the way the Japanese military was then battering the Chinese in their war. Some 800 rooters went from Norfolk to the city on the Appomattox, along with Brady and his band from Portsmouth. After the win, both groups walked back to downtown Petersburg, the Norfolk men in great glee and those from Portsmouth in an opposite state of mind. During the game, several men from Norfolk engaged in impromptu boxing matches with toughs from Petersburg's notorious Fifth

Ward before police restored order. The Norfolk reporter assumed the Norfolk fans were happy despite their discolored eyes and bloody noses. In the next game, Petersburg avoided a sweep, Foreman besting Fry, to boost the lead to five games. Undeterred, Norfolk continued to win about as many as it lost, as Petersburg fell below par for a time.[16]

In the middle of August, Sommers traded a part-time catcher and sometime third baseman to Roanoke for Harry "Stonewall" O'Hagen, known as the "King of the Kickers," apparently vying for that title with George Kelly of Petersburg. Catcher and team captain Ernie Hodge negotiated an arrangement that allowed Roanoke to demand the return of O'Hagen any time before September 1, if the two former Norfolk players failed to live up to expectations, When that proved to be the case, Roanoke called for their old third baseman, but when Sommers came up with a financial incentive, O'Hagen stayed in Norfolk.

At a critical juncture of the season, the Staunton team disbanded. Baseball men in Newport News and Hampton and one of Norfolk's owners, subsidized by Camden Sommers, picked up the franchise. A few days before Sommers made the deal for O'Hagen, the Peninsula club acquired John McCloskey, an outfielder and a former minor league manager, and Harry Truby, a second baseman. Both had played the early part of the season in the now-defunct Southern League. The owner of the Roanoke club sold McCloskey for $500 despite knowing that he had "by far the greatest baseball general that has ever struck the state," because he realized his club could do no better than third place. McCloskey seems not to have played many games, if any, for Roanoke, but because he signed a contract, Sommers had to come up with payment to the Roanoke owner. After Newport News bested Norfolk in a game with the two former Southern Leaguers in the winning lineup, Sommers moved both Truby and McCloskey across the Roads to Norfolk, the latter to act as captain as well as manage his club. Norfolk farmed out McCreary to Newport News. Newport News then materially helped Norfolk by beating Petersburg three straight.[17]

Games between Petersburg and Norfolk came close to resembling armed conflict. In early August, the Farmers and their fans came to Norfolk in force aboard twelve train cars. They made so much noise that no one could hear the umpire. The "frenzied" Petersburg captain George Kelly, ran into rival players, and the principal owner of the Goobers became embroiled in a controversy with Sommers, who refused a personal bet with Harrison for $1,000 on the outcome of the pennant race, although he continually claimed that Petersburg had little chance of winning. At one point, Sommers called for Harrison's dismissal from the league; another time he pointed out that betting was illegal under league rules, not to mention state law.[18]

Despite losing seven of eight games to Richmond and making 20 errors in one three-game series, Norfolk remained very much in the race. In late August, baseball fever reached levels never seen before and rarely seen again in Norfolk and Petersburg. The new armory on City Hall Avenue (where revivalists sometimes held forth and now the site of MacArthur Mall) became a surrogate site for away games. Fans paid 15 cents to see actors, properly attired, play out each incident in games reported over the wire. The audience for these enactments ran as high as 900. Petersburg had a similar, but less elaborate, setup at its Chorus Hall.

Toward the end of August, even though Norfolk had a decided edge in the contests between the two, Petersburg held a commanding five-game lead. An Appomattox reporter pointed out that his club added a couple of top minor league players to its roster for the stretch run and predicted Petersburg's lead would soon grow to 10 games. He also advised the Norfolk correspondent to the national magazine to desist in his "funny stuff" and concentrate on the fact that Norfolk resided in third place in the league standings.[19]

In late August the pennant race heated up even more as Richmond reeled off seven straight wins to jump back into contention. Norfolk also won several games as Petersburg lost six straight, capped by a 12–2 loss to Norfolk. Petersburg suspended Foreman for indifferent play, some even accusing him of selling out to Norfolk. In response, Foreman defended his honor in a letter to the newspapers. A few days later, after no one found any evidence of bribery, Petersburg allowed Foreman to return.[20]

As August waned, Sommers shored up his pitching, bringing in Charles "Big" Petty, formerly with Washington and Cleveland of the National League, and H.H. Hunt, a student at Vanderbilt with connections to Memphis of the Southern League. With these acquisitions, a Norfolk reporter projected that Norfolk would win the race by one game over Richmond and three games over Petersburg.[21]

Norfolk did edge ahead in the league standings on August 28 with a 59–38 record, but Richmond immediately set Norfolk back with a lopsided win. Newcomer Petty failed miserably, partially because "Tiny" Hodge had trouble handling his fast ones. Colliflower, who had been playing outfield regularly and pitching on occasion, then lost a close game to Richmond, 2–0. During that fray, umpire Ed Clark displayed an obvious bias, even in the view of the Richmond people according to the Norfolk newspaper. After one especially galling call, O'Hagen tore the mask from the umpire's face. An "excited and angry mob," led by a "pugnacious policeman in uniform who wanted to smash O'Hagen in the face," surrounded the players, but order was restored with no bloodshed. The third baseman later explained that he did not intend to assault Clark, but grabbed the "mask, the insignia of office, from the umpire's face to show his disgust for him and to proclaim to the public that he regarded him as an unfit person for the position." The umpire called the game after the seventh inning, claiming it was too dark to play. The next day, with Clark still umpiring, Norfolk lost again at Richmond. In a game on September 1, with the same umpire now working the bases, the Clams managed a 6–6 tie with the Colts, despite "several rank decisions against Norfolk." In that affair, plate umpire Sandy McDermott refused to accept a written protest from Sommers about the base calls because, as he later explained, he feared the crowd would think it was some form of payment. "Paderewski" Hunt pitched credibly before some 4,500 at Richmond, with 900 at Norfolk's Armory watching "replays" on a Saturday afternoon.[22]

The Clams then moved on to Lynchburg, where they lost again, this time 4–1. According to one account labeled "Another Game of Growl," umpire McLaughlin verbally abused Hodge, who had not spoken to him, declaring that he "would get even with" players from D.C. In the first inning he called Hodge out on three balls "over his head which he made no attempt to hit." Indeed, he called O'Hagen, who also hailed from the nation's capital, out three times on strikes, despite which the usually volatile O'Hagen kept his cool. With the bases full and two men out, the umpire did the same to second baseman Truby, one pitch being over his head and the second missing by six inches, whereupon Truby threw his bat at the umpire, "hitting him a glancing blow in the side." Harry went to jail to await court action the next day. One Norfolk newspaper thought his actions unwise but stressed provocation. Kissinger pitched well enough to win, but errors and rank decisions allowed the Hilltoppers to score four times, Norfolk's only run coming when Colliflower doubled in a runner who had to throw off the rival third baseman who clung to him "around the neck" as he lurched toward home plate. The Norfolk reporter considered this behavior "the dirtiest exhibition of ball playing yet seen in the league." In this instance, even McLaughlin reluctantly ruled interference and allowed the run, to the annoyance of the Lynchburg press.[23]

The next day's headline read "Won Against the Umpire." After the game on Monday, McLaughlin boasted that he had won the game for the home team and would "repeat the performance today." When Lynchburg broke through with three runs in the third, it looked like the umpire would have his way, but except for that inning Petty placed every ball directly over the center of the plate with such velocity that the batters could not hit the sphere squarely. In the fifth inning, Norfolk wracked Kit McKenna, who had been throwing wildly but walking no one, for eight hits and five runs. When Captain McCloskey, the only Norfolk player Sommers authorized to speak to the umpire, carped at his third strike call in the fifth, the umpire threw him out of the game, supposedly the first time that had happened to the quiet right fielder in 10 years as a professional. Even though Norfolk won the contest 6–4, that evening McCloskey, insulted by the abusive language, called on the hung-over umpire at the hotel and gave "him a severe thrashing." The next day a sober McLaughlin called an objective game, won by Norfolk 9–1.[24]

Newspaper accounts regarding Truby and McCloskey vary greatly. No mention of the umpire's inebriation appears in the account of these games in the Lynchburg daily. A brief editorial comment, probably written or at least sanctioned by Carter Glass, owner of the Lynchburg newspaper, part owner of the Lynchburg professional club and a future U.S. senator, sharply criticized *The Landmark* for relying on Camden Sommers to ascertain what happened. According to Glass's newspaper, the umpire walked halfway from in back of the mound toward home plate to warn the second baseman to desist from complaining. When Truby continued, only then did the umpire eject him, whereupon the former flung his bat into McLaughlin's side. The injured umpire continued his work, as Lynchburg's chief of police and an officer escorted the defiant Truby to jail, where he posted bond. The Lynchburg paper considered Truby and O'Hagen "birds of a feather."[25]

After the McCloskey incident, the Lynchburg press sharply criticized Sommers for surrounding himself with a "lot of toughs of the worst description." Only Hodge, Hauptman, Colliflower and Fry were exempt from this status. *The Landmark* allegedly presented a sanitized version of this affair, much to its discredit, while the other principal Norfolk daily reported the poor behavior in a less partisan fashion.[26]

At this point, Norfolk stood in third place, between five and six games back of Petersburg. In the meantime, Petersburg defeated Richmond enough to force the losers back to third place. And then the Farmers lost several contests. Suddenly, Norfolk was in a showdown series with Petersburg, with five fewer wins but two less losses than the Farmers. But Fry, trying to hold a 2–1 lead in relief of Kissinger, instead absorbed a 17–7 loss against the Farmers in Petersburg.

The only good news for Norfolk that day was the firing of umpire Ed Clark. The Petersburg press roundly condemned the action, and saw it as part of the Norfolk-Richmond-Newport News conspiracy. Sommers had either released or threatened to fire Clark several times earlier that season. Even when Truby played for teams other than Norfolk, he had complained about Clark, who started the season as a pitcher for the Hill Climbers.[27]

The next day the Clams recovered to win, 8–6, under most unusual circumstances. As the teams prepared for this crucial game, the fans in Petersburg took note of the article from a Lynchburg paper, describing McCloskey's arrest by local police and payment of a court-imposed fine for "a cowardly attack" on the umpire. As a result of the article, Petersburg fans had even more negative feelings about their Norfolk adversaries than usual. In a later meeting of league officials, Sommers charged that Harrison issued passes to 25 "Fifth Ward toughs" carrying "sticks, sling shots and boxes of fireworks." The chief of police dispersed them to various parts of the field, with ten being assigned to a spot about ten feet behind the Norfolk bench. The game had to be delayed several times as rockets and cannon crackers came onto the diamond.

Captain Pop Lanser, "as honest a ball player as ever played on a diamond," observed that he had never seen such an outrage in fourteen years as a player. "We had to flee for our lives; it reminded me more of a war than anything else," as "every rowdy in Petersburg" sought revenge. When "a tough" tossed a "whistling bomb" at Sommers, a nearby policeman said nothing could be done. After the game, a revolver-wielding Petersburg policeman conducted the men to safety outside the park, but toughs attacked the coach on the way to the hotel, as "policemen stood by watching the dirty attack without making any effort to protect the players." Spaine blamed the failure to intervene on a police chief that also happened to be "one of the owners of the local club." Still later, the team had to hide from mobs that roamed the streets, looking for visiting ball players to prey upon.

Fearing for their lives, the Norfolk players stayed that night in Richmond. When Norfolk failed to show up in Petersburg for the contest the next day, the umpire called a forfeit, the decision later being overturned by the league. Once he returned to Norfolk, the young collegian, Hunt, said that he was "honestly glad to get back with my life."[28]

Although both of the main newspapers in Norfolk stressed the danger of the moment, the Petersburg paper downplayed the incident, claiming that "several small boys" tossed some missiles (over-ripe vegetables and dirt balls) at the players in their tallyho as they passed a street corner outside the park. But the police, "with great firmness and determination," restored order. The writer reminded readers of the previous treatment of Petersburg players in Norfolk and urged that nothing happen that might seriously tarnish Petersburg's reputation as a "peaceful and orderly community." Winning one ball game — "or, for that matter, the pennant"— paled in comparison to retaining the honor of the community. Reporters in several Virginia cities other than Norfolk followed Petersburg's lead in minimizing the danger and also in chiding Sommers for not bringing his club to play in Petersburg the next day, contending that he wanted to postpone a showdown until he could secure another National League pitcher.[29]

Norfolk papers also claimed that Harrison laughed as the crowd became unruly and never offered any sort of assistance to the visitors; also, that he had been miffed when an alleged crooked umpire had been relieved of his job after the first game of the series. The captain of the Farmers tried to bribe Petty to throw the game, but the pitcher spurned the offer. Sommers claimed that Harrison gave free passes to thugs armed with firecrackers. Harrison denied all the charges but did admit to letting people bring firecrackers to the game. That had been done before with no ill effects, but because of the most recent experience would not be permitted again.[30]

At this point, even though Sommers was still president, the league decided that none of the postponed games would be made up, a decision that gave league-leading Petersburg a distinct advantage. Some Norfolk reporters called for an extension of the season in the hope that several Petersburg players would return to college, thus giving Norfolk an advantage.[31]

When Richmond came to Norfolk, Sommers urged his players to show no discourtesy to the visitors. "They are our guests; let us treat them as such." Norfolk, he noted, could "not endorse the lawlessness of Petersburg by similar acts of violence. Let us have order and let the best club win." With the Richmond players possibly overwhelmed by such courteous treatment, Norfolk won the game, 19–6, with the president of the National League in attendance. Nick Young thought Norfolk was somewhat deficient in base running, making one wonder whether they simply wore out in scoring so often. The Richmond players, receiving even more gracious treatment from the locals, reciprocated by losing two more high-scoring affairs, as Norfolk "feasted on Crow." The locals wanted to play a fourth game, but the visitors demurred playing a rescheduled affair on the grounds that one of its pitchers had been injured in losing the first game of the series.[32]

Standing a game and a half behind Petersburg, Sommers planned to go with Petty in all three remaining games of the season, all scheduled in Petersburg, where the mayor now promised police protection. The manager may have had little choice in the matter, as Colliflower had blistered a finger throwing too many curve balls against Richmond, Kissinger had become ill, Hunt had an emergency at home, and Fry had been ineffective lately.

According to several reporters, even though the standings as posted in the newspapers and in future publications disagree, Norfolk still had a chance to cop the pennant by one percentage point if it could win two contests. As it turned out, Petty lost the first game, 6–2, with three errors proving disastrous. Nearly four years later, a member of the Norfolk press blamed Petty, a $250 "mountain of flesh," for losing the pennant. Having lost the first contest, Petty, having an early lead in the second game, suddenly yielded five runs in the seventh followed by a home run against reliever Hunt, who had returned from his trip. The home club rallied for nine runs in two innings, eight of them earned. In the meaningless finale, with Hunt doing the hurling, the Clams won 10–6, leaving Petersburg after seven innings to catch a train. Most of the players stuck around Norfolk to play against some local amateurs to raise money to cover Herr's hospital costs.[33]

The Petersburg press praised its triumphant team and thanked John Brady and other residents of Portsmouth for their support. In a congratulatory note, Brady wrote — "Rah, Rah, Rah!/Sis, Boom, Bah!/Petersburg-Petersburg/Ha, Ha, Ha." Brady seems to have gotten the last laugh on Norfolk.[34]

In 1940, Win Clark, who played his first year in professional ball for the Staunton and Peninsula clubs in 1894, reminisced that he became familiar with Norfolk as a result of his trips to the city to play ball. Something about Norfolk "fascinated me and I suppose that is why I finally decided to make Norfolk my permanent home." He described Camden Sommers as a "man of great personality and fine mixer" and among the first to use advertising to encourage interest in the game. Clark also confirmed that the Norfolk owner subsidized the club on the Peninsula, the team Clark played for in 1894.[35]

Although lacking official statistics, a reporter thought Kissinger ranked second to Foreman as the best pitcher in the league, while Ed Tate for Richmond did somewhat better than Colliflower as the league's best hitter. Even though fielders now all had gloves, the greater distance between the pitcher's slab and home plate allowed more sharply hit balls and thus caused an increase in errors. On one occasion, Norfolk won a game despite making 12 errors. Very few games produced low scores.[36]

The 1894 season set a standard for controversy, excitement and violence that would be hard to exceed. But that would not necessarily be so because of lack of effort.

A Disputed Third Place Finish (1895)

Over the winter, Norfolk's fans learned that pitcher Kissinger moved up to Baltimore in the National League. So, apparently, had Jack Corcoran, who joined his brother in the top level of pro ball, but by the start of the season the shortstop returned to Norfolk. In January 1895, responding to criticism in a national magazine that he failed to keep experienced players, Sommers said he advanced money to Hodge, Colliflower and O'Hagen, but he released Hodge from his contract, being unable to match an offer from Ted Sullivan's Texas club because the Virginia League had a lower team salary cap of $800 a month. O'Hagen might also be lost because Louisville seemed willing to offer him a salary that Sommers could not match, but the blustery O'Hagen came back. Colliflower signed with another league team, but also later returned. In a wise move, the league appointed neutral judge Samuel B. Witt, Jr. from Fluvanna Court House to fill the league presidency.

The new season brought Jack "Corkie" Corcoran, the volatile Harry O'Hagen, speedy Harry Hauptman, and a recovered "Big" Ed Herr, along with a slew of newcomers to wear the new team uniforms of gray and blue plaid with maroon trim. One could pay $20 for a season ticket or $12.50 for ladies and others. Every Monday ladies could enter free. Game officials wore blue trousers and white shirts with the letters in blue spelling out the word "umpire" over the breast.[37]

In the pre-season, Ted Sullivan's Dallas Steers, with Hodge and Thornton and three other Virginia Leaguers, edged out Norfolk 6–5 at League Park, before a few hundred. But they also lost, 19–3, much to Sullivan's dismay. The New York Giants pounded Norfolk, 25–8, after defeating Portsmouth by a much smaller margin. With Norfolk down by 21 runs, the never-say-die O'Hagen drove a hit to right field and scored an inside-the-park grand slam when the ball became lost "among the carriages," suggesting that the fence must have been a considerable distance from home plate. After these heroics, Norfolk lost to Lancaster of the Eastern League 8–7, in a game lacking "snap" and played before a thin crowd. The Philadelphia Phillies kayoed the Clams 20–1, as Portsmouth bested Lancaster on the same day. Because Portsmouth lost to Ed Delahanty and the Phillies by only 15–10, comparative scores indicated that Norfolk might have trouble with the sister city which now had a league franchise. The Washington club of the National League also defeated Norfolk, 10–5.

So many major league clubs passed through the ports along the Elizabeth heading to their home parks after training at various places in the South that one evening more than one hundred professionals stayed at Norfolk's hotels such as the Purcell House and the Atlantic Hotel. Sommers put his club up at the Mansion House for the season.[38]

Norfolk made a decent showing in holding the Boston Beaneaters, considered the best team in baseball, to a 13–6 margin. The Baltimore Orioles, a team that usually either won or placed second in the National League (a twelve-team association at the time), cruised by Norfolk, 15–1. The Orioles had John "Mugsy" McGraw, the notorious third baseman, "Hit-em Where They Ain't" Willie Keeler, Hugh Jennings, young Kissinger, as well as Warrenton, Virginia's Walter Brodie, who slapped out four hits in this game. The second match between the two clubs proved to be quite a contest, with the Orioles barely prevailing, 12–11, in 10 innings before but 200 freezing fans. McGraw drew heavy hissing from most of those for his obnoxious behavior.

In 1895, neighboring Portsmouth outmaneuvered Newport News for the sixth spot in the league. John Brady, known for his weight and wit, and M.W. Jenkins, the club secretary, were the club's principal owners. "Genial and wide awake" Charles T. Bland, the city editor of the *Portsmouth Star*, served as the official scorer, but he soon resigned his press post to take over as general manager of the club. "Bat N. Ball" sent in "Portsmouth Pennings" or "Portsmouth Pointers" to one of the national magazines. The club nickname varied between "Truckers" and "Grangers," both named for the numerous farmers in the area.

Portsmouth management built a new grandstand that held 525 fans along with bleachers that seated some 1,600. As was true with nearly every new park, owners and reporters considered it the finest in the state. Brady put 25 men to work on building the fences, grandstand and bleachers early one Monday morning in late February and expected the project to be completed within three weeks. In a slightly revised scheme, management split the stands so that ladies and their escorts would have half the seats. The wooden facility, standing at the corner of Godwin and South streets, was supposedly accessible to the rest of the city via streetcars. Before the season, when the traction line backed off building a spur line right to the park, Brady announced plans to run his own omnibuses from the ferry, Navy Yard, and other points.[39]

In the pre-season, the Truckers beat the Texans, 14–12, after losing 13–10, before some 1,000 fans. The New York Giants then whitewashed the Gray and Green before some 500, which was no great shame as the locals faced three of the "greatest pitchers" (one of them was Amos Rusie) in the country. Portsmouth then defeated the local All-Americans before some 2,000, 11–4, with some of the Portsmouth amateur club having the same last names as the Portsmouth independent football players of that era. The crowd was largely composed of young ladies, who appeared fashionably dressed in support of Portsmouth's finest young men, each of whom had an estimated 100 female admirers.

Among those Brady recruited was outfielder Dennis "Reddy" Cleary, who played for Norfolk the previous year and later in the Pennsylvania State League. Others included Phil Vetter, William Brandt, Edgar Leach (Petersburg's pitcher), Ralph "Old Soldier" Joanes, who played for Norfolk the previous year and who died of consumption at Newport News the next year, and another local, William Hargrove. With another Virginia Leaguer, "Dickie" Knox, in the fold, Portsmouth seemed on a par with any team in the league.

Brady's most important recruit by far was Edward C. "Pop" Tate, Richmond's captain the previous year. A Richmond writer pointed out that Tate saved many games that season "not only by his heavy hitting and splendid coaching, but by his valuable headwork." Only one Richmond player had more home runs than Tate. Possessed of a "keen eye" and observant of the "smallest points in the game," Tate also worked for the "general welfare of his team" and had concerns about the "individual rights of the players." Knowledgeable residents of Richmond believed local management made a "grave mistake" in letting Tate go.[40]

On April 15, the regular season commenced before an excited home crowd of well over 3,000 at Portsmouth's League Park, with the home club prevailing over Norfolk, 14–10. Many of the city's children wore the team colors — green and gray — as did most of the ladies in the stands. In the return opening match at Norfolk, also lost by the Clams, the reporter complained about the failings of the umpire and the "youthful pluguglies," who pelted the Portsmouth players with stones after the game. Norfolk, however, rebounded to blast the visiting Petersburg Farmers twice in retaliation for the previous year's outcome.

In mid–May, even with the loss of Tate, Richmond led the league with a 21–5 record, well ahead of Lynchburg, with Portsmouth a bit above .500. Norfolk sported a dismal 10–19 record. Even so, that record was good enough for fourth place, as Petersburg and Roanoke did even worse. The league clearly had two levels of play, with the lower division performing much more poorly than those residing in the first three spots.

In response to the team's poor performance, Sommers signed on Purcell, a catcher, who after a supposed critical remark about his field play, struck reporter Jack D. Tanner in the face without warning. The two then fought a "rough and tumble," with the catcher ready to strike his opponent in the face with his foot when the groundskeeper stopped him. Tanner refused to press charges. He wrote for several small papers, principally the *Daily-Pilot,* for which there are no extant copies for the time, so we don't know the negative comment that so infuriated the catcher. One of the other writers warned ballplayers that scribes might stop reporting games if such action recurred. After behaving badly in this episode, a raging Purcell seriously injured a black bellboy at the Mansion House one Sunday morning. Hotel management ordered the ballplayer from the premises, and the bellboy hired a lawyer to bring charges against his attacker. Purcell also once threw down his catcher's mask, and stalked from the field of play, when Captain Corcoran criticized his play. Despite such behavior, Sommers failed to release him.[41]

During May, the Clams dug a deep hole for themselves, falling into the cellar at 13–31. Losses in that interval included a forfeit incurred when the team failed to come up with baseballs to start a home game against the Roanoke Magicians (or Mountaineers). The mountain men followed that up with a 9–8 win, in a game started when baseballs mysteriously appeared after the home crowd rose as one to seek the return of their money. In that game, the victors came back from an 8–1 deficit to win in ten innings against Ed Herr. The only win in that span turned out to be a disputed triumph over those same Magicians, who stalked from the field when substitute umpire (the regular umpire had become the victim of an errant pitch) Willie Wynne, a sometime Norfolk player, called out a Roanoke runner coming in from third after a wild pitch caromed off the back stop exactly 90 feet to the waiting catcher, who tagged the runner. The reporter opined that league rules stated that any ball that hit the backstop automatically entitled runners to advance one base, but he doubted the Roanoke protest would be upheld.[42]

After enduring these losing ways, Camden Sommers, noticing the 50 percent drop in attendance, folks complaining of "Chinese" or "Yellow" exhibitions, and a salary cap now raised to $900 a month, accepted $2,000 from his former silent partner for his shares in the club. At a league meeting a few days before the sale, Sommers agreed to fulfill a contract with the Norfolk and Western Railroad to use its services exclusively. Sommers, it seems, had the players go to Richmond via the shorter route through Newport News on the tracks of the Chesapeake and Ohio. The N&W complained that they had given Norfolk steep cuts in rates only if they always used tracks it controlled.[43]

Principal ownership of the club now fell to Arthur A. O'Neill, Norfolk's famed state champion bicycle racer and bike shop owner. O'Neill's first act was to release catcher "Scrapper" Purcell, and his second was to buy the team new uniforms (black with the word "Norfolk" printed in white). The new owner wanted to hire umpire Charlie Mitchell as manager, but when the players raised a fuss (they'd already urged the league president to fire Mitchell), O'Neill opted for umpire W.S. Hoggins as an interim player/manager. About a week later, the light-hitting Hoggins incurred a forfeit when he failed to bring his team across the Elizabeth to play Portsmouth. A few weeks afterwards, O'Neill turned to Pop Tate to guide the club. Portsmouth's Brady had recently released the overweight and not so nimble Tate despite objections from some parts of the press corps in the sister city. Tate's "knocking" younger players also might have influenced his removal.[44]

The league schedule was built on natural rivalries. Richmond played a disproportionate number of games against Petersburg and the Roanoke Magicians or "Mountaineers," as they were sometimes dubbed, often contended with the Lynchburg "Hill Toppers," "Hill Climbers," or "Tobacconists." As natural rivals, Norfolk and Portsmouth faced each other some thirty times that year, and Norfolk lost fifteen out of the first twenty contests. Portsmouth received a prize as the Elizabeth River champions about two-thirds of the way through the season.[45]

Norfolk lost the especially important July 4 morning contest before some 3,000 at Portsmouth, where steady Edgar "Eddie" or "Adonis" Leach outdid three Norfolk hurlers, including Ed Herr. A Norfolk reporter compared the "vaunted predictions of the hundreds of Norfolk rooters" who went across the river for the morning contest to Shakespeare's *Midsummer Night's Dream*. In honor of the occasion, he gave Norfolk a new name — the "Crows," a dubious honor he had been trying to give to Richmond. The Portsmouth newspaper started out calling Norfolk the Clams, switched to Crabs, and ended up with Crows.

The second game of the doubleheader on the Fourth, held in the afternoon at Norfolk, had to be called off in the fifth inning because hundreds of unruly fans occupied a good bit of the playing field, despite the efforts of the players to force the "disgusted crowd of genteel ball cranks" away from the playing area. The afternoon contest at Norfolk featured O'Hagen reverting to form, when he tripped a player heading around third base. The ensuing brawl led to an injury to Portsmouth pitcher Willie Brandt.[46]

A few weeks earlier, a Petersburg judge had fined O'Hagen $2.50 for hitting umpire Charlie Mitchell in the back of the neck with his glove after the latter fined him $10 for disputing a call. (Umpires fining players was a common practice in those days.) The third baseman said he did not think the thrown glove could possibly have hurt the umpire, but the judge disagreed, and admonished O'Hagen to maintain self-control, but such was not in O'Hagen's nature, at least in the long term. Just before that incident, a Norfolk reporter had praised the third baseman for his improved demeanor when he assumed the team captaincy.

During the July 4 afternoon game, Pop Tate angered Portsmouth fans by forcing them to move farther away from the foul line than the distance required of Norfolk fans. Although the Crows tied their rivals with their last at-bat, the season at its halfway mark looked like a total loss for Norfolk.[47]

Tate took over the club around the middle of June, with Norfolk about twenty games below .500. At that time, O'Neill bet Brady $100 that Norfolk would end up no lower than third in the league at season's end. Nearly everyone conceded that the Richmond Bluebirds would easily win the pennant, but interest focused on the fight for third between Norfolk and Portsmouth.[48]

Through most of July and August, Norfolk sometimes moved to within 13 or 14 games of .500 only to fall back. A reporter for one of Norfolk's dailies had the Bluebirds "swoop down" on the Blackbirds in a shutout loss to Richmond played before a large crowd in Norfolk, as a big contingent of denizens from the capital city squared off against local residents. A Huntersville constable arrested two blacks fighting each other, one wielding a stiletto, the other a hatchet, each a fan of the contending clubs. On August 20, the Blackbirds' record stood at 39–60 following a 7–6 loss to Roanoke, a club vying with Norfolk for last place. Around that time Norfolk placed sixth in fielding and fifth in hitting among the league's six clubs.[49]

During this down time, Norfolk's reporters expended a good bit of ink complaining about the inadequacies of the umpires, especially those that the secretary of the league, a resident of Richmond, put on permanent duty in the capital city. Even when this particular secretary quit, his replacement, another friend of Wells, Bradley and company, was expected to hire only those who were friendly to the home club. After one of them officiated at a Richmond game at Norfolk, he returned to the capital, vowing never to umpire in Norfolk ever again. O'Hagen and Tate claimed they had not *really* threatened his life if he did not reverse a call against their team.[50]

Despite so-so results, the club showed positive attributes. It dominated league-leading Richmond in head-to-head contests. New players such as Henry J. Cote, Sam Mills and Frank McPartlin, the latter from the Rochester club, plugged holes in the team at catcher, second, and pitcher respectively. The club decided against releasing Ed Herr near the end of July, probably because he had won about as many as he lost — a rare trait up to that point of the season. The big pitcher went on to win six of his next seven decisions. One of those wins came against Lynchburg's famed future major-leaguer Al Orth. Newcomer lefty George Weeks finished with 35 decisions, but only a 16–19 record.

As might be expected with Portsmouth and Norfolk closely contending, the two clubs carried on controversies. One involved Sam Mills, who after running away from a team in Evansville, Indiana, took an advance from John Brady then signed a contract with Norfolk, much to Brady's displeasure. To make room for Mills at second, O'Neill planned to switch Norfolk's regular second baseman Ambrose McGann, on loan from John McCloskey's Louisville club, to the outfield. Rather than accept the new assignment and under the impression that he could drop his affiliation with Norfolk after a certain date, McGann signed with Brady's club. O'Neill persuaded Nick Young of the National League that the deal violated his contract. It all worked out when Evansville decided not to continue blacklisting Mills because he wasn't worth the fuss. Once Norfolk knew that Mills could play, the club permitted McGann to stay with the sister city.[51]

Statistically, Mills and McGann were very similar, so one only wonders why after playing about .500 under Tate in July and most of August, Norfolk surged to win 15 of the next 18 games. After a 3–2 win over Roanoke in early September, the soaring Crows improved to 52–63, good for fourth place ahead of Petersburg, which had sold ace pitcher Johnny Foreman to Pittsburgh.

Though Portsmouth was four games below .500, it still looked like a long shot for Norfolk to overtake its neighbors, but McPartlin shut out the second-place Lynchburg Hill Climbers and Weeks followed by beating them, 9–6. After the McPartlin win, a headline proclaimed that the Crows were "in Fine Feather and Fly Far Ahead." The reporter praised the virtues of these particular Crows, who once stood on the "very lowest branch of the percentage tree" but now were "within just a few twigs of the third highest limb." No longer were they ordinary birds but must be considered "new world" crows, a much better breed than the older species. A day or so later, when Norfolk narrowly moved ahead of Portsmouth in the standings, the reporter had the Crows land on the third branch of the tree. But Portsmouth resumed that particular perch the next day, when Norfolk lost to Lynchburg while Portsmouth tied Petersburg. The Truckers then took three straight from Lynchburg at home, while the Crows did well in winning two of three from Richmond in the capital city. With the home team now holding a one-game edge over Norfolk, the Portsmouth newspaper bragged as if the season had ended, saying "Poor Norfolk! There may be another season next year. When that time comes, if better ball players are secured and better luck is engaged, third place may be in her grasp." But when Norfolk beat the league-leading Richmond "Hustlers" two of three in the capital city, the Portsmouth people heard "whisperings" that the Crows bought off the losers.[52]

In the first game of a showdown series between the two rivals, Norfolk easily triumphed, 11–2, putting the two teams in a virtual tie with two games remaining on the schedule. In the second game of the series, Brady refused to accept Charlie Mitchell as the arbiter on the grounds that he had not officially been reinstated in the league. Brady possibly recalled a game earlier that season, when Mitchell, tired of hearing Brady complain, stalked off the field. It also may be that the Portsmouth owner had concerns about Mitchell's close relationship to O'Neill. For their refusal to play, Portsmouth presumably sustained a forfeit, the traditional ceremony of nine pitched balls having been performed. With no game in the offing, fans howled. Brady now decided to play a game. Despite Mitchell's public announcement to the contrary, owner O'Neill went ahead with a contest convinced that it was an exhibition and, therefore, would not count in the standings. When Portsmouth won, the reporter at the

Portsmouth branch office of the *Virginian* ignored the forfeit and claimed a third-place finish for his team.[53]

On the last day of the season, the Crows apparently took over third place by winning, 6–3, in a game that was officially terminated after six innings. When Norfolk scored several runs in the seventh with more runners perched on the bases, Portsmouth fans, objecting to an umpire's safe call, started to fight with Norfolk supporters. As the toughs, even using clubs, assaulted each other, the umpire called the game for Norfolk. With order restored, John Patrick Thornton, not seeing his glove in center field where he left it, pursued his Portsmouth counterpart. The latter, finding the glove in a nearby wagon, returned it, but the two squared off after a verbal exchange. A hotel detective from Port Norfolk then slugged Thornton with a blackjack. Thornton went amok, striking at nearly everyone in sight before finally being subdued by his own mates. A Huntersville constable arrested the detective, as "pandemonium reigned supreme."[54]

After the season ended, league officials discounted the Portsmouth forfeit and counted the second game as a loss for Norfolk. However, Portsmouth did not finish third, despite its percentage of .472.44 (60–67) to Norfolk's .472.00 (59–66). It seems more than likely that the moguls would not have reversed the results of the game had they known it would change the final standings. One can only wonder whether anyone raised the point about Norfolk forfeiting a game to Roanoke in early June and then playing another game when new baseballs showed up. Norfolk absorbed two losses that day, but technically the second game was an unscheduled affair and thus should not have counted. A meeting in Lexington to deal with the matter went on for hours as the delegates massaged the numbers. The committee consisting of O'Neill, Jake Wells and John L. Watson, the latter representing Portsmouth, finally agreed that no one occupied third place or two teams did. One can only wonder if anyone won the $100 bet between Brady and O'Neill about whether Norfolk would end up third.[55]

Whatever the case, the Portsmouth "Grangers," aided by the absence of several Norfolk players, took three straight from Norfolk in a postseason series for a special cup, with 60 percent of the gate going to the winning players. So Portsmouth acquired two cups that year. Captain John T. Brady, owner and sometime manager, received a silver-and-gold-lined cup bearing the inscription "Frank H. Gale's prize cup, won by the Portsmouth baseball team from Norfolk, in the inter-city series, Virginia League, Season 1895." The other side featured a diamond with nine men filling positions with a batter at the plate. Brady also secured the Chapman and Jakemen cup, a representation of three bats as a stand with a baseball for a bowl, for winning the postseason series. Just as in 1894, Brady ended the season on a happy note— just the opposite of the view in Norfolk.[56]

That season, Pop Tate batted an amazing .530 during one sustained stretch. Although he was overweight, he could still steal bases fairly regularly. He was widely regarded as a fair fielder, and the press nearly everywhere praised him for his congeniality and baseball acumen. In explaining Richmond's failure to re-sign him before the season, his release by Brady during the season and O'Neill not re-signing him for the following year, one can only surmise that he either could not get the most out of the youngsters or had to be paid too much.

Lynchburg led the league in overall hitting, with Norfolk coming in second (.263) and Portsmouth fifth at .238. For Norfolk, Corcoran hit .312, and fans voted him the most popular player, for which honor he received a gold watch and chain. Will Hargrove won that honor for Portsmouth, although he only hit .251. Despite his light hitting, Hargrove had a shot at the majors in Baltimore. Later, a newspaper in that city described the Virginian as "a big well-built young man," who displayed "hard, accurate throwing." As it turned out, he failed to stick in the majors; instead, he became a policeman in Norfolk and returned to Portsmouth the next season. In 1897, "Hargy" played for Richmond in the Atlantic League and did pretty well.[57]

Even though the Richmond press had worried about the loss of Pop Tate as player/manager before the start of the season, the Bluebirds dominated the race from the beginning, with only Lynchburg having even a remote chance of keeping pace. William Bradley hired Jacob "Jake" Wells, one-time major leaguer and more recently from the Southern League, to take over at first base and as manager. With younger brother Otto, Jake Wells would establish one of the biggest entertainment industries in the South, with main bases in Richmond and Norfolk. Wells' first foray in Virginia was in baseball. With his numerous contacts, he formed a talented and balanced aggregation, mostly players from the Southern League, including Jesse Tannehill, who would later pitch for Pittsburgh for several years. Wells also had Charles "Barley" Kain.

Kain, although an exceedingly talented player, had a problem with alcohol. After warning Kain twice when he showed up tipsy, Wells benched him without pay for several games after a third incident. At least on one of these times, Kain had been with McLaughlin, the umpire the Norfolk complained about the previous season. In a brief note, the Richmond paper made it clear that McLaughlin was not in proper condition to umpire the game, thus validating what Sommers had been saying the year before. The league finally released McLaughlin, who went to the Southern League.[58]

Having such a fine club did not make Richmond fans any better than those of the rest of the league. Early in the season in a game against Petersburg—actually a win—Richmond toughs inflicted a stone-induced head wound on Bob Pender, the Petersburg manager. Late in the season, the Richmond paper attributed two straight losses to the suddenly surging Norfolk Crows to fans who paid only 10 cents for admission to the bleachers. Even before the games began, these fans verbally assaulted their own players, thus breaking their spirit. The press suggested that Bradley charge the bleacher crowd the same as other clubs did to keep the riff raff out.[59]

Such low fares and a winning record, however, kept the stiles turning in the capital city. Almost from the beginning of the season, Sam Chowder and a cast of "little men" (apparently some sort of robots) acted out many of the away games at the city's Academy of Music. These shows sustained interest in the team at a high level through the long season. After the regular season, Richmond easily overcame second-place Lynchburg in the playoffs for the Nowlan Cup, but it lost a hard-fought series against Nashville for a perceived Southern championship.

Three Seasons in One (1896)

During the 1896 season, "Mate" Armstrong invited reporter Thomas Spaine to join the crew, including Captain Davis and George "Skipper" Cleve, on one of the trips of the sloop *Mary Jane*. Based on his nautical experiences, Spaine claimed that no one had "any better time than the jolly ball players," and so he dubbed them the "Crew of the Mary Jane." The name did not immediately grab the public's attention, but eventually several reporters began to call the team the Crew of the Mary Jane or more simply the Mary Janes or the Crew. In the meantime, what passed for professional baseball in Norfolk carried several names, some pretty silly. For much of 1896 it would be the "Seagulls" or just plain "Gulls," but even before Spaine circulated his story in a national magazine, a Portsmouth scribe happily reported in "Diamond

Dust" in the local newspaper that "the Mary Jane seems to have struck a snag as that noble ship is somewhat waterlogged."[60]

After some debate, Portsmouth received the title of "Grangers," doubtless due to members of the Patrons of Husbandry that resided on the outskirts of the city. At least one reporter insisted on calling the club the "Brownies," because of the color of their new uniforms.

During the winter, John Brady sold two-thirds of his stock in the Portsmouth baseball team to State Senator Henry Lee Maynard and John Watson. A few days later, Maynard introduced a bill that became law "for the preservation of order at race courses, fair grounds, baseball and football parks and other places where athletic sports are held." The act called for city police to have jurisdiction one mile beyond city limits. Off-duty police would have free entry to the sporting arena and be able to enforce the law should rowdy behavior arise, something that had happened frequently in the first two years of the Virginia League. When people in Portsmouth questioned Maynard's motives for calling for this legislation, Watson defended his partner, noting that the Portsmouth team realized no benefit from the act since the city charter already allowed city police to make arrests in Norfolk County one mile over the boundary. Under current conditions, the police presence at the games did not cost the taxpayers anything.[61]

In 1896 in Norfolk, O'Neill tapped Louisville's one-time sports editor and sometime saloon owner Claude McFarlan to become player/manager, and he began signing players in January. In response to criticism about the lack of quality of his recruits, the new Norfolk manager noted that Portsmouth had only signed two respectable candidates—"Lefty" Marr, as manager, and third basemen Joe Burke—along with several others from Cincinnati's amateur ranks. Portsmouth also had catcher Pat Rollins, who had started his career in Lynchburg in 1886, playing at the time with future umpire Charlie Mitchell. In March, about a month before the start of the league season, "Little Mac" asserted that he had put "together a good, strong aggregation of ball players" for Norfolk, "a good ball town," whose citizens "generally love the game." Portsmouth reporter Bland thought second baseman Jack Wentz had amassed pretty solid minor league numbers the previous year. George Pfanmiller and George Weeks might be able pitchers. And McFarlan himself was no slouch.[62]

The usual bric-a-brac accompanied the time between the seasons. The Norfolk men now sported two sets of uniforms—black ones with red trim and red-stripped stockings for the road, and gray with blue trim for home. O'Neill planned to enlarge the stands and put some dirt in left field. Management also now provided a clubhouse equipped with "baths and other paraphernalia for the comfort and health of the men." O'Neill even hired a physician, whose quarters were located in the new clubhouse. The press hoped that the traction company might put in tracks to link the park with the rails on Church Street, "two squares" (blocks) away. Fans, and one might add reporters needing to get downtown in a hurry to report on games, had to walk or run in the dust and heat to reach the cars at the end of the game. Traction company officials, however, did not think a spur covering two blocks would be cost effective. Newspapermen were pleased to learn that they would have a special box on top of the grandstand. Reporter Bland wanted everyone to know that the general public would be considered trespassers for entering these premises. For its part, Norfolk management, like its counterpart across the river, was determined to stop the rowdy behavior of the fans. The bill before the Virginia General Assembly would allow Norfolk police, like their Portsmouth counterparts, to supervise the games even though they were played in Norfolk County.[63]

With everyone in the right frame of mind, the season commenced. An excellent omen at the start was a surprise exhibition victory over Boston, 5–0, with George Pfanmiller in the box, putting the team "Knee Deep in Glory." It was only a six-inning contest, but the win came at the expense of Kid Nichols, the youngest pitcher ever to win 300 games and one of the greatest of all time. "MacFarlan's Pets" also did rather well in a game against the Baltimore Orioles, losing 5–3, but then they lost, 20–1, to the Orioles before some 800. McGraw did not even play, being a victim of typhoid. They then secured an easy win over New Haven when Harry O'Hagen, now playing for New Haven, charged across the infield to attack a Norfolk player who was then serving as umpire. McFarlan, noting his impending arrival, throttled him by the back of his neck and fell on him. Order finally prevailed before some 800 disgusted fans. Norfolk also succumbed to the Brooklyn Bridegrooms (later known as the Dodgers), 17–8.[64]

But what happened in Norfolk was child's play in comparison to what transpired in Petersburg when the Orioles went to the Appomattox River before they arrived on the Elizabeth. The visitors left the "Cockade City" without their share of the gate receipts when a mob chased them in an episode similar to what had happened in 1894 to Norfolk. Some Orioles, including Walter Brodie, headed out of state, when they heard the authorities from Petersburg planned to arrest them.

"The Agony Has Begun," the paper noted, as it began league coverage of the 1896 season, and explored President Cleveland's disinclination to help Cuban rebels. Streetcars moved some 4,000 fans just before the 4 P.M. starting time. Pfanmiller fanned a few in the Gulls' 7–4 victory over archrivals Portsmouth. Norfolk then lost the game in Portsmouth, but rebounded to take the rubber game of the series. At first, Norfolk played at .500 or a few games above that mark and held second spot in the standings through most of May, but the team never really challenged for anything better than second place before falling back in the pack.

As usual, management sought new talent. O'Neill secured pitcher Jake "Happy Jack" Gilroy from the D.C. club a few games into the season. On the last day of April, Gilroy won, 14–4, over Roanoke. He then won several more games and also did well hitting and playing in the outfield. O'Neill later acquired collegian Joe Corbett, the brother of famed world champion boxer "Gentleman Jim Corbett." The younger Corbett had played for Washington and now belonged to Baltimore. His solid work as pitcher and infielder surprised many who thought he was riding on his brother's fame. O'Neill also brought in hard-hitting catcher Frank Bowerman, but two injuries to his hand put him out of commission for a time. This infusion of new talent helped, but Corbett, Bowerman and a third player eventually headed off to Baltimore's minor league team in Scranton, though Corbett and Bowerman later won games for the National League Orioles.

The hiring of Corbett, Gilroy, and possibly Bowerman shows clearly that Norfolk had "farmed" players on its roster, even though a league rule forbade this practice. One of Richmond's best pitchers was also a farmhand being seasoned for Washington. A league meeting finally resolved the matter by allowing all the clubs to have no more than two such players.

Of the original crew, several did not remain for very long. McFarlan, in the face of contrary public opinion, farmed out C.F. "Frog Eye" Meredith, Frank Redding, Shirley Thompson and pitcher Richard Waite to the Kentucky State League. Quinn, a short-term outfielder, hit only .214 and was soon set adrift. The rapid turnover meant that by mid-season the club only retained four of the original eight men in the field on a regular basis. Only three players had fixed positions — McFarlan in center garden, third baseman "Monk" Ramp, and second-sacker Jack Wentz, the last two considered "conscientious gentlemen" by the Portsmouth press. Frank "Red" Armstrong caught and played several positions in the field.

Among the pitchers, Blankenship looked like a "wicked southpaw," but after doing well once or twice, he ended up playing in nearby Suffolk as a semi-pro. As one old sailor put it, as quoted in the sports column called "Music of the Spheres," the commentary section that accompanied accounts of ballgames, "that cruiser may be swift enough, but I don't like the way he shoots 'em from the port side." Blankenship's fielding percentage of .625, as published in the local press, was exceedingly poor by any standard.[65]

McFarlan also released lefty Fred Schmidt, even though he feared the pitcher might sign up with another league team. Schmidt won a game for Portsmouth against Norfolk 9–0, but it was a forfeit. Norfolk led at the time the Crew left the field, 5–0. In another contest, Norfolk scored several runs off Schmidt, then toiling for Petersburg, thus justifying McFarlan's judgment in disposing of him. Fred had just signed on to play for the semi-pro Suffolk club when he agreed to terms with a New England League club.

Around midseason, the club carried out a flurry of maneuvers, some of which caused controversy. When McFarlan started to use his younger brother (A. McFarlan) in the outfield, he released the fleet-footed Stephenson, who wanted to join Lynchburg, where fans had given him a silver-knobbed cane. A reporter thought the folks at Epworth Methodist Church would miss him. After playing in Suffolk for a short time, the fielder ended up in Portsmouth. Toward the end of the season, when he muffed a fly ball to help Norfolk win a game, rumors flew that members of each team were on the take. Reuben Carl Stephenson, taking umbrage at this assault to his honor, pointed out in a public letter that because McFarlan questioned his ability, the outfielder fought harder against his former team than any others in the league. He also noted that Norfolk at its best was a second-place club, and now Portsmouth was superior. In response, officials of the Norfolk club contended that Norfolk's earlier failure to take over first was largely due to Stephenson creating dissension.[66]

Even popular Bob "Lily" Langsford received his release. A reporter blamed the shortstop for one loss, when he tried for an unassisted double play instead of throwing the ball to Wentz. Langsford claimed the little second baseman was nowhere near the bag to receive his throw, but the reporter disagreed. Within a week, O'Neill replaced the culprit with Lamont (from Owensboro, Kentucky), who according to the reporter, looked like Langsford from afar. Clearly the reporter now felt sorry for raising such a fuss, as Langsford headed home, his professional season supposedly at an end. At the time of his departure, he was hitting about .325. Lamont in his first 25 at-bats managed but three hits. He also made four errors, suggesting some weakness in his fielding, the supposed reason for Langsford's release. Lamont finally stabilized, although he maintained a reputation for muffing easy chances.[67]

All-purpose Tommy Turner, who was especially adept at blocking runners returning to first base and had been Petersburg's heaviest hitter the previous year, also joined the exodus. Having shaved his mustache, he had his bag in hand about to leave town. The next day found him back in the field without his mustache, but he soon headed toward Richmond. When he later sought to become a league umpire, O'Neill objected on the grounds that Tommy could not possibly judge Norfolk games objectively.

By July 1, Lynchburg led the league by some seven games over Richmond. Portsmouth and Norfolk once again vied for third, with Portsmouth having a two and one-half game edge. Only three straight wins in late June over Richmond allowed the Crew to end the first half two games below .500.

Not satisfied with this mediocre result, McFarlan and owner O'Neill kept changing players. They brought on a new and "mysterious" first baseman who did not stay long enough for anyone to know his first name or his origins. Catcher and utility man Jim Ballentyne did okay for a time, but then received his release. McFarlan's brother Al batted only .159 in his first 44 at-bats, but eventually came around. Near the end of the first half of the season, with Bowerman injured, O'Neill took on Earl Thurston, the fellow Thornton had fought with the previous year in the last game of the season against Portsmouth. The catcher/outfielder hit .375 in a handful of games, but quickly dropped to below .300 when he developed a sore arm. In the latter part of July, he was replaced by Jocko Fields, who played out the rest of the season as the regular catcher.

Although Fields did well, his performance supposedly fell off as soon as his wife and child joined him from Atlanta, where the catcher had been playing in the Southern League. O'Neill acquired Fields because an overweight Armstrong missed an exhibition game at Newport News. One of the numerous bits of so-called poetry that permeated parts of the press at the time hinted that Armstrong was overly critical of his fellow players. Owner O'Neill fined him $50 and made him sit out several games without pay. Finally, Armstrong returned to play first base exclusively.

O'Neill and McFarlan also signed on Harry "Slats" Davis, who reputedly led the New England League in hitting the year before. Davis played in several games before the halfway mark, having but five hits in his first 27 at-bats. His fielding, however, was solid, and eventually his hitting came around, at which time he served as team captain. Outfielder George Cleve, who came on board about the same time as Davis and Lamont, hit solidly from the outset, batting .296 as of July 26.[68]

Among the pitchers, George Weeks left just after the season started, leaving George Pfanmiller, who was soon joined by Jack Gilroy. "Happy Jack," hitting at .252 in early July, raised his average to .310 a little over two weeks later based mostly on one game, where he went 5 for 7 at the plate. He even caught in one game when O'Neill punished Armstrong. Quite versatile, he also played outfield and even umpired at times. In limited duty, Joe Corbett hit close to .350, but went to Scranton. Around midseason O'Neill secured Joe "Doc" Sechrist from New Orleans. Near season's end, lefty Fred Clausen, another ex–Southern Leaguer, pitched a few games for Norfolk after being let go by Richmond. Eddie Leach, formerly with Petersburg and Portsmouth, held down a place in the rotation for much of the season. Also near season's end, O'Neill acquired Otis Stockdale, who pitched in a preseason game against Norfolk for Baltimore (his batterymate being Bowerman). When Richmond failed to pay him more than $65 a month, he left for home, but somehow Norfolk ended up with him.[69]

The press praised Claude McFarlan, and surely "Little Mac" must have been one of the better center fielders ever to play in the City by the Sea. Rival reporters thought he also tended to create turmoil on the field. The Portsmouth press, copying a Richmond account, maintained that in a game Norfolk narrowly lost against the Bluebirds, McFarlan taunted pitcher and future major leaguer Jesse Tannehill, yelling obscene remarks in the direction of the fans in the bleachers behind third base at West End Park in the capital city. In another version of the episode, Tannehill interjected himself into a discussion between McFarlan and Jake Wells, the two opposing managers. An annoyed McFarlan punched him, causing the crowd to swarm onto the field from the left-field bleachers, finally contained by the police. The Norfolk newspaper comment was part of a three-pronged denunciation of the way Richmond management controlled nearly everything in league affairs. Norfolk lost three straight games in the capital, but all the contests had peculiar calls or occurrences, from an umpire calling one runner safe even though he was out by at least two feet. In the last game of the series, the distance between the pitching slab and home plate varied up to 18 inches too short depending on who did the measuring.[70]

In a May game mentioned earlier, with Schmidt on the mound in Portsmouth, McFarlan refused to accept the much-respected I.T. Van Patten as an umpire, forcing the clubs to use a player from each team. When the Portsmouth man umpiring behind the plate threw a ball as hard as he could through the infield, manager Charlie Marr urged his runner to advance. When the runner, at Marr's insistence, refused to return to first after umpire Gilroy told him to, the Norfolk team, leading by several runs at the time, walked off the field. The club thus forfeited the game, to the disgust of *The Virginian* reporter, who excoriated McFarlan. A letter to the editor from a Norfolk fan defended the manager, maintaining that the game should have ended when the Portsmouth players would not accept Gilroy's call. But the Norfolk reporter, pointing to chapter and verse of the baseball rules, noted that Mac should have protested the game, but not left the field.[71]

Writing for one of the national sporting magazines, H. Salomonsky called "Watson, Maynard, Marr and Co.," the owners and manager of the Portsmouth club, the "pugilistic Pirates." At one point in the season umpires Sandy McDermott and Ed Cline wrote a letter to league President James McLaughlin, wherein they said they would never umpire in Portsmouth again unless police protection was guaranteed. A few weeks later, in a game against Norfolk, umpire Harry Mace, after being criticized by the Portsmouth manager regarding a pitched ball, stalked away from the game, saying darkness prevented him from seeing the plate. At the time, Portsmouth had just pulled ahead by one run. Some irate fans pursued Mace outside the grounds, and somehow (some reports imply coercion) convinced him to return to the ballpark. In the meantime the Norfolk players, already loaded into an omnibus, refused to obey Mace's command for the continuance of the game. Mace then called a forfeit, even though he had already called the game a tie. Mace allegedly changed his verdict after he got to Norfolk, but the standings show Norfolk taking a permanent loss on its record. And Mace's letter to McLaughlin published in the press clearly indicated a forfeit for Norfolk.[72]

After Norfolk romped over Portsmouth, a rhymster for *The Landmark* was so pleased with the "gilt-edged ball" of the "Skippers of the Mary Jane" that he produced a few stanzas in honor of the occasion, wherein he predicted they would take the pennant: "They don't believe in kicking, they play in sun — and rain–? They're wide awake; they take the cake/ Hurrah for the 'Mary Jane.'" (The use of the question mark is either a misprint or a subtle criticism.)[73]

After winning three of four games, the club soon ran into a lengthy losing streak. After righting the ship, the club improved to 20–18, but the press in Portsmouth insisted that the "wind is not blowing from exactly the right quarter to benefit the 'Mary Jane.'" Her crew seemed less than happy that its craft was "on the losing tack." This comment appeared in the Portsmouth press just before Spaine's explanation for the new name appeared in a national magazine.[74]

Even though no Norfolk fan could consider the season a success, residents had to be pleased when the club — whatever its name — pummeled Portsmouth 15–1, 9–6, 9–7, 11–2, and 14–10, while absorbing one admittedly lopsided 13–0 beating. Portsmouth's status as a "Jonah" for the city across the river, dating back to the previous year, seemed to have faded.[75]

Not only did Portsmouth fall on hard times, but the entire league looked shaky. Dark clouds had been hanging over the league since May, when the less financially endowed clubs (the entire league except Richmond and Norfolk) objected strenuously about the wealthier teams borrowing farm players from other clubs and exceeding the $850 monthly team salary cap.

A few weeks later, last-place Petersburg moved to Hampton. The traction company that ran between Newport News and Old Point and for which Captain Frank D. Darling served as president, expressed interest in helping, but Darling and James McMenamin, two men prominent in Hampton's fishing industry, agreed to finance the venture apart from the traction company. O'Neill convinced the two Hamptonians to accept the Petersburg franchise, and when the league failed to reappear the next year, the two sued the Norfolk owner and the Virginia League for $2,000 in damages. Nearly four years later, a Hampton jury exonerated Bradley and O'Neill from the charge of deception in the civil case.[76]

Richmond took over the league lead and carried it the rest of the way, with virtually no challenge. Lynchburg sold several of its best players to the majors—one to the Boston Beaneaters and two to the Louisville Colonels—but the athletic association, noting that the club was not too far behind the Bluebirds, planned to hire fresh talent. However, at that juncture, Roanoke, which had not been doing well either in the standings or at the turnstiles, disbanded. For a few days, Lynchburg baseball men, knowing they had a good chance to cop the pennant because their club won the first half of the split season, hung on. But having lost their natural rival, they decided to give up their franchise.

With the failing of Roanoke and Lynchburg, league officials ran a supplementary season. O'Neill suggested that Richmond be declared the winner of the second part of the season, and the remaining teams would play a third season. Should Richmond win that race, it would play the second-place contender in a seven-game set for the championship Nowlan Cup.

After winning the second part of the season, Richmond did less well the rest of the way, as both Norfolk and Portsmouth became more competitive. The revived Portsmouth Browns, with Willie Brandt back in the box (he temporarily left town over bad debts), Pete Hall managing and playing shortstop, and Joe Burke reverting to form at third base, overcame Richmond, beat Norfolk, and ran off three straight against Hampton.[77]

"The Mary Janes will be well ballasted once more," a local reporter predicted on learning that Norfolk might pick up new players from one of the now-defunct league clubs. But even with no new men, Norfolk beat Richmond three times in a row, 9–4, 5–4, and 21–9 during the third part of the season. Capital City players, reportedly annoyed for reasons never specified, threw the third game. When Norfolk went to Portsmouth, the umpire stopped two games because of darkness with the home team narrowly ahead and plenty of light left. On Labor Day, the clubs split, with Norfolk winning its home contest by a wide margin but losing to Portsmouth that morning by two runs. After Norfolk took two of three from Richmond in the capital city, Portsmouth and Norfolk finished the season by playing each other at Norfolk, with Norfolk trailing in the race for first place by two games.[78]

It is not normal to forfeit the same game twice, but in the first encounter at Norfolk, manager Pete Hall refused to accept the designated umpire, who declared a forfeit to Norfolk, 9–0. But as 4,500 customers became increasingly disgruntled, the two teams negotiated, and sportsreporter and umpire Fred Chisnell expunged the forfeit. Early in the game, Portsmouth's catcher Pat Rollins sustained a serious injury as Norfolk moved into the lead. At this point, Hall, now without one of his best players and claiming the crowd seemed ominous, called for an end to the affair, but the umpire maintained that police protection was sufficient. When Hall failed to have his players take the field in a timely fashion, Chisnell again presented Norfolk with a forfeit victory.

Norfolk then easily won the ensuing two contests and claimed the championship of the supplemental season. But league officials overturned the verdict in the twice-forfeited contest, thus leaving the two teams tied. When Portsmouth failed to put in an appearance on a field in Newport News, however, it absorbed another forfeit, this one not overturned.

Norfolk played Richmond in a postseason series. The latter won three of four, and when a crucial game at Richmond was postponed by rain, the visitors returned home. When Norfolk failed to show up the next day, the umpire declared a forfeit and awarded the home team the Nowlan Cup. Perhaps we should label 1896 as the "year of forfeits."

The first voyage of the Norfolk team known at least for part of the season as the Crew of the Mary Jane, although not a great success, ended up with a club playing well above .500 and exhibiting a fairly potent offense built largely around speed, with McFarlan the leading basestealer.

As the season approached its end, Portsmouth's Van Patten said unpleasant things about umpire John McCloskey and the treatment of his Brownies by Richmond and Norfolk when Norfolk, rather than Portsmouth, got to play for the championship against Richmond. He was also embittered by the announcement that Norfolk and Richmond planned to abandon the Virginia League and join the more prestigious Atlantic League. He attributed this action largely to W.B. Bradley, Richmond's top baseball man, but "Mr. Too" (O'Neill) went along with the arrangement, although he initially preferred reviving the Virginia League. Van Patten reminded everyone that the Virginia League still existed and the territories of Richmond and Norfolk remained a part of it, but that assertion proved moot. Efforts to continue the Virginia League in the more western part of the state failed, although umpire Charlie Mitchell did everything he could to organize the residents of Roanoke, Lynchburg, and Danville to join up with some North Carolina cities.[79]

With the Virginia League a thing of the past, Portsmouth owners helped organize a Tidewater League and even hoped to have Richmond take up a franchise. That did not happen, but Bland represented Portsmouth at an organizational meeting with delegates from Suffolk and Newport News. Officials worked on by-laws, rules and a schedule, planned to charge males 25 cents to sit in the grandstands and decided that no player could receive above $40 a month (with each club having only three professionals). The Tidewater or Southeastern League ended up with a team in Suffolk, two on the Peninsula, and another in Portsmouth. That league hired a handful of beginning professionals and mostly carried unpaid collegians, playing an 18-game schedule.[80]

4

Agony in the Atlantic League, 1897–1898

Once Arthur O'Neill decided to go with the more prestigious league, the Norfolk reporters solidly supported the move. Thomas Spaine reported that many residents of Norfolk, as in Richmond, were generally happy with the move to the new league. Only those two cities in Virginia had a big enough population to supply sufficient attendance for such an adventurous voyage. In October, O'Neill confidently petitioned the corporation court for an increase in potential capitalization from $5,000 to $8,000. The move would put the two cities in faster company, but it might also attract better-behaved crowds because of the absence of local rivalries. As a national correspondent opined, "Norfolk and Portsmouth have never agreed on anything, and I don't think they ever will." Arguments among the players, management, and fans turned off some of the "better class."[1]

Even though sacked as manager, Claude McFarlan stuck around to cover the center garden. Second sacker Jack Wentz and pitchers George Pfanmiller and Jack Gilroy were also among those who remained. The most important of the new players was William "Billy" Smith, a slick-fielding right fielder and manager. In leading Lynchburg the previous two seasons, his club had run reasonably close to Richmond in 1895 and had the best record in the Virginia League the next year, when the team had to disband after Roanoke withdrew from the league.

In the middle of the 1895 season, the main Lynchburg paper described his players as veritable Lord Chesterfields. However, Smith's relations with umpires, like almost every other manager, had sometimes been a bit strained. Early in the 1896 season, in a game at Portsmouth, an arbiter called a forfeit against the Hill Toppers when Smith, in objecting to a safe call on a runner that even the Portsmouth press thought might well have been out, sat down in the outfield and picked petals off daisies. After the umpire called a forfeit, an official for the Lynchburg Baseball Association criticized Smith, apparently convincing him to mend his ways for the rest of the season. But as the 1897 season progressed for the Norfolk club, Smith acquired a reputation for his number of ejections.[2]

The local press did its best to build up interest in baseball over the winter of 1897, as folks saw the Depression easing despite the Norfolk and Western Railroad's firing of workers. In the preliminary games, fans in Norfolk got a chance to see Ernie Hodge and Harry O'Hagen, both of whom now played for Newark, and Harry Hauptman, now with Ted Sullivan's Trenton team.

Smith's "Crack-a-Jacks" started off the preseason rather well in outhitting, but not outscoring, Washington of the National League, before some 1,500 at National Park. After a second respectable loss, the team came to Norfolk to set up headquarters in the Hotel Norfolk. The players were "all clean limbed, clever, sober chaps." C.H. Broome, the "energetic, aggressive, suave and business from the word go" financial manager, had done all that he could to secure success after attending the league meeting in Philadelphia, where delegates agreed not to use "farmed" players. Elaborate efforts were made to see that the press received official scores. Fred Chisnell edited the sports items for *The Virginian*, including the comments called "Bat N. Ball." E.M. Isaacs reported on Norfolk baseball to a national sporting magazine and also sometimes wrote poems for the local newspaper.[3]

The club changed the color of its uniforms to be more nautical. "Marine blue" trim accompanied the "stout gray cloth," along with the word "NORFOLK" in blue across the chest — all that went with blue belts and hats. Yet, early accounts called the club the "Gulls," rather than the Mary Janes. Whatever their name, they surprised many in April when they "almost scalped" the world champion Baltimore Orioles. The game ended in a 3–3 tie, called after eight innings due to darkness, with George Pfanmiller pitching an outstanding game and holding John McGraw hitless. Norfolk's fans hissed the third basemen for his "dirty kicking," which "made his own team sick."

A few days later after losing to the Brooklyn Bridegrooms, 11–8, the locals stunned the same club, also known as the Trolley Dodgers, 9–6, with Jack Gilroy and Eustace J. Newton in the box. The game was called after Norfolk scored six runs in the top of the ninth, at which point the "Bridegrooms then simply HAD to leave." The club also bested the Philadelphia Phillies, 4–3, with the press of the Quaker City blaming a green umpire named Chisnell. Based on these preseason performances, the local newspaper now asserted that Norfolk had "the best minor league team ever seen in the State of Virginia."[4]

The Atlantic League season began with a tie against the Reading "Brownies" before 3,000 at League Park. Newly elected mayor W.R. Mayo threw out the first ball and gave a "happy little speech," praising the team and the national game. The previous mayor, a temperance man, had been conspicuous by his absence from ballgames in recent seasons. In the next game, a lopsided win over Reading, Claude McFarlan swatted the sphere over the Katzenstein ad on the center field fence, and also hit another homer in the seventh. The owner of the clothing store awarded McFarlan a suit that must have been worth at least $2.48, which was P. Katzenstein's base price according to his advertisement, which also displayed sketches of the heroes.

Another easy victory over Reading, 13–3, hinted at a great season, apparently confirmed when Norfolk shocked Richmond in the capital, 11–5. According to one reporter, the game proved that Richmond pitcher Sam Leever did not have the necessary leverage, thus making "Archimedes a Liar." He went on and on about various scientific laws, suggesting that Leever, "a professor," knew something about physics. After Norfolk defeated him, a Norfolk writer noted that although Leever attained near "Napoleonic fame" in Richmond, he went from the "pinnacle of earthly glory to the bottom of the pit of human woe." Jake Wells supposedly said, "Give me a Leever, and I will move the world," but the Leever broke in Norfolk, without the world moving. Isaacs wrote a poem in honor of the event, crediting Shaffer's triple with unleashing the Norfolk attack.

Now with a new name in honor of one of their owners, the "Brooms" enjoyed a "sweep" of a series, one of the few times anyone could use the word in describing a Norfolk series all season. The early record seemed to confirm a belief in Norfolk and other cities in the league that the Brooms would win the pennant.[5]

Reality soon set in. Richmond took the next two and although "Happy Jack" Gilroy shut out the "Cherubs," 1–0, Norfolk began to play .500. At home they split, winning a 7–6 contest in front of some 5,000, a "Funeral March" for Richmond. Lefty Newton, equipped with a fast-moving curve, won one game in a series against Paterson, but the visitors also prevailed in at least one encounter. Norfolk beat Newark twice with Pfanmiller and Newton both pitching shutouts. Despite these high spots, Norfolk stood in fifth place in late May with an 11–11 record, only three games off the pace.

During May, "Bat N. Ball" (probably written by Fred Chisnell), now appearing as a column in Norfolk, conducted a relentless campaign against umpire Tom McNamara, who fined several Norfolk players without informing them, allowed prolonged discussions on the field, missed calls on foul balls, and either did not know the strike zone or could not see the path of the ball. Even though he once mistakenly took a hit away from Richmond, he usually sided with that club, especially on its home field, leading manager Smith to dispatch a letter detailing his offenses to Chisnell. He, of course, published it. The Richmond press initially defended McNamara, but later at least one of that city's dailies confirmed Chisnell's diagnosis. Ed Barrow, the president of the league, soon handed the umpire his release. Maintaining that he resigned, McNamara also took issue with Chisnell's claim that he had robbed Norfolk of a home game against Richmond, noting that anyone who cheated Norfolk out of a game in its own park "might as well say his prayers." The Norfolk club usually got "everything in sight" because of "a newspaperman named Chisnell." As might be expected, the columnist got in the last word, by noting in a headline that McNamara was "Talking through His Hat."[6]

In a recurring theme reporters berated umpires. Even before the season started, a reporter castigated Harry "India Rubber" Mace for turning down a job as umpire in the Atlantic League because he feared for his life umpiring in the Old Dominion. The previous year in Portsmouth, Chisnell alleged, Mace displayed cowardice when he forfeited a game to that city, only to change his verdict to favor Norfolk once he crossed the river. Midway through the season, Mace started umpiring in the Atlantic League, but President Barrow would not assign him in either Richmond or Norfolk. The Norfolk press delighted in copying complaints about him from the northern press. Overweight umpire Ed Cline also came under heavy fire.[7]

Spaine noted that "home fans have little use for a losing club and do little reasoning." But Spaine himself discovered all sorts of weaknesses, especially on the first extensive road trip. The players hit spasmodically and ran the bases ineptly. On the positive side, the pitching proved adequate, especially the work of Jack Gilroy, who "seems to have been in possession of the graveyard rabbit's foot, as he was lucky enough to win every game" so far. Moreover, Jack was hitting at a .370 clip.[8]

Unfortunately Gilroy suffered severe health problems. After recovering the year before from typhoid fever to win five of six games and become one of the team's best batsmen of 1897, Gilroy developed a problem with his appendix, suffering considerable pain as he pitched. Finally, deathly ill, he went to St. Vincent's, where he survived an operation but remained sick for weeks. It turned out nothing had been wrong with his appendix; instead, he had kidney disease that never responded to treatment. "Happy Jack's" reporter friends started a fund with a $5 contribution and urged others to help defray the costs of his hospitalization. After Gilroy died in early August, the manager and players passed the hat at a game to help cover funeral expenses. Gilroy's death was a loss from which Norfolk never recovered.

In addition to Gilroy, several players incurred malaria-like symptoms, with shortstop Danny Leahy playing through until his recovery.

Through the next month, the Brooms lost more than they won, dropping to sixth place, although they remained but three games below league-leading Lancaster in the loss column. Richmond was a game and a half behind Norfolk in the tightly packed league standings. When Norfolk was suffering, the Richmond press piled on, with the notation that many Richmonders planned to accompany the team for its next engagement in Norfolk to "see the wreck of the good ship Mary Jane." *The Virginian* responded that although the Mary Jane was undergoing some "needed repairs," the ship "will be in such good fighting trim" that it would be able to repel its "threatened destruction."

Richmond did win two of the three contests, but the Norfolk reporter accused umpire Buck Carlin of losing his eyesight as well as his brains in the rubber game of the series. The umpire reportedly even bragged to a Richmond reporter how he had turned the game around for the visitors. Carlin later resigned because of mistreatment in the City by the Sea.[9]

A first baseman and a leading hitter in the Texas League, Charley Shaffer proved to be too short for a first baseman and a dud with the bat. But Al Weddige and Jake Weihl became so upset about Shaffer's forced departure that they sulked, leading management to fine them for insubordination. In searching for Shaffer's replacement, Broome found Jim Knowles. At the time of his hiring, Knowles, once an Atlanta Cracker who hit .322 and .367 in the two previous seasons, was umpiring in the Eastern League. Although he occasionally hit the ball with authority, he proved too slow afoot. Once his lack of movement on the basepaths prompted his own teammates (Weddige and Weihl) to yell at him. With Knowles a failure, Broome turned to Pop Tate, who was also umpiring. Norfolk fans perked up when they heard that the greatest hitter in the history of the Virginia League would once again wield his mighty bat. But although he hit tolerably well (.326), he only scored one run, suggesting that he had slowed considerably. Broome then signed George King Kelly, the obstreperous manager for the Farmers in 1894. Injuries hampered him the previous season and he surely was well past his prime, but he still exhibited a lot of pep. Near the end of the season Norfolk brought back Henry Cote, capable of both catching and playing first base. So Kelly had a chance to play outfield.

The club started the season with Jack Heydon as a backup catcher, but management lowered his salary, complaining that he was not in shape (in one game he muffed two straight curves, allowing the opponents to score). When he refused to accept the new arrangement, the owners released him, and he soon ended up in Reading, where he played that season and the next year. After his departure and a subsequent tailspin, some "patrons of the game" publicly criticized the club, saying he had been the best catcher on the staff.[10]

Pitching was a problem. Lefty Eustace Newton did well enough so that early in August, the Baltimore Orioles supposedly paid the club $700 for his contract, the deal to take effect at the end of the season. The sale surprised one reporter who noted that Newton gave up more earned runs than others on the staff. Broome found a new pitcher nearly in his backyard (Suffolk)—a young "country boy" named John Bishop, who had recently tossed a no-hitter followed by a two-hitter against Norfolk's best amateur teams. The Suffolk manager, who had signed the pitcher to a seasonal contract, objected to the deal, and threatened an injunction to prevent him from joining Norfolk unless Cunningham came up with $100. How the Norfolk owner resolved that issue is unknown, but Bishop won his first professional contest, 4–3, over Paterson. Although Bishop pitched well in most of his outings, he lost more than he won.[11]

Fred Clausen came upon a bad spell, forcing Broome to release him. The pitcher finished the season in fine form with the Lancaster Maroons, the pennant winners. The Norfolk Brooms remained seriously deficient in pitching until they signed W.T. MacFarland, who the previous year won more than twenty games (newspaper box scores provide a lower but still impressive record) at Lynchburg. McFarland gave Norfolk hope by beating Hartford, 3–1. That came only a day or two after Bishop lost to Hartford, 1–0. Fans heartily approved hiring Willie Brandt, once Portsmouth's ace. But even though he lost a game only by 2–1, a reporter thought his changed delivery would lead to too many walks. Brandt played a minimal role for the rest of the season.[12]

Early in the season, it looked like Richmond had little hitting and solid pitching, and Norfolk appeared to be strong offensively. But now the low scores indicated that Norfolk's lack of hitting might be its Achilles heel. Everyone had a theory of what was wrong. At the end of July, a Newark newspaper attributed Norfolk's sixth place in the standings to poor judgment in always trying to drive in runs with base hits rather than using sacrifices.[13]

As often happens in these circumstances, the Norfolk Baseball Association endured major shakeups. Arthur O'Neill resigned as president. Two directors also quit. E. Harvey Cunningham took a more active role as the secretary, with Broome now serving as president. Broome and Cunningham tried to create a more formidable team, but Broome become ill, supposedly losing forty pounds in a matter of weeks due to the stress. In the middle of July, C.W. Diem, acting as an intermediary for two other investors, bought out Broom's half of the team for $2,500. Cunningham, however, soon assumed full ownership of the club, a move praised by the press in the belief that he would procure more talent. Win Clark, commenting in 1940, recalled Cunningham as "one of the game's finest and most liberal owners."[14]

The press started calling the club the "Cunning Hams," but fortunately that phase passed rapidly. Although a Newark reporter insisted on consistently calling them the "Oyster Shuckers," at least some of the reporters in other league cities used the term "Crew of the Mary Jane." A Hartford writer thought the crew put up a "sorry showing," especially in batting, running, and fielding in a game in the Connecticut capital. Except for George Kelly they acted like "dead men." A week or so later Kelly sustained a cut in a fight with the umpire after a game in Hartford.[15]

With Richmond being Norfolk's main rival in the league, fans followed closely the comparative standing of the two clubs. Despite MacFarland winning most of his outings and Bishop and Pfanmiller occasionally winning, the record stood at 36–39 toward the end of July. A brief burst pulled Norfolk one game over .500 (at 47–46), but then a steady decline set in. Richmond had started off well behind Norfolk. Wells let so many of his players go that folks talked about forming a team from the released players for a benefit game in Richmond. After obtaining Chauncey Stuart from another league club, the "Johnnie Rebs" or "Johnnies," as the *Richmond Dispatch* called them, steadily improved and around midseason pulled in front of the so-so Norfolk club.

Letters and news clippings out of Richmond frequently joked about the bad behavior of the Norfolk team and its supporters. In one such assessment, reproduced in the Norfolk newspaper, a scribe complained about McFarlan's desire for a scrap with Richmond's diminutive third baseman Norman Elberfield after a close play at the plate. Although many Norfolk fans did not like the unseemly action of the crew of the Mary Jane, the "rough element goes in for just such playing." But the Richmond infielder had a mean streak and may well have instigated McFarlan's actions.

A missive appearing in a Manchester, Virginia, paper noted that baseball in the seaside city was "a thing of horrors and evils and with attending catastrophe." Visiting teams should, the author opined, "be armed with crow bars for bats and have their pockets full of cannon balls." They also needed ammo in their belts plus some cavalry and artillery nearby because "the crew of the badly damaged craft, the 'Mary Jane,'" always went for "the win by crook or hook — but mostly by crook." Only someone with "nerve, iron jaws and well developed sinews, with plenty of life insurance, should he be married, dared to umpire in Norfolk." Excited cranks in the bleachers at times "simply jump over the fence and proceed in an undignified manner to demand an explanation from the umpire or the player." It was well worth twice the price of admission to see the spectacle, except supporters of rival teams seemed to be an endangered species." Bat N. Ball furiously denounced these anonymous comments as "the vilest, most outrageous and thoroughly venial [sic] and blackguardly calumny that was ever penned."[16]

At the end of the season, Richmond sold Elberfield to the Philadelphia Phillies, where he attained a reputation as one of the most combative players the game would ever know. After playing for several major league clubs, he finished his career with Brooklyn in 1914. After managing in the minors for many years, he reappeared in Norfolk for a visit, allegedly for the first time since he had played for Richmond thirty years earlier. The city had changed so much since 1897 that "the Tobacco Kid" had a hard time finding his way around the city, but he had apparently forgotten that he played in an exhibition game in Norfolk in 1910.[17]

An incident where shortstop Dan Leahy hit William "Hargy" Hargrove in the face during a game between Norfolk and Richmond did nothing to improve relations between the cities and their reporters. But in this case Hargrove's occupation as a policeman in Norfolk between seasons may well have hurt Leahy's standing among locals. Leahy ended up with Richmond the next year, where he was Hargy's teammate. In 1904 Leahy died in a gunfight in a Texas saloon when Hargrove was a detective at the Monticello Hotel in Norfolk. Hargrove also helped out with the area's amateur baseball.[18]

Other clubs and their fans in the league were less than angelic. The Newark team, with the volatile O'Hagen leading the league in hitting, was known in Norfolk and Richmond as the "Mosquitoes" or "the Thugs." Bat N. Ball believed the New Jersey manager cheated by employing players from the New York Giants. Although newspapermen in several cities criticized Newark management for pressuring umpires to give their team an advantage on the home field and inferred that Newark's players did not always behave in a gentlemanly fashion, the principal Newark newspaper rarely mentioned the club's misbehavior. But a riot one Sunday at Shooting Park in the suburb where Newark played caused that community to ban future games on the Sabbath, an action praised by a Newark editorialist. One of their players punched a 14-year-old boy in the face, breaking two teeth. The pitcher then eluded police and returned to Newark, thereby becoming available for his next start in the rotation.

In Reading, when the assigned umpire failed to arrive on time, a popular local ballplayer angered the Paterson catcher so much that he threw a ball at the umpire's head, missing it by inches. As the Reading players ran from their bench, one of them angrily threw a ball directly into the catcher's face, smashing six teeth. Richmond sometimes caused problems. As reported in the Newark press, when Norfolk bested the home club 8–6, some 1,800 men and boys yelling "mob him" chased umpire Charley Snyder off the field. Police found a rear exit to allow him to escape. At Lancaster several of the Richmond "Cherubs" went after an umpire with Chauncey Stuart calling for his colleagues to "spike him." The Johnny Rebs soon found themselves surrounded by a mob which rained blows on Stuart and another Richmond player. A Richmond newspaper noticed that Sam LaRocque, Lancaster's French-Canadian second baseman, once threw a ball at an umpire's head, indulged in excessive bench-jockeying, and had a fistfight with Richmond's shortstop Stuart, all in one game.[19]

In a curious cultural connection that ran counter to the prevailing trend, the press and fans from Norfolk and Lancaster created a mutual admiration society. Early in the season the Lancaster writers thought Norfolk had one of the strongest clubs in the league, and even hoped that both Norfolk and Richmond, the two Southern clubs, would do well. But after Richmond and Lancaster battled each other in early July, Lancasterians confined their sympathy to Norfolk. For their part, the fans and newsmen in Norfolk applauded and publicly praised the Lancaster club and took great delight when the Pennsylvanians pulled in front of Newark and went on to win the pennant. When Norfolk defeated Lancaster at the latter's field late in the season, ending a 21-game winning streak, the Lancaster press expressed pleasure that at least it was the Norfolk club that did the honors. The fans, however, yelled "thief" and "robber" to the umpire the next day, when Norfolk won again. A story that surfaced the next year concerned manager Frank Rinn's rabbit foot, which had been given to him by a Norfolk "street urchin" that greatly admired the Lancaster club. Rinn attributed that keepsake to his club's success.[20]

As the season wound down, Spaine opined that even if the Baltimore Orioles moved "here for a season, we could not win a pennant." Now the cry was "Wait Till Next Year." "All the home cranks can do now is hope for better results in '98, but this is very poor consolation indeed."[21]

Norfolk's 1897 club: William Smith, far right in top row. The seated player in the lower right closely resembles a sketch of Dan Leahy (shortstop), who later died in a gunfight in a Texas saloon. Other players likely include Claude McFarlan (center field), Al Weddige (third base), Jake Wiehl (left field), Jack Wentz (second base), Barney Snyder (catcher) and George Pfanmiller (pitcher), all of whom played the entire season. Owner C.H. Broome appears dressed in a suit (National Baseball Hall of Fame Library, Cooperstown, New York).

Norfolk finished sixth, well behind principal rival fourth-place Richmond. George Pfanmiller won the last home game. Bat N. Ball lamented that he would no longer hear the tenor voice of Jake Weihl, a .293 hitter, in left field, watch big Al Weddige (.326), who was reputedly the best third baseman in Norfolk since the deceased Johnson (an insult for O'Hagen) fighting pop fouls, nor see Danny Leahy (.277) at shortstop or Claude McFarlan (.310) roving center field. Jack Wentz (.255), the fielding whiz, would be returning home to work in a brewery.

After winning its last home game to sport an almost respectable 57-60 record (still ahead of the Paterson Silk Weavers in the standings), the Crew went to Richmond, along with a few diehard fans on a Chesapeake and Ohio train. But the Mary Jane was wrecked by scores of 17–3, 15–2, 15–8 and 12–3. With Manager Smith suffering from pneumonia, the club collapsed in every sense. After being ejected during one of the one-sided losses and with police in pursuit, McFarlan scaled the left-field fence, landing in an adjacent garden, where the groundskeeper kept several dogs. The ashen-faced outfielder then jumped back over the fence. After losing four games in Richmond and winning three of five games at Paterson, the club completed the season by losing three of four each at Hartford and Reading, and then losing the last game of the season at Lancaster, thus ending the first voyage in the Atlantic League, with a record of 62–73.[22]

Near the season's end columnist Spaine, noting the loss of money largely due to weak attendance, pointed out that Norfolk's residents would do well to emulate Portsmouth with its spirit, patriotism and pride. Of the eight teams in the league only three—Richmond, Newark and Paterson—made a profit. Richmond's greater population and low bleacher prices and Newark and Paterson's use of Sunday games were largely responsible for this situation. Even community-based Lancaster, whose club won the pennant, went into the red by about $1,500, but the sale of one of its players cut the deficit by half. The Philadelphia Athletics, which had trouble finding a home field and competed against the major league Phillies (for a time the two shared the same park), found it best to move some of its home games to Paterson and Newark and take a portion of the Sunday gate. Eventually they stopped playing at home, becoming the "Wanderers." Barrow and company agreed to move the club to Allentown for the next season.[23]

To boost attendance, Reading signed up "Gentleman Jim" Corbett, who lost the world boxing championship just before the start of the baseball season. Corbett played first base for Reading in one game and then switched to the Philadelphia club, where he helped as the Athletics tied Richmond in both games of a doubleheader. At Norfolk, he failed to make a hit, muffed an easy fly and made another error as the visitors lost 9–2 before several thousand customers. He then played for the Paterson club at home on a Sunday, securing two hits and making no errors. Wherever he played, attendance markedly increased, but because he likely received about $400 per appearance, it would be difficult to determine his overall financial benefit for the teams involved.[24]

As the season drew to a close, Cunningham planned to spend time in "deep meditation." Some owners wanted to replace the two southern clubs to reduce travel costs. When rumors circulated that Richmond and Norfolk might lose their franchises, Cunningham tried to convince owners in Richmond to re-create the old state league. Although they seemed so inclined at first, the Atlantic League kept the southern clubs and Richmond decided to stay, compelling Norfolk to do the same.[25]

Having accepted the idea of sticking with the Atlantic League, the Norfolk owner believed that the real Jonah for Norfolk was lack of a first-class ballpark. During the season, Billy Smith noticed all kinds of problems with League Park. Fans found the task of walking, and sometimes wading, the two blocks from the trolley to the stadium a bit tedious, so the press wrote about building a new park closer to the traction line. It seemed likely that the Norfolk Street Railway Company might acquire shares in the club and help build a park next to the tracks. In March, just before the next season started, a new park materialized with a grandstand holding some 800 fans and a bleacher capacity at 1,750. With one entrance fronting on Princess Anne Road, its location was not far from the site of old Gymnasium Park.[26]

In the off-season Cunningham sacked Billy Smith, who at the time was still suffering the effects of either typhoid or pneumonia. Smith had started off the season in St. Vincent's Hospital and at its end he could be found in the same place. A Richmond newspaper applauded his dismissal, noting that while the "clever little man" could be charming and always behaved himself outside the ball grounds, on the field Smith was "a wild Indian, a mixture of baby and rowdy rolled together ... when he thinks the umpire is against him." Atlantic League fans, however, took kindly to the Tennessean, known for his spectacular catches, as an outfielder. Whatever his assets, he did not remain on the roster.[27]

"War fever" gripped the country following the sinking of the *USS Maine* in Havana Harbor in February 1898. This incident, and the continuous failures of Spain to change its treatment of Cuban rebels, led President William McKinley to call for a declaration of war against Spain just a week or so before the baseball season commenced. As the press focused on the coming war, Norfolk assembled its crew under new manager Charlie Jewell, with Bishop, Weddige, Wentz and McFarlan returning along with many newcomers. Included were George Fox, who caught for Philadelphia the year before, first baseman Bill Klusman (Western Association), experienced shortstop Bobby Wheelock, veteran pitcher Harry Staley, who had a stint in the majors, one-time Petersburg and Pittsburgh lefty Johnny "Brownie" Foreman, and outfielder Bill George, who hit .340 for St. Paul the previous year. Sometime in March, the club purged itself of Weihl, Snyder and McFarland.

An easy win over Montreal, a lopsided one versus a collegiate club, and a 14–11 loss to the Boston major-league club suggested that the Norfolk club might be of about the same caliber as the year before (as usual, the local press thought the club was the best ever), but neither assessment turned out to be accurate.

The Oystermen or "Shuckers" as they were known in several cities (not Newark, where they were called the "Crew of Mary Jane") commenced their regular season just after the United States formally went to war on April 25. Five days later as Admiral George Dewey led his Asiatic Squadron in subduing the Spanish fleet near Manila, Norfolk started the season with a 7–2 win over Paterson on the home grounds, with Johnny Foreman pitching well. Losses and wins then followed each other in roughly equal amounts amid several rainouts.

Without warning, and even though the team record stood in third place with a tolerable 8–6 record, Cunningham released manager Jewell. Just before that move, the sports editor for one of Norfolk's dailies criticized the "convivial habits" of some of the players. The image of a $200 outfielder doing a "Japanese juggling turn" for five minutes in trying to handle a groundball, and infielders throwing balls into the right-field bleachers instead of first base intimated that Jewell's men lacked discipline. When Jewell failed to live up to his name, Cunningham took over as manager. First baseman Bill Klusman assumed command whenever Cunningham went to find better players.[28]

A local reporter claimed that Norfolk was "the worst town in the league for a ball player." An element "desires the home team to lose against anybody." Another large group frantically favored the locals but berated the players for even a minor miscue. Only a small minority sat in silence when things went wrong and cheered when they went right.[29]

For the local baseball team, the situation went along tolerably well until about the midpoint of the season, even though a batted ball to "Brownie" Foreman's hand took the one-time major leaguer out of action. Backup catcher Jack Berger was hitting .350, Weddige was at .339, outfielder "Snapper" Kennedy was at .321 and Klusman batted a respectable .294. Wentz hit .271 and shortstop Wheelock carried a .241. Fox, at a .226, was doing okay for a catcher, but McFarlan was far off his usual pace, batting but .218. Cunningham, after accepting his poor hitting for a time, released him. He soon signed on with Newark and later moved over to Hartford. As might be expected, his triple led to the local's undoing in one game, but "Little Mac" did not light up the league after his departure.

Norfolk picked up Dicky Knox, who once played for Portsmouth, where he had been criticized for his bad attitude. He hit a home run and a triple in a game against Richmond, but despite these heroics, he did not stay. Scott Hardesty, who earlier played for Paterson before being traded for Kennedy, covered right field. The Paterson press accepted the Hardesty deal because the older and more versatile Kennedy became their regular shortstop, receiving ample press plaudits there until he committed four errors in one game. Later on, when he managed to err five times in one game, and a reporter noticed his errors often occurred at critical moments, Paterson arranged for his release. When Richmond let Barley Kain go, Norfolk convinced the fast outfielder to join the Mary Janes. He lasted for a few games, but then went into business back in Richmond. Somewhere along the way Cunningham dispensed with Bill George and Jack Berger, both of whom ended up with other league teams. Early in August, management signed Charlie Marr, former manager in Portsmouth and more recently an outfielder with Hartford and first baseman for Allentown, to help in the outfield.[30]

After Foreman's injury, Cunningham shored up his staff with a pitcher supposedly out of the Southern League. Later, he brought back C.H. Donnell, who had moved into the amateur or semi-pro ranks in Elizabeth City after failing to make the grade at the start of the season. Deep in June, Cunningham re-acquired E.J. Newton after his release from Reading. The 21-year-old lefty arrived in time to participate in the great collapse, wherein he managed to lose some 17 games while winning but three.[31]

In the early part of the season, the local ball club did tolerably well, at least compared to the Spaniards. They failed to prevent the Americans from invading Cuba, as 600 marines landed at Guantanamo Bay on the same day that Norfolk prevailed over Lancaster 2–1 to bring its record back to .500. When reporting the negative results of a game in June, a local reporter compared a seven-run batting assault against George Pfanmiller to the rapid-fire "bombardments of Manila and Santiago."[32]

Norfolk writers were not the only ones to weave the war into their baseball accounts. Norfolk succumbed to Richmond on the last day of May, 5–3, with Bishop taking the loss. In describing the game, a Richmond writer praised Norfolk for putting up a "gilt-edge specimen of the national sport," but although the Bluebirds "didn't exactly bottle them up, as Mr. Schley had done Cervera, they gave them royal battle, such as Dewey would have done."

"The Commodore of the Mary Jane's crew" (Bishop) faced a "terrific bombardment ... didn't show the white flag, however; he just kept throwing hot ones until the fight was over, and then Cunningham telegraphed home, saying 'We fought a good fight, but were vanquished because our ammunition was not so powerful as was the enemy's.'" Even when no game took place because of rain, one writer had "old man Jupiter Pluvius with his large hitting battery of 13-inch guns" bombarding the city.[33]

During the war, the Southern League disbanded, allowing Norfolk to pick up Morris "Farmer" Steelman, who had previously played for Richmond. Some potential players were not available because they volunteered for the military. One-time Petersburg and Norfolk pitcher Eddie Leach and the catcher from the Petersburg's 1894 Virginia League championship club were located at Camp Cuban Libre with the Fourth Virginia, preparing for action. Although very few professional ballplayers joined the army, the war, plus terrible weather, sharply cut attendance. As one Atlantic League reporter saw the situation, many of the most loyal fans had volunteered for war service and those that joined the home guard spent their free time reading bulletins about the battles rather than going to the ballpark. The National League, and probably every league in the country, suffered from the same adversity. National League President Nick Young talked about "huge chunks" of gate receipts being lost due to the war.[34]

To attract more fans, the Atlantic and some other minor leagues resorted to employing female curiosity Lizzie Arlington to pitch five innings or so in exhibitions between clubs. Lizzie did not do strikingly well in Norfolk, but in a couple of towns she shut out the hitters, though one scribe inferred that the players let her off easy. She even scored a questionable hit through the second baseman's legs at Lancaster.[35]

When John Bishop shut out Hartford, Norfolk once again evened its record as American forces prepared for the big invasion at Daiquiri. Norfolk hoped to better its record on the first Sunday in July by winning at Reading, but its management decided not to challenge Pennsylvania law against playing professional ball on the Sabbath. By July 4 that year, when Norfolk split a double bill with Richmond in the capital city, Teddy Roosevelt's Rough Riders and black regiments, among others, had forced their way through Spanish defenses around Santiago. At the time, Richmond led the league with a record of 31–22. Its ace, Jake Chesbro, beat Norfolk 6–2, a day or so later, growing stronger as the game progressed. Chesbro would later join the New York Highlanders (Yankees) and win over 40 games in 1904.

The series in Richmond, which ended a 14-game road trip for the Crew during which they won seven games, left Norfolk with a mark of 28–29. Back home, Norfolk lost two of three against the Bluebirds as Chesbro beat lefty Newton, with Bishop getting the locals their only win. After a series against Allentown in which Bishop won 2–1, the record stood at two games below .500. That was followed by a split of a doubleheader against Lancaster on the day the Spanish surrendered Santiago.

Through July and much of August, Norfolk slowly rode a "toboggan downhill." Richmond swept a series, with scores of 7–1, 2–0, and 7–0. Obviously hitting was not the Crew's forte. Finally, after losing another game at Hartford, Newton won a game against the same team, 3–1, but Pfanmiller lost the next, 3–2. The Newark newspaper described one loss as "Crew of Mary Jane Wrecked in Inhospitable Port of Richmond" and another as "Crew of the Mary Jane: It Sails into Its Home Port, Covered with Barnacles and Goes Down to Bitter Defeat."[36]

In mid–August a local paper assessed the team and its 36–53 record. Not since the "palmy days when Doc. Sommers had a team here," the reporter lamented, had the attendance at the games produced an extra dollar in the pockets of the owners. But 1898 was the worst year in the club's history. Captain Cunningham "with grit to spare, built a park, put a first-class team in the city and from the fall of the flag has lost money." Cunningham put more money into finding players than any other team in the league but had the worst team. The Norfolk writer hoped that the state league might be revived, or that Portsmouth could take Hartford's place in the Atlantic League, hinting that one of the reasons for the decline of interest in Norfolk might be the absence of the bitter rivalry between the sister cities. A Lancaster reporter attributed the team's failure to the captain's inexperience and his paying too much to his players.[37]

As usual, controversy tarnished the league. Denny Long, the Reading manager/owner, was at the center of several of these. He seems not only to have mistreated his players, but also to have dealt fast and loose with some of the other clubs. Most particularly, he failed to show up with his team in Paterson one Sunday, having instead decided to host an exhibition against the Hartford Cooperatives. The league decided not to allow his forfeit to Paterson stand, but he was fined $117 by a local judge for being in violation of Pennsylvania law. The Hartford players were also fined the same amount when they returned for their next series in Reading. There is no indication that Long made up the difference.

Once in Norfolk, he ordered his team off the field just as the Crew took the lead, claiming that both clubs had agreed to a time limit. The umpire agreed, and Norfolk's protest to the league went for naught. And, because Norfolk once did something quite similar to Lancaster, the locals had little to complain about.[38]

The usually good relations between Lancaster and Norfolk became strained. Trouble started when Norfolk won two of three in the City by the Sea after the Maroons had lost three straight in Richmond. In a planned doubleheader, the two managers agreed to a time limit for the second game. Just as Lancaster scored the go-ahead run in the top of an inning, the umpire abruptly ended the contest, time having expired. A few weeks later, on Norfolk's last trip of the season to Lancaster, acting manager Klusman complained to umpire Tommy Phelan about Maroon fans sitting in the shade of the eave of the stands behind the catcher. Phelan forced them to move and then ordered the Norfolk players not to stray from their bench, located under the hot sun. In the first game of the series, won by Lancaster, 14–0, the umpire ejected Scott Hardesty for arguing. That decision had no bearing on the loss, but under rules imposed by the league at the start of the season, Hardesty had to sit out more games. Klusman protested Hardesty not being able to play the next day, inducing the umpire to declare a forfeit in that contest, but then the teams played a doubleheader without Hardesty participating. The clubs also played another contest on the second day after his ejection. When umpire Phelan refused to let Hardesty play in that contest, Klusman again protested to Ed Barrow, contending that the rule meant that the player had to sit out two games, not two days. Several newspapers reported that Barrow agreed with Klusman, but the Lancaster commentator said the league board of directors would not ratify such a decision. That body did not decide the matter during the season. In a possibly related action, Barrow later fired Phelan.[39]

Norfolk's precipitous fall and Lancaster's rise in the standings started about the same time. Norfolk lost four of five games that weekend, and also incurred the forfeit. One can only wonder how a club could forfeit and still lose two more games in one day. Clearly, one of the later affairs should have been considered an exhibition, the result not counting in the standings. The Norfolk club and those competing with Lancaster for the pennant questioned at least two of Lancaster's wins. This forfeit might explain the discrepancies in Norfolk's record that year, as noted in various sources.

Later in the season, an Allentown writer kidded Cunningham, pointing out that he had to drink ice water to head off a fit when the usually reliable Steelman threw to one of the Allentown men, thinking he was third baseman Weddige (how he mistook someone in a maroon hat for a Mary Jane is anyone's guess) and thus helped the "Mercury (Lancaster) base ball club" win the game. But "Jack" (why he called him so is unknown) Cunningham was a manager his men all swore by and not at.[40]

Once it became clear that Norfolk would likely end up in the cellar, Cunningham traveled with only nine players, thus compelling pitchers Newton and Pfanmiller to play in the field. A reporter in Lancaster noted that the Norfolk owner violated a rule that required ten men on a traveling team, and jokingly wondered if the rather heavy-set and middle-aged captain might play in a pinch.

The captain, after releasing Hardesty because he was too expensive to keep, also sold his best pitcher, John Bishop, to Richmond. Because he grew up in that city and the club was now vying for the pennant, Bishop welcomed the deal, as did Richmond fandom. The Bishop deal may also have further strained relations between Norfolk and Lancaster, a club that at about the same time incurred the unplanned departure of former Mary Jane Fred Clausen, who had won 11 of 15 home games. Manager Frank Rinn quickly signed up Fred Schmidt, released by Richmond when it secured Bishop. The Maroon men were obviously quite pleased when Schmidt beat Richmond, 9–7, and they also expressed pleasure when they later knocked Bishop from the box, even though Richmond won the game. Although Schmidt won a couple of games, by the end of the season Bishop had won five of six decisions and his acquisition is what likely carried the Cherubs into first on the last weekend of the season.[41]

In the waning dog days of August, Norfolk lost three out of four to resurgent Allentown, five straight (including two doubleheaders) to Hartford, a Sunday doubleheader to Newark, and three more to Reading before finally blasting the Reading "Coal Heavers," 14–4. After one of the losses to Reading, a Norfolk newspaper issued a fake ad saying, "Wanted — a ball team to represent Norfolk that can win a game now and then." The team that had won but two of the last thirteen seemed "dead as a doornail."

After a 6–5 loss to Reading, one sarcastic reporter mused, "Norfolk had a narrow escape from wining a baseball game yesterday." Then when Norfolk surprised Reading, he remarked, "Think of it ye baseball cranks! Norfolk has in fact won a game." But then the club reverted to form, losing to Paterson in another Sunday twin bill before finally winning on the Passaic River field, 5–3. Of course that was followed by three losses to Richmond, Bishop and Chesbro doing the honors for the winners in a twin bill. Finally coming home, the club split with Reading and then amazingly won two of three versus Hartford. In his last two starts Pfanmiller shut out the opposition.[42]

In the end, Norfolk came away with a record of 47–78 (one source says 79 losses), deep in the cellar. Richmond won the race at 78–43. In effect, the Virginia teams sandwiched the other six teams in the league between them, with Norfolk serving as the bottom piece of bread. This fact did not escape the attention of the local reporter, whose report on the last day of play stressed the poor results in Norfolk but also pointed out that every team but Richmond suffered a "disastrous year financially." One source, however, contends that Richmond may well have lost money, but the new ownership that had taken over from Bradley had enough members to spread the loss.

The Norfolk reporter praised "Captain" Cunningham, who demonstrated "true grit." While Newark endured a players' strike when the owner fell behind in paying salaries, Hartford had to let its players operate as a co-operative (Newark did something similar). Denny Long, the manager/owner of Reading, cut his labor costs by fining players for poor play. Cunningham, meanwhile, didn't fine for poor play and went $2,000 in debt.

Hard luck haunted the team from the start, but the members of the Crew bore the main responsibility. This "aggregation of supposed first-class players were never in the hunt." Goldbricked from the start, "the man whom (Cunningham) secured as manager ("W.A." Jewell) did not know a base hit from a bat bag, and other men whom he signed as stars turned out to be frosts."[43]

The reporter exempted four men from criticism: George Fox, who caught every game except when he split a finger, outfielder/catcher Steelman, second baseman Jack Wentz and pitcher George Pfanmiller. Why the commentator (probably sports editor Bailey) kept Al Weddige off the list is a bit mysterious, as the third baseman hit a credible .298 that season. Wentz, the fielding whiz at second base, saw his average drop to .234, reflecting a not uncommon trend for the team as a whole. Especially notable was the team's drop in extra-base hitting.[44]

One is struck by the comparative absence of violence on the part of either players or fans that year. Careful scanning of newspapers from all the cities in the league produced only a handful of violent acts. Off the field, the Reading manager fought off one of his own knife-wielding players. In another episode, hoodlums known as the "Frog Hollow gang" of Reading, celebrating several wins at home against Richmond by accosting the Bluebirds as they were leaving their hotel just as the Lancaster club arrived. When told to leave the front of the hotel, the miscreants began to throw half-bricks at the players from both clubs and other guests of the hotel. The Lancaster catcher sustained a deep head wound. As the players engaged in fisticuffs with their adversaries, the police happened on the scene and arrested one of the players. Justice eventually prevailed, as several assailants were prosecuted.[45]

At a meeting at the start of the year, most of the owners had pledged to combat rowdy behavior. Indeed, fan misbehavior at the ballparks seems to have been minimal, with no one from Richmond or any other city commenting on Norfolk's unruly crowds. Focusing on the war with Spain possibly had a salutary impact. Smaller attendance and general lack of excitement may have contributed. Given the triumph of the Lancaster players, widely known for their congeniality, the year before, it would probably be going too far to claim that Norfolk could have profited from more passion.

After the poor showing, Cunningham once again pressured Richmond baseball men to help organize a state league. But Richmond, having won the pennant, preferred to defend its flag, which the team would do in overwhelming fashion. The owners of the other teams in the Atlantic League decided to bear the costs of traveling to only one Virginia location in 1899 — Richmond — probably because the Capital City usually attracted reasonably large crowds. That meant Norfolk would not be a member of any league, nor have a professional team, in 1899.[46]

5

Hampton Roads at the Turn of the Century, 1900–1901

In August 1899, the Virginia League reorganized during a meeting inside Jake Wells' office at the Bijou Theater in Richmond. About a month later, delegates elected officers during a session in the new Monticello Hotel in Norfolk. E. Harvey Cunningham, the driving force behind re-creating the league, became president and treasurer, while one-time newsman Hugh L. Cardoza of Richmond became secretary. G.B.A. Booker, the "enterprising manager" of the Opera House who was about to take over in the same capacity at the new Academy of Music in Newport News, represented the City of Shipbuilders at this session.

A Thanksgiving meeting at the Jefferson Hotel in Richmond revealed that only four teams had paid their dues, but Petersburg and Hampton soon came up with the necessary funds. The owners rejected the idea of making an eight-team association by including Danville and Roanoke because the original idea was to cut down on travel costs by covering the most densely populated section of the state.[1]

The circuit would include Norfolk (population in 1900 of 46,624), Richmond (83,050), Portsmouth (17,427), Newport News (10,205), Petersburg (21,810) and Hampton (2,764). The low population of the crab capital of Virginia suggests that Hampton would have trouble keeping up with the other teams in the league. Its fan and financial base, however, extended into Elizabeth City County, which housed another 12,000 or so. Anyone starting a club in Hampton also hoped to appeal to several hundred military men at Fort Monroe and to a similar number of veterans at the Soldiers Home. League owners set a salary cap, made plans to contact players from the now defunct Atlantic League, established a fund to pay salaries for competent umpires, and began work on the 1900 schedule.

Portsmouth began assembling its team at the end of March, with a large complement of players from the Texas League. At least seven of its expected contract players, all with better than .300 averages, plus their catcher/manager Pete Weckbecker, came from Texas. Included was a second baseman with the intriguing name of David Crockett. When Crockett moved to another team, Win Clark became the second baseman. A native of Ohio, Clark had been starring in the Texas League for several years. Although he did not hit for high average or for much power and stole few bases in 1900, he did field well and had the qualities of a natural leader. Charles "Sham" Myers held down first. Jim Murray would lead the league with 11 homers and 126 hits, including 15 triples.

Texas southpaw "Big Chief" or "Injun" Luitich (aka "Baldo") became the mainstay of the Portsmouth staff. Sporting gray and green uniforms, they became known as "Brady's Bunch of Boers," a name initially used by "Jolly" Ed Ashenback, the manager of the Hampton club, in recognition of owner John T. Brady and the people of South Africa, then engaged in a war against the British. At the time, many Americans were also aware of the "Boxer" Rebellion in China, but no one used that as a nickname for a team.[2]

Norfolk's team included John "Phenomenal" Smith, a former pitching great who lost his edge when the pitching rules were changed in 1893. More recently, he led Hartford in the Atlantic League and later managed and played outfield for Pawtucket, Rhode Island, and Portland, Maine. A New England newspaper considered him "the best, by far, the best, minor league manager in the business." The team, dressed in white and green, became known as the Phenoms, but the name Mary Janes, despite the color conforming more to the countryside, also resurfaced as a nickname, especially for the reporters in Portsmouth.

On paper, the team looked about the same as Portsmouth's, except many of its players had played professional ball in New England rather than Texas. Jim Smith, a flashy shortstop who had played at Hartford for "Phenom" in 1898, had batted .310 in 62 games in 1899. Second baseman William A. Spratt, a one-time Atlantic Leaguer, had batted .325 in the New England League. Nathan Pulsifer, who coached baseball at Bates College in Maine, started out as the left fielder. Smith signed up Patrick J. Conway to play first base, but McGraw's Giants put in a claim for him, and arbitration gave the nod to the New York club. When the season started, Norfolk had "Reddy" Armstrong, the original "Jolly Tar" who hit .360 in 70 games the previous year in a different league, covering the initial sack. John Smith, who had long ago given up regular pitching, had hit .386 in 96 games in Portland. At least three recruits came from his Portland team and two from Taunton, Massachusetts. Pitching looked secure with Tom Flannagan a winner of 18 of 28 decisions and Harry McCloud a winner of 18 out of 23, both at Portland. Christy Mathewson had batted .275 but had won just eight of 20 decisions pitching in Taunton the previous season, though a national magazine rightly thought he possessed "great promise and (was) an all-round athlete."[3]

The *Virginian-Pilot* reporter must have been a bit confused, for after printing Mathewson's name correctly when first introducing him to the public, he changed his name to "Chris Matthews" when the season started. The *Landmark* called him "Matthews" in giving an account of the first game of the season, switched to "Mathewson" for the second, and later returned to the first name. The Portsmouth paper also published his real name for a time, but eventually reporters there succumbed to the error. The Newport News paper persisted in providing his right name even longer.[4]

In the preseason analysis, the Bucknell College student looked the least likely of eleven candidates mentioned to succeed. But under the tutelage of John Smith, he developed rapidly. Mathewson supposedly taught himself to throw his future famous "fadeaway" the year before at Taunton, but it seems likely that the experienced Smith must have imparted something to the 19-year-old collegian, for the astonishing record of the "Boy Wonder" at Norfolk in 1900 contrasts with his accomplishments the year before.

Norfolk played Binghamton, New York, and Wilmington, Delaware, in the preseason. Both Portsmouth and Norfolk crushed the Baltimore All Americans, 10–1 and 19–7, respectively. Against these amateurs, Mathewson started the game in center field and went 2-for-5 at the plate. He also pitched in relief, allowing one run. Norfolk beat the Old Points, a semi-pro team from the Peninsula, 17–1. Because neither Portsmouth nor Norfolk played tough competition, it was difficult to assess just how creditable they would be in the new season.

The Virginia League season commenced in Norfolk on Monday, April 30, with Mayor

The famous Mathewson contract: Manager John Smith recruited Mathewson after watching the athlete play football for Bucknell in the fall of 1899. After the young pitcher gained fame with the New York Giants, William Hannan mounted the contract on the wall of his office so he could cite the $90 a month to prospective players for the Crew. Hannan probably also exhibited it at the College Inn, the pool parlor which also served as the headquarters of the club in 1909 and 1910 (National Baseball Hall of Fame Library, Cooperstown, New York).

C. Brooks Johnston, who was in good standing with the regular Democrats, tossing out the first ball before 3,000 fans at League Park. With Norfolk leading Portsmouth, 8–7, in the last of the seventh, the visitors put two men on base with no one out and Mathewson relieved McCloud. All eyes turned toward "the tall form of the new pitcher as he walked on the diamond. His athletic build won him favor before he pitched a ball." His first pitch "might have been shot out of a six-inch gun," given its speed. "It was a pretty strike; so was the second. And the third, too, went over the home plate within the right longitude, and [Baldo] Luitich threw the stick down in dismay." Fans "not only threw their hats in the air but jumped up themselves and fell over each other in the bleachers." Despite these heroics, both Win Clark and another Portsmouth player registered hits to put Portsmouth ahead. Norfolk, however, rallied in the eighth to take a 10–9 lead. In the ninth, although he gave up a walk, Mathewson's speed seemed to increase with each pitch. Running the count to 3–2 on the last batter, Mathewson ended the contest with a strikeout.[5]

Mathewson's encounter with Clark became the basis of legend. Almost 60 years later, Bill Cox, writing a column for the *Virginian-Pilot* on the occasion of a ceremonial dinner for Clark, claimed that as the player manager (Brady managed the club at this point in the season) for the Portsmouth Truckers, Win got three hits off Mathewson in that first game. Clark reputedly said "And you know I never was real close to Matty after that." A somewhat different version of the same episode has Clark getting a base hit against the future famous pitcher and razzing Matty from his perch on first base. Matty told Clark that would be the only hit he would ever attain against him. An examination of subsequent box scores, however, proves otherwise. The next day, the second baseman connected for another single off Mathewson. Moreover, near the end of May, when Portsmouth beat Matty, 5–4, Clark connected for three hits, including a double. He also stole two bases against Norfolk's ace. It is true that he failed to hit Matty after that, but he only had four more at-bats against him. A broken pinky sidelined Clark for several games, carrying him well past Matty's July departure from Norfolk. Overall, Clark hit .250 against the big man. Because Clark hit less than .250 against the rest of the league, his success against Matty seems particularly striking.[6]

On the second day of the season, in Portsmouth's home opener, Mathewson pitched again and carried the Mary Janes, 5–3, giving up but two earned runs. "That boy Matthews (sic) gives promise of being a valuable jewel and he has a fine chum in (catcher Harry) Nelson," one reporter opined. The Truckers then recovered to take Norfolk twice, once in each city, the youngster not pitching in either contest. In the fifth match between the two, Mathewson gave up one earned run and six hits in a 4–2 home victory. Norfolk's Mark Tierney then shut out Portsmouth at its park, 22–0, giving Norfolk a record of 4–2, with Portsmouth just the opposite. Mathewson had won three of Norfolk's first four triumphs.

Hampton then tagged Mathewson for five earned runs but lost, 8–7, before some 500 at Riverside (River View) Park on the Peninsula. After a 10-inning tie with Hampton, Norfolk pummeled Petersburg, 15–7, at League Park, with Harry McCloud on the slab. Meanwhile Portsmouth twice beat Richmond, which had previously been undefeated, giving Norfolk a share of the league lead.

After Mathewson carried Norfolk over the Farmers the next day, 11–2, yielding no earned runs and scattering 10 hits, Tierney and a new man, lefty Harry Dannehower, won low-scoring games. On Confederate Memorial Day, Mathewson won, 12–6, over Richmond, going 4-for-4 at the plate and giving Norfolk a league lead it never relinquished. "Cross Fire" Flannagan then shut out Richmond on a 5-hitter and Dannehower beat the Bluebirds, 3–2. Mathewson then gave Richmond but one earned run and three hits in a 6–2 triumph. Richmond finally won its first game over Norfolk, 4–2, with McCloud taking the loss.

Norfolk rose to the top of the standings amid rumors that the association was not drawing enough fans. With pitchers to spare, the Mary Janes released Tierney to bolster Petersburg. After a poor start, the Boers stabilized. The day after a solar eclipse in late May, Portsmouth edged Norfolk and Mathewson, 5–4, at its League Park before 1,200. It was his first loss of the year, even though Mathewson allowed but one earned run. Norfolk reeled off several victories with Dannehower and Flannagan doing the honors, the latter before some 1,800 at League Park, where the rowdies raised their ugly heads (a fairly rare occurrence that year), with no official umpire present.

With Norfolk running well ahead of all the other clubs, Mathewson and lefty Dannehower cruised by Newport News for two wins. The next day, McCloud found himself behind, 8–5, in the last game of the series, when Mathewson relieved him in the fourth inning. A Garrison finish, with both pitching and "daring base running, saved the day," 9–8. After winning three at home against the Builders, Norfolk took two of three at Newport News, with Mathewson winning the rubber game. Then Richmond "captured the crew of the Mary Jane," 3–2, Dannehower absorbing the loss. But Flannagan proved too much for the Bluebirds the next day as the two teams reversed scores. Richmond then won the rubber match, 4–3, over Dannehower.

With Norfolk still holding a four and one-half game lead over the club from the capital, it then swapped wins with Hampton. In a 1–0 victory "Matthews" pitched a no-hitter, "beyond a doubt the greatest exhibition of ball playing ever seen on this diamond." Only one base on balls prevented Mathewson from pitching a perfect game. Indeed, he faced but 27 batters. In Norfolk's last at-bat, "Father" John Smith's hit drove in Jim Smith. With a subsequent loss against Hampton, Norfolk's record stood at 27–8, more than five games ahead of the second-place Crabs.

At this time, the Petersburg club folded, forcing Richmond out of the League. Norfolk was declared the champion, and four teams — all abutting on Hampton Roads — began a new season. In the reorganization of the league, John Brady of Portsmouth became the new president, with Harvey Cunningham as vice president/treasurer and Hunter Harvey as secretary. The Hampton club had no representation among league officers, but it is quite likely that the governor of the Soldiers Home had some role in keeping the Crabs afloat.

At the start of the new season, Portsmouth drew first blood by beating Norfolk, 5–1, Dannehower taking the loss. The reporter there gloated over beating the "champions," but Norfolk returned the favor the next day when Mathewson won, 4–2, before 600 at Norfolk. Frank Morrissey of Portsmouth, however, mastered Flannagan, 1–0, to win the rubber game of the series. Norfolk then whipped Hampton, with Mathewson yielding but two earned runs on the Peninsula. Flannagan followed this win with a 6–4 decision. Wins against the Shipbuilders helped out, with a Newport News paper calling one a victory for the "Norfolk Stevedores." Back in Portsmouth, Dannehower prevailed before 800 enemy fans, 2–1. Matty also took care of business against the Boers with a 3–2 six-hitter. After a victory along with a loss, the Phenoms and Mathewson lost to Hampton, 1–0, in a "heart disease" game, with the press still ranking the Pennsylvanian as the hero of the game. One commentator said he was "the best pitcher this section of the country has ever seen." The Hampton pitcher won despite giving up nine hits. A Newport News newspaper described it as "Crabs white-washing Stevedores."[7]

Norfolk won seven of its first 10 in the new season to pull in front of Newport News by one game. It then split several series with the Builders and Boers, the last loss on July 3 being a 13-inning, 2–1, nail biter, with Flannagan pitching well. In the first game of the series,

The pennant-winning Mary Janes of 1900: Although the *Virginian-Pilot* newspaper on November 6, 1921, failed to name one of the players in the back row, the likely members, from left to right, are Harry Dannehower (pitcher), Frank B. "Red" Armstrong (center/infield), Tom "Crossfire" Flannagan (pitcher), secretary Norris, Christy Mathewson (pitcher) and Ben Beaumont (first base). Second row (seated) includes William B. Spratt, club owner, Captain Harvey Cunningham, John Smith (right field/manager) and Nathan Pulsifer (left field). The first row includes Charles "Barley" Kain (center field), Mike J. Sullivan (third base), Harry Nelson (catcher) and Jimmie Smith (shortstop). The presence of Kain and Beaumont indicates the photograph was taken in late June or early July, after the team had captured first place in the first part of the pennant race. Shortly after this photo was taken, Mathewson left for the start of his major league career (National Baseball Hall of Fame Library, Cooperstown, New York).

Luitich beat Flannagan for Portsmouth, but the biggest crowd of the season saw the White and Green hammer lefty Deacon Morrissey in the finale.

On July 4, Norfolk lost the morning game in Portsmouth, 7–2, with Dannehower the losing pitcher, but in the afternoon encounter at Norfolk, Matty gave up but five hits in shutting out the visitors. That victory started a skein of eight straight wins and included an 8–2 triumph over Hampton by Mathewson. The performance made a reporter wonder if the young pitcher, now 18–2, "would ever lose" again. The faithful leader of the rooters in the left-field bleachers, James Smalley, kept things humming with his "melodious voice," yelling for Matty to "shoot 'em over," which was exactly what the young man did. Norfolk wracked Tierney, now with Newport News, for 17 hits, and in the next game Matthews won, 10–3, giving up no earned runs. The streak ended with Flannagan losing, 2–1, to Portsmouth.

At this point, with Norfolk having won 18 of 26 games in the new season, well ahead of anyone else, vultures from North Carolina circled the Peninsula, promising up to $80 a month for recruits. Tierney and other Shipbuilders left the league. Three Hampton players had previously left the club, but management there kept the team operating. The Newport News franchise collapsed, and with no natural rival, Hampton surrendered its franchise. "The League is Dead—small attendance kills baseball in Virginia," the headline read. It looked like the end of professional ball for several years.[8]

As the second part of the season came to a halt, owner Cunningham sold Mathewson to the New York Giants. In a little over half the season, the future Giant great won 20 and lost only two. Although it is difficult to pin down his earned run average from existing box scores, he yielded less than an earned run a game. In his "farewell" he gave up seven runs, five of them earned, but won 10–7, when he rattled out three hits, including a double and a triple. "Matthews" made seven hits in his last 13 at-bats to raise his Norfolk average to .306. He had seven triples to go along with a homer and a slugging percentage well above .400. As the season progressed Smith had him playing in the outfield when he was not pitching.

A controversy arose over Mathewson's move to the big leagues. Cunningham signed a deal with Andrew Freedman of the New York Giants for $2,000 for his release. The next year, Mathewson actually began the season in Cincinnati, whose owner, John T. Brush, also owned stock in the Giants. An editorial in a national sports magazine suggested a possible conspiracy, but Brush insisted that he claimed Mathewson in a draft with the understanding that the Giants had returned him to Norfolk because he had not lived up to expectations. After Mathewson suffered through three poor outings (no decisions), Brush traded him to the Giants for an established major leaguer. Cunningham took the matter to big-league officials, claiming collusion between the two major league teams. The Norfolk owner eventually received some compensation, although the amount is not known.

John McGraw, who later took the helm as manager of the Giants, claimed he taught Matty how to judge the hitting abilities of rival batters, which accounted for his considerable improvement. Years later, Norfolk fans recalled that the Pennsylvanian greatly improved his control in their city by throwing balls through hoops secured from a barrel factory near League Park.[9]

After Christy's departure, strange though it may be, Norfolk and Portsmouth launched the season's third phase, playing on into the first week of September against each other. On July 23, Norfolk players rode on a couple of trolleys over "every inch" of the railway track, save for Lambert's Point. At every crossing and street corner, as they rode in a trolley, they heard cheers, even on Queen Street (later Brambleton Avenue), where about half the blacks "did a genuine cake-walk to the music of the Seaboard Air Line band." At League Park the two teams listened to speeches from representatives from the city and the club and then watched Norfolk management accept the league trophy for winning its first pennant. A large white flag "proclaiming the locals the champions of Virginia" then rose on "the pole in center field as the band played the Star Spangled Banner."[10]

Then with Flannagan (the Portsmouth paper called him "Turkey") toeing the slab and with most of the same players that had started the season except Mathewson, Norfolk shut out Portsmouth. Tierney, returning from his sojourn in Petersburg, Newport News and North Carolina and playing outfield for Norfolk, went 4-for-4, though he remained primarily a pitcher.

Not long after the season commenced, Portsmouth's Brady changed managers and personnel, changes necessitated by petty jealousies and excessive "boozing." When Clark returned to play after his injury, Brady allowed him to act as manager. Although a Norfolk reporter rebuked Clark for letting his players smoke on the bench, the team did reasonably well. Discipline and releasing John Patrick Thornton, who played for Norfolk years before, seemingly did the trick, and with the return of "Old Tacks" Allen (only 16 or 17 years old at the time), the solid play of Jimmie Murray, "Big Bill" Kemmer, and several pitchers, the Boers seriously threatened the supremacy of the Mary Janes.

Norfolk endured only minimal turnover, at least compared to previous and future clubs. Smith retained his starting roster of three pitchers and seven fielders until Armstrong split open two fingers while substitute catching. Nonetheless, he continued to play first base for several days. But after seeing him make several errors, Smith elected to go with Ben Beaumont, who had played with him at Pawtucket in 1897. When Armstrong reappeared on the roster, he had been moved to the outfield.

Center field posed problems for most of the season. The original enlistee, in his first season in pro ball, disappeared even before preseason, and his replacement proved to be a light hitter and soon left the ship. McCloud, considered the top pitcher at the start of the season, also played center field, but managed to hit but .136. Smith briefly went with Ed Pautot in the outfield, but after collecting just two hits in 20 at-bats, he showed up in box scores for Newport News, where he had started the season at second base.

Late in the second phase, Mathewson's classmate from college, Yenter Weidensaul, came on board. He had been delayed three weeks due to an accident. Weidensaul did pretty well, but left about the same time that Matty departed. After Richmond disbanded, Barley Kane played several games in the outfield as a Mary Jane. After the regular season ended, Smith had George "King" Kelly, who had played for Norfolk in 1898, play outfield for a few games.

The batting order also remained nearly the same for the first month, but as the season progressed, Smith sat out several games, apparently due to his wife's illness. William Spratt and Nathan Pulsifer sat out a game or two at different times, with the latter covering third base in the absence of the former. This stability stands in sharp contrast to most Norfolk teams in the Atlantic and Virginia Leagues both before and after 1900.

The team offense relied on solid hitting and good speed, with the first six men in the regular lineup all solid hitters. Catcher Nelson, normally batting seventh, hit in the .240s. Only the eighth spot in the order and sometimes the pitcher's spot exhibited weakness at the plate, except when Mathewson covered one of those slots. In addition, the local press considered Norfolk the fastest team in the league, an assertion pretty much corroborated by box scores.

But without Mathewson, Norfolk became an average ballclub, and the third phase of the 1900 season became quite a race. Despite Norfolk's dominance over most league teams, Portsmouth had managed to beat their river rivals in eight of 20 contests during the first two phases of the season, a much better showing than any other team in the league. Of Norfolk's 16 losses, half of them had come against Portsmouth.

Fortified with several players from disbanded teams, Brady and Portsmouth challenged the sister city. Smith stuck with seven members of the season's opening-day fielders plus Ben Beaumont at first base. Ed Ashenbeck, one time Hampton hero, came on board for one or two games late in the series. To make up for the loss of Mathewson, Smith acquired "Brownie" Martin, the one-time Boer and later Hampton pitcher, and had Flannagan and Tierney rotate with him. But when Martin lost most of his outings, Dannehower returned and rotated with the other two. At least one of the regular pitchers also played regularly in the outfield, with three pitchers sometimes in the lineup when injuries or circumstances forced the removal of one of the regular fielders. Tierney even played shortstop in at least one contest. After a few weak performances, Martin returned to Portsmouth, where his nickname, "Brownie," befit the color of that club's uniform.

With Luitich, O'Brien, and John Landrum (from one of the departed league clubs) pitching well, Portsmouth edged ahead in the season series, but Flannagan, Dannehower and Tierney won enough to keep Norfolk in the race. After 15 games, Portsmouth led in the series, 8–7. A 4–1 victory put the lads from the sister city two games up, but Norfolk swept a doubleheader from Brady's Boers in early August, just as the newspapers reported that the British had the Boers on the run in South Africa. Amid drought, two weeks of cool weather and then 100-degree days, rumors of a plot by Nihilists to kill the recently re-nominated President William McKinley, and reports in the newspapers about the progress of the international army that was making its way to the relief of the foreign legations under siege in Peking by the so-called Boxers, Brady's boys played the Phenoms through August, first one team and then the other moving a game or two above .500 in the standings. And, indeed, the newspapers did report the standings, with only the two teams mentioned, each having the mirror opposite of the other, unless, of course, they were tied.

One of the keys to the outcome of the race transpired in early August, when outfielder Red Gilligan returned to the Old Dominion after leaving the North Carolina League where he had gone when the Peninsula clubs folded. On his way to join the Norfolk crew, he somehow ended up in Portsmouth and became a Brady boy. Cunningham claimed he had a prior arrangement with Gilligan and refused to play a scheduled game. Whether it was money, the fact that Gilligan's brother was already ensconced at shortstop with Portsmouth, or some other reason, Gilligan stayed with the Boers after Cunningham supposedly received some unknown consideration.[11]

In the fourth week of August, Portsmouth made its move, beating Norfolk 3–2 and 2–1, the first in 13 innings and the second contest taking only one hour and thirty minutes. Portsmouth's record now stood at 17–14 and Norfolk's was just the opposite. With its third loss in a row, Norfolk appeared headed "down the toboggan."

Keeping fans interested in watching game after game between the same two teams proved no easy matter. Fortunately, the clubs were evenly matched, which provided some natural excitement. But management also promoted benefit games, whereby some local charity received part of the gate receipts. Thus on one August day in Norfolk, money went to help finish the statue of Johnny Reb at the head of Commercial Place in Norfolk. That game, won by Luitich, gave Portsmouth its three-game lead. The next in Portsmouth provided funds for the rebuilding of St. Paul's Catholic Church in that city. Lefty Dannehower gave up only three hits in a 9–0 win for the visitors.

With the disbanding of the league, both teams had to rely on players or local citizens for umpires. Reporters occasionally praised the stout-hearted souls who took on this task, but after a 6–3 Portsmouth victory near the end of July, the Norfolk paper blamed the result on the umpire's "near sightedness." This comment appeared just after the same reporter remarked several times that the Portsmouth correspondent for the same newspaper, who gave accounts of all the games played in Portsmouth, kept blaming umpires for nearly every one of the smaller city's losses. The reporter for the *Portsmouth Star* once humorously hoped that one of these men was a better stage carpenter than he was an umpire or a "terrible accident" would befall the Academy of Music, where he was employed.[12]

As the season drew to a close, management sought the services of well-known boxers (not the Chinese variety) to act as umpires, mostly to boost attendance and not necessarily to raise the quality of officiating. Norfolk brought in James J. Jeffries, then world heavyweight champ and later known as "the Great White Hope," before he failed in his effort to regain his championship in 1910 from black boxer Jack Johnson. Three thousand people, ten times the number that had been showing up, appeared at Norfolk's League Park assuming they would see the great pugilist calling balls and strikes. Instead, Flannagan watched the plate while Jeffries did the bases. When the latter stopped his work, Flannagan got to call the game by himself, a not unusual state of affairs. According to *The Virginian-Pilot* reporter, the Portsmouth team and especially Captain Win Clark, put on the "baby act" and forfeited the game. The fans screamed, wanting something for their money, so Jeffries agreed to box a trio of three-minute rounds and donned his boxing regalia. The exhibition pleased no one, the fans feeling they had been deceived. A day or two later, Jeffries did umpire before some 1,500 at Portsmouth, where spectators paid 25 cents for the privilege of watching the proceedings.[13]

As the long season ended, Norfolk won two games at home, lost 10–1 at Portsmouth, but recovered to win 3–1 at home, with Dannehower on the rubber. That left Portsmouth with a 21–20 lead in the series. When Smith pulled his team from the next game over the selection of an umpire, 300 fans became a bit embittered. The same reporter who had previously criticized Clark for complaining about Flannagan as a neutral umpire suggested that "Phenom" Smith had been having his way nearly all season on the matter of selecting umpires. The only one he really liked, it seemed, was Flannagan, who also occasionally pitched for him as well.

On the morning of September 3, Portsmouth finally won the deciding game and the coveted cup at Portsmouth, 4–1, as Dannehower lost to Martin. "The old gladiator" John L. Sullivan umpired the bases. Win Clark later took credit for bringing both Jeffries and Sullivan to Portsmouth, noting that he brought in Jeffries in his first year as world boxing champion to box four rounds and then umpire at first base. Jeffries then said he had a friend who needed work and it turned out to be John L. Sullivan. The newspaper attributed the presence of the bulk of the crowd to the famous boxer, who was warmly welcomed and who doffed his cap in appreciation. He also took away $89 more than Jeffries had. The victory gave Portsmouth a 22–20 edge in the series with but one game to play, that being the same afternoon. In that anti-climatic contest, Portsmouth eased by Norfolk, 9–0, as Sullivan called balls and strikes objectively and encountered few beefs (who would dare argue with the great John L., especially with the game being meaningless). How close were the two teams? No one at the time seemed to have noticed that had Portsmouth won one more game against Norfolk, the record for their 62 encounters that season would have been 31–31.[14]

A Norfolk reporter took the occasion to praise the local team, noting that at the end some players were performing at unfamiliar positions, but fans would certainly like to see John Smith and company represent the city the next year. *The Virginian-Pilot* also took "the liberty to extend the thanks of the sporting fraternity to owner Cunningham for his determination in keeping his team until the close of the season."[15]

The Virginia–North Carolina League of 1901

Professional baseball survived in Hampton Roads through part of the next season but not as part of the Virginia League. In 1901, Norfolk participated in the Virginia–North Carolina League, a six-club circuit that included Norfolk, Richmond, Newport News–Hampton, and Portsmouth plus the North Carolina cities of Raleigh and Wilmington. In January, the newspaper reported that Edward M. Ashenback held the Newport News–Hampton franchise, now merged into one club. Ashenback, who ran the Hampton club the previous year, and Hunter Harvey from Newport News sought to field a competitive team. The problems of the previous year, they thought, were due to the uneven quality of teams in the league and the failure to play quality major-league teams in the exhibition season. Although they lacked a first-rate club, the people of Newport News had come out in considerable numbers at Riverview Park. Harvey expected them to do the same for the new league. Railroads into North Carolina promised special low rates. Harvey refused to accept any players with bad reputations. Ashenback predicted that new baseball rules that counted the first two foul balls as strikes and made the pitcher yield a ball whenever he tried to pick a runner off base would speed up games, possibly cutting many to about an hour. The first modification, along with an enlarged strike zone, remained, but the ball call soon disappeared.[16]

Baseball men lamented the death of John Brady, the original president of the new league and owner of the Portsmouth club. Ashenback eulogized him as "one of the greatest and most original characters that has been my pleasure to meet in my baseball career." Brady's "unique coaching out of the grandstand would convulse one with laughter." Although the umpire was his deadliest enemy, after the game was over "he would be the same genial Brady that made him so popular throughout the entire East." A very charitable man, "his purse was ever open to those in need. Peace to his ashes."[17]

When the Norfolk club assembled in the spring, only five of the regulars from the previous season came on deck (Dannehower, Armstrong, Jimmy Smith, manager John Smith and Nelson). New men included E. and T. Gilligan who both had played for Portsmouth in the last part of the previous season. E. Gilligan, a second baseman, took over as manager (technically he captained the club with owner Cunningham, who was also president of the league after Brady's demise, labeled the manager) when Smith returned to the New England League. Home-based in Manchester, New Hampshire, Smith led that league in hitting.

Portsmouth politico Charles T. Bland and Williamson Smith became the new owners of the Portsmouth Baseball Club. Hoping that the financial losses of the previous year could be avoided, Win Clark stayed in Portsmouth as manager. Although Clark reported the loss of Baldo Luitich, he had Buck Weaver, Jackie Volz, a pitcher of promise, and Brownie Martin. The Portsmouth men would be attired in new brown uniforms, with white trim with a "big fancy" white letter P over the left breast along with a white belt and white-and-brown striped socks. A $5 season pass would be offered to ladies, whose attendance was likely to make the men play a "faster and more gentlemanly game" and curb arguments among excited spectators.[18]

Norfolk looked weak in the exhibition phase that year, losing to Georgetown College, 10–3 and 21–7. But the Potomac lads had a crackerjack college club, and the Norfolk men had practiced very little at the time. The "Skippers" honed their skills against the Artillery from Fort Monroe, and did respectably against Boston and Brooklyn, losing twice to the former and once to the latter, but with reasonable margins of defeat. Only a few hundred fans showed up to these contests, possibly due to the weather, but mostly because of a lack of interest.

Portsmouth absorbed a 16–1 thrashing from the Brooklyn Superbas (Dodgers), but otherwise looked capable of matching Norfolk once the season started. The capture of the rebel Aquinaldo, a turning point in the campaign in the Philippines, attracted considerable public interest, but no more so than whether Portsmouth would capture the pennant under the command of "General" Win Clark.[19]

Despite their comparatively poor showing in the exhibitions, the Norfolk Skippers opened play on April 15 by beating Raleigh, led by manager George "King" Kelly, with former Norfolk men Harry Hauptman and George Weeks also playing for the visitors. James "Waggy" Small (sometimes called Smalley) led the fans in cheering in the stands, while Chinaman Charlie Lee organized the yelling in the eastern bleachers. Norfolk soon won the first seven and split the next six games to keep well ahead of second-place Newport News–Hampton.

With Portsmouth in dead last, having lost twice as many as it won, the Portsmouth owners paid their players a half month's wages and told them their pay depended on gate receipts. Having sunk $1,500 into the team, they could not afford to lose anymore. In eight home games, attendance averaged but 366, with 40 percent only paying 15 cents, the other 60 percent paying 25 cents. Cold and rainy weather had not helped, along with injuries to several players. The owners hoped to find a buyer for the team. In the meantime the schedule would continue, with the exception of the next game, which would be transferred to Newport News because its dry-dock company had declared a Saturday holiday. Even though Harvey Cunningham complained about limited revenues, he offered to subsidize Portsmouth.

Several weeks later, after falling from first to as low as fifth place in the standings, Norfolk recovered after a small mutiny on the part of the players. They made Spratt, who materialized after the start of the season, their new chief skipper. In a Memorial Day doubleheader at Portsmouth, the Skippers beat the Brownies twice to stay competitive in the league race. According to a press account, Norfolk scored the winning run in the first game when an umpire failed to detect that a ball hit to the outfield was actually three feet foul. The crowd rushed toward him, but the police managed to secure him under the grandstand. Umpire Harry Staley, who pitched for Norfolk in the dismal 1898 season, later admitted he was too quick in making his decision, but that apology did not deter someone from kicking him.[20]

The award for being the rowdiest player had to go to Reddy Armstrong, who also played on the first Mary Jane club in 1896. It seems that the league also welcomed back Ed Clark, the notorious umpire of the 1894 season. Win Clark thought he was an objective arbiter, but folks in Norfolk had their doubts. In a series against Richmond in Norfolk, Clark assessed fines against Armstrong in three straight contests. On one of these days, the two engaged in a minor physical encounter. The next day, when Clark assessed another fine on the talkative Armstrong, the latter blackened both of Clark's eyes and bloodied his face, forcing him to leave the game. One of Norfolk's reporters excused this outburst on the grounds that Clark never fined complaining Richmond players. They urged his removal from the staff, but the Richmond press, depending on the testimony of a traveling salesman, labeled Armstrong a troublemaker. Whatever the circumstances, Armstrong, after doing rather well at bat, disappeared from the Norfolk lineup and returned to being a policeman.[21]

Although the Norfolk press usually called the local club the Skippers, the reporter for the Portsmouth daily called it the "giant crew of the 'Mary Jane'" when Norfolk shut out its visiting neighbor. The reporter talked about his team being "swallowed by rushing waters" in the Staley-Cunningham pond, Staley being a reference to the umpire Portsmouth had the most trouble with. Three days later the crew of the Mary Jane threw a "harpoon into the Orphans," as Norfolk won several games against its chief rivals, some doubtless due to Clark abandoning his home field advantage just to make ends meet.[22]

The North Carolina papers got into the spirit behind the Mary Jane. When the Norfolk team lost in Wilmington, another seaport city, they "landed on the shoals," and when they won, 8–5, they were a "full-rigged vessel." The Raleigh newspaper bragged that the "Skippers from Norfolk were shipwrecked," when they lost to its Redbirds, 7–2.[23]

As the season wore on, Norfolk slumped under the guidance of Captain Ed Gilligan as a revived Portsmouth club, under Win Clark, whipped them in five of six. Having been demoted from his captaincy, Gilligan asked to be traded to Newport News, so that he could be under Ashenback again. As a result of the deal, Cunningham acquired pitcher William Slagle. The Shipbuilders soon prospered, for with at least six former Norfolk men in their roster, including Al Weddige, they moved up the standings and even briefly moved into first place. A week or two after his brother's departure, T. "Red" Gilligan, Norfolk's most powerful hitter, headed to New Orleans where he helped the Pelicans rise from last place in the Southern League standings. Norfolk signed on "Big Bill" or "Little Willie" Kemmer, who had been released by Portsmouth. The club was also fortified by the reappearance of Nathan Pulsifer from the previous year's team, and the acquisition of Phil Meade, a one-time Raleigh player. Norfolk then closed on Newport News and the league-leading Wilmington Giants as the first part of the split season neared its end, with the Old North State club visiting both Portsmouth and Norfolk for its final games. The visitors caught a break when Win Clark, who was in the process of moving his team to Charlotte, failed to find enough players and forfeited a game, making it necessary for Norfolk to defeat the Carolinians three straight at home. When the Skippers managed to win but two, they lost out by one game. By taking the finale, 1–0, with former Portsmouth pitcher Frank Morrissey winning the game, the Mary Janes edged Newport News for second place.

Just after the first half of the season, the Norfolk press played up an impending baseball game supposedly between two teams of women then on tour. During the big buildup, a signal corpsman sent a message to Captain Cunningham aboard the vessel "Relief," then located off Cape Henry, seeking his assurance that he did not plan to have his professionals use League Park on the day scheduled for the much-anticipated contest. Because Norfolk had a game in Richmond that day, Cunningham scotched the rumor. The headline for the game noted that the "Ladies turned out to be Laddies." Several bloomer-attired local men, including a few who had been playing baseball for nearly thirty years, attracted a few thousand spectators, few of whom were annoyed by the deception, as the game receipts went to Jacksonville Florida, then in the grip of an outbreak of yellow fever.[24]

As the second part of the season got under way, the Newport News club moved to Tarboro, North Carolina, the action attributed to a strike at the shipyard. The newspaper urged Norfolk fans to support the Skippers and owner Cunningham so the same fate would not befall Norfolk.

In the abbreviated second half of the season, just as Norfolk pulled one game ahead of two other clubs, Richmond, mired deep in last place in the standings, went "up the flue." Hints of their impending demise appeared a few days earlier, when the Carolina clubs complained that their share of the gate in the capital city failed to cover travel costs. Management there took the pittance from the gate and spread it thinly among its own players, leaving none for the visiting club.

The local press pointed out that ever since William Spratt replaced Ed Gilligan as captain and manager, Norfolk played much better ball. The Crew once more led the league, one game up on Wilmington. The cadre of faithful fans took pleasure in saying "I told you so" but it required "more than a few to support a first class ball team like Norfolk." Cunningham, noting the absence of sustained support and likely concerned about not having any natural rival like Richmond or Portsmouth and facing increased travel costs, disbanded operations. The Virginia–North Carolina League now became entirely composed of teams from the Tar Heel State.[25]

Harry Dannehower headed to New Orleans, where his 14–6 record enabled the home club to finish the season a respectable fourth. In an ironic postscript, William Spratt, Nathan

Pulsifer, Phil Meade and William Slagle joined several other former shipmates from the Mary Jane on the Tarboro team. On several occasions, they played the Charlotte Hornets, essentially the old Portsmouth club, still led by Win Clark. In one doubleheader, the Hornets forfeited *both* games when they argued too vigorously with an umpire. The change in landscape seems not to have changed the essential nature of the old rivalry. The North Carolina League season lasted almost through August, at which point the Raleigh Senators (Redbirds) stood far ahead in the standings, with Tarboro also playing well above .500. Wilmington, after its solid earlier performance, fell on hard times and vied with Charlotte for the cellar of the four-club league. Raleigh had easy pickings in the playoff between the winners of the split seasons.[26]

Back in Norfolk, baseball enthusiasts had to be content with watching a variety of amateur and semipro clubs until 1906. In the summers, the Norfolk collegians, including Jim Barry, played a fairly extensive schedule against fairly stiff competition. But they only played about twenty games a season at Lafayette Field, built primarily to host college football contests. A considerable number of fans, both black and white, also watched "good baseball at Lafayette Field" on a day in late May 1904, when the Red Stockings shut out the Philadelphia Giants after losing the first of the series in the middle of the week. In a comparatively rare coverage of contests among blacks, the white press in this instance recounted the Stockings' win, the reporter praising the "battery work of both teams" as "the best seen here in quite a long time." Despite the "brilliant infield and outfield plays" and "exceptionally good" attendance, the white press ignored the results of the last two games of the four-game series. A few weeks later, the press reported a Red Stocking 9–6 win over a "white aggregation" of stars from the District of Columbia. We know all too little about these teams, but George Wright, who played in 1905 for the same Red Stockings, was later widely regarded as one of the greatest black players.[27]

6

The Era of the Dead Ball, 1906–1910

As the 1905 baseball season ended, William M. Hannan Jr., who had guided the Norfolk Collegians, tried to form a Tidewater League consisting of either four or six teams of semi-pro players, all from the Hampton Roads area. Hampton raised $1,200 for such a team and planned to put $800 into leasing grounds and $400 for equipment. Newport News, with a new ballpark on its casino grounds overlooking the James River, would be ideally set up for such a league. But Hannan faced two problems. First, many colleges stopped letting players receive payments, reducing the source for much of the talent for Hannan's league. More importantly, a strong move toward re-creating a Virginia state league surfaced. For a time Hannan insisted that two such leagues could co-exist, but in 1906, when Norfolk and Portsmouth joined the Virginia League, he became the general manager and vice president of the new baseball corporation in Norfolk.[1]

Revival of the Virginia League (1906)

The new Virginia League included Richmond, Norfolk, Portsmouth, Lynchburg, Danville, and Roanoke. Otto Wells became the president of the corporation in Norfolk, while his brother Jacob (or Jake) of Richmond, a one-time professional baseball player, served as league president. Both of them ran an entertainment empire that frequently encountered legal trouble because they ran programs on Sunday — or tried to.

Win Clark, the former Portsmouth manager who had most recently played in the New England League, came on board as the Norfolk skipper. Seven New England players arrived on the Merchants and Miners steamer from Boston. The Bay Line brought in a couple of Baltimore men, and the C&O Railroad carried three from the Midwest, including pitcher Bill Otey from Ohio. Clark made a deal with Wells that allowed him to keep 25 percent of the sale price for any of these players. Wells had no idea the club would earn $5,000 in that manner.[2]

Club management soon had workers at Lafayette Field, on the east side of Church Street, enlarging the grandstand, replacing lockers and installing a water pipe next to the playing area. They also built a boardwalk from the trolley line on Church Street to the main entrance of the city-owned park, which had been built primarily for football four years earlier. The facility stood just north of the Norfolk and Western line that ran to Lambert's Point.

Norfolk proved helpless in the preseason against the offerings of Cy Young, losing 7–0.

The club split with Patterson, New Jersey, and played "Chinese ball" (a term of the era used to describe a sloppy, unprofessional game) against Richmond College. They also lost to Norfolk College, 4–2, and to the Baltimore Orioles, 11–7, in another poorly-played game.

Yet they received an endorsement from one of the greatest fielders of all time, Baltimore shortstop Hugh Jennings. A cog on multiple pennant-winning teams, and a refined man who was a favorite with reporters, he thought Norfolk was better than Portsmouth, where the Orioles nearly lost their feathers before winning, 4–2, after romping in their first encounter, 10–3. Norfolk did clobber the Old Point team and beat St. John's College (Annapolis) and the University of North Carolina. But it was a so-so preseason, and attendance, even against Boston, ran in the low hundreds, although 500 came out to see the game against the collegians.

On April 26, some 5,000 fans, doubtless concerned about the news of the San Francisco earthquake and fire, watched the "Tercentennials," named in honor of the exposition that would take place north of Norfolk the next year, beat the Portsmouth Truckers in the season's opener. In the traditional opening-day parade, the players distinguished themselves in attractive uniforms, with the old "English style" N on the front of their shirts. In a typical Dead Ball Era game, the Tars ground out a 2–1 victory.

In his account of the game, a Portsmouth reporter noticed the absence of Waggy Smalley, "the well known rooter imported from the insane asylum at Williamsburg." Presumably the man could not escape from the place for the occasion, he opined. At first blush, this comment sounds like a joke, but a committee of prominent residents that bore newspaper nicknames like "Reddy," "Peggy," "Flathead," "Kicking," and "Sour," met with Governor Claude Swanson and urged him to temporarily release James Small from Eastern State Hospital in Williamsburg. The inmate was no great threat to society — unless mischievous boys taunted him — and even roamed about the Colonial Capital during the day. During his stay in Norfolk, he would be under the care of local politicians.

Why Smalley failed to come to the game was not disclosed, but his absence disappointed many fans. The Norfolk press praised him as "the greatest baseball rooter Norfolk has ever known." When Norfolk played in the Atlantic League, his favorite yell was "Rap it round his neck, Fanny," a reference to pitcher George Pfanmiller or even a few years earlier, "Put it over the fence, Colly," in urging Colliflower to connect for a long one in 1894. He originally sat in the stands, but soon moved to the bleachers, always sitting in the same spot, where his rooting was "sweet music to the ears of the onlookers." The account failed to mention that police had cause to eject him from the premises in the past. In the absence of Smalley, the role of chief cheerleader fell to someone named "Goo-goo," who occasionally also had to be ejected from the grounds.[3]

In the second game, played across the river, Norfolk prevailed before some 2,000. Eschewing a straightforward account of this engagement, a Portsmouth reporter observed that the Mary Jane had "clear sailing from the third inning on, she having sailed the course twice without any serious interference, after which her crew dropped anchor." The team "remained in harbor until the sixth inning, then the cable was again slipped and the noble ship visited three more ports." Overall, "the good ship Mary Jane had a quality voyage, but landed with a little canvass left to the good." In the ninth inning the Truckers, true to their name, "dug up a couple of small potatoes." This mixture of seafaring and farming metaphors produced a 5–2 win for the Crew of the Mary Jane, a name which now resumed its rightful place with the club. A third win over the Truckers, this by a lopsided score, reduced the losers to "grubbing potatoes." In "Diamond Dust," the commentator urged the Truckers to "get a move; turn over the soil, and sow some ginger."[4]

Charles Bland, principal owner of the Portsmouth team, awarded season tickets to the persons who came up with winning nicknames for his team and its new ballpark on Washington Street, as well as a description of the new uniforms. Suggested nicknames included Sailors, Gamecocks (presumably in honor of the many cockfights that took place in back of the Navy Yard), Runnymedes, Reveres, Dreadnaughts, Scalpers, the Crawfords (for the fellow who founded the town) or Bland's Dragoons. Potential names for the park included Merrimack or Pocahontas; others thought Bland ought to honor himself or possibly Jefferson, Lincoln, Lee or Stonewall Jackson. Or it might be named for its location, such as "South End" "Southside Park" or "Washington Heights," the latter because of its comparatively high ground. Noting the nearness of three trolley car lines (Gilmerton, Crosstown and Piedmont Heights), another contestant called for Carline Park. The proposed color of the uniforms ranged across the spectrum.

The final choices were never publicly announced, but one spring day, the "Truckers" defeated the nine of the *USRS Franklin* (a receiver ship) before some 800 fans. No one had recommended that name among the dozens received, but that was the name reporters picked. A few years later, Portsmouth Athletic Park officially became Washington Park and its tenant, after being "Pirates" for some time, officially resumed the "Trucker" label after Bland left the business.

Despite the big buildup, things did not go well for Portsmouth in its first year. After losing three straight to Norfolk and four overall, Bland replaced manager Ernest C. Langraf with Barley Kain. Toward the end of May, Bland picked up a new bunch of players and his team showed marked improvement, beating Norfolk 5–4 on one occasion.

But on Memorial Day that year, some 5,000 watched "Steamboat Bill" Otey beat Portsmouth, 5–3, as part of a doubleheader win for Norfolk. As Portsmouth's record plunged to 10–27, frustration mounted in the strangest ways. Bland, a state legislator, threatened to make policeman pay admission to the games because he was so dissatisfied with their inability to prevent youngsters from sneaking in without paying. The police responded with a boycott. On another occasion, Portsmouth fans mobbed umpire Frank Newsome who, in the apparent absence of police, was saved from harm by the timely intervention of a naval paymaster and the mayor.[5]

Across the river, Norfolk won its first seven contests and held the league lead for several weeks despite losing several games to second-place Lynchburg. As late as Memorial Day, the club remained tied with the Shoemakers at 19–8, but losses to Portsmouth over the next two days allowed Lynchburg to slip in front. Lefty John Stanley at 10–1, John Leonard at 8–3, Bill Otey at 6–3 and Harvey Brooks at 3–1 were all doing well through much of May. Clark led the full-time hitters at .322, with Jack Dingle excelling in scoring runs.

Both shortstop William "Red" McMahon and Clark behaved badly at times, both being somewhat addicted to swearing. In three of their first six games at the Richmond Lawmakers, one or both were ejected. A scribe noticed that manager Clark had already been removed at least once before reaching Richmond. McMahon went to jail for one of his offenses, and on one occasion Clark was so irritated with an umpire that he was "literally foaming at the mouth."[6]

A few weaknesses among personnel surfaced. Neither the opening-day left fielder nor his backup proved adequate. Shortstop Billy Wynne also had to be replaced. After tinkering with a replacement outfielder, Clark found a small and inexperienced catcher who could rotate with George Edwards, leaving Art Evans to play outfield. That allowed Charlie "Dutch" Seitz to move from left field to short, but Clark had to send the new catcher to Tarboro for more training. Edwards also headed to Tarboro to avoid being forced to return to New England, where a ballclub had a prior claim for his services. Learning of this situation, Portsmouth manager Barley Kain paid $5 to the claimant, and Edwards ended up being a Trucker. Portsmouth fans were pleased that their club had acquired a catcher who excelled in grabbing foul balls. Clark signed on veteran catcher Oscar Foster who received praise for helping Bill Otey and year's later publicity for killing himself while intoxicated.

Despite a 25-11 record, Norfolk still trailed Jack Grim's Lynchburg club by two games. Then the Crew slumped a bit. Stanley lost as many as he won in the next 10 decisions and Jack "Dutch" Leonard lost six of his next eight. Harvey Brooks, thought by some to be the best amateur pitcher in the state, was demoted to Tarboro, leaving Norfolk with but three regular starters. Earlier in the season, one of the expected starters, Fred Huntington, sustained an injury that required him to undergo electrical treatment, after which he went to Tarboro for rehabilitation. He never made it back into the Norfolk rotation.

In late July, the club rebounded. Leonard and John Stanley pitched successive shutouts against the league leaders at Lynchburg, after Norfolk had lost the first game of the series. Stanley, with "southpaw cunning," also shut out the Danville Bugs with almost flawless fielding support. The exception was a play in which Red Head McMahon, thinking that new first baseman John "Telephone Pole" Wiley stood "a few inches shorter than the Norfolk Railway and Light Company's smoke stack" that loomed over the park, threw wildly into the bleachers. Wiley had replaced D.C. Benbow, who despite several long hits, had not hit for high average. At that point Lynchburg had a record of 50-25, Norfolk stood at 43-29.[7]

The August heat and humidity encouraged tensions to mount. After one game, Clark was criticized for being "addicted to profanity," even in the presence of ladies. During another, "Red" Foster and "Red" McMahon went looking, unsuccessfully, for an especially inept umpire to teach him a lesson. When "Dutchy" Seitz obstructed catcher George Cowan of the Richmond Lawmakers from throwing out a runner at second, a frenzied mob, unaware that the umpire had called the runner out, descended onto the field and had to be driven back by police. The Richmond fans jeered Clark and company.

The next week, when Richmond visited the City by the Sea, the capital city press cited verbal assaults on Richmond fans. Norfolk reporters claimed no one was accosted and the affair amounted to nothing more than a few boys tooting horns in celebration of a Norfolk win. Later that month, Lynchburg police had to come to the aid of umpire Pat Rollins in the last of the ninth of a 1–1 battle after Cowan blocked McMahon but dropped the ball. Curses and worse rent the air.[8]

Lafayette Field was also the scene of an assault that had nothing to do with local players, fans or anyone connected with the club. Phil Hinton, an injured Richmond catcher, was standing at the soft drink stand when former umpire and fight trainer Frank Newhouse walked up to him, said something about hearing that Hinton was looking for him, and punched him in the mouth. Newhouse clearly blamed the catcher for his dismissal as an arbiter, but league secretary E.N. Gregory pointed out that several clubs in the league had complained about Newhouse's performance. Despite such behavior, Newhouse later resumed his career as an arbiter, moving to the Sally League on the basis of Win Clark's recommendation that he did not let players push him around. Newhouse was even considered for major league duties.[9]

The loss of some key players during August caused Norfolk to slump. Catcher Arthur Evans, who had been accused of loafing after a loss at Roanoke, turned out to have a broken thumb. Before the end of the season, Wells sold ace pitcher John Stanley to the New York

Highlanders — supposedly for $1,000 — but Clark Griffith later tried to wriggle out of the deal when Stanley went into the high minors.[10]

On Labor Day, the Crew revived to take two from Portsmouth, winning the morning game at Portsmouth before 4,000. New pitcher Gus Bonno beat Robert "Smiling Dutch" Revelle, a one-time Navy Yard workman who had played in the local amateur league the year before. Norfolk eked out the afternoon game behind Otey, 2–1, before 2,500 in Norfolk. The Crew then won games against Richmond and completed the season with a couple of additional victories over sister city Portsmouth. After one of these, some 2,500 fans, equally divided in their loyalties, brawled.

Despite those losses, Portsmouth extricated itself from the league cellar to finish ahead of Roanoke. R.E. Shuman anchored the Trucker staff with a record of 19-15 and Robert Revelle pitched nearly as well. Lynchburg ended up playing .667 ball nearly the entire season. Norfolk, just shy of ten games behind, came in some seven games ahead of third-place Richmond.

When Norfolk last fielded a professional team in 1901, William McKinley was president and although he increased America's role in world affairs, he did very little to expand the role of the federal government in the domestic economy. By 1906, the dynamic Teddy Roosevelt, having taken office upon the assassination of McKinley, favored full participation of the federal government in regulating the economy and called for a big buildup of the nation's navy. With the energetic Roosevelt at the helm, the national economy boomed at a furious pace until 1907, when a financial panic dampened prosperity.

In the same period, the so-called "Dead Ball Era" came to dominate the national game. The sport, like a form of American music known as "ragtime," was at least theoretically full of pep and ginger. But, unlike American society, baseball offensive strategy was more conservative, relying extensively on infield hits, bunts and stolen bases. In 1900, the Mary Janes had at least four .300 hitters playing more or less regularly. The 1906 entree, after the changes to the pitching rules plus the widespread use of the spitball, only had one person in that category, Win Clark at .303. The earlier club had two more .280 or .290 batters, but the second-best average on the later team was Lester Dingle's .260. The 1906 club scored 397 runs in 112 games; the 1900 aggregation scored 385 runs in about half as many contests.

Team averages, even for the best hitting teams in the league, fell well below .240, nearly 30 points lower than the 1900 championship club. Because owners and umpires had long kept used balls in the games as long as possible, the physical condition of the ball had little to do with this trend.

The changed rules did speed up ball games a bit, but nowhere near what Ashenback had predicted. The 1907 and 1908 Norfolk clubs averaged about an hour and forty-five minutes to complete a full nine-inning game, while the 1897 team needed an hour and fifty-three minutes. Given the elimination of free fouls, the general decline in offensive output and fewer defensive errors, it is surprising the difference was not greater.

After toying with calling the club the "Tercentennials" at the start of the 1906 season, reporters generally reverted to the Crew of the Mary Jane. Most often in headings, game accounts and sports columns the team was simply "the Crew." That trend continued the next year, but more and more frequently the players were the "Tars," an obvious name in a port like Norfolk. In time, Tars became the preferred description, with the original name occasionally appearing. At least one Richmond writer occasionally used the tercentennial name almost throughout the season.

A Tercentennial Pennant (1907)

In preparing for the next season, Otto Wells put little effort in improving Lafayette Field because attendance had been so poor the year before. The press later disclosed that every team in the league finished the year in the black, so his comments should be taken with some suspicion. Writers speculated that the younger Wells, just like his brother Jake in Richmond, had too many conflicting businesses. He was deeply involved in several theaters, the amusement park at Ocean View as well as partial ownership of the ball club. He considered selling the team to investors in Newport News but wanted $6,000, not the $4,500 offered. G.B.A. Booker of Newport News raised $4,500 and when fans in the City of Shipbuilders offered to bankroll the project to a greater extent, Booker claimed he had plenty of financial resources. Baseball enthusiasts on the Peninsula were quite put out with Booker when he failed to make the deal. And so for the want of $1,500 Norfolk remained the port of the Mary Jane.[11]

Once committed to keeping the club, Wells told the players that no rowdy behavior would be tolerated because it kept respectable fans away from the games. Wells also worked on making a better rental arrangement either with the Athletic Field Association or directly with the city of Norfolk, the property's owner. Later in the season, in an attempt to keep costs down, he demanded that league owners adhere to a salary cap of $1,200 a month. Ironically, no club — including his own — came within $300 of that figure.[12]

The Crew of the Mary Jane won the pennant in 1907, the same year the world celebrated the tercentennial of the first successful English settlement in the New World with an exposition on 340 acres of land at Sewell's Point, later the Norfolk Naval Base. A lot of effort went into the enterprise, and even though it was not a financial success, it turned the world's attention to the area. Prospects for the exposition and Norfolk's ball club seemed bright when the exposition and the baseball season opened in April.

Expo management put on numerous sporting events, such as collegiate and military baseball games, plus a wide variety of other activities. Other entrepreneurs arranged for even more events outside the grounds, not all of them savory. Competition for the entertainment dollar seems to have been offset by the huge number of people that flowed through the area between April and November. Before the season, Hannan hoped the Crew would play at the new athletic field at the exposition, but no professional contests took place there. As the baseball season progressed, streetcar service to the ballpark was sometimes a problem because of the transportation needs of the exposition, as was finding housing for the home players and for visiting clubs. Despite the negatives, the excitement of the times blended rather well with the optimism prevalent at the ballpark.[13]

Just before the season a reporter assessed each of the managers in the Virginia League. Jack Grim, the pennant winner at Lynchburg, had a "luscious grin when his team did well, but never smiled when his team went on a toboggan slide," his personality alternating between Dr. Jekyl and Mr. Hyde. During the season Grim got into a fight with one of his own players, who claimed the manager refused to pay him for his last day of service before being released. Several years later Grim, accused of assaulting his wife (his mother-in-law testified that his behavior was very erratic), went into an asylum in Marion, Virginia, where he died. But in 1907 Grim knew baseball and could be counted on to field a solid team in the Hill City.

In Richmond, Charley "Big Chief" Shaffer, who performed for Norfolk and Paterson in the Atlantic League in 1897, played the part of "the clown of the league," but he also had long explanations when his team lost and tended to brag a lot when he won. Shaffer knew more than how to "hitch-em up" (his antics during a game). He could field and hit occasionally, and knew how to handle youngsters. He likely would make Richmond a good team, but not a pennant winner, in the estimation of the Norfolk reporter.

Manager Charley Moss in Portsmouth, a graceful fielder but a grandstander, tended to make easy chances look "like the daring exploit of a north pole explorer," but like the others he had "yards of experience" and knew how to select good youngsters.

The "pugnacious, touchy and scrappy Winsome [win some] Winn Clarke," Norfolk's manager the previous year, pushed his men like a slave driver, rarely giving praise and often getting a lot out of inferior material. Despite having a mild disorder in believing everyone was his enemy, he was the ablest manager in the league and would surely make Roanoke a contender. The reporter failed to mention Clark's penchant for swearing, perhaps because it was such a common failing among players and managers, or that on at least one occasion the previous year Clark pushed an umpire. In the heat of battle in 1907, he would strike an umpire with a left hook in response to cursing by the arbiter, quite an irony given his reputation. An edict issued by the league absolutely forbidding touching an umpire may have been due to Clark's actions.

James McKevitt of Danville, who played well for Jack Grim at Lynchburg the previous year, usually kept quiet except during a ballgame when he bull-headedly believed only the umpire caused his team to lose. On the positive side, he knew how to judge talent and drill his players.

As to the new manager of the Crew, Robert Pender had a reputation for being too gentlemanly and too easy on his players. This was the same "Dad" Pender who had played and managed for several years in the Southern League and in the earlier version of the Virginia League in 1894 for pennant-winning Petersburg. One might just as well drop a brick wall on him as persuade him to criticize one of his men. If the players were not the type that needed a "lash of curses and fines," then the Crew would do well. He knew the game and could play it himself. Another reporter found out that he only hit .211 the previous year at Charleston in the South Atlantic League and placed sixth out of sixteen in fielding at first base, so questions arose about his talents as a player.[14]

At the start of the season "Old Sea Dog Pender," noting he had an "evenly balanced team," got right into the spirit of a Mary Jane moment by saying how glad he was to commence hostilities with Portsmouth. It will be like "feeding a bulldog on gunpowder and whet our appetites for that Roanoke Bunch of Lobsters." Pender then responded to Roanoke manager Win Clark, who told a reporter that Norfolk was nowhere near as good as the previous year, by saying

> That bluffer Clark has been throwing hot air around about the Crew and this port. I'm itching to measure marling [sic] spikes with his bunch. When we get through with him, he will feel like furling his sails for the season. After the opening series, Dad Clark and his bunch will feel like ship-wrecked mariners who have lived for a fortnight on bilge water and stale sea biscuits.[15]

On another occasion Pender bellowed, "Shiver my timbers," saying that the Crew was the best "lot of lads ever to trod the timbers of the old tub." The situation offered the "genuine smell of salt brine." Pender planned to take the wind out of the sails of all the braggarts in the rest of the league.

Like the admiral in the Gilbert and Sullivan play *HMS Pinafore* who constantly noted that he had "a right good crew," Pender predicted that a his team would be "on deck when the gong sounded and a "pennant will fly from the mast of the good ship Mary Jane when the season is over next fall." "Sea Dog" surely won the award for making the most nautical comments ever by any Norfolk manager.[16]

The preseason provided only a few contests of interest. After feasting off local amateurs, Otey and a reliever shut out Yale before some one thousand fans, followed by victories over Elmira and Altoona. The Tars also edged out the Norfolk Collegians, 7–6, but the club did not do so well against Wilmington of the Tri-State League.

On paper, the Norfolk team looked okay, with only a few gaps. The club had "three midgets" in the outfield — Seitz, Jackson and Dingle (only played in a few early-season games) and an infield composed of "Redhead" McMahon at third plus manager "Doc" or "Dad" Pender in the infield, Billy Wynne at shortstop to go along with Bill Otey and a couple of other promising pitchers. Early on, the club sold Wynne to Sumter, South Carolina, for $250, although he ended up playing for another league team.[17]

Pender thought highly of pitcher F.B. Matney, who reminded him of Christy Mathewson, but although the young man showed promise and won a game or two when the entire team faltered early in the season, he disappeared from the roster sometime in late May not to return until 1908 — and then not to stay. Matney had pitched one shutout and won one in relief, but he had lost games with scores of 3–2, 4–1 twice and 2–1. After being rattled for 13 hits and losing 8–1, his name stopped appearing in the box scores, with no explanation. Although some confusion exists over his batting average at the time of his departure, he was likely hitting in the high .300s and had been playing in the outfield on occasion.

The Crew, attired in white uniforms with black trim, started the season with a victory over Portsmouth before some 4,500. But Portsmouth rebounded to beat Otey the next day in its park before some 3,000. Soon, the Crew trailed undefeated Richmond by several games and resembled the Russian navy in its recent loss to the Japanese fleet. The Roanoke Tigers, under Clark, easily defeated Norfolk, despite Pender's eagerness to play them. In describing one 6–3 loss, a reporter noted that Pender's "crew sailed in clouds." A Richmond scribe noted that the "Mary Jane is Still Aground" and "Another Hole in the Good Ship," "Little Hope Now for Pender's Crew," with "Another Hole in the Craft," and later still as Norfolk took another loss, "Poor Old Crew." Had "Sea Dog" Pender been keeping a ship's log, there would have been numerous negative entrees.[18]

With a record of 3–15 something had to be done, short of turning the ship around and returning to port. When the shortstop who had replaced Wynne pulled a "bonehead" play by trying to tag the runner rather than throwing the ball home on a double steal, the club released him. For a time, Pender played McMahon at shortstop, but he and the manager sparred and he was released. Charleston, South Carolina, picked him up, but he eventually ended up in Portsmouth. Finally, Norfolk secured George "Heinie" Manion (whose name was also mentioned in connection with the 1906 Norfolk club), a refugee out of the New York State League. He came originally to play third base, but ended up being a fixture at shortstop, supposedly even attracting attention from higher up in professional baseball's pecking order. That he ended up hitting in the .180s suggests that one really did not have to hit particularly well as a shortstop to succeed in baseball during the Dead Ball Era.

Gus Ruhland eventually became the regular at third base, and Bert Haas, acquired from Lynchburg in a trade for Arthur Evans, took over from Pender at first. Pender then played some at second base, but after a conference with Otto Wells, he benched himself for several games. When his much faster and more agile replacement failed to hit well enough, however, the manager returned on a regular basis. George Edwards came over from Danville to become the regular catcher.[19]

With the changed personnel, the Crew began to win games on a regular basis. It eased by the Richmond Colts, leading a cartoonist in the local paper to sketch "Pop" Shaffer, the

Richmond manager, occupying a hospital bed, all banged up and "Dreaming of Revenge." The doctor, while discussing the patient's hallucinations, says "He's Pretty Far Gone."[20]

Despite winning more often than losing after the disastrous start, at the end of May Norfolk still sat deep in the cellar. Danville led the league, nine games ahead of Norfolk. On Memorial Day, Portsmouth took a doubleheader from its neighbor. The headline summarized the season thus far, saying "Truckers Punch Holes in Craft Mary Jane." Portsmouth fans were "all smiles — tears on this side of river."[21]

Shortly afterwards, with pitcher John Fox doing well, Norfolk defeated Portsmouth and Dutch Revelle, "the boy with the smile that will not rub off," 2–1. After a win against the Roanoke Tigers, a cartoon in the newspaper showed a bear with the title "Old Sea Dog Pender's Crew Eating-Em-Up Alive," subtitled, "Helpless in Paws of Crew." The sailors had become wild animals, thoroughly mauling Clark's club in the Magic City of Roanoke, with Norfolk's record rising to 12-18. Another win, the team's third straight, came the next day and the newspaper featured another cartoon, this one mixing fewer metaphors. Two wins at Richmond, with the second one eliciting a cartoon showing a wide-eyed Shaffer in the midst of a cyclone, brought the Crew ever closer to jumping over Richmond and out of the basement. But Richmond held off that fate for a time when they beat "Big Lanky" Fox in the capital. Before that loss, Fox had won four straight, but the other Norfolk pitchers were all below .500.[22]

On June 18, "Richmond Thrust a Harpoon" into the Mary Jane, prevailing at Norfolk, 2–1. During the game a frustrated Gus Ruhland objected to a close call so strenuously that fans from the right-field bleachers descended onto the field, throwing empty bottles at base umpire Andy Stanton. Police prevented any injury. Ruhland later apologized for egging on the mob, but a shaken Stanton said he would no longer umpire.[23]

On June 21, when Richmond lost to Portsmouth and dropped "with a bump" back into last place, Norfolk's John "Tanglelegs" Fox bested the Danville Bugs, 4–1. Cy "Big Boy" Cummings, the right fielder who started the season as a pitcher, provided most of the wood for the occasion. At that point, Norfolk's record stood at 20–22, with Portsmouth, at 25–22, holding on to first place. Only seven games separated first from last in the league standings.

On July 4, while the Expo drew its biggest crowd since Opening Day (some 60,000), the crew took both games from the Truckers before over 4,000 in the morning game at Norfolk's Lafayette Field and 3,000 at the afternoon game in Portsmouth's Athletic Park. The double victory provided "sweet revenge" for the drubbing Norfolk absorbed on Memorial Day. Now Norfolk evened its record, tied with Portsmouth for third place in the standings, two games behind first-place Danville. When Norfolk defeated Portsmouth the next day on the latter's field, a crowd went after the umpires. Owner Bland, the sheriff, a policeman and a detective saved the arbiters by escorting them to the clubhouse. But as the umpires and their protectors sneaked out of a side entrance, a crowd of boys, casting bricks and stones, chased them down the tracks of the Seaboard Line, the two umpires taking refuge in the Young Men's Christian Association Building on High Street.[24]

When Otey beat Lynchburg, 13–1, before some 1,300, the Crew climbed into first place with a 29-26 record, leading Lynchburg by one percentage point. The team had risen from last to first, using a three-man pitching rotation of Ray Jordan, Bill Otey and John Fox. By consistently winning a few more games than it lost, Norfolk pulled ahead, amassing a record of 44-33 by early August.

Meanwhile, Bland of Portsmouth hoped that a Richmond stock company would pay him $4,000 for his sinking pirate ship. The sometime politician had gone to considerable expense to have holes filled in the outfield, the infield graded and rolled and other amenities added to the premises, but all that seemed in vain because the team did so poorly. Although Portsmouth played respectably enough early in the season, it lost one particularly well-attended game when a boy ran from the crowd to intercept a ball being thrown by the Pirate second baseman to first to complete a double play.

Management also released Martin Walsh, one of the future greats in the league, to Danville. That deal, and a lot of tough luck, sealed Moss's fate as the club sank in the standings in the second part of the season. The newspaper noted that Portsmouth still had fine players such pitcher Ivan "Pete" Loos. Late in the season Win Clark came from Roanoke to manage the Truckers after rumor had him headed for Richmond to replace Shaffer. A newspaper in the capital praised Clark's aggressiveness, although someone pointed out that when Clark managed the Crew the preceding year, Richmond fans thought the adjective that best described him was "rowdy." Within days of coming to Portsmouth, Clark slapped an umpire who uttered a "vile epithet" at him.[25]

The Danville press thought the word "rowdy" could best be applied to player/manager Pender, catcher George Edwards, and shortstop Heinie Manion for the Crew. In a game at Virginia's textile center, most of Danville's fans agreed that the umpire incorrectly called safe one of its players in a close play at the plate, but excused the error on his location at the time of the call. The visitors howled, but finally went back to playing the game. Then "a slight drizzle" and heavy clouds made "it a little dark" but not enough to force a cessation of play, at least in the minds of a local reporter, but Pender demanded an end to the game with Norfolk in the lead in the sixth inning. When Danville went ahead by two runs, "Dad" Pender "set up his howl," cussing at Willie Handiboe, the umpire a Portsmouth mob went after earlier in the season. When an ejected Pender moved too slowly, the umpire ordered him off the premises. Pender seemingly moved to attack the arbitrator, being restrained by his own players. As the police escorted Pender off the lot, "Dippy" Edwards, "the crazy catcher" made a few remarks to the umpire, for which the latter ordered his removal. As Edwards moved toward the umpire in a threatening fashion, "Big Bill" Otey restrained him. At some point Manion threw dirt in the umpire's face and incurred the same fate as the other two. The three culprits of the Crew each received a $5 fine, and Norfolk, with an insufficiency of players, forfeited the contest. The Danville writer called it all "pure childishness."[26]

On the same day, a Richmond mob became upset when Harry Truby, another ex-Norfolk player, called a forfeit against the home club for its dilatory tactics in trying to stave off defeat against Roanoke. Several policemen had to come to his aid, but, of course, could not prevent him from being assaulted by those vile epithets. The Portsmouth daily gleefully carried the account, particularly since its ball club had behaved itself, at least on that particular day.

Norfolk added to its rowdy reputation when it acquired a new pitcher. Sylvester D. Loucks started out in Danville, but faced suspension into early August for striking an umpire, whereupon that club released him. When he returned to the league, it was to play for Norfolk.[27]

Portsmouth helped out Danville a good bit when it sent Martin Walsh, one of its best pitchers (17–11 at season's end) and a pretty fair hitter (.274). Walsh, an effective spitball pitcher, won several key games for Danville. However, near the end of the season he lost a game in Richmond when one of the men from the capital city (no one ever admitted to the deed) enlivened the ball with some pepper or hot sauce, so that Walsh kept burning his tongue when he tried to moisten the ball with his saliva. The umpire, though admitting that the ball had been "doped," refused to exchange it for another, perhaps in the belief that using the spitball was a dirty tactic, a view held by some fans and reporters.[28]

The "good ship Mary Jane struck a snag" in losing to Danville, 4–3, on August 14 before 1,800 fans, but were still 10 games over .500, having defeated Danville in the first two games in the series. Otey shut out Richmond, Jordan lost in the Capital City and Fox lost to Lynchburg. At least one game ended in a tie — in Richmond before 10,000. At the end of the month the "Sea Dogs," nine games above .500, still led the league. They then surged, particularly against Portsmouth, rising to 60-44, compared to Danville, at 61-52.

Although attendance remained at reasonable levels largely due to the success of the team, management occasionally tapped into events at the Exposition to add to the audience. In the middle of August, the Crew and the Exposition celebrated Carolina Day. Before going to the ball game, the governor of North Carolina, reminiscing about his friendship with slave children, spoke at the Negro Building. A large delegation of Down Homers boosted attendance to some 3,000 for the ballgame.[29]

During this entire phase, management did not stand pat. In early August, the club pedaled Roscoe "Cy" Cummings, whose batting average had plummeted, to Lynchburg for pitcher Sheff Moore. The latter, however, saw limited duty on the Mary Jane. Near the end of the season, Cummings returned to the coast, Norfolk paying a minimum amount for him in the knowledge that a higher-level minor league club was willing to part with many times the amount Jack Grim received. Pender also picked up pitcher Sylvester Loucks and William Fetzer from rival Danville. Fetzer, a hard-hitting left-handed outfielder, reputedly gave Norfolk the best outfield in the league. Well before that deal, Hal Bertrand (Bertram) came from an undisclosed location, belatedly replacing Matney in the rotation and often doing well, as Pender returned to a four-man rotation. Steve Griffin, a solid second baseman, replaced Pender in the last two or three weeks as Norfolk clinched the pennant.[30]

Richmond and Danville raised objections to the acquisition of George Paige in early September. The new pitcher, after defeating Portsmouth in his first outing, set a new strikeout record versus Danville before some 3,000 on a weekday. In the four games Paige pitched, he was overpowering in three of them. Despite the protest, Pender insisted on using Paige before another 3,000 on a Saturday afternoon. Paige hurled a shutout, giving Norfolk a 62-44 record to Danville's 61-51. A headline read "Danville Beefs, Colts Howl in Vain."

When Richmond and Danville conspired to take away Paige's wins from Norfolk's records, Norfolk management released a letter claiming that Danville took such action to cut into Norfolk's lead while Richmond did it to keep higher attendance figures. Despite pleadings, a rump session of the league voted to take away the wins from Norfolk. Local owners noted that the meeting lacked a quorum because Norfolk, Portsmouth and Roanoke did not send anyone, but a Roanoke proxy proved sufficient even though its representative supposedly later recanted his actions. Norfolk argued that the player in question, although he had not received a release from Charleston of the South Atlantic League, had waited all season for assignment and transportation money, neither of which came. Technically, the player belonged to Denver and was on loan to Charleston. Manager McKevitt considered signing him, but, having found out his status, decided against it.

Whatever the specifics, one day Norfolk had 66 wins in the standings listed in the newspaper; the next day the number stood at 63, despite having beaten Lynchburg. The next year, Paige took his dispute with the Denver club to the baseball commission. In 1911, he finally made it to the majors, but did not do well.[31]

Norfolk's residents long remembered this wonderful season when the city sponsored the Exposition and won the Virginia League title. In 1932, W.N. "Bill" Cox, a sports columnist new to the area, heard several stories about the famous year. One had "Squire Otto Wells," the principal owner of the team, giving all the players derby hats for taking a series in Richmond late in the season. When the Crew had the four games taken away, the players feared they might have to return their hats. Cox also mentioned that the Crew lost 14 straight games to start the season, but ball scores from the newspapers of the day prove that Cox was misinformed. Cox also thought infielder Steve Griffin, secured late in the season, was ineligible, but nothing in the newspapers in 1907 dealt with that possibility.

Although labeled by *Sporting Life* as the Virginia League champions for 1908, this array of players actually ended the 1907 season as the pennant winners. From upper left they include pitchers Ray Jordan, S.D. Loucks, Bill Otey, John Fox and Hall Bertram, catcher George Edwards, first baseman Bert Haas, third baseman Gus Ruhland, shortstop George Manion and outfielders Roscoe "Cy" Cummings, Charlie Seitz, R.F. Dingle and Jimmy Jackson. Catcher Herb Smith participated in only a half-dozen games, but starred in the 1908 season (April 4, 1908, issue of *Sporting Life,* courtesy of Thomas R. Garrett).

Another Cox story suggests that the season all boiled down to the last game, with Norfolk needing a win over Portsmouth to secure the pennant. In the ninth inning of a scoreless game at Lafayette Field, Win Clark yelled to his third baseman to watch out for a bunt. The Norfolk batter obliged by laying one down, but the infielder, dashing to grab the ball, became so excited he threw it into the stands, allowing Norfolk to win the pennant. According to this tradition, Portsmouth fans presented "Brother Clark" with a union suit as a reward for managing the locals.[32]

Cox may not have created these stories from whole cloth, but he did embroider them a bit. Norfolk did clinch the pennant by winning a game with Portsmouth, 1–0, with Bill Otey the winning pitcher. As described in the press at the time, the contest took place several days before the end of the season. In it, two straight batters bunted for Norfolk, and in both cases the balls were so well placed that the fielder had no chance of throwing the runners out. In the first instance, the Portsmouth pitcher threw wildly, allowing Manion to advance to second. In the case of the second bunt, the third basemen threw the ball despite having no chance to beat the runner, and ended up allowing the winning run to score. The reporter at the time assured everyone that the two wild throws were legitimate errors and did not indicate any collusion on the part of the Portsmouth players to throw the game.

After clinching the pennant, Norfolk won two more games from Portsmouth while Danville lost several times. In the season finale, Red McMahon lost his temper and was ejected, a befitting end of the season for him. Norfolk ended up with the same number of wins as Danville, but with 10 fewer losses, even with the disputed games taken away. No single game had really mattered that much. Norfolk could even have been given losses through forfeit by league officials for Paige's games and the Crew would still have been the champions.

A post season assessment of the league's pitching in a national magazine pointed out that Norfolk had Bertrand with the second-best won/lost ratio in the league. He was knocked out of four or five games, but sustained few losses. He also won several times in relief, entering games when his team trailed. His wins could be attributed to the ability of his mates to rally, the major factor that enabled Norfolk to capture the pennant. The writer attributed Bertrand's performance to his being Jewish, saying he was evidently "born in the right stage of the moon to bring good luck."[33]

After the regular season, Norfolk played a postseason series against Charleston, the South Atlantic League champ. Only one game received press coverage, a 1–0 victory with "Kid" Jordan tossing the shutout. Coverage of this game inferred that the Crew had lost a previous encounter. The next day, the Crew conducted a benefit before some 400 fans in its last appearance, where they competed in various contests, like throwing the ball. When outfielder/pitcher Cummings incurred an injury, George Manion won the event.

Sometimes on Sunday

Early in the 1907 season, Wells and Hannan pointed out that the Exposition planned to operate on Sundays (it turned out not to be the case) and asked for the chance to talk to the Tidewater Ministerial Union. In May, after Hannan failed to show up at a scheduled meeting, the ministers said that their congregations would boycott weekday games if management tried to play on the Sabbath. Norfolk County officials said they would arrest ticket sellers, players and anyone else who participated in any way. Rain fell in torrents the night before, making the field unplayable and forcing the postponement of the first scheduled Sunday game, against Lynchburg.

A few weeks later, management scheduled a Sunday exhibition game against a semipro team from Newport News. *The Pilot* reporter, sympathizing with the Crew, noted that hundreds of fans in Norfolk wanted professional baseball on the Sabbath, it being the only day they had a chance to attend. Supporters of Sunday ball claimed that the game was "no more harmful than scores of other amusements and pastimes permitted in Tidewater Virginia every Sunday during the summer" (on any given Sunday, at least four navigation companies advertised in the newspaper for special tours on the Sabbath). They contended that greater attendance at ballgames on Sunday afternoons would sharply reduce imbibing in local saloons at those times. A recent decision in a Richmond court (the Idlewood or Wells case) suggested that Norfolk County authorities really could not stop a game in progress and arrest players. All the constables could do was to bring a complaint to a local magistrate.

Whatever the potential legal ramifications, Protestant ministers and laymen met at various churches on the Sunday preceding the scheduled game and denounced in "unmeasured terms this purpose on the part of the baseball management to thus openly violate the sanctity of God's Holy Day." About 60 delegates representing over 30 churches, including clergy and laity, formed a Law and Order League, equipped with constitution and bylaws, to prevent desecrations of the Sabbath. They assigned a committee to write a letter notifying all that they would encourage a boycott of weekday games should local baseball moguls persist in playing on Sunday.[34]

Because League Park then resided in Norfolk County, Norfolk city police played no role in preventing ball games on Sunday. Technically they could have, because under Norfolk's city charter, police had authority one mile beyond city limits. But custom dictated that county officials handle the situation. Norfolk County's Commonwealth Attorney, Captain Richard Coke Marshall, after failing to reach a Tanner's Creek constable by phone, made his way to the local justice of the peace office in Huntersville (the part of Norfolk County where the park was situated), and prepared a written order to have all the participants arrested. Just to be certain he was on the right side of the law, if not the Lord's, Marshall re-read a recent court decision that moderated the blue laws slightly, but not so much that professional baseball on Sunday could be tolerated. Marshall thought that Sunday games would give the sport "the worst kind of black eye in these communities and for fear of injuring their own enterprise, I was in hope that the baseball people would not schedule any more games for Sunday."

Management proceeded with the idea only to be washed out in their efforts. "The rains of Heaven" having assisted him in his efforts to "see that the law was carried out," Marshall intimated that he was prepared to take action should the owners schedule any contests on the Sabbath. The combined threats from the church people, Marshall and nature worked, for management scheduled no more games on the Sabbath, at least in the immediate future.[35]

Wells received little support from newspaper editors on the matter. An editor for the Portsmouth daily urged the baseball men to pay attention to the "sentiment" of the "Christian people" in these communities, for such folks could make things "decidedly uncomfortable" for those who tried to "engraft the foreign idea of Sunday sports upon this section." Hundreds of men in both cities enjoyed the contests, but most of them would reject the game if played on Sunday. Management would do well to take such patrons into account when they calculated profits and losses. If that did not suffice to convince the owners, then Marshall's threat should give them pause. That the Portsmouth club had not even suggested games on Sunday was "much to their credit." Portsmouth owner Charles Bland vigorously opposed Sunday games, as did manager Moss. The next year the state legislature changed the law on Sunday closings, making the infraction a criminal not a civil matter and raising the fine to $5 from $2.[36]

"Amateur ball" (where a few players received money under the table) proved to be different. In 1911, eight local clubs formed a Twin City League. Teams from fraternal, neighborhood and military clubs such as the Naval Hospital and the receivership *Franklin* vied for a championship. In the second year of competition, the league introduced Sunday baseball. Most of that season, the Naval Hospital hosted games on the Sabbath. In one such encounter in early June, some 2,500 fans "delighted with Sunday baseball," watched as visiting Franklin (the receivership club) eked out a 12–11 victory over their host. After reading about the large crowds attending these affairs, the Tidewater Ministerial Union in an "animated" meeting complained about the number of drug stores that opened on Sunday and the games being played on federal property. Although local police might be able to close drug stores, it had no control over what happened at military installations.[37]

Sabbath games went on, with local reporters periodically mentioning the large number in attendance. On Easter Sunday 1913, the surgeons at the Naval Hospital defeated the crew of the *USS New Hampshire* in a non-league affair held before some 3,000, with "not a few of the spectators ... gaily clad in Easter toggery ... the flowers worn by the fair ones [being] enough to stock a florist."[38]

Accounts of Twin City League games also occasionally note the amount of money wagered on these affairs. When the Franklin overtook the Naval Hospital for the Twin League title by winning a doubleheader (this one on a Saturday) at the end of September 1912, a reporter estimated that about $5,000 changed hands. Along with Sunday ball playing, such misbehavior irked the Law and Order League.

The First Shall Be Last (1908)

A Biblical prophecy took place at the end of the 1908 season when the Crew of the Mary Jane sank into last place. At the start of that season, as one might expect, the press and the people expressed optimism. (Of course, so did William Jennings Bryan, a few weeks later, when he decided to make his third bid for the presidency. A newspaper cartoon showed the "Great Commoner" ready to bat, with a fan yelling that he already had two strikes on him, a reference to Bryan's two previous losses in his presidential campaigns. Bryan got the nomination, but lost the election to William Howard Taft. Bryan knew Biblical prophecy, but unlike Norfolk's baseball team, he never reached first place.)

A picture of the "Skipper of the Mary Jane"—"Sea Dog" Pender—appeared in a prominent place in the press in early March. Although Bonno and Stanley had been drafted to higher levels of professional ball and Bill Otey had signed with Roanoke, management thought its new men were promising. A Lynchburg writer quoted in the Portsmouth daily, however, thought that with the loss of Otey, the Crew would "strike a calm" during the season.

As the season unfolded, the club struck several calms. Not knowing the future, locals looked forward to piping the Tars on deck and the start of a new season. In April, *Sporting Life* honored the "Norfolk Baseball Club" by arraying pictures of the individual players around "R. Pender, Mgr.& 2dB" with the phrase "Champions for 1908" underneath Pender's picture. The pictures were those of the 1907 squad.[39]

Adding to the optimism was the construction of a new ballpark in February 1908. Billy Hannan and Otto Wells debated about whether to build a new park or put money into the one at Lafayette Field, owned by the city. As described by a reporter, "after taking in the beauty of the landscape" as they wandered about the 18th Street area amid truck farms dormant for the winter, the two started across the field, where they encountered a drainage ditch, filled with ice, which Hannan, in attempting to cross, fell through and from which he emerged with mud above his knees. That was the place where the two decided to build their park, and within a week the mud began to fly.[40]

Dozens of fans submitted possible names for the facility, including Tidewater, Twin City, Spalding, Metropolitan, Lee, Jackson, Wells and Dixieland, to name a few. In the end, the Norfolk Athletic Field, located on the south side of 18th Street halfway between Granby and Church Streets became known as League Park. Hundreds of fans came out to see the park under construction.

The structure was but a block or so from Church Street, as all the other enclosed parks had been, but it was west of that thoroughfare and its main entrance was located nearer Granby Street. A western entry gave access to either side of the grandstand. One side was for ladies and their escorts, the other for smokers who might want to take off their coats. Boxes were situated in the stands directly behind the catcher and held opera-style chairs, an innovation for "this section of the country." Reporters sat next to that section. The bleachers, consisting of 10 rows, extended 200 feet on each side of the field next to the stands. Management set aside the left-field bleachers for "dusky rooters" led by Charlie Seltz. The modern one-story clubhouse had hot and cold water and tin showers. The lockers, dressing tables and other furniture could compete with the Waldorf-Astoria, a reporter thought.

Hannan and Wells thought nothing could be too good for the Virginia League champions. The diamond was laid out so that the late-afternoon sun, as it came closer to the western horizon, made life difficult only for the defenders on the right side, not those on the left, as was the case at Lafayette Field. With its weatherproof grandstand, the entire establishment had a "metropolitan" appearance. With a nucleus of players returning and a new park, Otto Wells and Billy Hannan thought attendance would skyrocket.[41]

Otto Wells got into quite a fracas with his brother Jake and other league officials over the schedule. An outlaw league tried to take advantage of the dispute by enticing Norfolk to put a team in its new association. After a suitable interval, Jake Wells agreed to a modification of the schedule so that Norfolk and Portsmouth would not play quite so many games against each other at the beginning of the season. Norfolk and Portsmouth also had fewer conflicting home dates. But the upcountry teams of Danville, Lynchburg and Roanoke balked at any advantages for the Tidewater clubs. So fractious was the meeting that the moguls forgot to turn the pennant over to Norfolk. When it finally arrived, the team had a grand parade through downtown and out to the new park, followed by some politician's remarks and the hoisting of the flag. That proved to be the highlight of the season.[42]

Fans coming on the streetcars for the games disembarked from 18th Street and made their way over a platform to one big entrance located on the Granby Street side. Whites going to the ballgames would usually come to the park over the Granby Street line rather than the one along Church Street. On Opening Day, trolleys on the Bay Shore Line that went to Ocean View left the corner of Granby and Plume every 20 minutes, while the Riverview Line departed the corner of Granby and Main Street every 20 minutes. That meant that a trolley would be moving along Granby every ten minutes. Cars also serviced Church Street.

Unfortunately, after this big buildup, the weather failed to cooperate, and the game ended in a tie, amid sloppy conditions. The next day some 3,500 watched the Truckers easily beat back the Crew at Portsmouth, followed by a 5–2 victory over them at Norfolk the next day before some 3,500.

Three weeks into the season Norfolk had an 8–7 record and a little later, the club had split 24 games. Then the "Sea Dogs" surged, their pitchers delivering five shutouts as Norfolk rose to first place at 17–13. But on Memorial Day, they succumbed to the Truckers twice, followed by three more losses to the same club. To add insult to injury, in a 6–4 win for Portsmouth, its manager, Steve Griffin, struck Norfolk shortstop Jimmy O'Neil in the face, jumped on him and then kicked him for supposedly blocking the path to second. Most fans thought the shortstop was merely catching a thrown ball.[43]

After these winning and losing streaks, the Mary Janes treaded water for some time. Halfway through the season Norfolk had a 29-32 record compared to 25-33 for Portsmouth. Entering July, a reporter claimed that there was "something radically wrong with the Norfolk team." The club seemed "wholly lacking in that inspiring element known as ginger." But after a victory the next day, he thought everything was fine.[44]

On July 4, the sister cities split a double bill. Portsmouth then endured a terrible tailspin. With a record of 31-47, the club fired Griffin and replaced him with Andy Lawrence, one of the players. Just as Portsmouth began to improve, Norfolk went into a slump, losing seven of eight games to league-leading Richmond in the middle of July. On August 1, Norfolk stood at 38-49, Portsmouth at 35-47 after reeling off four straight wins. A few days later, Norfolk dropped a pair at Roanoke while Portsmouth beat cellar-dweller Lynchburg twice, putting the sister city ahead of Norfolk.

As usually happened when things went awry, the team changed personnel. Earlier, when Norfolk traded Cy Cummings to Columbia for pitcher Dan Friend, a reporter thought that the two clubs were "swapping lemons." Management also released popular third baseman Gus Ruhland, replacing him with Tommy Toner from the Cotton States League. With Jimmie Jackson on the sidelines and wanting to move Seitz to the infield, Norfolk signed on Walter Brodie, a star with the Baltimore Orioles of the National League in the 1890s who played with Portsmouth earlier in the year, batting a respectable .283. Although Brodie was nearly on his last legs, reporters thought his knowledge of the game might help the team. Several weeks later, Pender released or traded lefty Dan Friend and Chenault (great speed but wild), and later let Brodie go as well.[45]

Pender sold catcher Herb Smith to Atlanta for $2,000, contending that George Edwards, a mainstay, spent too much time on the bench. But Edwards, the star from the previous year when he led league catchers in fielding percentage, only played sporadically due to several broken fingers. After a long slump by the team, a fan in a letter titled "What's the Matter with Norfolk?" claimed that the team lacked dependable catching, especially evident in a recent Richmond series when the capital city club stole numerous bases. Art Evans, who played as a Tar in 1907 and then joined Roanoke, received his release from the Chicago Cubs and looked like he could fill the void.

At the start of the season Norfolk fans hoped that George Cowan, who had been replaced as manager of the Richmond Colts, might join the club as he wintered over in the City by the Sea during the off-season. But Cowan stuck with his old team and helped Richmond win the pennant.

In late July, after the swoon against Richmond, Norfolk acquired seven new players, mostly from an expired New York league: Jake Warner (shortstop), William (Howard) Rhynders (first base), Charles Donahue (third base), William Gannon (outfield), as well a new battery of William Savage and Scanlon Morgan, and another pitcher. The club released Jimmy O'Neil, the shortstop from Boston who had done well earlier in the season. The club dispensed with the services of first baseman Bert Haas and moved outfielder Jimmy Jackson to a reserve role.

After the new aggregation got off to a poor start by losing three straight to Roanoke,

Portsmouth politician Earl Wright penned a poem, wherein Pender, the "gallant old seadog" with a pennant flying high over the center-field fence, after "cruising along all summer," concluded "his Tars wouldn't do."

> Just exactly what the trouble is I really cannot say,
> though I hear that some handle schooners, for which they don't get any pay;
> I shall pack up my duds quite shortly for a trip to the Empire State
> and enlist a new bunch of Jackies from deckhand clean on to first mate;
> and when I return with that gang, sir, mark now what I tell you is true,
> all ball cubs in dear old Virginia will dread Dad Pender's new Crew.
> He landed his new tars in Roanoke; they went at a very fast clip,
> but the Highlander crowd got busy and scuttled the Mary Jane ship.
> Since then they have drifted and drifted from fourth to the bottom gone down,
> and more trouble is likely to follow as our Truckers are coming to town.

Even though the Mary Jane still floated, its crew could expect "four more holes in her hull this week," after which it would need to enter a dry dock.[46]

During this time, when the Crew was not performing particularly well, the press spiced up its coverage by inserting poems (or something that might pass for them). In early August, the *Landmark* unleashed "Mabel" on an unsuspecting public: "The boat it rocked, the wind it blew, and the waves rushed o'er the table. For the Danville bunch had trimmed the crew — Say, ain't it awful Mabel?"

The account went on to note three losses and the "Crew's fall from the gable," which also rhymed with Mable but had nothing to do with a ship. The scribe even wondered if the Crew would "be able to hold last place at this swift pace." The next day, "a little rain ... saved us all a little pain." "He who watcheth o'er us prevented, just in time, this ducking of the sailors in the briny, briny, brine."

When the Tars lost the next day, the account of the game began with still another offering, which in part lamented:

> Say, quit your kidding mister, cause it ain't no fun for me
> to see those sailors flounderin' in the Truckers' Sea.
> But that is just what happened, why bless your mother's chicks,
> The sailors only made one run while the farmers gathered six.[47]

Not to be outdone, the Norfolk afternoon daily responded with a poem titled "Is It So?" by C.E. Arnold, a Norfolk advertising man. It questioned why the Tars were underachieving, seemingly in agreement with the comment about schooners in Wright's poem. They missed easy flies, could not even touch hard-hit ones, but they were "past grand masters at putting down the high ball."

> What's the matter with So-and So? Let an easy one go by;
> Bet he wouldn't have done it had it been filled with Raleigh Rye.
> They'd never miss mint juleps, or a glass of mild and mellow;
> For that's the brand that helped to land the Champions in the cellar
> Couldn't get the needed hit, so reads the daily news
> But have a lovely average when it comes to hitting booze.
> If someone asks "How stands the Crew?" Just answer, my dear fellow,
> And say, "You'll find them with the booze, away down in the cellar."[48]

As Norfolk's record worsened and it looked increasingly like the club was headed toward the league basement, a revised version of why Norfolk was called the Crew of the Mary Jane surfaced. According to a Richmond newspaper and re-published in the Portsmouth paper, some years earlier the team went on an outing on a ship by that name. But unlike the earlier account, the men were having such a good time that they traveled out into the Atlantic and were much delayed in returning for their game that day. By the time they arrived at the field back in Norfolk, fans had gone home. It was just as well, for the overindulged men were better for "bed than ball." The Richmond writer admitted no authenticity for the tale, making a reference to Uncle Remus in a parting remark.[49]

In addition to the concern about excessive drinking, newspaper accounts occasionally mentioned the inadequacies of umpires, the problem of people betting on games (a practice that sometimes led to fights in the bleachers) and bribery attempts on players and umpires. Norfolk had their share of these discomforting behaviors, but other cities in the league and all of baseball were not exempt.[50]

Bob Pender eventually resigned. Wells responded to a public clamor in accepting the resignation. "Old Dad" Pender, instead of sulking about the situation, stayed in Norfolk and presented awards to the players at season's end. In subsequent seasons he umpired league games, and although occasionally criticized in news accounts, he kept a reputation as an objective official. In August, second baseman Jack Bonner took the helm of the nearly disabled Mary Jane.[51]

No move, nautical or otherwise, kept Norfolk out of the cellar. Last-place Lynchburg, beset by numerous squabbles early in the season related to owner and manager Jack Grim, began to creep out of the basement. They even put their new manager Al Orth, the "Curveless Wonder" of major league fame, on the mound. Although he beat Portsmouth once, he lost to the Tars in one of the Crew's few victories. With only a few games left in the season, Norfolk defeated the Danville Bugs twice, as Lynchburg lost a game, seemingly pulling the Crew out of last place for good. But the Tars then lost two to the Bugs as the Shoemakers won the same number over Portsmouth. After losing two of three to Lynchburg, Norfolk split its remaining games with the Truckers.

At season's end, Richmond ran way out in front with an 87-41 record. The Capital City team was led by manager Perry Lipe and former Portsmouth pitcher "Sunny Jim" Revelle, as well as undefeated ace and future major leaguer George Quinn. Attendance in Richmond that year exceeded 400,000 and topped several major league clubs. Danville, paced by Martin Walsh and his 30 wins (by far the highest number in the league), placed second. Portsmouth led the second division. Lynchburg edged out Norfolk for fifth place at 52-78, losing one less game than the Tars. Norfolk's Crew would have to wait for another voyage to redeem its honor.[52]

One-Half Plank Shy of a Load (1909)

In the off-season, Otto Wells sold out his interests to a local syndicate headed up by hotel keeper Charles H. Consolvo, with Hannan continuing as secretary. Even the Portsmouth press expressed enthusiasm for the change, predicting that the "good ship which foundered frequently last year should be able to buffet the worst of the gales that sweep around the Virginia circuit this summer."

Win Clark returned to direct the Crew following one of the most bizarre, harrowing seasons any manager ever endured. While guiding a team in South Carolina, Clark was knifed during a drunken rage by one of his own players, John C. Bender, the brother of famous major leaguer Albert "Chief" Bender. He returned to his farm on the outskirts of Norfolk to recuperate and was added by Wells at Consolvo's behest.

Ned Cheshire became the business manager. Clark considered him the sharpest business managers he ever worked with. Combined with the presumably capable Consolvo as president, management was expected to run a tight ship.[53]

Over the winter, Hannan and Clark opened a large pool hall on the corner of City Hall Avenue and Granby Street. Called the College Inn Billiard and Pool Association, it featured the heaviest tables available. It also contained all sorts of sports memorabilia, such as the flags of all the major football powers in the country. Among the baseball items were pictures of past Norfolk professional teams, including the championship club of the previous year. The College Inn would also serve as the team's headquarters, from which club news would emanate.[54]

Charles Bland, who returned as one of the owners of the Portsmouth club, supported Hannan as a potential president of the Virginia League in the belief that Jake Wells was too preoccupied with his numerous businesses. Everyone, including brother Otto, assumed that Jake did not want to keep the position. They were wrong. Hannan remained with the Tars when Norfolk broke a logjam that went on for 10 ballots and voted for Wells.[55]

In February, the Crew began the process of "Scrubbing [the] Deck of the Mary Jane." Clark persuaded management to put down grass in the infield, making the park the only one in the Virginia League with such adornment. The national press later noted that, "Norfolk's park is the Forbes Field (the new home of the Pittsburgh Pirates) of the Virginia League, in having the only green infield." The grass went well with a "restful green hue" new coat of paint. The "pretty grandstand" would soon have uniformed attendants. The home uniforms for the players were white with red trim and white stockings. A band of red circled the arm with the letter N in white inscribed therein. The white cap featured the word "NORFOLK" in red letters. A similarly designed uniform of gray with blue stockings sufficed for road games. A local reporter, despite the odd colors for sailors' home uniforms, pronounced everything "shipshape" on the "Deck Scene of the Mary Jane."[56]

Genial Charlie "Dutchy" Seitz returned for another season, as did Paul Ellinger, William Savage, Jimmy Jackson, William Rhynders and Jack Bonner. "Steamboat Bill" Otey also reappeared after a year's absence. He was joined by several newcomers: pitchers W.T. "Jack" Temple and Sam Hartman, outfielder Ed Mullaney, catcher C.H. "Red" Munson and infielder Heine (Heinie) Busch. R.H. "Happy" Chandler, who played for the Peninsula club in 1901, came as a catcher and ended up playing first base and three other positions at different times. Harry Galvin became the regular catcher, at least at the start of the season. In a striking contrast to the previous year, nearly all these players stuck around for most of the season. Jake Volz, another former Virginia Leaguer, joined the Crew after the club picture was taken. Perhaps mindful of his assault the previous year, Clark assured everyone that none of the players had a problem with alcohol.[57]

The Crew enjoyed a successful preseason, beating Altoona, Elmira and Yale University; Portsmouth, meanwhile, had trouble in exhibitions against two professional teams.

As part of a strangely concocted exhibition series that featured a game between Yale and the New York Giants, Christy Mathewson returned to Norfolk for the first time since playing there. Mathewson pitched the first half of the Giants' 7–1 win over Yale, and the Eli defeated the University of Virginia. The Tars defeated Yale, but did not play the team with which they had the most in common, the Giants.

Hannan kept the original contract signed by Mathewson—$90 a month—and often pointed to it mounted on the wall when negotiating deals with players who wanted too much money. In recalling his first appearance in a Norfolk uniform, "Big Six" said he gave up four or five runs and greatly exaggerated the weakness of his performance. He failed to mention that he won the game. The reporter who told the contract story said that Christy played in 1899 (apparently the year the contract was signed) and in another column claimed he played in 1895. The Mathewson mystique was certainly developing at a brisk pace.[58]

The 1909 season started as usual with Norfolk playing Portsmouth, the Crew winning 9–4 before some 6,000 at home. In an early-season victory over Roanoke in the Magic City, umpire Pender "rendered a decision that" so enraged the locals that he had to be placed under police protection, with angry fans in pursuit all the way to the jailhouse door. By mid–May, the Crew stood third in the standings behind Danville and Richmond. In a 9–6 win over Richmond deep into the season, Clark hit the team's first home run, "a mighty swat" which like a rocket, bounced "over the fence" (a home run under the rules of the time).[59]

Pitching remained the most important element in these contests. Otey won several games, but Volz didn't produce as hoped though he tamed Richmond in the Capital City in front of some 5,000. "Long" John Fox found trouble gaining traction. A later assessment claimed that Fox was one of those pitchers who had but fair speed and only a roundhouse curve, yet consistently maintained a better than .500 record. Fox was drafted several times for the big leagues, but "convivial habits" supposedly prevented him from sticking. Tom Foxen of Portsmouth beat Fox, 1–0, at Portsmouth before 3,500 a few days after Fox had won over the same team, 2–1.

There was no telling when or how trouble would start. Tar first baseman Happy Chandler once kidded Roanoke manager Frank Shaughnessy about the latter's abuse of umpires. That led the manager to curse Chandler, who in turn grazed his glove across Shaughnessy's face, drawing blood from his lip. Fans rushed the field, but order was restored after the umpire removed both men from the game. Later that night at the Monticello Hotel, where the Norfolk player resided for the season, Chandler "spoiled Shaughnessy's physiognomy" before the crowd in the lobby broke up the fight. The Roanoke manager claimed he had been sucker-punched. The game, rendered secondary by all the boxing, ended in a 6–6 tie.[60]

Norfolk had trouble defeating Portsmouth that year, not an unusual state of affairs. On July 1, the Truckers "ripped two planks from the Mary Jane's hull," 5–0 and 2–1. The Truckers again swept the Tars on July 4, with some 7,000 coming for the afternoon contest at Norfolk, by far the largest ever to attend a baseball game in Norfolk. Unfortunately, the Norfolk and Portsmouth Traction Company had but one car on hand as the game ended. After waiting at 18th and Granby for an hour, several hundred disgruntled folks walked over to Church Street to ride the other line, whose ran cars just as rarely. It seems that the traction companies had assigned all available cars to the Ocean View division to take care of the resort business.[61]

At midseason, with "old" Jack Bonner hitting .340, "Old Mull" Mullaney .320 and Chandler .306, Norfolk had three respectable batters, with Charlie Seitz (said to be playing the "game of his life") nearly as high. Even pitcher/outfielder Jack Temple occasionally helped out, winning three games with his timely hitting. Late arrival and power hitter Sis Hopkins batted a solid .274 for the year and once slammed a home run that threatened to hit the nearby brewery. In the second half of the season, most of Norfolk's leading hitters saw their averages drop, though Seitz stayed hot. Even so, the team led the league with a .255 average in early July and ended up just below .250 for the entire season, a marked improvement over the previous year. Seitz eventually led the league. With only a day or two left in the season, Norfolk had three of the league's leading basestealers, with Seitz and Chandler placing one-two in that category.[62]

By comparison Portsmouth had no regulars near .300. Highly-touted Tom Guiheen played in all but two games and managed but .219. One regular, who appeared in 110 games, ended up at .158. The "dead ball" was certainly alive and well in the sister city, if not in Norfolk.

Toward the end of July, Roanoke forged ahead in the league standings, with Norfolk trailing in third place at 42-38, four games behind. The Tigers were led by first baseman "Buck" Pressley out of the University of Virginia, and Clemson's Joe Holland. Both were medical students. About half the club had collegiate experience and thus the press dubbed the team the "College Tigers." Roanoke purchased the anchor of its staff, Walter Doane, from Atlanta.

In the dog days of August, Fox bested Foxen of Portsmouth, 3–2. He also pitched a shutout a week or so later over Portsmouth before a thousand customers, but Otey lost in the city across the river, 6–1.

Norfolk then made its move, closing in on Roanoke. Brilliant fielding allowed Fox to win, 2–1, over the Richmond Colts as part of a doubleheader sweep. On August 17, Norfolk moved to within one-half game of Roanoke, but just as it looked like Norfolk would overtake the Tigers, the Tars lost two home games to Danville. Fox got the Tars back on track with a shutout to complete the series, and then Norfolk's Volz beat Roanoke, 2–1, before 3,300 at home. The Crew beat Roanoke, 6–5, before some 4,500 in an exciting 10-inning fray, meaning that Norfolk had tied Roanoke in the number of wins but still trailed with one more loss.

The losers protested the game, claiming that the umpire ended the game in the top half of the 11th inning just after the Tigers had tied the contest. The umpire reported that it was too dark to continue, but the visitors claimed that the umpire made his decision because Norfolk fans intruded onto the field, making it impossible to continue to play. League officials supported the umpire.

With excitement now running high, the two teams moved into September. On Labor Day, Norfolk edged out 3–1 and 3–2 wins over Portsmouth, with Fox winning the home game before some 5,000. But earlier losses meant that Roanoke still held a two and a half game lead. Otey then shut out Portsmouth and Fox bested Bobby Vail, 1–0, after Temple won, 3–2. With the finish line fast approaching, Roanoke still clung to a one-half game lead. Again, Norfolk eked out a win over Portsmouth as Roanoke only managed a split against Richmond. Portsmouth lost to the Tars so many times that "A Handful of Loyal Rooters" in Portsmouth accused the Truckers of "listless and indifferent playing." "If we must lose to them, let it be on the square," they complained.[63]

With both Norfolk and Roanoke having 73-49 records after the last game of the regular season, headlines noted the necessity of a playoff. The Tars celebrated their finish by attending the theater. But a game won against Portsmouth the previous day was protested by Roanoke after it learned that Consolvo insisted on a previously postponed game being played in Norfolk, even though the schedule called for Portsmouth.[64]

A Norfolk reporter opined that if Norfolk lost out "through any technical decision, it will be the greatest blow professional baseball has ever received in the city." But during a 10-minute league meeting in a smoke-filled room at Richmond's Murphy Hotel, Roanoke's protest was upheld, as was President Jake Wells' decision to give the pennant to Roanoke. Wells contended that he sent a telegram to Consolvo forbidding the moving of the game to Norfolk. Two-thirds of the league members had authorized the movement of the first game of the doubleheader and thus refused to sustain Roanoke's protest, but because Consolvo disobeyed instructions regarding the second game, the Mary Janes lost a chance to win the pennant. Consolvo complained that Wells informed him too late to allow time to publicize the change of venue.[65]

Norfolk's afternoon daily maintained that Norfolk's fans took the news "gracefully." Based on any fair-minded assessment of the documents provided in the press, no one could conclude that Wells had even intimated that Consolvo could move the disputed second game. A second telegram said absolutely the game had to take place in Portsmouth and even frowned on the change of the first game unless the original schedule had been incorrect. And so by a mere half-game, the Crew lost the chance to win the race. After the season, an irritated Consolvo resigned as president of the Tars, but still retained ownership of much of the stock in the corporation.

Although a much smaller victory, Norfolk captured the first leg of the new Paul Gale-Greenwood Company Cup, on display at the company's store on the corner of Granby and Main, offered to the team along the Elizabeth River that won the most games from the other. To keep the cup, however, a team had to win the season series two out of three years.

The season proved another frustrating one for the Truckers. Things became so bad in the sister city that the owners contested the city tax, but the mayor fined them $20. The team lawyer maintained that Virginia law did not allow football and baseball games to be taxed unless the city charter specifically permitted the practice. The mayor disagreed.[66]

In a curious denouement, the league considered dropping Roanoke the next year, largely on the grounds that it was too costly to do business in the Magic City. Roanoke may have won the pennant, but its crowds were too small to cover the cost of sending players over the mountains. This disclosure undermines Win Clark's assertion, made almost 50 years after the event, that the Virginia League caved in to Roanoke's complaint because it feared Roanoke would leave the association if it failed to be awarded the pennant.

In 1959, when Frank Shaughnessy was president of the International League, Clark reminded columnist Tom Fergusson about the episode. Not only did Fergusson confuse the story by having Shaughnessy act as an official of the Virginia League, the entire yarn seems suspect.

Once again, the press expected Wells to resign as president of the league, hopefully to be replaced by Billy Hannan of Norfolk. Once again that did not happen.[67]

Keeping Their Heads Above Water (1910)

The next season, with Win Clark still at the helm, another mix of old and new faces assembled around the Ides of March to prepare for another voyage. Bill Otey, "Happy" Chandler, catcher Red Munson, shortstop Henry "Heinie" Busch and center fielder Ed Mullaney were among the returnees. Pitching seemed especially strong with Otey and "Long John" Fox, plus the signing of Carl Walker, considered the best University of Virginia pitcher ever. Not far into the season, Clark signed Martin Walsh, already one of the best Virginia League pitchers.[68]

In the preseason, the Tars played well, although losing, 7–2, against the visiting Washington club. of the American League, which spent part of its spring in training in Norfolk. In addition to the great pitcher Walter Johnson, the visitors included catcher Charles "Gabby" Street, whose chief claim to fame to this point was catching a ball dropped from the top of the Washington Monument. A few years later, Street would become a manager in the Virginia League in Suffolk.

The Tars also lost a couple of games that spring to the New York Giants. On April 4 the Tars lost, 3–0, with a new Norfolk lefty showing good form with a spitball, but once the season started, he disappeared. In the second game against McGraw's men, the Giants won more handily, having been embarrassed by the close score the day before. That second day, the

Catcher/manager Charles Evard "Gabby" Street, who played in an exhibition game in Norfolk in 1910, is best known for catching a baseball thrown from the Washington Monument, though this weak-hitting but savvy backstop also had a lengthy career with several major league clubs. After serving as player/manager for Suffolk in 1920 (p. 156), he eventually became manager of the St. Louis Cardinals from 1929 and 1933, winning pennants in 1930 and 1931 and the 1931 World Series (National Baseball Hall of Fame Library, Cooperstown, New York).

Crew faced Christy Mathewson, with some 2,500 fans extending him a rousing welcome. The two runs credited to the Crew were not scored off what many Norfolk fans considered the best pitcher of his time. (That night Matty and McGraw were playing pool at the Monticello Hotel before a large crowd when a well-dressed gentleman inquired about them just as Matty missed a shot. A spectator said, "They are with the New York Giants," to which the inquisitive one asked "And who are the Giants?" The astonished audience almost as one responded that they were professional baseball players, leading the visitor to reply, "Well I hope they can play ball better than they can billiards.")[69]

Just before the start of the regular season, Clark stirred up some controversy by proposing that the league dispose of Roanoke and Danville and replace them with Petersburg and Newport News. "Half Nelson," the Richmond scribe, ignored Clark's real reason for such a proposal, the reduction of travel costs. He accused Clark of wanting to get back to the "good old days" (1894), when rooters for Norfolk and Petersburg "drank 'licker'" and furiously fought each other. Such a remark looks like a thinly veiled criticism of Clark and his reputation of pugnacity. But by 1910, he had calmed down considerably.[70]

Clark started the season with lefthander Carl Walker on the mound. Walker had thrown a no-hitter for the University of Virginia and Norfolk had outbid Lynchburg for his services. Folks in the Hill City complained when he would not accept payment of $250 a month, grumbling that Norfolk must be paying him at least that much, an amount that far exceeded the salary cap of $150. But Clark claimed he had not broken any rules; it was simply that the young man preferred to play in the City by the Sea. So confident were Clark and Consolvo in Walker that they even considered trading Long John Fox or Bill Otey. Walker won several games and even had some outstanding performances, but he failed to pitch regularly the full season, probably because of an injury induced by overwork.

In the first two contests against the Truckers, the Tars tied a 10-inning affair before some 4,000 and then rolled, 13–4. Several games ended in ties or inclement weather interfered, and finally when the club started to play games on a regular basis, it lost more frequently than it won.

In the second week in May, the Crew lost three straight to Danville, followed by two losses and a tie to Roanoke. Pitching and defense were serious problems. "There is something radically wrong with the Crew," one writer opined. When the pitchers had their stuff, the team lapsed on the field. When the fielders did well, the pitchers let down. Such weakness would cause problems at any time, but in the era of the dead ball, it could be fatal.

Whatever the case, the club finally got back on track by defeating Richmond and Portsmouth, winning two out of three from each. A Garrison 7–6 finish over Lynchburg gave the Crew some confidence as May approached its terminus. In the Memorial Day twin bill, the Tars and Truckers split, each winning on the other's home grounds, with 4,000 attending each game.[71]

In early May, Portsmouth correspondent and one-time pro player Joe Burke complained that league umpires allowed spitballers and other slow pitchers too much time, leading to "public disgust with their tediousness." Sometimes games with less than 10 runs scored actually took over two hours.[72]

In the second week in June, Alan C. Omohondro, the president of the Norfolk Athletic Association and a city councilman, ended the policy of allowing policemen to have free passes for games. As in Portsmouth previously, the police protested by boycotting the games. Policemen, Omohondro contended, sat in the stands where they were not needed instead of the bleachers where rowdy behavior was more likely. Even though the park was located in the county, which had no regular police, the law allowed Omohondro to request police, when a large crowd might attend. But the policy meant the club would have to pay for private guards for most contests. The day after this information surfaced in the newspaper, as if on cue, fans flooded onto the field. Ed Mullaney and Happy Chandler persuaded the crowd to return to their seats. Another account of this fracas said only one spectator ran onto the field (hoping to slug a special policeman); this writer was more concerned about all the swearing.[73]

In early June, Norfolk swooned again, losing three in a row to Richmond and scoring but one run. Now hitting was suspect, but the Colts forfeited the next two (once when they failed to bring two pitchers and their starter was ejected for excessive arguing). Walker regained his winning ways with 2–1 and 4–0 victories over Portsmouth, as Norfolk swept the series. Portsmouth, however, defeated Walker in his next outing, 1–0.

Shaking up their lineup to induce more runs, the Tars won, 11–5, over Lynchburg. The Shoemakers, however, recovered to hand the Tars an 8–6 loss. The reporter excused the overall recent lapses to the fact that Otey was sick and Fox had left, suffering from something called the "Bugs," or "Raymond's Disease" (named for major leaguer "Bugs" Raymond who went AWOL). The absences left Walker and Walsh to carry on. One newspaper even had a picture of the infamous Raymond. As could be predicted, Walker developed arm trouble, probably from overuse, and was lost for the season.

Norfolk recruited a deaf mute from New York who did poorly his lone start, with the word "dummy" in the headline in one paper, but another reporter blamed poor fielding for the loss. After all this, Norfolk had a record of 19-25, a game and a half above last place Lynchburg and a couple of games below fourth-place Portsmouth.

Over the next few weeks, Norfolk picked up new pitchers, Jim "Subway" Vance and "Jim Jeffries" Fletcher (named such by the fans because of his size), as well as a new catcher. Righty Vance won the morning part of the holiday doubleheader on July 4, shutting out Portsmouth in a game held in Norfolk.

If the Tars had troubles, they paled in comparison to what was occurring in the neighboring city. Although the Truckers were almost respectable on the diamond, dropping below .500 only toward the end of June, their management ran into a rough spell. Sometime earlier, Richmond businessmen invested in the Portsmouth franchise simply to keep it afloat. The Portsmouth organization, experiencing low attendance and several rainouts, failed to pay its players for some time, and the men would not report. Had civic-minded citizens possessed the club, Portsmouth apologists believed, the club would have received more support. Whatever the merits of that argument, the league stepped in, transferring several Portsmouth games to Norfolk in the belief that it would face legal problems with the current owners of the park if games continued to be played in Portsmouth. The league also dug into its sinking fund and made restitution to the players, telling them the "ghost would walk" after a game against Norfolk, which incidentally the Truckers won, 1–0.

At a meeting at on the veranda of the Ocean View Hotel one Sunday afternoon, league representatives turned down a proposal by Dr. Vernon Brooks to keep the team in Portsmouth. When Brooks said he could pay over $1,000 to cover league expenses but would not reimburse Richmond interests, the officials approved the idea. But Gus Williams of Roanoke and President W.B. Bradley of the Colts later declined to sign the contract. In a published affidavit, Brooks exonerated both Williams and Wells, claiming Bradley was the chief culprit in turning down his proposal. Bradley persuaded the rest of the league to have Jack Grim take over the franchise and move the team to Petersburg. An editorial in the Portsmouth daily placed blame principally on the outside owners, claiming they lacked local pride. Residents of the sister cities condemned the loss of the franchise.[74]

Given the situation the Portsmouth club faced, the July 4 morning game took place in Norfolk, when tradition usually placed it across the river. The low attendance of about 1,000 may have been due to the turmoil connected to the impending demise of the Portsmouth club. Jupiter Pluvius, the Roman God of rain, caused the cancellation of the afternoon contest, probably a fortuitous event. Had it been played it would have been overshadowed by the boxing match in Reno, Nevada, between black boxer and world champion Jack Johnson and Jim Jeffries, the "Great White Hope." Hundreds of people went downtown to hear megaphone announcements in front of the newspaper offices, starting around 4:30, about the same time the afternoon game was supposed to take place. The rain apparently had little impact on cooling the crowd that assembled there. Johnson's convincing win sent whites into hysterics in many places, including downtown Norfolk, where black residents, returning from the beach at Sewell's Point, were set upon by a mob of sailors and young thugs in one of the worst race riots in the city's history.[75]

A short time later, the Tars released Bill Otey, at the time hospitalized supposedly with typhoid fever. The embittered "Steamboat Bill" left the hospital and Norfolk, saying he would sign up with "a real team." It turned out to be the Washington Senators. His career as a Tar started in 1906 when he won 19 games, posting five shutouts. In 1907, he led the team to a pennant, winning 22 and shutting out opponents 10 times, which even in the era of the dead ball was quite an accomplishment. The next year, he did not join the team until almost the end of the season, pitching instead for Roanoke. Then in 1909, he worked in over 40 games as a Tar but won only 13 of 28 decisions. Until he became sick during the current season, the 6-foot-1 side-wheeler had been the mainstay of the staff, splitting evenly ten decisions. His release hinted at considerable callousness on management's part, although they likely disapproved of a lifestyle that caused him to die from syphilis in 1931, which was shown to have been contracted many years earlier in Norfolk.[76]

After the mid-point of the season, the Tars went through a long stretch through the middle of July where they won but one game — over Roanoke — showing a record on the 26th of 34–41 and, flirting with fifth place in the standings. Toward the end of July, Norfolk secured another win from Vance, 1–0, versus Danville. Even though Danville recovered to beat Vance in the next game, Norfolk soon showed signs of life, reeling off two straight shutouts, with Ryan and Vance doing the honors. At that point Norfolk closed to within four games of .500.

Early August brought more agony. Danville, now managed by former crewman Steve Griffin, won two contests, 3–2 and 4–0. Finally, Vance shut out the Bugs and Ryan reeled off four shutouts in six games. He was doing so well that the New York Americans bought the rights to him, but he did not immediately depart for more northern climes. After Vance and Fox lost a double bill to Roanoke, Ryan threw shutouts against Danville and Lynchburg. He also beat the Shoemakers again, sewing them up, 4–3.

The Tars persisted in their upward struggle to respectability, as Martin Walsh finally got his act together to beat Richmond, 6–2. Vance, who ended up with a 16–7 record, got plenty of hitting help against the Lawmakers, 10–3. "Phenom" Ryan then beat Richmond again, 4–2, to bring Norfolk to within three games of .500 as the league entered the stretch run. Walsh won again, this time over Roanoke, and then Ryan blanked the Highlanders, 1–0, and thus deprived them of a chance for first place in the standings. Ryan and Vance won the two games on Labor Day.

Danville, in dire financial trouble, raised much-needed funds through a public subscription. Its directors also transferred two players to Cleveland, an action that caused manager Steve Griffin to resign. Despite all the controversy, the Bugs held on against a rejuvenated Roanoke club and won their first Virginia League pennant by four games. The Mary Jane cruised in third, with a record of 59–56, taking three of four from Petersburg to end the season.

One reporter ended the season in an upbeat frame of mind, noting that Sam Wasserman and his special noise-making machine were already preparing for another season. Members of the "Left Field Bleacher Buster, Knockers and Squeezers Club" were too "dyed-in-the-wool" to keep down for long. Another reporter, however, focused on how disappointed Norfolk fans were in the overall showing.[77]

Just after the season ended, reporters speculated that shortstop Heinie Busch or possibly outfielder Wilbur E. Murdock might manage the team the next year, as Clark seemed destined for another assignment. Reporters considered the popular shortstop a good "inside man." As it turned out, Busch managed the Petersburg team and Clark crossed the river to manage a Portsmouth team in an entirely new league.

In assessing the 1910 club's performance, pitching held up fairly well, weakness resting largely in light hitting and the worst fielding in the league. Batting at .289, Murdock led the club, with Walsh posting a .277 average and Munson a .269 average. Murdock also led the team in extra base hits (close to 40), well above anyone else in that department and making him the winner of $100 (five $20 gold pieces) given by a local company. Murdock was so excited about winning the award that he could not hit a lick in the final game. Unlike most of their mates, Jimmy Jackson and Jack Bonner fielded nearly flawlessly, but they only lasted half the season. Happy Chandler's average dropped way off to .219, and his name would no longer grace the box scores of future Crews.[78]

In head-to-head engagements, Norfolk held its own against Richmond and Roanoke, pretty much breaking even with these two rivals, but Danville lost only five games to Norfolk all season. Richmond fared little better against the Bugs (Red Sox). The Crew did hold a sizeable advantage over Portsmouth/Petersburg (19 and 12), but no one mentioned anything about the special cup, presumably because the old rivalry no longer existed once the team moved to Petersburg.

After the season, reporters confirmed that rookie pitcher "Phenom" Ryan was really William Schaub, who captained both the football and baseball teams at Mt. St. Joseph College in Baltimore and played professional ball in West Virginia before coming to Norfolk. He used an alias to avoid losing his status as a college amateur. In practicing football back in college, he sustained a head injury. The next day, complaining of chest pains, he went to the infirmary, where he died from pneumonia.[79]

In the first five years of the revived Virginia League, Norfolk had scored one first-place finish, two seconds, one third, and one last place. Despite its miserable showing in 1908, the club won 53 percent of its games during the period. The Crew that won the pennant in 1907 hit but .223 (standing second in the league in that category) and sustained a slugging percentage of .265, lower in both respects than the 1909 version, which posted averages of .249 (highest in the league) and .290, respectively. But the 1907 club also stole some 350 bases, compared to about 270 by the later Crew. Indeed, no Norfolk team ever stole more bases, although the 1914 club, winners of another pennant, came pretty close. Even the best hitting clubs in Norfolk did little to ruin the reputation of the Era of the Dead Ball.

7

"The Tide of Victory Ebbs and Flows," 1911–1914

During the 1910 season and immediately afterwards, negative comments about the configuration of the Virginia league were abundant. In late August, many locals urged the elimination of both Danville and Roanoke because of the cost of travel and the small gates offered there. Win Clark pointed out that it was difficult to keep teams on the road, noting that even Richmond only once paid more than $400, with the amount usually well below that level. Because Richmond charged just 10 cents for seats in the bleachers, its total gate was often small despite having by far the biggest average attendance in the league. But with the largest population base in the league, Richmond was the only club in the league to end up in the black. The "Virginian League Muddle" persisted well into 1912.[1]

After the 1910 season, a new baseball association was formed in Portsmouth with George R. Parrish as president, with I.T. Van Patten running operations and ready to upgrade Athletic Park. These men wanted re-admission to the Virginia League, but others thought it best to create an eight-team league with four teams located in Hampton Roads, as had existed for part of the 1900 season.[2]

A Rival League and Another Second-Place Finish (1911)

Consolvo, still associated with the Norfolk Athletic Association and doubtless still smarting from the embarrassing finish of 1909, demanded reduced salary limits or changes in the schedule to allow Norfolk to make some money. Should anyone want his franchise they could have it, he grumbled. The owners of the upstate teams hoped others would take over the Norfolk franchise. If current management would not lease their field, then build or rent a new diamond, they urged. If that failed, then move the franchise to Newport News. Certainly the Newport News fans would do no worse than those from Norfolk, it was said.

Jake Wells, who supposedly had resigned as president, groaned about how some people refused to work for the good of the league. He assumed Bradley, the Richmond owner, would stand with Lynchburg, Danville and Roanoke. Things looked bleak for the future of the league. Some thought those three cities should look into the possibility of inviting Staunton or Durham, North Carolina, to join them. In any event, the westerners believed it cost no more than $1,200 a month to field a team, and if Consolvo could not find a way to raise that amount, he should get out of the business.[3]

A week later, it looked like Danville might be dropped, with Portsmouth getting its franchise. Again, it seemed likely that Jake Wells would resign and Billy Hannan of Norfolk would take over as president of the league. But Gus Williams, a University of Virginia man from Roanoke, became the new president instead. Consolvo and Hannan secretly sold out to Roanoke resident H.C. Elliot, a friend of Williams, purportedly for $6,000.

When Williams sabotaged efforts to bring Newport News and Portsmouth into the Virginia League, residents of those two cities started a movement that caught on like "wild fire," leading to the formation of the Tidewater League. Hannan's departure from the Norfolk club and his failure to attain the presidency of the Virginia League, along with Win Clark's lack of a job, were among the reasons for creating the new league. Hannan assumed its presidency, and insisted on a salary cap of $1,200 for the entire season for a full team. Clark became the manager of the new Portsmouth club. Norfolk would soon have two professional teams — one in each league.[4]

That year, the Virginia League, still rated Class C in Organized Baseball, decided to cap club salaries at $1,400 a month, with each team allowed thirteen players plus a manager. But because most managers made between $200 and $250, the actual payroll cap ran closer to $1,600 a month. Even though all contracts had to be inspected by league officials to make sure of adherence to the salary cap, reporters suspected that players received hidden financial help.[5]

The Tidewater League soon organized the Norfolk "Rookies," managed by Steve Griffin, who had recently guided Danville most of the way to a Virginia League pennant. Portsmouth, led by Win Clark, became the "Marines," the name derived from the new park's proximity to the Marine Barracks at the Navy Yard. The old baseball man I.T. Van Patten served as president of the new Southside Park Corporation, with a potential capitalization of $9,000. One writer thought "Recruits" better than "Marines," because almost all the players were expected to be first-time professionals. Once the season commenced, Portsmouth reporters reverted to the old name — "Pirates." Newport News resumed being the "Shipbuilders," Elizabeth City was the "Tar Heels," Suffolk, managed by the former Tar outfielder Ed Mullaney, became "the Nancies" for unknown reasons. Old Point found no nickname, but its people did revamp Army and Navy Field, near the train depot in Phoebus.[6]

Reporters forecast trouble for the old Virginia League, and particularly for the franchise in Norfolk, where fans disliked the secretive ways of the outside owners. Fans seemingly had a bias for the new league.[7]

Portsmouth soon had a contractor working on its new park on Cossack Street, South Side Park, just south and east of the old one. The new facility stood between 9th Street and the Gilmerton Car Line, which ran along the third-base side of the field. Because the principal streets were not at right angles, the diamond had to be shifted toward the street on the right-field side. Two sets of bleachers ran down the first base side, with a longer set beside third base. These bleachers ended about half way down the outfield; otherwise they would have intruded onto the field or encroached onto the streets. South Side had more room in left field and left center than earlier ball fields in Portsmouth, but its right-field fence was closer to home plate not only at the foul line but for several yards into the playing field. As the new park materialized, the city razed the one on Washington Street and sold its wooden fence, grandstand, and bleachers at auction with plans to turn left field into a site for a public school.[8]

As the preseason began, controversy immediately erupted. The National Association of Baseball Clubs told one major league club that it could not play a game against the new team from Newport News because the Tidewater League had been declared an outlaw league. Officials told a Montreal team already practicing at Newport News to move its instructional grounds and not to play the local team, or be subjected to severe penalties. A team from Trenton, New Jersey, however, after hearing the order from Secretary Farrell of the National Association, simply changed the name of their opponent in Newport News to the Independents. But the players were the same ones that were called the Shipbuilders. They played the game at Casino Park, with one of its sides facing the James River. It had a new eight-foot fence divided into even lengths covering some 400 feet on each side of a square. The fence and the new bleachers could be easily dismantled. It served as the field for the home team, whatever its name.[9]

As soon as the season started, the Norfolk manager in the Virginia League tried to lure a player away from Newport News. The director of that club, G.B.A. Booker, asked Hannan to allow him to break the salary cap to retain his shortstop. At that very time, Hannan was trying to make a deal with the National Association to prevent contract jumping. Hannan considered taking legal action, but because that might endanger his bid for recognition as a legitimate league, he did not follow through. It is unlikely that Hannan countenanced outbidding the rival league, but the Norfolk manager got some bad press in the process. Curiously, the wives of managers Steve Griffin and Charlie Babb got along well and supported each other's clubs in home games. The local press carried their pictures sitting together in the stands.

In the 1911 season, manager Charlie Babb "appeared on deck" to lead the Mary Janes. The columnist of "Heard in the Fo'castle" kept prodding him for details about the new talent. The information dribbled in, as Babb roamed Kentucky and Arkansas. After arriving in Norfolk, Babb issued the details of his expected roster. Only Martin Walsh of the 1910 squad would be retained; all the rest were new. George Block, Jack Law, George Kircher, James Poole, Joe Finneran and Johnny Dodge would stay with the team for most of the season; an equal number had their names (or perhaps some aliases) listed, but they never made the roster. Kircher and Poole formed what folks called the "Blue Grass Battery" (both hailing from Kentucky), but Babb also signed on two other catchers, who played all season, with two of the three catchers alternating in the outfield or at first base.[10]

In the preseason Boston's National Leaguers played the Norfolk Tars, leading them 2–0 when rain ended affairs, with but 250 attending. The New York Yankees had less trouble with the Tars, winning 12–5, with Jack Warhop, a future Tar player/manager, yielding few runs, and Dodge, the shortstop for the Crew displaying a "good head." The Tars took Altoona to the tune of 16–9, but lost to Yale University, 7–4, in a ragged contest before but 300. Whether this low attendance was due to weather, competing horse racing, or general ill feeling toward the Virginia League is hard to know. Cold weather on Opening Day allegedly kept the crowd to a little more than a thousand, the Tars beating Heine Busch's "Gooberites" from Petersburg. But the Portsmouth paper maintained that at least two-thirds of the spectators had been given free passes.

Unable to use League Park, the home of the Tars, the Rookies played at Lafayette Field, overcoming the Portsmouth Marines, 6–2, before some 2,100, roughly twice the number that showed up to watch the Tars. Norfolk, with but a 9–7 record, soon gave way to Newport News as league leader. The Nancies did not win as many games as their fans hoped, but Suffolk citizens were pleased that all their players had habits better than the typical professional ballplayer.[11]

Tidewater League president Billy Hannan soon axed Griffin as manager of the Rookies because the latter bad-mouthed the league, which was not an alliance of separate corporations but a company with different branches. In his search for a better job, Griffin kept saying things such as "Our league is about done." Hannan found out about this sabotage when Griffin, indiscreetly enough, used league postal services. In dismissing him, Hannan claimed Griffin also ruined relations with most of his team.

Before angering Hannan, Griffin scrapped with umpire Jack Henshaw at Old Point. Bad relations between the two started when Griffin complained about Henshaw's calls at a game in Norfolk, which led to the latter's resignation as a league umpire. Then at Old Point Henshaw, the prizefighter and boxing instructor from Phoebus, happened upon Griffin and hit him in the face. The latter responded in kind and the two started slugging. When they fell to the ground in a clinch, the one-time boxer "like a mad bull dog," bit one of Griffin's fingers. At this point the crowd broke up the fight and Griffin repaired to a nearby drug store for cauterization. A passing policeman issued both combatants summonses to appear in the mayor's court the next morning.[12]

Buck Hooker took over managing duties in Norfolk, and the Rookies beat the Shipbuilders, 3–2, at Casino Park in "the fastest played and most brilliant battle of the season." Norfolk moved to the top of the league with a record of 23-12. Portsmouth placed second 21-14. Newport News stood at 20-14, with Elizabeth City, Suffolk and Old Point trailing.[13]

Meanwhile, the Norfolk Crew was running away with the Virginia League, with 31 wins and but 11 defeats. Even so, attendance often fell to less than 500. Five Tars were batting over .300. Babb himself carried a .322 average, while two of his pitchers, Martin Walsh and Joe Finneran, did even better as hitters though with far fewer at-bats. Norfolk continued its winning ways into early June. Walsh, now becoming quite the hitter, clubbed the longest home run ever at the park, thrilling an unusually large crowd of 1,100. He also won six of seven pitching decisions. Jimmie Poole (11–3) and Finneran (10–3) were more than holding their own.

Then came an amazing three-week swoon of 14 losses in 15 games, allegedly brought on by players having to pay fines out of their own pockets. Norfolk still managed to stay close to the league lead. Bush's Petersburg club administered a 2–0 shutout the day the Norfolk record fell to 32-22, as the Tars hitting woes continued. Over the next week or two, the club showed some improvement and regained first place, splitting a doubleheader on July 4 with last-place Danville.

On July 1, catcher Block, Babb and outfielder Joe Staub were all hitting above .300. Pitcher and pinch-hitter Walsh came in at .288. Jack Law and Johnny Dodge hit .250 and .244, respectively. Staub had 16 doubles and five triples to lead in extra-base hits. Kircher's 20 steals led that department.[14]

In the meantime, Elizabeth City secured the services of Portsmouth collegian Davis Robertson, a former star at Portsmouth High School and currently a student at North Carolina A&M (now North Carolina State). Robertson had pitched for the Elizabeth City team in the Albemarle League the year before. Without Robertson, Elizabeth City had been playing about .500; now they seemed unstoppable.

The Norfolk Rookies and Portsmouth Marines split their July 4 doubleheader, by which time the league was disintegrating. The last standings printed in Norfolk's main daily newspaper appeared on July 5, when Hannan suddenly declared Elizabeth City the winner of the first part of a split season. Elizabeth City demonstrated a marked superiority with its 44-23 record, with the Norfolk Rookies five games back and Portsmouth two games in back of them. Suffolk ended up at .500 and Newport News did not lose any more than Suffolk, but won five fewer. Old Point came in a distant last at 16-50.

Although the newspaper in Newport News continued to carry the standings of the second half of the season on a regular basis, Norfolk and Portsmouth fans lost interest. Hannan and company blamed the league's troubles on the weaker than expected attendance in Portsmouth and Norfolk, cities that were supposed to provide some cushion for the league. In a desperate maneuver, Hannan moved the Norfolk club to Hampton. The residents of Crabtown expressed less than enthusiastic financial support for the enterprise, but enough of them showed up at the games to keep the club alive—for a while.[15]

Occasional scores suggest that a league minus several former members persisted through July. On August 2, a Norfolk newspaper announced its formal death, noting that such a circuit surviving up to July 4 "was miraculous." After Elizabeth City folded, the league carried on with four teams—three from the Peninsula and one from Suffolk. At the end, Suffolk had the best record.[16]

Attendance had been improving some in the Virginia League even before the demise of the Tidewater League. Some 1,300 watched Norfolk beat Roanoke, 11–10 on July 2, giving the Tars a 36-26 record, and permitting them to regain the lead from Roanoke. The Crew split two games with Danville on July 4, drawing some 1,500 for one game and 2,500 for the other, the latter number possibly underestimated by some 500. Even with the addition, those numbers fell a bit short of the usual level for the traditional holiday games, but they were certainly an improvement over what the club had been averaging.

Even the comparatively small number attending both games of the doubleheader taxed the capabilities of the traction company. As described by a reporter, fans made it to the park "because they were able to squeeze and jam and hang on the steps and fenders. If any baseball extras were run, Three Fingered Brown of the Chicago Cubs could have counted them on his salary paw, and then not have been crowded for room."[17]

Norfolk continued to do well on the playing field for a time. Walsh helped beat the Roanoke Magicians one day by pitching well and also hitting a circuit rider, and thereby got his picture in the paper. Toward the end of July, Walsh had to leave town for a few days when his wife became ill.[18]

In mid–July management changed policy to allow blacks to enter through the main gate of League Park because it had closed the entry in right field when blacks were moved to the left-field bleachers. Even though blacks now came through the main entrance, they still bought tickets at segregated booths and thus whites and blacks did not stand in line together. Despite that restriction, a writer expressed concern that blacks and whites commingled when they entered the ballpark and said "I will not allow my wife to further attend games for fear that in the rush of a big crowd she might come close to a black person." Given the sparse attendance thus far into the season, another reporter doubted that would happen. Writers also criticized management for permitting blacks to sit in seats formerly assigned to whites in the left-field bleachers, with only an imaginary line now separating the two races.[19]

In early August, President Williams indefinitely suspended first baseman Jack Law, supposedly on the bad advice of umpire Bob Pender. Law claimed that the incident started with his laughing when Pender failed to detect that a rival first basemen had dropped a ball and later after Law snickered at being called out on strikes when the ball sailed far away from the plate. Reacting against the suspension, hundreds of indignant fans signed a petition to the president of the league threatening a boycott. Some of Law's mates said they would not participate in the next road game, but Law convinced them to play. It turned out that Williams was disturbed with Law not because he baited an umpire, but because he openly criticized his team's Roanoke officials, claiming that L.E. Johnson, the top man with the Norfolk and Western Railroad, was part owner of the Roanoke team. Williams responded that Law had lied, but he said nothing about the implied criticism about the connection between the Norfolk and Roanoke teams. Fans and reporters believed that secrecy about ownership caused the controversy and wanted to know why Williams did not punish Frank Shaughnessy, the manager of the Roanoke club, for making disparaging remarks to several Norfolk players about president Williams. Faced with a deluge of protests, Williams finally fixed Law's punishment at a five-day suspension and a $25 fine. Despite the end of the suspension, Norfolk, for undisclosed reasons, went for the remainder of the season without Law, a steady hitter equipped with "octopus-like" arms that greatly assisted his fielding. After trying a couple of experiments with replacements, Norfolk acquired light-hitting Henry Foiles. Whether Law ever paid his $25 (a pretty stiff fine in those days) is not known.[20]

Even after the Law suspension, Norfolk clung to a one and one-half game edge over fast-rising Petersburg. But in one week without Law, Norfolk won but one out of six contests, the Goobers ran off seven straight wins to take a big lead. During this stage, Babb secured Johnny Shaw, an infielder from Petersburg, but the young man hit poorly. The Crew also picked up Cy Pierce, a pitcher, who as a visiting Colt had developed a rapport with local colored fans. But Richmond had released him for a reason — wildness — and he did not help the cause. Black fans often criticized Shaw, Law as well as Babb. Norfolk also acquired Portsmouth's best outfielder after the demise of the Tidewater League, but the new recruit played but little. Management delayed in acquiring one-time Tar Ed Mullaney, the manager of Suffolk, and so he only played in only eight games, posting a .370 mark.

During the remainder of the season, the Tars took three in a row from Lynchburg, but lost two of three to Roanoke, followed by three straight losses to Richmond. In one of the wins Walsh, pinch-hitting for Foiles at the request of the fans, poked a double and scored when Finneran sacrificed him to third and Babb drove him in with a hit. Then they won five straight, including four over Danville. Petersburg, however, took three games from them, all low-scoring affairs, at which point Norfolk had little chance to win the race as the Crew now trailed the Goobers by five games with but six to play.

The press blamed one loss on Walsh's wildness, but as he lost, 2–0, something more might have been said about the lack of hitting. The reporter also grumbled about the small attendance (2,000) in light of the importance of the two games that day. Norfolk did take two from Petersburg, but on Labor Day, before a fairly slim crowd, Norfolk split with Danville, as Petersburg did the same in its doubleheader. The Goobers ended the season in first place by two and one-half games. Vance, a former Tar hurler, finished 11–0 and materially helped Petersburg's cause. Roanoke finished third at 62-54, followed by Richmond, Lynchburg and Danville.

The fans that year added to their reputation for bad behavior. They often threw soda bottles onto the field when something irritated them, even at their own players. The practice became so common that the Tars supposedly lost a game against Lynchburg when, with the bases loaded with two out in the ninth inning, one of Shoemakers launched a high pop foul fly between third base and home plate. As Johnny Dodge and George Block converged under the descending ball, manager Charlie Babb yelled "Dodge," intending for the infielder to make the play. But both players thought he meant to watch out for a coke bottle and they ducked, thus missing the ball. The visitor then smashed a double to drive in the winning runs. The story may well be hokum, as newspaper accounts of games against Lynchburg offer no confirmation. No matter, the story reinforced the legacy that Norfolk fans were quite unruly.[21]

In 1911, the Pickwick Club opened on Main Street, almost opposite the Academy of

Music. Owned by a corporation, with Norman Hoffheimer its president and manager of the combination saloon, billiard parlor and spacious site for wrestling matches and the like, the Pickwick also became a hangout for folks interested in professional baseball. Instead of finding out the results of the World Series by standing in a big crowd in front of one of the two daily newspaper offices, members of the club could watch the results of the New York Giants-Philadelphia Athletics championship coming in on teletype as they played billiards. With Clark and Hannan no longer involved in local professional baseball after the 1911 season, the College Inn closed the next year. Whether the Pickwick picked up the memorabilia to adorn its walls is unknown.[22]

Tabulations at the end of the season revealed that George "Bruno" Block, from Paducah, led the Tars and the league with an average of .330, but Walsh, Babb and Staub also did well at the plate. It was a fairly respectable showing, but averages were generally up everywhere that year, as a livelier ball began to phase out the dead-ball era.

Just after the season, James E. Barry, probably with his brother's backing, supposedly took an option to buy the club from Elliott and Gus Williams. An enterprising young business man, Barry had played both football and baseball at the University of Virginia and the University of North Carolina. He had also starred for the local collegians during the summers. At one point he had been tabbed as a member of the Crew, but for unknown reasons, he never joined the club. With his supposed option, Barry commenced combing college teams in Virginia and North Carolina for young players who wanted to become professionals.

The O'Neill-Barry Company, which both he and his brother owned, sold athletic supplies and had long supported amateur athletics in the area. As a personal friend of Williams, Barry figured he could bring ownership of the team back to Norfolk. But just as the young man never became a member of the Mary Janes, he did not become one of the principal owners in 1912 for reasons not fully explained by the press.[23]

League Machinations (1912)

One would think that with the end of the Tidewater league, normalcy would return, but it did not. At a December meeting, delegates suggested that the Virginia-League would be better off without Richmond as long as W.B. Bradley led that franchise. In January 1912, Bradley evidenced a considerable penchant toward compromise when he said he would accept anyone the Norfolk club, represented by Dr. J.R. McCrary and Charley Shaffer, cared to nominate for the presidency of the league. Bradley would, however, not agree to oust any clubs from the association.

After two unsuccessful attempts to have a league meeting, representatives from Lynchburg, Danville and Richmond cast their votes for a new president, while Roanoke and Petersburg voted for the incumbent Williams. The first three clubs prevented Norfolk from voting by proxy, even though vice president Bradley from Richmond, then presiding as chair, ruled that the Norfolk vote would be counted. Petersburg and Roanoke delegates then walked out of the session.

Sometime later, Petersburg, Roanoke and Norfolk delegates met in Petersburg at a session boycotted by the other three teams, all claiming that the issue of the presidency had been decided at the previous meeting. The three teams that met at Petersburg on January 15 made Williams president and notified the other owners to inform the league within a week whether they planned to continue operations. Lynchburg, Danville and Richmond declared such actions to be "illegal and tyrannical," and a violation of their property and "reservation rights." They took the matter before the National Board at a meeting in New York. After listening to several lawyers, that body decided that under the constitution of the Virginia League, no election for president had taken place. The board sent Dr. F.R. Carson to mediate the next meeting of the Virginia League. Williams, objecting to the participation of a board representative, held a meeting even though Carson requested a delay to allow him to attend.[24]

At a subsequent meeting at Lynchburg with all six clubs represented, Carson had a lengthy and acrimonious private meeting with Williams where the latter refused any possible compromise, including one in which Williams could act as president but the opposing faction could name the secretary and treasurer. Following that encounter, Carson met with representatives from Roanoke, Petersburg and Norfolk, where their delegates took turns berating the National Board. With league clubs "hopelessly divided," Carson declared that the proceedings of January 15 were illegal and ordered a new election, demanding that Williams desist from acting as presiding officer, his term having expired. The Williams faction refused to concede the matter. As soon as John H. Farrell heard Carson's report, he accepted the three complying clubs as true representatives of the Virginia League. And based on Article 5, Section 4 of the National Association Agreement, Secretary Farrell decided that Roanoke, Petersburg and Norfolk were "guilty of conduct detrimental to the general welfare of the game" or in violation of the letter or spirit of the National Association Agreement, and thereby were suspended from enjoying the privileges and protection of that agreement.[25]

Arbiter Carson gave Lynchburg, Danville and Richmond protection under the National Agreement along with Newport News, Portsmouth and Suffolk — in effect, recognizing an entirely new league. If interests in Petersburg and Norfolk wanted to join, they could petition for admission. In this scenario, Roanoke faced extinction in professional ball unless it could join the Appalachian circuit. Williams now appeared out of a job as president of the league and his Roanoke team also lost its franchise. Norfolk, with its ties to Roanoke, also looked vulnerable.

Writing to the national press and complaining that the public had only heard one side of the story, Williams enclosed minutes of the two meetings in question and a copy of the letter sent to him by Farrell. These documents purportedly proved that Farrell never gave directions for an election and that the minutes showed sharp discrepancies from what Carson reported. Williams contended that his faction, in having a meeting to select a president, followed the rules of the National Board. The three clubs in question and Williams had yet to receive any notification about Carson's coming. Williams believed the other three clubs were in defiance of the board. No one had "greater respect for his superior officers and law and order than myself," but he also thought that the board's action was without precedent and rewarded "a disorganizing element in the Virginia League," thereby opening "the way for much trouble and dissension among the minor leagues."

Then Williams, a former football player and coach at the University of Virginia, gracefully exited the stage, in a "manly acceptance" of defeat, by notifying new league president Jacob O. Boatwright of Danville that he would cooperate with him for the sake of the league. Williams planned to continue to direct the Roanoke ball club, whose franchise was saved by these actions, but would concentrate on his law practice and keep an eye on his various businesses in Roanoke. The press of that city remained convinced in the rightness of his cause.[26]

After more back-room maneuvers, the Virginia League (with its old name) now operated under president Boatwright. While all this was transpiring, Bradley tried to have Newport News replace Roanoke. Representatives of the Peninsula city were invited, along with those of Suffolk, to attend a session at the Monticello Hotel in Norfolk dealing with membership. When league officials decided not to add any teams, a delegate from Suffolk let loose a barrage, saying, "Like a lot of Negroes we have been kept standing around the hotel corridors and lobby all day, never even given a hearing, and now are told that we cannot get a franchise in the league.... Suffolk has been treated discourteously."[27]

That was mild compared to the reaction of Abe Horwitz, the principal owner of the potential Newport News club, who fired off a protest to the National Board. The complaint had its effect, for Farrell said no matter the configuration of the new league, the City of Shipbuilders had to be in it. And so when play started that spring, the league had eight teams and Newport News was one of them — and so was Portsmouth, instead of Suffolk.[28]

After the season commenced, several teams conspired to bounce Danville and Roanoke, the original complaints about poor gates and high transportation costs resurfacing. The other clubs claimed they were losing $250 every time they went to those two cities. When Danville forfeited its franchise because of weak attendance and the related poor performance of the team, the Bugs took to the road and became known as the Orphans. At that time, several delegates held a secret meeting at Ocean View, with neither Boatwright nor representatives from the two teams in question invited. At first, the moguls considered simply replacing Danville, but when Suffolk's citizens, likely still smarting from being snubbed earlier, showed no interest in joining the league, they instead dropped Lynchburg and Danville.

Danville businessmen did not care; baseball had been losing money for over six years. But Lynchburg, though mired deep in last place without even 10 wins on the season, objected and took its case to the National Commission, which decided against interfering in the matter. Roanoke's ownership of the Norfolk team doubtless had something to do with not eliminating the team from the Magic City, even though travel costs there from Tidewater certainly exceeded those to and from Lynchburg. The dispatching of Lynchburg has the earmarks of a conspiracy because the original news reports claimed Roanoke was the intended victim. But with Norfolk controlled by Roanoke interests, it would never cast Roanoke out of the loop.[29]

Following a lead provided by Bradley, a reporter met H.C. Elliot of Roanoke, who told him he had owned the Norfolk club for some time, but had sold it at the end of the previous season to Dr. J.R. McCrary for some $5,800. Elliot had bought the club as part of a deal to support Williams, not for personal gain. To show how much of a Williams man he was, Elliot even supported the decision about Jake Law the previous year, even though that may have cost Norfolk the pennant. But when Williams lost the struggle for the presidency, McCrary sought and received protection from the National Board and thus Norfolk regained its franchise in the new league. Elliot kept mum on his ownership because knowledge of it might have hurt his business interests in Roanoke. McCrary supposedly now owned the franchise, but that testimony proved highly dubious in the light of subsequent disclosures in the press. Despite these revelations, Elliot's name shows up several times whenever lists of minor league owners were published. What happened to Barry's supposed option to acquire the club is unknown.[30]

Otherwise, the 1912 season was business as usual. Charley Shaffer now managed the Crew, replacing Babb who had ascended up the minor-league ladder. Shaffer's comical acts helped pass the time, but fans hoped he would have better results on the field. Portsmouth, with Bland back as franchise owner, hired as manager Lou "Count" Castro, a former player and manager in the Southern and the South Atlantic Leagues. Castro was expected to bring some Georgians with him — folks like Bill Douglass and Lee Garvin — along with Martin Walsh. With Garvin and Castro, the Portsmouth Pirates had the two of the best-known comedians of the Southern League. Both Norfolk and Portsmouth seemed well endowed with humor. They would need it. Sometimes when the two clubs played each other, the reporters grumbled that Castro and Shaffer, another comical character, insulted each other and the players with insider jokes, so although everyone knew the identity of the butt of the commentary, they had no idea what the remarks meant.[31]

In Norfolk, reports noted the arrival of a mix of old and new players, including cool-headed Joe Finneran, the fire-balling right-hander, and lean and lanky lefty "Jim" Poole, "who had been in the forecastle for a number of seasons." "Jack-of-all trades" infielder Johnny Dodge, "the Tennessee Chicken," signed as did popular left fielder Joe Staub. "Pop" Shaffer, now "navigating the good ship Mary Jane," planned to have fleet-footed George Kircher behind the plate. Charlie Curtis, a former refugee from the Tidewater League, also returned, although a court case concerning his status was still unresolved. New members of the aggregation included Lewis Woods, an Oklahoman who demonstrated some ability, and infielder Jack Hinton (aka Summers).

Shaffer released Alvie LeBraun even before preseason started, but the catcher would later return. Stan Bigbie, who saw limited duty the previous year, looked to be a good prospect at first base. Some fans hoped George "Scrap Iron" Cowan, now no longer a Colt, might become the catcher for the Crew, but instead he became an umpire. Outfielder Guy Titman received his release after playing a few games, after which Portsmouth picked him up.

No matter their names, the Norfolk club would be dressed in new gray uniforms in the latest fashion, designed to make "lady-killers" out of the players. "Military collars will add the nautical touch to the outfit, imparting the jaunty air that is necessary to sailors of the deep blue main, while blue trimmings and stockings will carry out the color scheme."[32]

Across the river, Count Castro's Pirates looked especially strong in pitching, especially with Erskine Mayer, who played in the Southern League the previous year. Not only did he secure Walsh, the former Tar, the "Count" also acquired Dutch Revelle, the Richmond pitcher who started his professional career in Portsmouth. Having failed to make the grade in Portsmouth, he came to Norfolk, where he soon also received his release and ended the season at Newport News.

In the preseason the New York Americans (Highlanders or Yankees) defeated the Tars, when in the seventh inning, Charley "Silent" Lusky, once considered by a Richmond writer to be the best catcher in the league, threw wildly trying to nab a runner and the ball became lost in a pile of lumber that sat in front of the right-field bleachers. Why a pile of wood should occupy this place is a mystery, but such things simply add to the aura of these ballparks. A fair ball occasionally became an inside-the-park home run when a fielder could not find it in tall grass.[33]

After struggling through the preseason, the Crew cast off the season with a home game against the promising Pirates of Portsmouth. President Charles Bland expressed disgust with the "Trucker" label and persuaded reporters to use "Pirates" for the name of the club. Norfolk's Jim Poole proved an easy target as the Pirates shelled the Crew, 10–5, before some 2,500, a smaller crowd than expected due to threatening weather. The next day, readers learned about the arrival at New York of victims of the sinking of the *Titanic,* along with other details of the worst disaster in American maritime history, such as the shortage of lifeboats and the band playing "Nearer My God to Thee" as the ship started to sink. In describing the "scuttling" of the Mary Jane, the reporter perhaps unintentionally linked the game and the *Titanic* tragedy by noting the participation of 200 to 300 hundred loyal black "cranks from Portsmouth" whose "joy was almost savage, often hysterical, and finally took a religious turn" and ended with the singing "a funeral dirge ... a burial anthem for the Tars."[34]

Virginia League fans came to a drastically remodeled Lafayette Field. Toward the end of 1911, the Virginia Railway and Power Company purchased the site of old League Park on 18th Street for new and larger barns for its trolley cars. The owners of the Norfolk Baseball Association likely did not mind the termination of its lease almost a year before its expiration as they were not at all sure they would retain the franchise. After securing the franchise, they ordered workmen to dismantle the seats in the grandstand and move them up Church Street to Lafayette Field. A newspaper item suggests that passengers left the streetcars and walked across the railroad tracks to reach the ball yard, but surely the traction line corrected this deficiency at some point.[35]

As originally constructed, Lafayette Field had white fans making their way directly off Church Street, through a wide main entrance located behind the new grandstand and near a small area for autos and carriages. Blacks came through a tiny passage to the far right, next to the railroad tracks and went to the their designated bleachers that were separated from the grandstand in right field. But just after the 1911 season, when the Rookies of the Tidewater League ceased playing there, the city changed the entire seating arrangement to avoid having the sun glare on the left fielder. The old grandstand, located in the extreme corner of left field, now became seating for blacks, thus giving them at least three times the seating of the old bleachers.[36]

The new arrangement, however, failed to satisfy the Norfolk baseball management. The old grandstand jutted into the outfield 302 feet from the plate, making coverage of the area by the left or center fielder a precarious business. From home plate to the right-field fence at the foul pole was 290 feet, but the fence quickly reached far greater distances just a few feet inside the foul line. The park could be converted to use for football games by simply putting portable bleachers directly opposite the existing sets of bleachers in left field. In the spring, workmen took them down and used the wood for fencing and planks to repair the baseball park.

In Portsmouth, the new Bland Park, constructed on the old grounds of the Atlantic and Danville Railroad at the "extremity" of Washington Street, was also quite a piece of work. Bland wanted to return to the old site because it was nearer the center of the city. In the middle of the 1912 season, President Boatwright sent Al Orth, the old major leaguer, manager, umpire, and Washington & Lee baseball coach to check it out. An unbelievable number of home runs (for that time anyway!) were exiting the premises. Visiting teams protested that the short left-field fence allowed the home team to win too many games. Carefully placing his tape as straight as possible along the third base line from home plate to the left-field fence, Orth calculated a distance of 255 feet, 6 inches (21 feet and 6 inches more than regulations required).

The fence in right field stood some 325 feet from home plate at its shortest distance. The Bull Durham sign in deep center was 365 feet away from home plate. By comparison, the ballpark in Richmond used by the United States League measured 320 feet and 376 feet, dimensions considered too small by a Richmond correspondent. At Portsmouth, "Home Runs Galore," was the headline for the August 12 game. Petersburg won, 6–2, with both teams using lefties.[37]

In Newport News, former Lynchburg manager Jack Grim became owner and manager of the Shipbuilders. Within a few weeks, a new ballpark emerged in the East End of the city with a grandstand at the corner of Wickham Avenue and 28th Street. Its diamond sat directly northeastward of the stands, as prescribed by baseball men. The ballpark was situated where corn grew the previous year and the furrows had to be leveled out to make the terrain suitable for baseball. Up to fifty automobiles could park along the left-field line.[38]

The Pirates drew first blood once the regular season commenced, but the Tars retaliated the next day in Portsmouth, 9–8. Revelle absorbed the loss in front of 4,000, a crowd quite a bit larger than the one that showed up at Norfolk on Opening Day. A little later in the season, after the Pirates again beat the Crew, their record stood at 18-15 while Norfolk was slightly better at 20-16. They both trailed league-leader Petersburg (22-12). The removal of Danville and Lynchburg near the middle of June left all six remaining teams with records above .500. The surviving league teams made short work of the remains of the two defunct clubs, Norfolk acquiring lefty Frank Gordon and Steve Gaston from Danville and Alvie LeBraun from Lynchburg.

In its first season back in the Virginia League after a brief hiatus, Portsmouth held its own for at time — indeed, the best it had ever done, possibly because of the shape of the field but more likely due to good pitching. Toward the end of June and into early July, the Pirates enjoyed a hot streak. At the midpoint of the season the Pirate record stood at 37-26, good for third place. By comparison, fifth-place Norfolk managed to win but one more game than it lost.

By July 9, having won four of five (the only loss coming at the hands of young Burl McCrary, who secured his only win that year for the Crew, 2–1), the Pirates pulled ahead of Roanoke. In the middle of July, Portsmouth's record soared to 45-30 to put it well ahead of second-place Roanoke. Norfolk struggled along in fifth place just one game above .500, while Newport News rested in last at 33-44. At this point, Portsmouth pitcher Erskine Mayer sported a phenomenal 17-3 record. The Pittsburgh Pirates and Philadelphia Phillies expressed interest in picking up his contract, which was owned by Atlanta.

Norfolk enjoyed a few good moments that year. Pitcher Joe Finneran hit a home run to spark a win over the Danville Bugs in a game played at Peanut Park in Suffolk before 2,000 fans. "Sidna Allen" Woods bested the Shipbuilders early in the season before some 2,000 at Norfolk. The nickname stemmed from an incident that year in the Carroll County courthouse in Hillsville, Virginia, where members of the Allen clan shot several court officials and bystanders after their leader was found guilty of obstructing justice. Sidna Allen, the son of the clan leader, was one of the participants in the shootout, and at the start of the baseball season "the outlaw" was the object of an extensive search.

The reporters called the pitcher "Outlaw" Woods, possibly because he had once played ball for an outlaw league. Whatever his nickname, Shaffer released him when Gordon and Gaston joined the club. He ended up in Portsmouth right about the time the Pirates lost their momentum and soon thereafter lost to Norfolk, 17–9.[39]

In first place in mid–July, the Pirates lost their bearings, sustaining one defeat after another. By the end of the month they had lost nine of 13 contests and fell into fourth place at 49-39. Roanoke regained first place, with Petersburg and Richmond close behind. In August's dog days, with Mayer winning less frequently, the Pirates continued to experience rough times. They soon stood only three games above .500, as even Norfolk passed them with a 60-52 mark. At that point the three Hampton Roads teams populated the second division of the six-team league. The Busch-led Petersburg Goobers had a small lead over Richmond and Roanoke.

With a week remaining in August and Portsmouth not doing particularly well, Castro had a falling out with Bland. The president of the Portsmouth Baseball and Athletic Corporation wrote to the Count in Richmond, pointing out that his players were "failing to live up to contract ... by not giving the best possible service in return for the money disbursed in salaries." Bland also mentioned Castro's drinking in a saloon and inferred that he was embezzling funds. Castro fired off a telegram saying he had gotten "word from President Taft saying you wished me exiled from the United States. Go to it. I will see you personally when I return. You are trying to take the players' money and everybody knows it. Send my release if you want to or do anything else, as I am paid as of to date." Bland, thinking the count was not trying to be funny in spite of his reputation, and fearing that Castro planned bodily violence, sent a mediator, and the two more or less made up. Castro, however, did send a complaint to the league, calling for a full investigation to clear his name and the reputation of his players.[40]

The team stabilized in time to finish 65-63, just behind Norfolk. The Crew, according to a national magazine, ended up 68-65, despite a double loss to Portsmouth in early September, which one newspaper described as "Pirates Board the Good Ship," winning 4-0 and 4-2 before 1,800.[41]

The Roanoke Tigers, 81-55, pulled ahead of Petersburg to win the flag by a game and a half. Roanoke, despite poor attendance, managed to win its second league pennant in three years. Petersburg had led the league by a game and a half games at the time Danville and Lynchburg lost their franchises

Newport News remained mired in last. Lacking fan support, Jack Grim pulled out of the City of Shipbuilders toward the end of the season and left Abe Horwitz and others to pick up the pieces. On the way out of town, he neglected to sign a statement to drop all rights to any income from the sale of players. League officials belatedly fined all Grim's players $5 for carrying out an unauthorized strike against their manager. Horwitz hired Buck Hooker to guide the Shipbuilders the rest of the season. The strain showed on Grim, who had apparently absorbed a $4,000 loss. He began to exhibit mental problems.

In 1912, Steve Griffin, Richmond's player/manager, led the league in hitting. Jesse Becker led Portsmouth in hitting with a .325 average. Lacking batting support, Mayer lost five of his last 12 decisions, including a 1-0 loss to Poole in early August. Nonetheless, he ended up 24-8.[42]

For the Crew, Johnny Dodge, a solid fielder, hit well enough at Norfolk to play in the majors the next year for the Phillies. At the end of that season, they released him, but he caught on with Cincinnati. He spent the 1912-13 winter in Vaudeville performing with Lefty Miller, who also played with the Tars. Noting Dodge's acting career, a national sports rag satirized his lack of success against big-league pitching.

Finneran led Norfolk pitchers with 18 wins but also suffered 15 losses. The Phillies purchased him and he played in the majors. Left-hander Frank Gordon's winning streak allowed Norfolk to rise to several games above .500. Steve Gaston also occasionally helped out with a win. After the season, Norfolk swapped Poole for Jack Shenn in a deal with Savannah, but Poole ended up back in the Virginia League to compete against his old team.[43]

Meanwhile, those playing in the Twin City League sometimes advanced to the Virginia League and even higher. In 1913, George Weller, the best "slabster of the Saints" (the receivership *Franklin* stationed at St. Helena) pitched briefly for the Crew of the Mary Jane and went to the Cleveland organization. William E. "Swat" Mundy got a chance with the Red Sox after playing for Portsmouth. Earlier, while playing with the "Surgeons" of the Naval Hospital, he hit a bases-loaded home run in the 11th inning, his hit soaring on a line just a foot or two above second base but moving with such velocity that before an outfielder could track the ball down, it passed out of the field and rolled across a street and along a gutter. Swat led the Twin City League in hitting .419 that year. Since Mundy was a potter from Ohio, one suspects someone at the Naval Hospital paid him to ply his other line of work in Portsmouth during the baseball season.

Another product of the Twin City League was Guy "Rebel" Cooper, "an ordinary seaman" aboard the *Franklin*. Bill Hannan, one-time secretary of the Crew, took the big right-hander to see Clark Griffith. In 1913, Cooper beat the Crew for Petersburg where he became known as the "Admiral of the Appomattox." Later he made the majors with the New York Americans. That "an ordinary seaman" did not join the ranks of the Crew aboard the Mary Jane or at the least become a Portsmouth Pirate must have saddened folks along the Elizabeth River.[44]

A New Ballpark for Cellar Dwellers (1913)

Early on, Shaffer signed up 22 "youngsters," only four of them returnees from the previous season. A reporter in a national magazine correctly pointed out that many of these young men would be traded, sold or simply released before the start of the season. In limiting the number of returnees, Norfolk was following a league policy aimed at avoiding "old-timers." Such a policy brought "a greater amount of coin to the treasuries of the various clubs" by allowing more player sales and drafts at season's end. The reporter also believed that interest in baseball was at fever pitch, as the various teams representing battleships at the local navy yard had begun their season and a fast-paced amateur league had been organized. He believed that "all things considered, it appears as though the season of 1913 will be the best that ever came to Virginia."[45]

The preseason brought Christy Mathewson and the New York Giants, winners of the National League pennant the previous year, to Lafayette Field. The game's only real highlight occurred when Gus "Germany" Schrader walloped a Mathewson offering over the head of Fred Snodgrass in center field. The drive doubtless reminded folks that the Boston Red Sox had won the previous World Series when, with Matty on the mound, a fly ball hit Snodgrass on the head. The Tars lost, 10–4, but some 4,000 got a big kick out of the hit. Otherwise that preseason, Connie Mack's Philadelphia A's pounded Portsmouth pitching, 19–5, before some 3,000, and Mack's aspiring youngsters beat the Tars twice, once by shutout. Earlier in preseason, Washington beat the Tars, but only 4–3.[46]

The regular season started in traditional fashion with 3,500 seeing Norfolk beat Portsmouth, 6–2, after appropriate ceremonies, Skipper Shaffer's crew overcoming Lee "Captain Kidd" Garvin's Pirates. Garvin had replaced Count Castro when the latter somehow injured his arm officiating at a wrestling match. The Pirates' lineup included William "Swat" Mundy and Harold "Gene" Hudgins, two local men. After losing the opener to Norfolk, the Pirates performed much better, playing well above .500, while the Tars struggled. Finally, "after eight days of defeat-engendering discord, the harmony of victory" was heard once more on the good ship Mary Jane as the Tars overcame the "pestiferous Pirates" also known as "Garvin's bold buccaneers."[47]

Despite that win, Norfolk dropped like a rock in water in the standings, posting but eight wins in its first 24 decisions. Newport News managed just half as many wins as Norfolk, although it did achieve a tie against Petersburg at Horwitz Park. One month into the season, only the fact that the Builders started the season with 18 losses kept the Tars from being in last place. The first four wins for the Builders that season all came against the Tars.

When things settled down, Portsmouth seemed vastly superior to any of the other Hampton Roads clubs, yet the Pirates were in fourth place. The Portsmouth press described the Norfolk contingent as "completely demoralized" in early May. Things became so bad that Shaffer refused to coach at third base in one game, presumably because no runner ever got that far. Garvin, perhaps in a humorous vein, protested Shaffer's appearance in a game at Portsmouth when he came out in a Norfolk home uniform. Ultimately, Shaffer turned over the manager's job to outfielder/catcher George Kircher, who would lead the league in steals that year.[48]

At this time, Gus Schrader carried a .338 average to lead the Tars, while Garvin posted a .327 to lead Portsmouth. When Norfolk's Harry Damrau was injured before the season, then could not find his batting eye when he returned, Shaffer released him, spoiling one of the season's best stories. Earlier, Damrau used a bat that belonged to the 1885 Norfolk club in the Eastern League to drill the game-winning hit against a supposed former major-leaguer for Portsmouth. The Petersburg club, masterminded by Busch, picked him up.

Later in the season, one of the few solid contributors, outfielder "Wee" Keller (his batting average had just dipped below .300), became upset when his July 1 paycheck had been docked $10 because an umpire mistook him for George Kircher in assessing a fine. When Keller refused to play until he received back pay, management fined him $25. In W.J. Callan's cartoon on the matter, a concerned fan said to Keller, "S'Matter Keller. Don't leave us like that. You're one of the best we've got," to which the player responds "You're wrong son. I ain't worth ten dollars to the club." As he packed his bags to head back to Ohio where he was a machinist, Keller was sold to Busch and Petersburg for $200. Damrau and Keller helped the Goobers win the pennant.[49]

The Tars continued playing musical chairs most of the year. They released Roy Whitcraft, who immediately joined the Pirates. Numerous other names might be mentioned, but suffice to say that a huge turnover rate usually goes with last-place teams. In one case, general manager Shaffer made arrangements to bring in a pitcher from the Midwest. After paying for his own transportation, the man pitched one game and received his immediate release. He had to borrow money from the Portsmouth manager to get home.

Kircher, the new Norfolk manager as of May, reported late to duty that season because a flood inundated his house in Louisville. As proof, Kircher sent a picture to Shaffer, showing him calmly sitting on the edge of his roof with his feet dangling in the water. At the time Kircher took over, the Crew sported a less than glittering 11-25 record. On his first day on the job—an 11-4 loss to the Portsmouth Pirates—the new manager exchanged punches with one of the Pirates who did not take kindly to some of Kircher's foul language.

As the Tars flirted with last place in the standings, a cartoonist presented a series called "A Glimpse in the Fo'castle and on the Poopdeck," which among other scenes showed a player hanging upside down in a barrel labeled "white wash" with a 6-0 score and Petersburg manager Busch standing nearby singing "Everybody's Doing it." Another scene showed a Newport News player lying next to signs that read "Last Place" and "Welcome Mary Jane." An aeronaut holds on by one hand from a swing attached to a descending balloon, with an animated character called "Jinx" harassing him. "Bonehead Playing" and "Poor Hitting" tore holes in and deflated the craft. A third scene concerned the recent Memorial Day twin bill when the Tars were lucky enough to split with Portsmouth. And another frame praised Gus Schrader for propping up the team with his big bat. "Schrader's Trusty Weapon" kept the team from doing even worse. One of the characters says, "Brace up kid. This is no way for an old sea craft to flop."[50]

Once in the basement, the Tars looked destined to stay there for some time; nonetheless, management opened its new field. Despite the major renovation of Lafayette Field the previous season, the Norfolk Baseball Corporation, represented by President J.R. McCrary and Secretary/Treasurer Charles Shaffer, purchased some 52 city lots, with plans to build an entirely new park. Under the original plan, the ball field extended 450 feet going east/west along 20th Street and 400 feet running north/south. Even though reporters continued to describe the park as located near 18th and Church Streets, it clearly stood more than one full block north of 18th Street (19th Street did not exist). The new car barns of the Virginia Railway and Power Company occupied the site of the ballpark built in 1908, directly south of 18th Street. Fans coming to the games via 18th Street walked north along a block of residences to reach the main entrance of the new park.[51]

McCrary and Shaffer wanted a regulation-size park, with a grandstand sufficient to hold 3,000 located at the western end of the field, making right field the sun garden. Overall, the facility could hold 7,000, and would, supposedly be the biggest in the league after Richmond. It would be easily adaptable for sports besides baseball. Under the original plan, a cinder track would encircle the playing field. Showing receptivity to a changing world of transportation, the owners would provide space for those who drove their cars to watch the games from their vehicles, thus making the park a drive-in facility.[52]

Needing time to build a new park, including tearing down the fairly new grandstand at its old park and moving it to the new one, the Norfolk Baseball Corporation negotiated a 60-day lease for Lafayette Field. The agreement with the Lafayette Field Corporation received the consent of the municipal government, the owner of the property. That body, however, proved to be a problem over another critical issue.[53]

As management worked on the new park despite its recent overhaul, remained an object of scorn. One reporter did not think a future park was a sufficient reason for subjecting fans "to inconvenience and discomfort" in the interim. Patrons still found the boardwalk to Church Street in need of repairs and even worse, "there seems to be no desire on the part of the management to make those repairs." The reporter also pointed out that other parks had easy access for autos and carriages, which was not the case at Lafayette Field.[54]

Relieved of his duties as field manager, Shaffer supervised construction of the new park to be ready in June. The press praised "Pop" for his devotion to duty in working every day to ensure the completion of the facility, but the plans for a grandiose park never materialized. Perhaps city fathers refused to allow the club to close off Rugby, a short street (apparently a street only on paper) that cut at an angle across the northwest quadrant of the property, coming to a dead end at the right-of-way for the Norfolk and Western coal line that ran to Lambert's Point. With a much smaller tract of land than originally available, management was forced to move the entire facility a bit to the east and cram it into whatever space remained. The facility was, therefore, a far cry from the original proposal.[55]

On the plus side, the infield drained well and featured an impressive nearby grandstand. But the left-field fence resided only 235 feet from home plate, challenging even the park in Portsmouth as having the shortest distance between the two markers. Even worse, the right-field bleachers for black fans jutted into the field of play. A ball hit into them counted only for a double, but a hit over the second fence was scored a home run. Moreover, the fence between those bleachers and the ball field did not yet exist, so fans intruded into the official field of play during the first game. When coal trains passed, so much smoke covered the outfield that it was hard to see the flight of the ball.

Just as Norfolk scheduled its first contest in the new facility, a storm dumped so much rain on downtown Norfolk that the paper talked about City Hall Avenue becoming City Hall "Canal." Not only did the rain postpone the game, it exposed the lack of drainage in the outfield and accesses to the park. No one could reach the flooded front entrance. In nearing the entrance to the bleachers in left field, one had to traverse either "Lake McCrary" or "Pop"

Shaffer's Lake, named by the fans. In addition, the outfield contained numerous holes and uneven spots, meaning water remained in pockets. Another lake covered the area behind the catcher. To make matters worse, no boardwalk yet existed. A reporter, watching a doubleheader against Richmond, described the new park as a "turtle back rising from the surrounding marshes in the vicinity of Church and Eighteenth streets." The park, like many newly constructed ships, needed some finishing touches, although it came "down the ways fresh from the splash of a champagne bottle dashed against its sides by a fair young maiden." During the first game, it "received its baptism of hits, errors, and runs."[56]

A scribe in Richmond was even more critical, using words like "joke" and "abortion" to describe the place. He blamed Norfolk's municipal leaders for impeding progress. The Norfolk press said nothing about the failings of the city fathers and council records fail to enlighten. It may well be that the Norfolk Baseball Corporation simply failed to push the right political buttons in a timely fashion. The Richmond scribe also took the occasion to say that Norfolk was the worst city in the country in supporting the national game. For a city half the size of Richmond, but far bigger than other communities in the league, Norfolk failed to measure up. The league, he thought, ought to consider giving its franchise to Lynchburg. "Somehow or other, things always break badly in Norfolk," he intoned.[57]

As the "Tars christened the new ballpark at Church and Eighteenth streets," the "Hillsville Hurrah," a future major-leaguer born in North Carolina but raised in Carroll County, Virginia, and otherwise known as Yancey Wyatt "Doc" Ayers, "had not the least sense of the propriety." Given that the Norfolk club was supposed to be sailors, one would think they could have done better in this environment, but the 9–1 thrashing by Ayers and the Richmond Colts was not entirely unexpected, because Ayers won 29 games that season

In another cartoon, W.J. Callan reviewed the Virginia League contests held on July 4 under the label "The Tide of Victory Ebbs and Flows." As usual, Norfolk and Portsmouth split their games that day, but the Mary Jane did a lot more ebbing than flowing that year.[58]

In the middle of the season, Norfolk acquired Mark Stewart from Roanoke. Stewart started the season at Washington and Lee, for whom he played when the Generals took on Yale University at Lafayette Field in the spring. Norfolk fans were likely unimpressed with Stewart's hitting ability as he went 0-for-4 against the Eli and struck out with the bases loaded and two out in the last of the seventh with the score 5–2 in favor of Yale. The Generals barred him from continuing to play when they discovered he played pro ball the previous summer. At first, Stewart played with Roanoke, but a trade brought him to Tidewater. Cincinnati soon put Stewart under contract for $3,000 but allowed him to stay in Norfolk, where, as a left-handed batter, he was credited with several home runs over the fence in right field.

Pitching woes accompanied the general decline of the club. Steve Gaston broke his leg just after he dropped one game below .500. Stingy management suspended him without pay. Before that, the team docked him for spending time with his deathly ill sister. Fans had a high regard for Gaston, who sang and also played the pipe organ at Cumberland Street Methodist Church. When apprised of the situation, Secretary Farrell wrote a public letter, noting that injured players had to be paid. Norfolk management paid Gaston and even reserved him for the next season. The Newport News doctor who tended to the pitcher's leg must have done something wrong, for later in the year, surgeons had to re-break the leg so that it could mend properly.[59]

George Weller, a former "Saint" with the receivership *Franklin* based at St. Helena, lost three games, mostly due to lack of support. His talent, however, was sufficient to encourage a scout for Cleveland to sign him to play at Toledo, thus becoming the fifth graduate of the training station or battleship clubs to reach the majors or high minors that season. In the early part of the season, the club released Charlie Saxe, who had been underperforming. Toward the end of the season, it let new pitcher R.E. Dye go after he lost several games. At season's end, Charles Burden, a deputy sheriff in the offseason, came on board. Another newcomer, "Big" or "Shoulders" Bernhardt, proved solid enough. They joined Lefty Weeder and Jack Shenn, both of whom won about as many as they lost, to form a creditable four-man rotation.

Portsmouth pitching included Clem Howell, who took five of six decisions. By the middle of July, Emie Herbert, a Missourian, improved his record to 11–4. Endowed with a deliberate demeanor and a deceptive drop, along with a "cool and collected" presence on the field, Herbert did so well that a scout persuaded the Reds to give him a shot at the majors. This deprived Portsmouth of an able pitcher but made the team more financially solvent. The sale of Herbert, followed by the peddling of John Verbout to Jersey City and Bill "Swat" Mundy to the Boston Red Sox, upset some Portsmouth fans, but the Pirates had little chance of changing their position in the standings at the time. Several of the Tars were likely happy about Verbout's departure, for he had defeated them on numerous occasions over the previous two years. In early July, however, "Verbout left his 'Indian sign' back in Portsmouth and absorbed a 7–1 licking, being relieved before the third inning ended."[60]

In late June, the heading blared, "Skipper Ryan on Deck Now," as the Tars once again changed managers. Ray Ryan took command and the Norfolk owners brought in several men, including shortstop "Dolly" Gray and second sacker Eugene Steinbrenner, who had been playing for Wheeling, West Virginia, until its league collapsed.[61]

As the season wound down to its sorry conclusion, one of a series of cartoons on Virginia League matters showed a Pirate slamming a bat with a score of 2–1 imprinted on it down on the head of a Tar who was trying to move out of "that cellar." Obviously the cellar-dweller did not make it in part because Tars castoff Dye threw a no-hitter at them for Portsmouth.

At the end of the 1913 season the results from the perspective of the residents of Hampton Roads were much the same as in 1912. Their three teams placed in the second division of the six-team league. Only this time Portsmouth headed that list, with Newport News next and Norfolk a game behind the Shipbuilders. Petersburg, with solid pitching from Guy Cooper, Harvey Brooks (a 1906 Tar), and Harry Hedgepeth, eked out a pennant over equally impressive Richmond.

With only a few days left in the campaign, the Tars beat Petersburg twice after the Goobers had won 13 straight, an indication that Ryan had "shaped the disorganized Tars into a fighting machine." But the writer, somewhat in contradiction, also blasted management for signing more than 50 men in the course of the season. Each supposedly defective player was replaced by one no better, but Norfolk now had six positions covered by batters who hit above .250. Ryan himself was no slouch, batting .326 in limited duty. Mark Stewart, "the College Colossus," looked like a good bet to make the majors. Kircher, who stole 74 bases and hit .271, looked solid. First baseman Gus Schrader hit well most of the year ending up at .262, with the crowd in the last home game rising as one to applaud him for his untiring hustle.[62]

Keeping the nucleus of the club for the next year was not to be. McCrary traded Schrader to Winston-Salem. "Big Jack" Shenn, despite a 15-17 record, had a deal pending with the Pittsburgh Pirates, but it looked more likely that he would end up, along with Kircher, with the Baltimore Orioles of the International League. Management let Richmond sign Ryan as its manager. When the team assembled the next spring, only pitchers Burden and Gaston would be on deck, along with Stewart, who failed to catch on at a higher level, and shortstop Eugene Steinbrenner.

The Last Shall Be First (1914)

The outcome the 1914 season proved that most anything can happen in Class C baseball, Biblical prophecy, and the voyages of the crew of the Mary Jane.

McCrary, through Elliott who now had $10,000 invested in Norfolk and much less than that in Roanoke, persuaded William "Buck" Pressly (the spelling of which changed to Pressley in 1915) to come over from Roanoke and "sail the Mary Jane," even though the player/manager was trying to finish his medical education at the University of Virginia and had already turned down an offer to manage the Richmond Colts. Once he reached the port of Norfolk, Pressley put mostly a new crew on deck, including shortstop Morrison "Molly" Morrison, who had played under him at Roanoke. Alvah J. "Gunboat" or "Steamer" Cockran resigned from the U.S. Navy, where he had been serving as a real sailor on the *USS Louisiana*, and came aboard the Mary Jane. Stewart and Steinbrenner were held over from the previous year, along with a recovered Steve Gaston and Charles Burden.

Before the start of the season, management persuaded the city council to temporarily close a street immediately north of the ballpark, thus allowing the club to extend its left-field fence some 100 feet. Now the shortest point for a home run would be directly down the right-field line. The club also agreed to a request from the "loyal" black fans to put a roof over part of the bleachers, thus encouraging black women to attend games.[63]

In preseason Chief Bender, pitching for the youngsters trying out for the Philadelphia Athletics, gave up hits to Swat Mundy, among others, and lost to the Pirates, 6–4. Then the A's turned around to beat the Tars in Norfolk, 5–4. In the next encounter between the same two teams, the Tars triumphed when Bender muffed a fly ball while playing center field.

In the offseason, Charles Bland sold out to a new corporation in Portsmouth. Dr. Vernon Brooks, the city physician and a long-time Pirates fan, served as the president of the Portsmouth Exhibition Company with Frank D. Lawrence as its secretary. They planned to bring back six of their old players, although their reserve list cited at least 10 names. Before giving up control, Bland expressed contentment about the Pirates schedule, which may have been a first for anyone from Norfolk or Portsmouth. Former major-leaguer Jesse Tannehill became the new Pirate manager after Joe Wall from Brooklyn failed to make the grade. Well after the season's start, new investors took over the organization, fired Tannehill and formally changed the nickname of the team from Pirates to Truckers. Tannehill appealed to the National Board for back pay, and won.[64]

On April 16, 1914, Norfolk started off the regular season at home by turning four double plays against Portsmouth, with Charles "Sheriff" Burden getting credit for the 7–0 win before 3,000. The next day the Tars again overwhelmed the Pirates, 16–4, with backup catcher Dick "Bull Durham" Ulrich delivering a bases-clearing double before some 3,500 at Portsmouth. From that point on, the Tars dominated the league, moving to a 15-3 record, the mirror opposite of their record at the start of the 1907 season, when they last won a Virginia League race.

Fans and players alike knew that destiny was with them when they scored three runs in the last of the fifth inning to win one game, 3–2, with torrential rains erupting just as the inning ended. In the midst of a 10-game winning streak, the managers of the restaurant at the Lorraine Hotel gave the players — and even the umpires — a steak dinner as a reward for their good work. The managers promised a turkey dinner for the next streak.[65]

Although they experienced a slight slump at the end of June, the Tars posted a 58-28 record just past the halfway point, overwhelming Richmond and everyone else in the league.

Newport News ran a respectable, but distant, 49–40 at the time. League moguls at first delayed creating a split season, and the teams went well into July before it was decided to designate July 1 as a starting point for second part of the season. McCrary of the Tars thought a plot must be afoot, whereby other league representatives held off as long as possible in the hopes that someone at some point might overtake the Crew. When that did not happen, officials pretended they had already split the season. Thus one day the Tars led the league with a record of 59-30, seven games better than second-place Richmond. The next day they led the league at 19-10, with the Roanoke Tigers in second at 17-11. It must have been pretty confusing for the fans then, and it certainly is today for anyone looking at the old newspapers.

No matter how one looks at the standings, Portsmouth brought up the rear for both halves. Throughout the season, Portsmouth got rid of some 60 members.

In contrast, the Tars stuck with most of its original crew, as Pressley kept roster changes to a minimum. Only two of the starting eight positions in the field changed. Early in the season, Pressley brought Frank Thrasher on board to replace outfielder Jimmy Tennant (a .299 hitter the previous year), a one-time Pirate and base-stealing threat out of Basic City (Waynesboro), Virginia. Tennant ended up back in Portsmouth. Management later demoted Charlie Allen, an outfielder from Phoebus, and replaced him with J.W. "Sis" Hopkins, a Tar in a previous incarnation who had spent time in the Southern League impressing people with long home runs. The club originally sent Alexander to Portsmouth, because Allen was considered fleeter, but then Alexander returned to hold down right field near the end of the season.

The pitching situation proved a little more fluid. Just after the start of the season, McCrary contracted for Cliff Markle, who won 18 games and lost 10 in a lower level the previous season, though the deal included a clause that Norfolk did not have to keep him unless he made good. Because he won over 30 games, Pressley had no desire to send him back. Pressley did have to do some maneuvering to find his fourth starting pitcher. A lefty came down from the Orioles, and a right-hander came up from Atlanta, but neither stayed long. Pressley also let Burden go and replaced him with Sam Hall, out of the Appalachian League. But although Hall proved occasionally solid, about half the time he blew up in the early innings, so Pressley released him to Portsmouth after initially suspending him when he balked about going to Georgia. Hall soon lost three times to his old mates, twice in low-scoring contests and once by a wide margin.

Around the middle of July, Pressley secured Charles "Rube" Humphries as his fourth pitcher. The newcomer also had the virtue of being a lefty, giving him a supposed advantage at League Park with its spacious left and center fields. Late in the season, Pressley brought another lefty onboard as a spot starter, but only used him once. He did not even appear in the group's season-ending photograph.[66]

In June, a controversy arose over the distance between home plate and second base in Newport News. The issue received some coverage in Norfolk, but it became front-page news in the City of Shipbuilders. After a series there in which he'd suffered several losses, Richmond manager Ray Ryan filed a protest with the league. Buck Pressley was drawn into the controversy when it was revealed that, with umpire Win Clark watching, he had stepped off the distance in a previous game. Noting a discrepancy, he bought a steel tape at a nearby hardware store and planned to secure a more accurate measure the next day. But he never followed through. He had the impression that something was amiss, but Clark later said he thought the distance looked about right. When Ryan, supported by at least two newspapers in Richmond, tried to get the losses thrown out, some reporters assumed that Pressley told him about the problem. When it looked like Pressley might write a letter to President Boatwright, saying that the base might be as much as five feet inside of where it should have been, the folks in Newport News bitterly criticized the once-popular Norfolk manager. It was assumed that he wanted to deprive second-place Newport News of victories to put greater distance between the two teams in the standings. Later, in a public letter, Pressley admitted to telling Ryan of his suspicions in a telephone conversation but only after Ryan had already taken action with the league about the matter.

A related rumor at the time claimed that Pressley had earlier tried to prevent Harry Matthews from being retained as the manager at Newport News. In a sometimes confrontational encounter at the Warwick Hotel in Newport News, including an unfriendly exchange between several Shipbuilders and Molly McMahon, Pressley said he had never tried to stop Matthews from being re-hired. He did say that he had not appreciated Matthews' verbal attack on his pitcher Parson Perryman the previous year. The rough language was an obvious effort to upset the religiously-minded Roanoke pitcher. Pressley also said he appreciated Matthews giving his club access to a new player. After all that, Pressley said he did not want his name brought into the matter anymore, but he also added that second base was not in the same place it was when Norfolk last visited the park. Thenceforth, Matthews became the "Diamond Doctor" in some parts of the press and the doctor became "Affidavit" Pressley in other parts.[67]

Right-handed pitcher Cliff Markle, "the Morristown Marvel," set the Virginia League single-season record for wins with 31 (only 9 losses). In September 1915, he debuted for the New York Yankees. In a sporadic career with the Yankees and Reds, he won 12 and lost 17, with a respectable 4.10 earned-run average. He never lived up to expectations created by his magical season with the Crew of the Mary Jane in 1914 (National Baseball Hall of Fame Library, Cooperstown, New York)

Matthews' club did fairly well in the first half of the season, coming in just a few games behind the Tars. Management there must have thought he could do better, for it replaced him, and the team did much worse in the second part of the season. The Builders had at least two outstanding players—big catcher Norm Glockson and "Rasty" Walters at third base.[68]

During the second part of the season, the Crew continued to win two of every three games, ending up 50-27. Although the accounting techniques left something to be desired, it looks like Norfolk had a

93-48 record over the full season, a league record. A day or two after league officials officially split the season, various European powers broke diplomatic relations, armies mobilized, and the "guns of August" opened up to start the Great War while the United States was still trying to figure out how to extricate its personnel from Vera Cruz. Through this time, the Crew of the Mary Jane sent salvo after salvo against adversaries in the Virginia League.

At 46-92 as the full season drew to a close, the Truckers from Portsmouth at least showed consistency in remaining in last place. Newport News did not do as well in the last part of the season as in the first phase. Its overall record fell to about .500. Petersburg, under "Herr Heinrich" Busch, never gained traction all year despite the mound work of Harry Hedgepeth. Roanoke made a run in the second half, but in three straight doubleheaders, two in the Tigers' own park, it was only able to achieve splits against Norfolk.

The Colts in the capital proved to be the most troublesome for the Tars, actually winning the season's series. They led the league in hitting, but even with ex-major leaguer Bill Foxen, future major-leaguer Burleigh Grimes and two other solid starters, they could not match Clifford Markle and company. Richmond swept the Tars in a three-game series at Richmond, but the Tars did the same to them on their home field to acquire an almost insurmountable lead before the end of August. In a typical winning contest, Humphries bested Grimes (23-13), 3–1. An eight-game win streak helped considerably. The club clinched the second half of the season several days before the last game that year. In the last contest, Norfolk again beat the Truckers, 5–3, in a game that took but 45 minutes, with Gaston's spitball mowing down adversaries even more rapidly than usual. Manager/first baseman William Lowry Pressley clinched the pennant himself on September 8, when he doubled to center field. The sometime medical man and former manager of the Roanoke club was just what the doctor ordered for the Tars.[69]

Markle amassed an amazing pitching record that year. At one point, the "Morristown Marvel," had 23 wins and but five defeats, and his number of victories kept going up. On August 20, he fanned 12 and gave up but two hits to beat Roanoke and win his 29th victory. He posted his 30th win on September 8, a shutout against Portsmouth, and soon followed with his 31st, the most ever by any pitcher in the history of the Virginia League.

In completing 32 games out of 40 decisions, he absorbed but nine losses while pitching 345 innings. This performance has to be the greatest ever over a single season by a member of the Crew of the Mary Jane, including Christy Mathewson, who had a loftier won-lost percentage but toiled for only half a season. Some experts thought Markle was another Mathewson, and had more in common than the initials of their first and last names. Like Matty, Markle excelled in throwing a "fadeaway." For a time John McGraw expressed interest in buying his services. Markle made the majors with the New York Yankees, but his temperament hindered his retention there.[70]

Three other pitchers toiled tolerably well. "Steamer" or "Red" Cockran once walked nine and struck out the same number in winning one game. For the season, his first in professional ball, he was 20-13. Spitball master Steve Gaston ended up at 22–9, throwing only 77 pitches in one 3–2 win over Petersburg. Charles E. "Rube" Humphreys, who joined the staff around mid-season, won nine of 15 decisions. Some thought the southpaw was about as good as Markle in setting league records in scoreless innings pitched and the number of strikeouts in succession.[71]

Not only did the Tars play well, but most Norfolk reporters thought they set a high standard of deportment for future Tars. Umpire Tom "Rainbow" Reynolds had doubts about that. Reynolds wrote a public letter attesting that Stewart had cussed him over being fined. The umpire ejected and fined Pressley for using the vilest words "that could come from the tongue of any person who had white blood in their veins." Reynolds also asserted that Stewart had on three occasions deliberately tried to hit him with a foul ball, and that Cochran abetted Stewart in trying to avoid arrest and thereby got himself arrested. It was commonly known, the umpire maintained, that both men "had bet $5 each that Norfolk would win the game over Petersburg."[72]

After Reynolds had Cockran and Stewart arrested, the two made bail for $50 and later paid court imposed fines. The Norfolk manager admitted to the press that he had originally been hectored into betting, but when informed of the league rule just as the game was starting, he negated the bet. After looking into the matter, President Boatwright at first suspended Pressley, but later fired the umpire. In the estimation of *The Pilot*, the move came three weeks too late. The reporter claimed that the umpire knew almost nothing about the game, having no breast protector, mask or pitch indicator when he started work. After the season, members of the press urged the removal of Boatwright for his tardy intervention in this matter and especially after he deducted league fines ranging from $10 to $20 from players' pay.[73]

If Reynolds did not appreciate the Tars, Frank Norcum, who umpired a lot of games for Norfolk, had a fairly solid reputation. But the next year a Newport News reporter recalled that toward the end of the 1914 season, Norcum, although generally competent, tended to side with the Tars. The reporter considered this favoritism a natural byproduct of not moving umpires around so they did not see the same team too often.[74]

In an anticlimax, Markle lost his stuff in a postseason series against the Carolina League champs from Winston-Salem. The team rode in a special Pullman car to Winston-Salem, where the Twins dealt Markle a loss, as one of their players touched him up for three home runs. Humphries won the second game, but in the third game, a heavy mist made it hard for Gaston to control his spitball. Back in the City by the Sea, fans gave Gus Schrader, now playing for the Down Homers, a big hand. Once again, Markle lost, this time 4–1. Now behind three games to one, Pressley planned to pitch Humphries in both games in an expected Saturday doubleheader, but Schrader's two hits helped the Twins beat the lefthander in the first encounter to end the series.

A month or so later, Pressley announced his retirement in order to resume his efforts to become a physician. Many years later, after driving a succession of Model T autos across South Carolina on behalf of his patients, he received an award as the best doctor in the United States. Morrison "Molly" McMahon took over as player/manager even though the national press assumed that either Lee Garvin or Harry Matthews, one-time managers of Portsmouth and Newport News, respectively, would get the position.[75]

Toward the end of the season, with attendance double what it had averaged the two preceding years and far better than the rest of the league, a bizarre controversy arose. H.C. Elliot, who told a reporter two years earlier that he sold out his interests in the club to McCrary, now supposedly sold the same club to a local capitalist and current club treasurer Flavius B. Walker, for $50,000 or $60,000 (including the ballpark and adjacent house lots). The deal became effective at the end of the season. A suspicious Norfolk press demanded the publication of legal papers giving details of the transaction to assure everyone that Roanoke interests no longer controlled the Norfolk club.[76]

Offensive statistics improved some during the 1909–1914 period both for the league and Norfolk. The 1911 club posted the highest average (.261) of the first two decades of the 20th century, but the 1914 club, even though it only hit .246, had a slugging percentage over .300, very similar to that of the 1900 representatives. It also placed second for all 20th century, Mary Jane teams in stealing bases.

8

Mary Jane at Low Tide, 1915–1918

As the 1914 season ended, much of the world went to war. Although the United States did not formally enter the Great War until April 1917, its impact could be felt long before then. In Hampton Roads, professional baseball lost ground as military baseball saw a substantial increase. But the full impact did not register until the spring of 1917.

No Five-Cent Cigar (1915)

In the early years of the 20th century, a nickel went a long way. One could buy a beer and even get something to eat for five cents in one of Norfolk's numerous saloons. But temperance people were hard at work persuading judges to reduce the number of bars in the city and making sure such places stayed closed on Sundays. It cost the same to ride the trolley or go to one of the new picture shows. In 1915, one could also ride the "jitney," a vehicle that ran along routes that supposedly supplemented the trolleys. But the price of a good cigar had risen to more than a nickel. Norfolk baseball fans had much to bother them as the team entered this era, including the rising prices for cigars. As things turned out at the end of the season, they could not even say "Close, but no cigar."

The tenth annual season of the Virginia League sparked considerable interest among the fans and the press in 1915. Suffolk and Rocky Mount, North Carolina, joined the association to go along with Newport News, Norfolk, Petersburg and Portsmouth. With the addition of Suffolk and Rocky Mount, North Carolina, the league acquired two comparatively small communities and lost its largest, Richmond. The North Carolina city contained about 10,000 people while Suffolk had just over 7,000. By comparison, between 25,000 and 30,000 residents lived in Petersburg, and fast-growing Newport News counted 20,000 in 1910 and 35,000 in 1920. At 7,000 residents, Suffolk had far less than 10 percent of Norfolk's total. The national press marveled that Suffolk could carry on, especially because the place had to resort to jitneys to move folks to the games.[1]

Richmond, by far the largest city in the commonwealth, withdrew from the Virginia League over the winter, paying a hefty $12,500 price for giving up its franchise. That came about because the Baltimore Orioles' Jack Dunn moved his International League team to Virginia's capital to avoid direct competition from the new Federal League, which was challenging major league baseball. Rocky Mount secured the Richmond franchise. In addition, Virginia League officials gave Suffolk the Roanoke franchise. These maneuvers meant that no team needed to travel more than one hundred miles one way to play a game.[2]

Baseball men in Portsmouth and Newport News were determined to make a strong bid for the pennant. Win Clark retired from umpire duty in the league to direct the Pirates of Portsmouth, a city directly influenced by the growing workforce at the nearby federal shipyard. Observers also thought that the big increase of war work at the Newport News Shipyard and concomitant prosperity would translate into greater interest in the shipbuilders of baseball.

Norfolk lost two of its leading pitchers from the previous year, but still had A.J. "Steamer" Cockran and Charles "Rube" Humphries. Cockran worked on his control over the winter by throwing balls at a knothole in a barn. Also, George Weller had matured some since a handful of appearances in 1913. Carroll R. "Buck" Barton, originally with Newport News, looked solid, but halfway through the season, Portsmouth would acquire him. Initially, the club signed an unnamed 20-year-old "giant"—6 foot 1 inch, 185 pounds—from the *USS Delaware* in the local league. They doubtless thought they might have another Cockran on deck, but this sailor soon disappeared.

Management got rid of pitcher Steve Gaston because he had allegedly urged his mates to strike for higher pay the previous year. Pressley had diffused that effort, but Gaston lost any reputation he might have had as a promoter of team harmony. It may well be that Tar management concocted the story to minimize fan criticism for axing a high paid, popular player. Whatever the case, Gaston ended up with Suffolk.

Originally, Norfolk traded Gaston for Carl "Dolly" Gray, an outfielder of "elephantine" dimensions who hit .321 with nine home runs for Richmond the previous season. But someone nixed the deal, leaving the Tars lean in the outfield, even with the league's most prolific hitter in center fielder Buster Thrasher.

After the season commenced, the club tried to obtain Clarence Berger after his release from Pittsburgh. But Newport News had claims on what some considered potentially the best young outfielder in the league. After verbally agreeing to sign a Crew contract, Berger delayed doing so and ended up in Newport News, leaving Norfolk with a large hole in its outfield. The club helped itself considerably by acquiring B. "Red" Stewart, who soon became a steadying influence, at least until Norfolk let him go to Suffolk.

Technically, the Crew still had their double-play combination, although manager and shortstop Morrison "Red" McMahon started the season on the shelf while he recovered from an arm broken in two places. The acquisition of first baseman Henry "Henerey" Foiles from Portsmouth for "Slim" Alexander and cash during the offseason, convinced one reporter that Norfolk had an infield worth $10,000. Norfolk also acquired catcher Johnny Mace to back up Mark Stewart, who even played shortstop in one of the preliminary games. The Mace deal led to another dispute with Newport News, though Norfolk got to keep Mace.

The Tars lost a preseason exhibition against the World Series–bound Philadelphia Phillies and pitcher Eppa Jeptha Rixey out of the University of Virginia, "the most elongated southpaw in captivity." A future Hall of Famer and winner of well over 200 games in the majors, Rixey bested them, 7–1. The Tars then bumped the Navy Yard, 11–4, at a time when the fleet was in and thousands of blue jackets hit hard pavement.

The 1915 voyage of the Mary Jane was less than a resounding success. It started well enough as 2,000 braved wintry weather in April to see the Tars, attired in "spotless white" uniforms trimmed in black, win the home opener against Portsmouth, which dressed in gray with white and maroon trim. Rube Humphreys proved to be in good form, winning 2–0 following opening ceremonies. Then the Crew lost an exciting 7–6 battle following appropriate rites in Portsmouth the next day. With somewhat improved weather, some 2,500 showed up, including "a hundred Teutonic fans" that served as real tars on the German cruiser *Prinz Eitel Frederich*. That vessel had recently taken refuge at Newport News for repairs and had then been brought to the Navy Yard and interned, along with its crew, under international rules of neutrality. Norfolk then won the rubber game at home the next day.

Impressed by several early-season wins, one Portsmouth reporter bragged that the local club was 100 percent better than the year before. Then the club fell back to near .500 as surprising Suffolk, nicknamed the Tigers, having inherited the Roanoke franchise, moved to the head of the league under Harry Welcher. (Welcher managed Roanoke the year before. Curiously, he was let go then brought back before the season started, along with several other Tigers.)

During a losing phase, the Truckers lost use of their grounds — old Bland Park. It was just as well, for the short left-field fence in the old park sometimes meant that balls hit over it only counted as doubles. They eventually went to Washington Street Park (it was officially called Athletic Park until 1916) just outside city limits, which was also endowed with a short left field.[3]

At first, Norfolk had trouble and fell below .500. The day after the newspapers reported the sinking of the *Lusitania* and the loss of more than a thousand lives, the Crew succumbed to Rocky Mount, 4–3, in 10 innings. With the season only a few weeks old, Norfolk rested in last place, though only one and a half games separated top from bottom. With the return of shortstop Red McMahon the club reeled off 10 straight wins to take a sizeable lead in the fight for the flag. After making three errors in his first game (a loss), McMahon soon became his old reliable self as he and Thrasher began to bunch timely hits in several wins. In a typical game in that stretch, a 2–0 win over Suffolk, the Tigers could do little with Cockran's offerings while the Tars touched Gaston for seven hits. Both teams were dissatisfied with the rulings of former Tar, now umpire, Gus Ruhland.

A former UNC athlete and veteran of the New England and Carolina Leagues, B.C. Stewart started his first game in the outfield as a Tar replacing Carl Saracino, a one-time outstanding sandlot player from Richmond signed by Walker late in the previous season. His release was due in part to his inability to take orders, a deficiency that could be lethal on a ball team or on a ship.[4]

This streak moved the club to the front of the pack in late May with a record of 18–12. But the Tars soon ran into trouble, dropping four in a row. In the Memorial Day doubleheader, the Pirates wrote a new chapter in Virginia League history when they beat the Tars twice, upsetting all precedents according to the reporter. Nothing like it would be seen again "until the Elizabeth River dries up, the grass grows knee high down the middle of High Street, and the Seaboard Air Line trains run on time." It would not quite be a day that would live in infamy, but it was pretty close, as the Tars lost, 4–3 and 2–0, stopping the recent strong showing in its tracks.[5]

Winning about the same number as they lost, the Tars struggled with Newport News and Rocky Mount for the lead. They took two from Portsmouth after the Memorial Day debacle, but lost three games to the Tar Heels at Rocky Mount to fall to fourth. That's where they stood on the day they hoisted their 1914 pennant and had to listen to a reform candidate of the Citizens Party stump for a state senate seat. After that, they returned temporarily to their winning ways to regain third place, where they remained for the rest of the first half of the season. The next day, the Tars took the Builders twice, thus letting Rocky Mount tie the latter for the league lead. On that occasion, *The Pilot* reporter opined that such "a lengthy piece of pasturing" had not been seen "since the days when rounders was played in the back lots."[6]

Near June's end, Buck Pressley rejoined the club to play a few games, with his medical career on hold while he was on his honeymoon. The club held a special day to honor his heroics the previous year and wish him well in married life. Near the end of the first half of the season, Newport News still held first, but by early July its 34–24 mark was one game shy of Rocky Mount's record, with Norfolk running third, five games back at 30–28. Portsmouth, Petersburg and Suffolk rounded out the standings.

Across the Roads, Carl Carnes assumed managerial duties for the Builders, who faced the Suffolk Tigers (aka Cats, Bearcats or Wildcats) to open the second half before about 3,000. A cheerleader who went by "Connie Mack" performed his usual antics with his high silk hat. Guests included Virginia's political boss, U.S. Senator Thomas Staples Martin, and twelve officers of the German cruiser, *Kronprinz Wilhelm*. Like its sister ship, the cruiser and its crew were interned in Hampton Roads. Early that season, Newport News reeled off several wins, including a 15–8 walloping of the Tars at Norfolk, a game in which Tar third basemen Bernie Cleveland hit the longest home run on record up to that time, though the distance wasn't divulged.[7]

As Norfolk and Newport News battled each other, a controversy arose between the two clubs. The Tars captured a doubleheader, with Cockran besting Roy Gardinier, 6–2, and Humphreys winning over "Dutch" Mullins, 6–5. Indeed, the Tars took five out of the eight games between the two, with Cockran winning all three of his starts. But the Tars lost all but two games to Rocky Mount.

In a "Sporting Comment," based on what returning fans reported happened at Norfolk, a Newport News columnist tore into the Tars. Norfolk fans, it seemed, were once again resorting to their "disgraceful tactics of last year." They not only went after the umpires, but Norfolk's leading fan, known as the "Horse Doctor," threw a bottle of soda pop at a Newport News pitcher, causing a near riot. Officials ejected the culprit from the park, but the man soon reappeared. The writer said a riot had resulted the previous year when the same miscreant did something similar. The columnist attributed the poor behavior of Norfolk fans, which he claimed surpassed anything that ever took place in Newport News, to the gamblers who openly bet on games. In the Peninsula ballpark, the newspaper contended, Horwitz acted firmly against gambling. Given that Newport News was due to entertain the Tars for a three-game series at home, it seems fortunate that these comments did not stir up fans in the City of Shipbuilders to carry out retaliatory measures.[8]

The debate resumed several days later after a comment appeared in *The Pilot*, saying that most Norfolk fans favored Rocky Mount in its race for first with the Builders, because the latter had violated the spirit of the league constitution since the beginning of the season. League officials failed to punish Portsmouth for exceeding the limit on the number of veteran players (a club could only have four players who had more than 15 games experience above Class C), but set a date after which the rule would be enforced. Later, when Newport News and other clubs appeared to be in violation of the rule, the league simply modified the requirement.[9]

In a Monday commentary based on reports from Norfolk fans who had crossed the Roads to see the game at Newport News, a Norfolk reporter described the supposed reaction of Newport News fans to Builders' shortstop Armando Seiglie, a Cuban. When the player threw down his glove and walked from the field after a couple of errors, the home fans supposedly made allegations about "the color of blood in Sieglie's veins," implying that he belonged to the "brunette part of Cuba's population." In a counterthrust, a Newport News commentator hoped "that all of the news published in the town of dead cruisers" was not as garbled "as this little bit of sporting news." Manager Carnes ordered Seiglie out of the game, but the player never threw his glove nor did the crowd utter racist remarks. The manager reinstated the Cuban several days later. Such comments on the part of the newspapers from the two cities about their respective baseball teams and their fans reflected an ongoing city rivalry that occasionally became bitter.[10]

Losing a home game to Norfolk left the Builders tied with Rocky Mount. After this game, several sore Builder fans gave President Walker of the Tars a "tongue lashing." Newport News then lost the crucial showdown against Rocky Mount, taking two of three from the Builders at the winner's home yard, and thereby winning the first half of the pennant race by one game. At this point, the Newport News club withdrew a protest about Norfolk having too many players in uniform for one of its games, thus enabling Rocky Mount to claim the first-half title. Builder fans could now root against Norfolk with a clear conscience. Had Peninsula people heard about the practice in Rocky Mount of fans giving incentive money to their players they might have been less sporting about relinquishing claim to the first-half title.[11]

The second half of the season brought more troubles for two teams in the league. Attendance in both Portsmouth and Petersburg ran quite low, with the former averaging not much above 100 fans other than on holidays or season openers. Reporters believed many clubs, including the Richmond representative in the International League (with AA status) drawing just above a thousand a game, experienced poor spectator participation due to the strains caused by the war.

The Baseball Association of Portsmouth, led by Dr. Brooks, gave way to another corporation with virtually the same name, led by W.E. Stanley, one of the top men for the Seaboard Railroad, and Isaac Van Patten, a long-time baseball man. With President Boatwright's help, the new company raised enough money to play out the season. The Fourth Ward Social and Athletic Club, an organization that favored undertakings that promised to better the city and elevate mankind socially, sent a letter to the new team president offering its "undivided support." Noting that its members from the south part of Portsmouth comprised largely of men in humble circumstances who could not invest financially in the team, the club supported events like Booster Day and promised loyal support with daily attendance. In his letter the secretary of the club hoped the efforts of the corporation to strengthen the team would be "crowned with success." The entire social club planned to go to Rocky Mount to root when Portsmouth triumphed in the second half of the season. In a postscript, the writer noticed that the Suffolk team seemed to have some sort of hex on Portsmouth. Although not a believer in superstition, he suggested that a "real dark colored rooter" bury a black cat, "out in deep center field by the Bull Durham sign, the next time Suffolk comes here to play." The writer agreed to supply the dead cat.[12]

Whatever the steps taken, Portsmouth showed substantial improvement. Lee Garvin returned for a brief time to take a position in the field and also act as a lieutenant for manager Clark. Management continued its search for players, usually looking south to the Sally League or to Florida, until it finally assembled a club that could compete.

In Petersburg, poor attendance in part caused by the war's impact on neighboring Hopewell, forced the team to forfeit its franchise. The huge DuPont Plant hired some 20,000 operatives, many working overtime. Such a business could not accommodate its schedule to allow times to watch ball games. Petersburg baseball management was so deeply involved in Hopewell that they sometimes forgot to pay the Petersburg players. League officials agreed to use the $800 deposit to cover most of the $900 owed to the players. They also chipped in more money to insure the survival of the team and announced that hereafter the club would be called the "Orphans." A little later, required to play all its games on foreign turf with a reduced payroll, they lost game after game. A disgusted "Herr Heine" Busch resigned, blaming the end of baseball along the Appomattox on the rise of nearby Hopewell, with DuPont providing thousands of jobs making gunpowder and other war materials, some of it doubtless being used to kill some of Busch's German relatives. Busch said "Hopewell killed baseball," because the residents of Petersburg "eat, sleep, work, and dream Hopewell."[13]

In a losing effort in Norfolk, typical for much of the season, a reporter described how McMahon's "crusty seafarers" proved "too cruel" to the "waifs from Petersburg," after Busch's desertion. But in another less praiseworthy effort, catcher Stewart got into a fight with a rival player and ended up paying a fine of $10 in the Petersburg police court, as did Norfolk pitcher Ira Nicks, who interfered with the arrest.[14]

A different story emerged in Suffolk, where the Tigers rose temporarily to the top of the second-half standings, in stark contrast to their last-place finish in the first half. The owners went into a financial hole, possibly as much as $5,000, just to have their community represented respectably in league play. For the small city, it was a matter of pride. Around the midpoint of the season, management brought in George "King" Kelly, who had first managed in the Virginia League in 1894 for Petersburg.

Two ex–Tars, outfielder Stewart and outfielder Charlie Allen, led the hitters, with some help from slick-fielding Fred "Snake" Henry at first base. Henry attracted a lot of attention as potential major-league material. Kelly's pitching staff consisted of three former crewmen: "Jimmie" Poole (18–14), Steve Gaston (9–18) and lefty Bert Graham (12–13), along with veteran Jack "Jap" Efird (18–11), a former Roanoke Tiger. All four of these pitchers gave Portsmouth a hard time, had an advantage over Rocky Mount in head-to-head encounters, and they often fought the Tars tooth and claw.

Norfolk fans long recalled two memorable battles against the Tigers. In August, the two battled a league-record 23 innings to a 2–2 tie when darkness interceded. Cockran and Poole pitched the entire game for their respective clubs. Both teams combined made but one substitution. In the 20th inning, with the bases loaded for the Tigers and no one out, Steinbrenner grabbed an apparent hit and threw out the runner coming in from third. Cockran induced the next two hitters to pop up. This game occurred after the teams had swapped extra-inning victories.

About two weeks later, the two teams played 22 innings, with Efird going the distance for the visitors and Nicks and Humphreys splitting pitching chores for the Tars. Again, the teams ended in a tie — this time 3–3. The sheer number of innings the two played against each other over a short span with only two verdicts must be some sort of record.[15]

The City of Shipbuilders did not do as well as it had in the first half of the season, placing fifth. Carnes resigned as manager in the middle of August, replaced by Brooke "Old Mud Hoss" Crist. By beating the Orphans several times at Newport News, the Builders managed to play almost .500 ball the rest of the season. Roy Gardinier posted a 20–17 record, George Mullins broke even in 30 decisions and Earl Hamilton won a lot more than he lost (14–5). Rasty Walters hit six home runs and averaged just a bit above .300 to pace the offense. The Peninsula press lost interest as September rolled around, but it did praise the league for surviving without Richmond, contrary to predictions in the Richmond newspapers.[16]

In a second-half game at Norfolk, Newport News shortstop "Signer Armando" Seiglie, the "Cuban Comet" got into a fight with "Buck" Thrasher of the Tars when the latter slid into second following a two-base error on the shortstop. After an exchange of words (Thrasher later said the shortstop swore at him) "before any declaration of war had been framed, Thrasher had one arm around the visiting shortstop's neck, while the other was messing up the Cuban's swarthy features." Teammates separated the two before any major damage. The "Charley Chaplain" umpire ejected them both, but "a squad of bluecoats, large enough to capture Mexico City" (United States troops occupied Vera Cruz at the time), seeing their chance to "get in the limelight," swarmed on the field and arrested the combatants. The Tars lost, 4–1, in an otherwise dull game.[17]

In a game at Petersburg before that city lost its franchise, Tar pitcher Ira "Ignatius Galliopus" Nicks was arrested for striking at a police officer during a fight. But the penalty could not have been too severe, for he won a game against the Goobers a day or so later. In another contest a new Tar outfielder Don Flynn turned an umpire around and booted him in the rear, but was not ejected. Third baseman Bernard Cleveland became so annoyed with being called out on the bases that he hit the umpire with the ball. The umpire didn't even eject Cleveland, but he also did not show up for the next game, leaving the two teams to appoint representative players as arbiters.[18]

Throughout the season, as usual, Norfolk acquired new players and got rid of those underperforming or being paid too much. Early in the season, the club secured Clarence "Dad" Foster, who did quite well at the bat, but when they brought on "Broncho" Flynn from Texas, management let Portsmouth have Foster. Foster could easily have replaced the light-hitting Foiles at first base, but his salary and veteran status meant the Tars could not keep him. He turned out to be a mainstay in the Portsmouth lineup and its drive for the pennant, along with Harry Damrau, another former Tar.

Flynn lofted a home run against Portsmouth in the sister city's park. Normally the reporter would not be impressed with such a feat because the left fielder in Portsmouth almost looked "into the third baseman's pocket." But this particular hit soared high into the air and dropped many feet beyond the fence. On another occasion, Flynn hit two home runs at Portsmouth. Since he only hit five homers for the season, he must have found that park inviting, unlike pitcher Nicks. He once allowed three home runs in one inning there.[19]

Norfolk opened the second half strongly. In a noteworthy game against the Nuts at Norfolk, Cockran bested Sammy Rice, who ended the season pitching for the Washington Senators. The game reminded local fans that the two had vied for the naval championship a couple of years before, with Rice emerging the winner in that particular contest.

After clinging to the lead almost to the end of July, the Tars fell back as Suffolk came on strong. With a little more than a week to play, Suffolk, 10 games above .500 held first place, with Rocky Mount and Portsmouth in hot pursuit. Near the end of the season, the Tigers fell back while Portsmouth soared, with Rocky Mount close. The Crew remained in contention, just a few games back, but the Tars could not overtake the leaders.

In mid–August, the club sold A.J. "Steamer" Cockran to Cincinnati. Cockran, 16–8, reportedly went for $3,000, with $1,000 paid up front and the rest to come should he not be returned to Norfolk. President Walker said he had to let Cockran go during the season because Cincinnati wanted him right away and he could not take a chance that the pitcher would become subject to a draft at the end of the season. He made that decision because in the previous year; he'd received only $400 for Cliff Markle.

Management also went through a long list of throwers in seeking four good starters. In addition to Cockran and Humphreys, who went 14–14 that year, the Crew at times included George Weller, Joe McManus, Nicks, Maurice Craft and one or two others. The team released Weller early when his record fell to a game or two below .500. Although Nicks lost a few more than he won, he could be relied upon in a pinch. Once, when the club was temporarily short-handed, he pitched a doubleheader against Petersburg, winning the first and losing the second. The Tars gave up on Barton when his record fell to 5–8.

"Molly" Craft, a gifted multi-sports Portsmouth athlete who worked for Win Clark early in the year, came over the river in early August to win a couple of contests in his first professional season. One game turned out to be the "Molly" and "Molly" show as Craft did the pitching and McMahon the hitting to win the game. Toward the end of the season after the Cockran sale, the Tars' four-man rotation included Humphries, Craft, Nicks and McManus.

Humphreys recovered from an injury and defeated the Orphans, 4–2, in a late-season game in which he did not allow a hit. The win followed victories over the "Wanderers" by Craft and Nicks to put Norfolk six games above .500. For most of the season, the pitching was adequate, with even a shutout here and there.

Cockran's departure did little damage to the Tars' record, but the Reds decided he was not quite ready for the big time and returned him to Norfolk after the Virginia League season. The stocky right-hander planned to spend the winter working on a better curve ball. His current twister was fine for getting out Virginia Leaguers but not adequate for the majors. On his return, he disclosed that Cincinnati only paid $500 directly to the Tars for him. The Reds would have paid $1,000 more had he made the grade.[20]

In other transactions, Walker sold Thrasher and Flynn to the Giants and Yankees for a potential $2,500 and $1,500, respectively. As in the Cockran deal, the final amount depended on how well the two performed, but in this case the two would play the remaining 17 days on the schedule for Norfolk. Walker was again trying to avoid losing players to the draft after the season ended when the return would be less. But once again Walker was thwarted in his efforts when the National Commission nixed both deals because they violated a rule that stated that no deals could be consummated with less than 20 days to the end of the season.

The Yankees were doubtless happy about the cancellation, for Flynn's batting average was dropping at the rate of about 10 points every week. At the same time, a doctor told the frustrated and sick Walker he needed to go to the mountains, the Norfolk climate no longer agreeing with him. One can only ponder whether stress may have contributed to his failing health. Walker's first full year as the principal owner of the Tars had brought numerous problems for the contractor.[21]

As August waned, a rejuvenated Portsmouth club, 11 games above .500, held a one-game edge on Rocky Mount and a two-game lead over Suffolk, a margin they maintained to season's end. They cemented their standing by winning the first game of the traditional morning-afternoon double bill with the Tars at home. Norfolk, although well down in the standings, ended the season with a respectable 35–27 mark (66–56 for the season). Oddly enough, the overall record of the Tars exactly equaled that of Portsmouth. If one combines the records of all the teams for the entire season, then Portsmouth and Norfolk tied for second place, well in back of Rocky Mount, a team that played good ball the whole year.

On the statistical front, Thrasher led the league in hitting and seemed destined for bigger things. According to an official publication, he pounded out 150 hits and a .348 average (another source says .333) to go along with 11 home runs. The next best hitter for the Crew was outfielder Hugh Whitted at .275, with one home run. Outfielder Flynn, who joined after midseason, came in at .258, after batting well over .300 in the first few weeks following his arrival. Reliable "Red" Cleveland batted .256 and led the team in stolen bases with 43. First baseman Foiles, shortstop "Molly" McMahon, and second baseman Steinbrenner managed to hit .242, .241, and .220 respectively, with the last mentioned pilfering 39 bases. Carl Eubanks, who replaced Stewart as catcher, produced a feeble .111 in 30 games. Catcher Stewart, who stoically played despite severe indigestion, hit in the mid-to-low .200s. Newcomer Eubanks did worse at the plate, but he supposedly knew how to handle pitchers better.

Over in Portsmouth, only two players — Harry Damrau and Vic St. Martin — played the full season. Damrau, who hit less than .100 in his brief stint as a Crewman in 1913, led the Trucker regulars with .288 (one source says .279) and either 10 or 12 homers. Portsmouth gave up a tiny catcher named Tee to secure Damrau, replacing him with a catcher named Jack Dempsey, who quickly became the idol of the Portsmouth fans early in the season. Left fielder St. Martin hoisted either 10 or 12 out of the park, depending which source one uses, and batted around .255. Foster, a Tar for part of the season, came in with a solid .295. Johnny Mace, who started out as the Tar backup catcher, eked out a .134 and had to be replaced for the stretch run.

Portsmouth also had Eugene "Doc" Newton, who batted .303 for part of the year. In addition, Manuel Cueto, a fleet-footed Cuban center fielder, batted .318 in 41 games. Overall, Portsmouth presented a more formidable offense than the Tars, even though the latter had more holdovers stay on the field for the entire season.

Portsmouth's winning ways in the second half of the season engendered considerable excitement along the Elizabeth River, even on its north bank. One "Jimmie Raincheck," whose column "The Morning After" occasionally appeared in the Norfolk daily afternoon paper, noted that "for the first time in the history of the national pastime" Portsmouth had won a Virginia League pennant. Raincheck admitted that the real pennant winner would be decided by the playoffs, but it was "the first time since the days of Billy Hargrove, Dick Knox, Pop Tate, Vetter, Leach and others back in the palmy days of '96 that Portsmouth has finished the season in the van."

As we already know from studying the 1896 season, Portsmouth stood third, or tied with Norfolk, and some of the players he noted played in 1895. But as he was a Norfolk commentator, we should praise him for at least knowing something about Portsmouth's past.[22]

Some 3,500, an overflow crowd, rabidly supported the Truckers in the morning game against the Tars on Labor Day that clinched the title. And now the same fans would cheer their team against Rocky Mount. Needing more seats at Washington Park, the club added an extra bank of bleachers along the right-field line all the way to the fence. These new seats would be exclusively for whites, with all the bleachers in left field now being turned over to blacks. Because of interest in the playoffs in Norfolk, Wells and Hannan ran an electric scoreboard in one of the theaters for those who could not attend the game. Across the Roads, a less than happy Horwitz withdrew his complaint about Portsmouth breaking league rules, thus allowing the playoff to proceed in apparent harmony. Portsmouth possibly kept about 18 players available, but only put 14 on the roster at any one time, placing the others in a sort of revolving suspension.

Although the Truckers' second-half triumph seemed to fulfill Biblical prophecy, Win Clark's men lost their playoff to Rocky Mount, to the displeasure of crowds at Washington Street Park that were well above those attending the contests in the Tar Heel state. The Down Homers, with Dolly Gray and Dick Ulrich leading the way, won the first three games of the series before Portsmouth won its first victory. The only North Carolina club in the "Virginia League" easily went on to win the pennant.

A Builder Pennant as the Mary Jane Barely Avoids Sinking (1916)

Over the winter, the Newport News and Norfolk newspapers continued their war of words over matters related to the Virginia League. In early January, an article in the Newport News

Daily Press blistered the *Ledger-Dispatch* for calling its negative forecasts over the future of the league "childish vaporings." The Norfolk newsman thought Abe Horwitz would somehow find a way to provide minor league ball for his city, and no one really missed having Richmond, whose attendance throughout 1915 in the supposedly superior International League remained miniscule. The Newport News reporter agreed with his Norfolk counterpart that the league could survive without the Capital City, but he thought that his insulting attitude toward the Peninsula made it look as though Norfolk, now the biggest city in population in the league, had assumed the typical tyrannical attitude toward other clubs once held by the city on the James.[23]

As expected, Boatwright resigned as president of the league and was replaced by Norfolk realtor Burrus Corprew, who soon let it be known that every club had to have someone trained in engineering go over the ball fields to make sure the measurements between bases, etc. were accurate. Once the season started, he offered a $10 reward for the umpire who could achieve the fastest games in the belief that the average fan did not want to watch a ballgame for more than 1 hour and 45 minutes. Otherwise, his office appointed the umpires with the qualifications or lack of same as heretofore.

The league set the standard $1,400 monthly salary cap for players with a maximum of $150 for any single performer, a roster never exceeding 14, and a specified number who had played at higher levels of Organized Baseball. The number of protests having reached record levels the previous year, complaints about violations would be turned over to a committee for arbitration.[24]

The spring of 1916 came along with a crisis over German use of submarines against neutral targets, incursions of Mexican bandits under Pancho Villa across the U.S. border, another season of minor-league ball for Hampton Roads and one more trip for the Mary Jane. Tar fans likely hoped that their team would not be torpedoed.

At the end of the previous season, reporters figured McMahon would not return, but he again took command. Cockran also showed up, along with Ira "Shot Gun" Nicks, towing his brother E.A. "Pop Pistol" Nicks. The younger Nicks did not stay long. "Red" Cleveland did not appear on deck because he had a tryout with Pittsburgh. Harry Welcher, former manager of the Suffolk Tigers, looked like an improvement as catcher, while Fisher Bruce, a star outfielder at Virginia Polytechnic Institute who joined the Crew briefly in 1915, returned with the hope that he could avoid an injury this time.

The Tars warmed up by losing to Buffalo twice and beating Durham two of three. They also defeated the Richmond Grays, an amateur club. In one of the Buffalo games, they scored a couple of runs against Guy Cooper, who recalled being paid $16 a month when he served at St. Helena Station a couple of years earlier, just before signing on with the Virginia League to start his professional career.[25]

Win Clark took charge of the new team at Hopewell, called the "8th Wonder of the World" as the city mushroomed near the big plant owned by the DuPont munitions makers. The Norfolk newspaper called the team the "Powder Puffs" or "Bombs," and as might be expected, one day they blew up the Tars. A few months earlier, a huge fire destroyed much of Hopewell, so that city was not immune from destroying itself.[26]

The promoters of baseball in this frontier-like boomtown (which celebrated its first anniversary as the baseball season was about to start) obviously thought they could entice DuPont employees to watch games after work, even though many of them were heading to their homes in Petersburg. Investors in the ballclub erected what they thought was the finest park in the league right next to the plant, near the main trolley line to Petersburg. In so doing, they took considerable risk, given that the DuPont Company warned anyone who would listen that should the war in Europe end, the plant would close shortly thereafter. As matters turned out, the war continued, but the Powder Puffs fizzled anyway. Their financial success depended on persuading Petersburg people to attend the contests.

Hopewell received the old Petersburg franchise, but when the citizens of Suffolk decided they could not take any more financial baths, the "Cockade City" on the Appomattox received the old Suffolk franchise even though its baseball people failed to support the team the previous year and despite being but a few miles from the Hopewell ballpark. The decision to let Petersburg have a team likely doomed any chance for baseball in Hopewell, because such a limited area would have trouble supporting one team, let alone two.

Before the season started, the Portsmouth paper carried numerous letters, all written by youngsters between the ages of 10 and 18, on the value of a city having a professional baseball team. Several of these appeared each day for over a week in response to the possibility of winning a prize of a season ticket to Truckers' contests. One 18-year-old thought baseball kept "greenbacks" in circulation within the city limit. It also increased the use of streetcars and jitneys. Rooters, he joked, wore out their throats by yelling, thus giving druggists and doctors business. Winning a pennant brought favorable publicity to a city. Team owners made profits, especially if their club participated in playoffs, when big attendance secured more receipts. A 15-year-old noted the "rich harvest" for railroads and steamboat companies.

Several others took pretty much the same or similar views. Publicity related to the club might add to the community's population because outsiders, noting in a sports magazine the number of people attending a contest, might assume a large population. On the non-material side, men might become so excited about a contest that they forgot their worries for the time being. Another writer believed both businessmen and laborers could benefit from the same escapism.

Another youngster said professional baseball benefited any city because it was a "clean and manly game" and "a great pleasure to sport lovers" of the participating and neighboring cities who read accounts of games in the newspapers, thus affording positive advertising. Above all, baseball was "an American game."[27]

One lad put his ideas in rhyme:

> Every merchant is busier, and that's the reason
> spring should be hailed as baseball season.
> Since cities with ball teams people must know
> in all the newspapers our city does grow.
> Over all the city this clean sport holds sway
> not letting youth from the right path stray.
> Boys and girls should attend every game
> as it will give Portsmouth greater fame.[28]

Most of the other contributors made the same points with different details. If and when Portsmouth won a pennant, one boy thought, the city would receive lots of coverage in *Reach's Baseball Guide*. "A town without a baseball club is a good place to have a funeral directors convention," he added. It was healthful to walk to the park and use one's lungs to support the team, but most importantly, he hoped to win the contest because he was tired of playing "the mole" to see games through the fence.

One 10-year-old, who recalled German sailors going to a Trucker game early the previous season, assumed these foreigners now had some idea about how Americans played, inferring that somehow that might help international relations. The writer went on to emphasize the virtues of being out in the open air and the community advertising that appeared in home and out-of-town media.[29]

Overall, it seems doubtful that anyone since 1916 has come up with better arguments for community support for professional baseball or any other sport than these teens and pre-teens. We, of course, hear no negative opinions about the subject, because the question had been phrased "Why Professional Baseball is of Value to a City?" One would not win the season ticket by taking the negative view. No one talked about the negative publicity of having a losing team, or the embarrassment of a player slugging an umpire, or club members or fans consuming the monthly liquor quota in one day and behaving accordingly.

In late March, Norfolk management complained about the short distance to the left field fence in Portsmouth, claiming it stood but "137 feet" from home plate. Because this number appears more than once in the press, it seems not be a misprint or an effort at humor. Portsmouth considered adding a 30-foot wire fence to make it more difficult to hit home runs. The alternative suggestion was to count anything hit over the fence as a double, as had been the case the year before at Bland Park. Why the people of Portsmouth persisted in building parks with such short left-field fences is anyone's guess. At this point League Park in Norfolk was rearranged so that both left- and right-field fences were exactly 270 feet from home plate at the shortest distance. Thus symmetry prevailed in Norfolk while something decidedly more disorderly characterized the sister city.[30]

Whatever the dimensions of its field or the height of the left-field fence, the Portsmouth club did quite well. It opened its regular season under new manager Jim Fox at Truckertown with a 4–2 win over Norfolk, before some 4,000 paid customers (4,300 overall). Ida Wyatt, a basketball player for Portsmouth High School, threw out the first ball. The Portsmouth reporter happily and aptly announced the result in the headline, "No Warning Given When Mary Jane Is Torpedoed," as Bob "Smokey Joe" Wood beat Cockran and Mollie Craft. "Howls of exultation could have been heard at Bowers Hill," the local scribe opined.[31]

The Truckers then took the home opener at Norfolk, despite the best efforts of "Middy" Hunt, whose minstrel show enlivened festivities deep in the right-field bleachers. Portsmouth opened the year with seven straight wins. They were 10–1 as Norfolk, rebounding after an initial three straight loses to Portsmouth, rose to 6–5. Before the start of the season, knowledgeable baseball men said Portsmouth and Newport News had far better overall talent than Norfolk, although the latter possessed creditable pitchers. This assessment proved accurate for Portsmouth but seemed to be mistaken regarding Newport News, which lost most of its early games. Soon, however, Fred Payne replaced Crist as manager and the Builders commenced a remarkable recovery — thus validating these prognostications.[32]

About the time Pancho Villa's bandits raided a Texas town, former Tar "Lefty" Graham beat his old mates, 4–2, for Petersburg. In a game against Hopewell, Fisher Bruce's triple drove in three to beat Steve Gaston 7–6, but in the next game the "Bombs" exploded for nine runs in the ninth as Cockran "ascended higher than any aviator trying for an altitude record would wish to go." In that game, Jack Bennett, once a crewman on the *Franklin,* yielded but two runs to the Tars.[33]

The Tars finally won one over the Truckers, in a game in which Manny Cueto, wrongly thinking the umpire had called a strike or possibly upset by a signal that he had just received a $5 fine for his objection, twice struck the arbitrator, once with his fist and then with the bat on his backside. A "stately convoy" of police escorted him from the field as the crowd yelled, "lynch the dirty roughneck." The next day, the Cuban's letter of apology appeared in print, saying simply that he had lost control in his zealous desire to have his team win. The umpire in question (Joe Rossano, a resident of Portsmouth and future president of the Virginia Federation of Labor) had to be temporarily replaced with representatives from the teams. The court assessed a $10 fine and the league suspended Cueto for six days, though he seems to have only missed a couple of games. Previous to this incident, the press had found shortcomings in Rossano's work. He had even gotten into a fight with a former umpire over his calls.[34]

While the Mary Jane struggled to stay afloat, things were going so well in Portsmouth in early May that Earl Wright, then a member of the corporate board of directors of the club, produced a poem to celebrate "Portsmouth's Winning Team." His opus dealt with much of the political culture of the time, and is here presented in modified form:

> It takes a lot to live these days, with foodstuffs climbing forty ways.
> To work all day and half the night, it does not seem it can be right.
> Still that's the funny way of life; we gladly all stay in the strife.
> One bright ray through the clouds does beam,
> cause Portsmouth has a winning team.
>
> They may catch Villa in a trap and erase his features from the map.
> A lot of soldiers yet may go to bust the land of Mexico.
> These rumors cause a bitter thrill, it makes some happy, some get ill.
> Through troubled nights we sweetly dream
> of Portsmouth and her winning team
>
> Sad Europe with her gory fields must grapple on till someone yields.
> The curse of war collects its toll while thousands die on honor's roll.
> To keep this on your mind is bad; it's bound to keep you blue and sad.
> Just let your features smile and gleam,
> and think of Portsmouth's winning team.
>
> Election time will soon be here, which causes some to stand in fear.
> To view the field with sad disdain, should Willie Bryan run again?
> Or Teddy with the famous Moose; they all may run but what's the use.
> Tis Wilson sure; he's sail the stream,
> home in front like Portsmouth's team.[35]

The poem appeared the same day as accounts of the Truckers' triumph over the Builders, 16–9, where the winners also pulled off a triple play because umpire Kennedy refused to call an infield fly with two men on and no one out.

After defeating Hopewell a couple of times, the Tars lost to the Builders, 12–0, on Confederate Memorial Day as Carl Ray applied a coat of "whitewash" to "the good ship Mary Jane." Another loss to the Builders left the Tars three games below .500. At this point, Tar management shipped manager McMahon, who was now hitting a woeful .167, to Winston-Salem. Bill Lindsay replaced McMahon in the short field. The club announced that Buck Pressley had agreed to leave his South Carolina medical practice and return to Norfolk to save the Tars. It would take him some time to make arrangements, leaving the job of managing in the hands of Eugene "Doc" Newton, a Portsmouth player the previous year.

As they awaited the arrival of Pressley, the Tars treaded water. By the end of May, Portsmouth had a commanding seven-game lead over Newport News, which was playing only .500 ball. Indeed, a few days later, only Portsmouth had a record better than .500. Norfolk, at 13–17, stood fifth, a game ahead of the last-place Powder Puffs.

Statistics released at the end of May revealed that Norfolk's top hitter, Harry Hartsell, ranked seventh among regular batters, at .317. Newton was the next best among the Tars, with an average of .274, followed by Bruce at .260. First baseman Casper Morpeth came in at a respectable .256 and Hugh Whitted at .250. Infielder Ed Sicking fell just three points below that.

Newton became renowned for his long hits while playing for Portsmouth the previous year, but he failed to sustain that reputation while playing for the Tars. Homer output among the entire team seemed particularly low, with several never hitting even one. Some experts thought Virginia League pitchers had found a new way to scuff up a ball on one side and smooth it on the other, thus causing a swift movement as it approached the hitters.

In early June, on the day the British and Germans fought a fierce naval battle in the North Sea off Denmark, the Truckers shelled the Tars, 11–4, leaving Portsmouth with a record of 27–20 compared to Norfolk's 17–20. Soon thereafter Newport News bloodied Cockran and Nicks in an 11–6 drubbing, but Eddie Pooray, who had won only four of 24 ball games for another Virginia League team the previous year, surprised everyone by shutting out Portsmouth, 2–0. A few weeks later, he shut them out again, 1–0. Portsmouth press members muttered that the Truckers were the only team in the Virginia League the Tars could beat.

Overall, however, Portsmouth had little to complain about, as both Wood and Lefty Alton tossed no-hitters, the former easing by Norfolk, 2–0. With a record of 25–9, the Truckers were far ahead of the rest of the league. The Fourth Ward Club celebrated by having an excursion to the Capes. They did not take the good ship Mary Jane on their outing.[36]

Meanwhile, the Tars struggled on, alternating losses with wins, as they awaited Pressley's coming. Finally, toward the end of June and amidst much fanfare, Pressley arrived at the embattled scene that was Norfolk. He let Morpeth continue to work at first base, and spent time coaching Craft on the art of pitching and instilling confidence in the young man.

Management thought it possible to persuade "Jap" Efird, who had won 18 games for Suffolk the year before and had been under Pressley's guidance two years earlier in Roanoke, to join the Crew. Efird had let it be known that, outside of the majors, he did not care to pitch professionally except in the Virginia League, and being a man of independent financial status, he expected to have his way. But Efird did not sign on with the Crew.

Pressley's arrival did not bring the expected miracle cure. Although the doctor predicted there was no way the Tars would continue to lose, the Tars lost at a higher rate than before he came. They did win his first game, 12–9, "hypnotized by his presence" and buoyed "by his cheers." But then with 7–2, 2–1, 3–1, and 3–2 losses to surging Newport News, their record fell to 24–32. Pressley told a Portsmouth reporter that the fiasco against the Builders featured the worst luck he had ever seen. As the first half of the season came to a close in early July, the Tars remained eight games under .500.[37]

Even worse, the Tars got off to a woeful start in the second half of the season, experiencing the worst July in club history. They again lost three straight to Portsmouth, including the July 4 double bill, but this time instead of rebounding with a few wins, they lost another four encounters before finally winning one. Then, they won only two of the next eight, making them one game worse than fifth-place Hopewell. Soon, their record stood at 7–22. Meanwhile, Newport News soared ahead of the pack, with only Portsmouth having any possibility of overtaking the Builders.

Statistics gathered just after midseason revealed considerable weakness for the Tars, particularly at the plate, but a lot of possibilities for Portsmouth. Cueto led everyone at .373 and Jim Fox posted a .364 average. For Norfolk, Whitted raised his average to .288, Bruce to .278, and Sicking to .266, but Morpeth dropped down to .227 and catcher Welcher remained mired at .165. After giving up on Welcher, the Tars tried another catcher who originally was supposed to go to Portsmouth, but he performed even worse. After mulling over the situation, Pressley replaced Morpeth at first base, moving the latter to the outfield temporarily.

Among the pitchers, Nicks had done well with seven wins and two losses. Craft, with limited pitching duty, was 3–1. Otherwise, only Eddie Pooray, at 7–6, was above .500. Cockran limped along at 7–9, pitching games that gave occasional glimpses of his former self intermixed with disastrous outings. Knowing he needed one more creditable thrower, Pressley acquired Steve Gaston from the soon-to-be disbanded Hopewell, where he went 7–10.

The Powder Puffs self-destructed near the end of July, forfeiting $1,000 to the league as the club disbanded. The league did nothing to revise the schedule except to eliminate Hopewell games. Then when Roanoke Rapids fielded a team, the standings changed again, with the North Carolinians saddled with Hopewell's dismal record. Yet, even after twice taking Rocky Mount, the replacement club disbanded, and standings changed for the third time. The absence of a sixth team in the league meant that all teams had three idle days every two or three weeks. Portsmouth filled those dates by playing crews from battleships and other local amateur or semipro clubs. The scores of these games turned out to be closer than most of those played against the substitute Tars that showed up in August.[38]

The only bright spot in July was Craft's performances. With an earned-run average around 2.00, he won six of seven, or all but two of the Tar victories that month. With an overall 8–2 mark and a .260 batting average, Craft stood out among the Crew. Craft did so well that Clark Griffith's Washington Senators purchased him for immediate assignment, thus leaving the Tars without its best pitcher. Rumors initially had Craft and second baseman Ed Sicking headed to the Chicago White Sox, but Craft went to Washington and Sicking eventually tried out for the Chicago Cubs.

In early August, about the time Portsmouth swept the Tars in one-run, emotional, low-scoring games, Pressley gave up and returned to his medical practice in Florida. Plagued by weak attendance, F.B. Walker renewed his call for reduced player salaries and almost disbanded the team. On August 4, the league announced that it would proceed with four teams. But after a fractious meeting, it opted to let Norfolk continue to play, albeit using mostly amateurs.

At the time, Norfolk owed its players some $1,400, which meant they had not been paid in July. Possibly the owners thought they did not deserve to be paid, given their penchant for losing. Possibly there was no money for payroll, given the town's aversion to watching inferior baseball. Unlike in other Virginia cities when support slackened, Walker was too proud to beg for subscriptions or special days. Norfolk was the only city to participate in every year of the Virginia League's existence, and the team had never failed to finish a season. Nor had the club ever resorted to begging fans to subscribe funds. And it did not this time.[39]

The Crewmen, as expected, refused to play without compensation. Moreover, they dispatched a telegram to the National Commission, demanding that the proceeds from the Craft and Sicking deals be turned over to them. Walker asked the league not to forfeit the Norfolk franchise and to release league funds to help pay the players. If the players wanted back pay, Walker said it could come from the commission. It appears that Norfolk had been operating with a double-contract system, giving the league one set of contracts that fell under the cap, but holding a second contract that offered higher pay. The league, of course, paid the amount called for in the first contract. The precise amount the players secured is not known, but the press considered the players' action a "strike" and called the amateurs that replaced them "strike breakers," although the name fails to fit the circumstances.

Most of the professional Crewman disbanded. Bruce headed to Richmond to play in the

International League. Morpeth found a spot in the New York State League. Doc Newton found a home as shortstop for the Truckers. Only Sicking, waiting on word about when to join Chicago, and Harry Hartsell stuck with the sinking ship, with the latter becoming the new manager. Sandlot players now took the cudgels to sustain Norfolk's honor.

The Mary Jane sank to 9–43 at the end of August. The amateurs officially won two games. Emmett Dozier won one game. A Portsmouth lad, J. Stewart, bested Petersburg and later seemingly secured an equally lustrous victory over the Truckers. Curiously, this win should have given the amateurs three wins, but it is not reflected in the standings in any of the newspapers, nor in league records. They lost a few games by close scores; mostly their deficits were in double digits, and they seldom scored more than two or three runs. On the same day that Stewart surprised Portsmouth in one game of a double bill, the once proud Crew of the Mary Jane lost, 13–1, in a "sad affair," providing considerable humor for the "astonished spectators."[40]

Even though fans in other cities applauded the gritty efforts of the amateurs, some of the amateurs, doubtless tired of the drubbings or committed to life outside baseball, deserted the ship. Hartsell merely rounded up new players and went on. Amazingly, the losses included no forfeits. In an unusual twist, 1,000 Norfolk fans showed up at League Park to watch Rocky Mount as the home team against neighboring Portsmouth on Labor Day, demonstrating "just how hungry the Norfolk fans are for real baseball."[41]

Meanwhile, Newport News came on strong to win the second half at 41–13 to give the Shipbuilders an edge over Portsmouth. The season proved to be the most successful ever for the Shipbuilders. In February, Abe Horwitz gave up chances of having a team in the league, but in March a mass meeting raised enough subscriptions to field a team. Management signed several new players, retained Roy Gardinier among others, and purchased new uniforms, with green now serving as trim. The club offered season tickets for men at $20, $6.98 for women, and 25-game packages for $5.[42]

After winning against the Buffalo Bisons of the International League, the Builders started the season on a losing note at Rocky Mount during a series in which Frank Walker apparently broke his leg. In the first home game, a crowd of some 4,000 (many others sitting atop nearby fences) watched a losing effort against the Petersburg Nuts. Before the game, super fan "Connie Mack," with his famous hat and otherwise audaciously attired, led a parade astride a white mule. Management originally planned to have him catch a ball thrown from an airplane, but such a feat would be a bit risky. The biplane took off from the nearby small boat harbor. The plane from the Curtiss Aviation School approached the ballpark then circled it several times, before the pilot made his last run. As the plane approached the field, the big crowd watched nervously as the plane descended to about a hundred feet, its engines making explosive sounds. Suddenly a ball, with a flag attached, descended among the players on the field. So far as anyone knew, this was the first time an opening pitch to start a season had been delivered in this fashion.[43]

After a disastrous start, Crist asked for and received his release, and the club hired Fred Payne to manage. Under his guidance, the club rebounded, as did Walker from his injury, for he belted two home runs in a mid–June game. After sweeping Norfolk in an important series and winning fairly regularly against other teams, Newport News posted a 38–25 record at the halfway point, compared to first-place Portsmouth's 40–19.

In the second half of the season, with Walker and catcher Harry Lake carrying the most of the batting chores of the club, Newport News forged ahead, much to the delight of its fans and press. The Builders posted 41 wins and but 13 losses, six games better than Portsmouth, with Rocky Mount and Petersburg playing .500 or one game above it. Portsmouth reporters grumbled about losing that one game to the "Make Believers" out of Norfolk and also a forfeit victory given to the Builders by the league when Petersburg failed to show up for a game in its own park. Finding the park locked up, the umpire sneaked in through a hole and officially gave the visitors the win. Petersburg police arrested him for trespassing.

Earlier in the season, Petersburg refused to play Portsmouth in the second game of a doubleheader after losing the first contest in 16 innings. The team also protested three losses at Newport News early in the second half of the season. The league concurred in the protest, but the National Commission overturned it. Just after this verdict, Corprew resigned as president, but it is uncertain whether that decision had anything to do with the outcome of the protest. After falling far back of the Builders just after the start of the second half of the year and barely playing .500, Portsmouth markedly improved its record. But although they closed the gap, they could not overtake the Builders, especially after the Petersburg protests were overturned and even though they swept their opponents in a late-season series.

Along the way, Newport News sold the rights to Walker to the Detroit Tigers, but he remained with the club for the rest of the season. At the end of the season, the St. Louis Cardinals drafted Gardinier and the Chicago White Sox acquired Lake. The $750 received took a large chunk out of the $2,200 debt the club accumulated over the season.[44]

Portsmouth also had at least one player headed to the majors — Manny Ceuto. The great Cuban center fielder joined the club the previous year after midseason and batted over .330. After hitting over .400 in Cuba that winter and receiving a diamond watch fob for his efforts, he made his way to the YMCA in Portsmouth. He maintained the plus-.400 pace for half the season, though he trailed off in the second half.

Despite saying that he would not raise money by selling off players, near the end of the season Stanley began putting out feelers with several major league clubs about purchasing the center fielder. Clark Griffith asked Portsmouth to send Cueto to the capital for a tryout. Griffith thought by so doing he had a commitment, but W.E. Stanley thought otherwise. When he received a solid offer from Cincinnati for Cueto to report after the minor-league season, he readily agreed. An angry Griffith said people like Stanley had no business running a baseball team. Stanley wrote a public letter defending his actions.[45]

Griffith's "gratuitous insult" of Stanley made the front page of the Portsmouth paper, which defended the local railroad man. The reporter thought Griffith's charge unfair, and there was nothing funny about it. "It has caused a wave of indignation in the Virginia State League that will not subside until the slander has been fully repudiated," he wrote.[46]

In his letter, Stanley explained that Nick Altrock, representing the Washington club, came to Portsmouth to look over Cueto, but left without offering a deal. Stanley then saw news accounts that claimed Griffith thought that Cueto must be at least 27 years old, too old to start a major-league career. While on railroad business in D.C., Stanley talked to Griffith, who confirmed his worry about Cueto's age but said he would be willing to have Cueto come to D.C. and play in two games on Friday and Saturday. If he liked what he saw, Griffith would pay $1,000 for Cueto.

Reluctantly, Stanley consented to this arrangement. While Cueto was in D.C., Christy Mathewson, manager of Cincinnati, offered a better deal. Faced with having to accept much less money at the end of the season if a bargain could not be arranged, Stanley accepted Mathewson's deal. "Baseball is a pastime and not a business with me," Stanley wrote, and so long as I care to continue to engage in it, it will take bigger men than Clarke Griffith to run me out of the game." Stanley said that Griffith was right about one thing — Portsmouth would never sell any player to the Senators.[47]

In assessing the two teams, Newport News had a higher team batting average, .247 to .225, but when pitchers and catchers were discounted, the two were much closer. Cueto and Walker respectively led the Truckers and Builders in hitting .321 and .319. The Truckers stole far more bases and had many more triples. Portsmouth also had more power. Left-handed hitter St. Martin contributed nine home runs over the season despite the longer distance to the right-field fence, while Moore had seven, Cueto had six, and several others produced smaller numbers. They had a decisive advantage with 47 homers compared to but 22 for the Builders. The small size of the park in Portsmouth undoubtedly influenced those numbers.

As usual, the press in the two cities battled each other. After the Builders moved into first place, people in Portsmouth grumbled about the possibility that Newport News management had exceeded the salary cap. J.A. Fox, a sports columnist for the daily paper in Newport News, sarcastically retaliated that one of the nice things about the possibility of the Builders winning the second half was that the people of Portsmouth, the good sports that they were, would not complain: "Oh no. Never! Not any more than if it was a tooth-pulling affair or something equally as pleasant." They were already resorting to the "old 'salary limit' gag." Everyone there talked about Newport News paying "anywhere from four to forty-four major leaguers," with all of them receiving "immense sums."[48]

Portsmouth had four dependable moundsmen while the Builders had only three, according to one reporter. That prognosticator seemed unaware that in a short series, the quality of the pitching might count for more than the quantity. Those three Builders were outstanding, with Gardinier at 17–7, John Voss at 19–5 (though he lost more than once to Portsmouth) and Carl Ray (on loan from the Philadelphia A's) at 19–7. Steve Gaston, the old Tar, also started for the Builders, but did not do particularly well. For Portsmouth, Bob Wood (23–9), possibly assigned to Detroit, was expected to win at least two games for Portsmouth. New pitcher Jack Orr, out of Auburn University, was undefeated in six decisions with the Truckers.

In the series opener, manager Jim Fox started Orr, who won a 2–1 decision before 4,000 in Portsmouth. The game's only blemish was the behavior of a "large package of Norfolk liquor, wrapped in human form," that tried "to bounce a pop bottle off the lion head of Umpire Kennedy." No one knew why he threw the missile, but police arrested the culprit. Fortunately, his throw was inaccurate.

With Portsmouth leading the series, Cueto snapped a bone in his left ankle trying to steal second. Dozens of Portsmouth fans visited him at the hospital in Newport News, when the next game was rained out. Based on a doctor's report, a reporter assumed the Cuban would not be able to play the next year, but he did — for Cincinnati. Third baseman Richard "Al" Moore, a sharp fielder, also sustained a broken finger in the same game. Newport News granted Portsmouth permission to hire "Molly" McMahon, Norfolk's former third baseman, who finished the season with Winston-Salem and had planned to join a touring team that fall.

In the game in which the two men were injured, Voss, thought to be vulnerable to Portsmouth hitters, had an easy win at Newport News, 6–1. After rain forced a postponement of the next contest, the Builders won, 2–0, and followed with another win back at Portsmouth. Now facing elimination, Portsmouth rallied behind Orr to win, 5–2, at Newport News, and captured the sixth game, 1–0, at home when one its weakest pitchers, Archie Pearson, came through with a gem.

The Builders and Truckers then repaired to League Park in Norfolk for the finale. A huge crowd, mostly from the two competing cities, watched as the Builders prevailed, 3–1, as southpaw Carl Ray bested another lefty, "Rube" Alton. Center fielder Walker went 4-for-4 and headed for a stint in the majors as some 5,000 fans made their way to the exits. During the contest, Newport News fans filled one set of grandstands; "home" team Portsmouth fans occupied the other, each side cheering plays that helped their respective teams.

After the Builders won the pennant, the Newport News paper editorialized about the "Lesson of the Pennant." Winning was good news, but the editor was more inspired by the loyalty exhibited by the local residents. Over the winter the franchise seemed on the way out, but a few public-spirited citizens acted in the nick of time to save it. During the season, when the team faded and attendance lagged, several men, acting solely for the benefit of the community, took considerable risk with "no hope of substantial gain." The editor found in this experience a lesson for the city and for the whole lower part of the Peninsula. Why not apply such faith and loyalty, both "powerful instruments for progress," to other aspects of life. Rooting for a baseball team proved to be a tonic, but why not root for all "local enterprises" and the city every day of the year? "There's magic in it."[49]

The Lost Season (1917)

In an assessment of the Virginia League, *The Virginian-Pilot* noted trouble brewing in the majors stemming from the work of the players association headed by Staunton, Virginia's David Fultz, a former Virginia Leaguer and major league player. The reporter figured that the Players Protective Fraternity had not opened up to Class B or C performers; thus the proposed strike would not directly affect the local situation. Owners in the Virginia League made it clear that they would impose heavy fines for disregarding the limits on salaries. They also decided to return to the full-season format.[50]

In 1917, Walker sold out his remaining interest in the Norfolk club, but kept ownership of the park. According to Win Clark, Walker simply turned over the franchise, the players, the uniforms, etc. to Clark, who then persuaded C. Moran Barry to assume the presidency, with his brother Jim also having a role.[51]

One of the brothers immediately ordered the reinstallation of the "Bull Durham" sign at League Park. Management also put grass on the infield, making Norfolk the only team in the league with such an adornment. It helped players and fans by reducing glare. In addition, management moved the grandstand back 40 feet, mostly to make more room for football in the fall, and it added new bleachers along the third-base/left-field line. Auto owners could park their vehicles in the now enclosed vacant lot next to the park to protect them from damage by stray baseballs and gang members that frequented the front entrance.[52]

The Barry brothers hired Arthur Devlin, a solid .300 hitter with major-league experience, to manage the club. Devlin, who also played, started his professional career at third base in the Virginia-Carolina League in 1901. He then went with the New York Giants and later with the Boston team in the National League. After managing in the Pennsylvania League, he came to Norfolk.[53]

Around the same time as both the Norfolk Blues and Grimes Battery returned from service on the Mexican front Devlin, having to start from scratch with no holdovers from the previous season, signed Jack Gillespie, Stanley Tinin, Harry E. Carraway, and many who would not be heard from in the local press again. S.A. Marable, from the Richmond semipro league and New Kent County, Virginia, came on board. Stanley Harris from Pennsylvania showed up with a recommendation from the great Hugh Jennings and immediately impressed a reporter as the "cleanest, surest and most polished infielder of the bunch."[54]

Devlin also signed Emmett Dozier, a local lad who played some in 1916, but Dozier's name did not show up in the early-season box scores. Lefty Louis Magalis joined the Crew and started several games. Devlin also tried out former Maury High School pitchers George "Beef" Treakle and his younger brother.

Before the season started, Devlin wanted to send $12 in transportation money to a player he had coached at Fordham College the previous year. Barry declined the request, thinking that he would rather have an experienced professional. Devlin then told John McGraw about the young man — Frankie Frisch, the "Fordham Flash." Baseball, like a lot of things in life, is often a matter of missed opportunities.[55]

The Tars prepared for the season by playing a couple of losing games against the Buffalo Bisons and then restricted games to contests against local amateurs. Norfolk's people thought they had a "strong lineup, with six youngsters and three veterans, even though they had "not set the world on fire" in the preseason.[56]

Once the season started, Ira Nicks, Harry Hartsell, and Fisher Bruce returned to give the club much needed experience. A reporter believed "Shot Gun" Nicks lacked proper handling in his previous stint as a Tar and expected him to do better under Devlin's tutelage.[57]

On the international front, German plots to persuade the Mexicans and Japanese to join them in the likely event of war between the United States and the Central Powers and renewed German attacks on American shipping forced President Wilson to proposed declaring war in April. About the same time, the Tars managed to defeat Maury High School, 4–0, but secured only a 4–4 tie against the St. Helena Saints at the latter's grounds in Berkley. The day after that contest, "Chico" Manila, a Filipino star pitcher for the Saints, joined the Crew.

After winning several games against local schools, Maury High ended its season prematurely, due to the impending war. A few weeks later, officials at St. Helena complained that they could not keep the same team in the field because of the turnover of military assignments. Soon after the declaration, Congress called up the naval reserves and discussed conscripting soldiers. That season and the one that followed were filled with excitement and anxiety, with young men either volunteering for military service or waiting for a succession of drafts to conscript them. Wilson urged sports programs to be continued as usual, but that would prove to be impossible.

A day or two before the Tars and Truckers launched the 1917 season amid the usual parades and other festivities, an American merchantman fired shells at the periscope of a German U-boat some 1000 yards away to attain the honor of firing the first shots in the war. Some observers thought one of these shells hit the target.

The fictional Tars could have used a similar salvo, falling to the Truckers 6–2 on Opening Day. Outfielder Carraway committed three errors to undermine Manila's excellent mound work.[58]

Although the Tars managed to send Jack Orr to his first defeat ever for Portsmouth a day or so later, the situation did not look promising for the Crew of the Mary Jane. The quality of Norfolk pitching seemed especially suspect. Newport News and Portsmouth, however, were both loaded with talent. The Builders quickly moved out in front with a 10–5 record and Portsmouth followed at 9–7. Although Lynchburg, now back in the league replacing Hopewell, lost to Norfolk, 7–1, in one game, the men from the Hill City still led Norfolk at 7–9 in the battle for third place. Petersburg and Rocky Mount brought up the rear in the standings.

Everything looked about as predicted when the newspapers suddenly announced: "Virginia League Dead." Four clubs, excluding Lynchburg and Norfolk, disbanded their teams after a four-hour meeting at the Monticello Hotel. The Portsmouth Field Sports Association folded first. Its president said that the organization simply could not continue to make a financial sacrifice for the sake of the community. The team put a first-class product on the field, and few fans came out to watch the games. At first, he thought the league might carry the franchise, which had been losing $40 to $50 a day, but the moguls decided otherwise. The Portsmouth owners presumably sold all the loose paraphernalia on the grounds and turned the proceeds over to the departing members of the club. C. Moran Barry tried hard to save the association, pointing out that the Elizabeth City Chamber of Commerce would take over the Portsmouth franchise. Barry and company expressed disappointment that the Portsmouth people had given them insufficient notice.[59]

With such a brief season, statistics were almost meaningless. But Crewman Harry Hartsell was hitting a sizzling .387 at the time the voyage prematurely ended. Carraway hit .409 for the first two weeks, but Harris only managed a .165. Stanley Harris, the slick-fielding Pennsylvanian, became better known as "Bucky" Harris, and eventually became the player/manager of the Washington Senators when they won two American League pennants and one World Series in the mid–1920s. Harris recalled that Norfolk had a fairly solid team, with Buddy Culloton, who later pitched for the Pittsburgh Pirates, on the staff. "We were sailing toward the pennant when the World War stopped us," Harris recalled. "When the league disbanded for the time being, all the Norfolk players went home to go to war."[60]

Because Norfolk actually was in fourth place when the season ended and Culloton did not play for Norfolk until the next year, Harris must have been confusing hope with reality. Harris sought to return for the 1919 team, as the fighting in France ceased and professional ball made a comeback. Norfolk management told him not to come.

Another Brief Voyage in Dangerous Waters (1918)

After the brief season, contractor F.B. Walker exchanged League Park "near the corner of Church and 18th Street," and neighboring property (four acres all told), with the Old Dominion Peanut Corporation, for an apartment complex elsewhere in the city worth $120,000. The company planned to erect a large plant to process peanut candy but delayed doing anything because of the muddled financial situation created by the war. As the war effort built up, the peanut men leased the ball field to the Norfolk War Camp Community Service, a semi-public agency that arranged for athletic contests and other forms of entertainment for soldiers and sailors. In 1918, the ball field became known as Red Circle Park, the name for numerous military-oriented amusement centers throughout the country.[61]

Because the war caused the demise of the league in 1917, theoretically, it should not have been able to revive for the next season, when the demands of Mars markedly increased. Yet play the league did, but with only four teams. The season started a month late and ended early.

With the populations of Norfolk, Portsmouth and Newport News growing so rapidly due to the war, and with the return of Richmond from its International League sojourn, the league attained Class B status. But the quality of play actually went down as more and more players became subject to the military draft. Not all able-bodied men were drafted during the summer of 1918, but the minor leagues carried on with several men the service exempted for physical limitations or other reasons. Just as the season started, the provost marshal decided that all professional ballplayers of draft age had to enlist or work in some useful occupation. The government did not consider playing ball a useful occupation.

Despite many obstacles, Barry campaigned for a four-team league at a meeting where the moguls arranged a 90-game schedule. The Crew encountered a snag when Barry found out that Red Circle Park officials required a percentage of the gate, but he worked out that detail.[62]

Skipper Devlin once again headed up the Norfolk Crew, and quickly went to New York to recruit among the semipro players of that city. He ended up with an aggregation from all over, including two players from Portsmouth, a Norfolk man, and only one experienced player — shortstop Pelham "Jack" Ballinger. Second baseman Rabbit Gillespie left the club for a time then returned to play well, and then fell ill to typhoid. Although Magalis also returned for a time, the mainstay of the staff was Buddy Culloton, who also played outfield. Former Tar "Red" Stewart returned to the outfield as well.[63]

The Tars started the season by beating the Richmond Colts two of three. The winning pitcher in one of these games, Culloton, a reporter predicted, "with a little more experience should make one of the Tars' best bets, if not one of the best in the league. He has plenty of stuff on the ball."

Even though Norfolk started the season on a winning note, the club's record soon swooned to 3–9, then to 3–13, and only got worse. "Smiley" Meyers managed a 7–2 win over the Colts at about the time the record stood at 7–18. Another win over the Capital City team reminded one reporter of "flashes of brilliance" of the pre–1915 team under Buck Pressley, but such praise was otherwise rarely merited.

The July 4 doubleheader against the Newport News Builders proved especially devastating. Acutely aware of the warfare prevalent in Europe, the reporter told the "sad story" in terms of "Devlin's shot-to-pieces Tars, with no reserves to call up, [and] forced to yield ground in two engagements, being ignominiously repulsed when they invaded the Builder's positions yesterday morning." After losing, 11–2, they permitted the enemy to "lunge into our own trenches" in the afternoon for a 6–3 victory. Fans hoped for a turnabout in the afternoon contest, with Culloton on the mound, but Culloton "proved to be easy pickings for the visitors and their heavy artillerymen began to drill holes in the atmosphere around League Park." Clearly, Norfolk needed to call in the marines.[64]

Despite the poor showing, a few days later, the stockholders in the Norfolk Baseball Corporation did not plan to disband the team even though Richmond and other cities showed clear signs of weakness. Devlin finally seemed to be moving the ship in the right direction, evidenced by a 3–2 win over Newport News. The reporter attributed the weakness in attendance throughout the league to the war, which had taken away "a great many of the men who would be the ardent fans." The league might have to resort to using the $2,000 forfeit in the event one team disbanded. But clearly that would not be Norfolk.

In the middle of July, after several more losses, the club revived some, winning five of eight on the road. But in the first game back at home, the Tars yielded to the Petersburg Nuts. The reporter, still insisting on using army metaphors, compared the reaction of the Tars to that of the Huns when they went "over the top" in the trenches and "found themselves in a hornet's nest" of enemy soldiers.[65]

On the last day of the brief season, and a day before the Allies drove the Germans across the Marne River for the final time, a *Pilot* reporter opined in an article entitled "Good Old Baseball May Die" that despite all the "gobs" of gloom, "no matter what happens, when all is well with America and the world again, the Virginia League will revive with peace, stronger and livelier than ever."[66]

During one of the many down times for the Tars, when Culloton yielded 12 runs in one game, the press played up the reappearance of "Pop" Shaffer, now an umpire. The reporter hoped Shafer would supply some comedy with his "hitch 'em up" routine.

Richmond edged Newport News by winning the last game of the rump season, giving the Capital City a title of sorts in its first year back in the Virginia League. The abbreviated 1918 season started well into June and ended before the end of August. The Builders, led by center fielder Tom Daughton with a .328 average, took an early lead, but in the end the Newport News record of 28–21 proved one game too few. Petersburg cashed in with a 27–22 record, just one game behind the second-place Builders. Only Norfolk, with a mark of 13–33, never effectively participated in the race.[67]

During the war and to a degree afterwards, military teams took over the ball grounds and fan interest. Because many of these clubs bore nautical names, it is only fair to consider them honorary members of the Crew of the Mary Jane. In March 1918, a newspaper noted that several big-league players were already training at the Navy Base. The Fifth Naval District Athletic Association organized at a meeting at the Navy Y, with Win Clark presiding. The War Camp people, in control of League Park, supported the military league by charging admission to non-military people.

In military pre-season encounters Davis Robertson, the former New York Giant outfielder from Portsmouth, served as the player/manager of the Minesweepers, who defeated an infantry unit, 10–5, at Horwitz Park in Newport News toward the end of April. The "Fliers" (Naval Air Station) beat the "Sawbones" of the Portsmouth Naval Hospital, 8–5, at the Naval Base. The "'Saints' [St. Helena] Riddled the Sharpshooters," as the Navy Yard overcame the *USS Iowa*, 4–2.[68]

Salivating over the prospects of reporting the actions of former major league players, *The Pilot* lined up a cartoonist or two and a formidable list of nationally known reporters. Included was James Tracy of the *Chicago Record-Herald*, who now edited a military magazine, and Tom Hanes, formerly with a Birmingham paper. With the professional Tars starting late that year and playing an abbreviated season, the area relied mostly on its military teams for entertainment. In the first day of action in league play hundreds of "raving baseball maniacs howled themselves half dumb" as the Navy Yard shot the "good ship Iowa ... to pieces," and the "Naval Base blew up [the] Minesweepers," Win Clark's "Tars" besting Dave Robertson's club.

In the next round, the Naval Base "Admirals" again sank the Minesweepers, 12–2, while the Naval Hospital lost to the Air Station and St. Helena triumphed over the Rifle Range, as the *Iowa* got vengeance on the Navy Yard. The Navy Yard battled the Quartermaster Terminal team that was composed of folks who worked for the company constructing the big army base at Bush Bluff (now the piers of Norfolk International Terminals). All proceeds from a game at Red Circle Park went to the Red Cross. The crew of the *USS Mississippi* proved too much for the Hospital, which won only one of eight.[69]

The Naval Base team looked the best as the teams continued to play about two times a week. With Rube Zellers, a future Tar, as one of the starting pitchers, the Naval Base amassed an unblemished record with 10 wins by early June, closely followed by St. Helena at 9–1. Clark's club, with Zellers on the mound, even defeated one of the top navy teams, led by Rabbit Maranville, one of the heroes of the Boston Braves in the 1914 World Series, in a contest played at Yorktown before hundreds of naval personnel.

The St. Helena Saints, however, moved to the front of the naval league standings. Five thousand fans packed into League Park — more than the professional Tars had seen in years — to watch the Saints overcome the Minesweepers. "Big Chief" Norman Glockson, the catcher for the Saints and former and future professional player for at least two Virginia League teams, went 5 for 5 to lead his team in a 10–4 romp. Even though a writer for *Navy Life* reported that the Minesweepers, with John Voss, another former and future professional on the mound, overcame the Navy Yard, St. Helena now held the league lead. Toward the end of July, Glockson led the regular Saint hitters with a .362 average.[70]

Robertson of the Sweepers, a star in the majors, performed very limited duty. In the middle of July, John McGraw offered him $7,500 to finish the season with the Giants, but Robertson rejected the offer. Although the military board deferred him from military service because of a bad knee, Robertson insisted on staying on as an agent for the Justice Department. Around that point in the season St. Helena's record stood at 18–1, with the Minesweepers at 13–5 and the Naval Base at 14–6.[71]

In early August, 6,500 came to Red Circle Park to watch St. Helena sink the Minesweepers, with Voss, the former Builder, losing 9–1. Nine Sweeper errors blew them out of the water. As St. Helena swept the Sweepers and claimed the championship, the Fifth Naval District organized its all-star team, which included lefty Joe Boehling from Richmond and Mollie Craft, two former major leaguers, as pitchers.[72]

9

Stormy Seas, 1919–1923

In 1919, Virginians faced a postwar world that included Bolshevism's takeover in Russia and its rise in Germany, Woodrow Wilson's ill-fated effort to erect an effective League of Nations and major labor strikes across the country. In the Old Dominion, the problems were runaway inflation, the return of flu-infected soldiers from France, race riots and shortages of just about everything but trouble. Faced with this situation, many Americans hoped for normality, including the return of professional baseball to Norfolk and other cities in the Virginia League. After a torturous postwar era that included a major recession, the nation entered the flamboyant 1920s, during which professional baseball experienced a golden age, at least nationally.

"Too Much Bender" (1919)

As soon as the Armistice was signed in November 1918, President Bradley of the Virginia League made plans for the next season, but all sorts of obstacles got in the way. As late as March, league officials had not figured out what cities would be represented. That month, Bradley convinced several Portsmouth residents to take initial steps in organizing a team. In the middle of March, with H.P. Dawson, city manager Earl Wright and a councilman or two playing influential roles, the citizens of Portsmouth formed a new baseball corporation and called for a mass meeting to raise funds.

Although the meeting raised about $4,500, planners estimated they needed at least an additional $2,500. They found it difficult to compete for funds against the Fourth Liberty Bond drive. Embarrassed that the small neighboring city of Suffolk, with fewer than 10,000 residents, had already subscribed $10,000, the residents of Portsmouth raised what they needed by mid–April. The club also worked out an agreement with the Portsmouth War Camp Community Service, which rented the Washington Street Park from the owner, the Southern Railway.[1]

The situation in Norfolk was simpler on the surface, because C. Moran Barry still ran an existing baseball corporation, but he again ran into problems leasing the ballpark. No one questioned that he could sublet the facility from the Norfolk War Camp Community Service, which in turn rented it from the Old Dominion Peanut Corporation. Most of the officers of the Community Service were willing to share the place for reasonable rates, but the two parties conflicted over scheduling. The Service wanted at least half of the holidays and every other week for its military programs. Later, the Fifth Naval District wanted to play every

Wednesday and Saturday afternoon. Possibly because a chaplain at the Navy Base played an active role in military sports, the military, after first playing on Sundays, turned to other days of the week for game times. Without Saturdays, Norfolk would not be able to play sets of three home games against league competition and would also not be able to schedule games on the day with the highest average attendance.

When the two sides seemingly came to terms near the end of March, a bold heading in the morning daily announced: "Course Clear for the Mary Jane's Cruise." But despite having Norfolk's city manager, a state senator and other politicos in his camp, Barry found it tough sailing to negotiate with the head of the Navy League. Two weeks later, the newspaper reported that the "Good Ship Mary Jane is Hard on Lee Shore." Barry, meeting with agents at the Officer's Club at the base, failed to convince them to accept the temporary schedule worked out by Virginia League officials. The morning paper reported: "The Norfolk ball club better known as the 'Mary Jane' has had hard sailing for some time, but last night owing to poor navigation or something, the cruise of the good old ship came to a dead stop, unless the chief engineer and the navigator can get together at the league meeting today and fix things up." The service league's firm stand hit the Norfolk baseball team and its league like a "bombshell" and caused the reporter to speculate that "the state circuit seems doomed to a rough ride in Norfolk in (the) event the Mary Jane attempts to weather the storm."[2]

Further negotiations finally produced the necessary arrangements. The Navy agreed to play earlier in the afternoons on Wednesdays and Saturdays, with the professionals using the standard 4:30 P.M. start time. Instead of giving military personnel a 50 percent discount on tickets, the Tars turned over one-fourth of all gate receipts to the military. (Portsmouth people later complained about sharing gate receipts with Norfolk for the latter's home games with the return from each ticket reduced 25 percent to pay the Norfolk War Camp Community Service before the visiting club could take its share.)[3]

Right before the season started, *Ledger-Dispatch* sports columnist Tom Jones argued that although the "Crew of the Mary Jane" might be an acceptable moniker for a smaller city, the club needed something new to go along with Norfolk's emergence as a "real city." Norfolk was some four or five times larger than at the turn of the century when the nickname first materialized. His suggestions included Corsairs, Buccaneers and Pirates (the old Portsmouth label). Jones finally settled on "Gobs," but Norfolk manager Bill Schwartz objected, few took the proposal seriously, and the press continued to refer to the Mary Jane and its Tars.

The players did acquire some new uniforms. For home games the Tars wore white with black trim, along with blue caps and stockings. Gray replaced white for away games.[4]

A few days after unknown anarchists sent several bombs through the mail intending to kill or maim prominent people, Norfolk commenced its 1919 season with its traditional opener against Portsmouth. Frank Lawrence, who by this time had taken over the ballclub, pushed the starting time in Portsmouth back to 5 P.M. to give Navy Yard employees an opportunity to attend. The Tars won handily, only to lose the home opener at League Park in Norfolk the next day, 5–3, before 1,100 fans, one-third of them from across the river.

Without much fanfare (far less than in Norfolk and Portsmouth), new league entry Suffolk opened its home season on May 10 against Richmond, already having lost a series in Newport News. Management promised a band and fun for the folks of Isle of Wight and Southampton counties, and generally made good on that vow. Special cars were dispatched to bring the players and fans back from Newport News. "Colored patrons, some of whom are the most ardent rooters and supporters of the game" also received better accommodations. The Suffolk club hired Rube Oldring, a former major leaguer, and thus became known as the "Rubes."[5]

On the Peninsula, George Barnes, who had been running the Builders after Horwitz reduced his role, appointed one-time Tar and Trucker Roy Whitcraft to manage. By the middle of April, Whitcraft, a shortstop, signed 21 men for tryouts. Few lasted the year.

On the day of a Norfolk victory over Portsmouth at League Park, one of several early wins, the city of Norfolk welcomed back from France the parading 116th Regiment of the 29th Division, composed of many young men from Hampton Roads and its environs. A few days later, the 111th Field Artillery, composed mostly of the old Norfolk Light Artillery Blues and the Grimes Battery out of Portsmouth, arrived home to further expand the local fan base.

Around the same time, James E. Barry, one of the principal owners of the Tars, presided over a meeting of the Personal Liberty Club, an organization that opposed the continuation of prohibition on both state and federal levels. Woodrow Wilson decided not to end federal wartime restrictions against production and consumption of wine and beer, but he changed his mind in the middle of the season so fans could now find solace when their team lost.

During May, Norfolk won three straight from its neighbors, the last a 7–2 win for Buddy Culloton. Portsmouth looked a little suspect at the start of the season, in part because their manager had to fulfill contractual obligations to coach at the Johns Hopkins University until the end of its season (May 23). As the season progressed, Portsmouth improved some and both clubs gravitated toward .500.

Toward the end of May, the Tars lost two straight to Suffolk, as the home-standing "Rubes" (Oldring hit .327 to lead the club) drew 1,400 and 1,300 in the two contests. As excitement reigned in Virginian's peanut capital. Portsmouth also swept the first two games of the last series in May, 9–4 and 7–3, before Norfolk turned the tables the next day, 8–5. After the double victory, a Portsmouth reporter talked about returning to the park in Norfolk "Red Circled Ocean ... upon which sails the leaking and sinking Mary Jane." The two split the official Memorial Day doubleheader, with Portsmouth securing an 11–8 triumph in the morning contest.[6]

Earlier that month, on the same day the 317th Regiment of the famed 80th Division (Blue Ridge) returned from France, the Tars edged out a 2–1 win over Newport News to bring their record to one above .500. Around this time the German government, facing possible revolution at home, finally agreed to sign the Versailles Treaty, formally ending World War I. But because the U.S. Senate failed to ratify the treaty, the United States technically remained at war. Just to add to the state of anxiety, elements of the American Army crossed the Mexican border on a couple of occasions in pursuit of bandits. American troops also occupied portions of Siberia and the Baltic region. During this critical time, with prices moving ever higher amid charges of profiteering, one of the few oases of stability was the national game.

As in previous seasons, the Portsmouth press engaged in sniping at its neighbor. One of its reporters insisted on calling Bill Schwartz "Billy Warts," also referring to him as "Stupid Bill." Whenever "Billy Warts" lost, he supposedly offered all sorts of excuses, though he primarily relied on bad luck. The reporter found no inconsistency in his own use of the same factor to explain defeats for his home team.[7]

Around mid–June, the old Philadelphia Athletic "Chief" Bender took the reins for the Richmond Colts (aka Bronchos). He also played outfield and did some relief pitching, and his team became known as the Richmond "Indians." Bender defeated Portsmouth in relief, 7–6. Later, folks in Norfolk gave Bender a "royal welcome," when he stepped up to the plate. The Tars won that contest behind Claude Edney, Schwartz forcing an ex–Tar to "walk the plank." But in an ensuing contest, Richmond bested Norfolk, 8–4, before some 1,200 at the 20th Street Park. Bender mixed his slow "Jazz curves" with an "occasional speed pill" in conquering the Crew.[8]

In the next contest, the Tars lost to Portsmouth, as the "Farmers" slugged out a 5–2 win, the Portsmouth reporter discovering a "leak in the good ship Mary Jane." Ballinger and another Tar were injured and pitchers Lewis Samuels and Edney were apparently out of shape. Portsmouth soon swept three straight from the Tars. A 2–1 loss to Suffolk brought the losing streak to five. Meanwhile, Portsmouth had won seven in a row to edge ahead of Norfolk in the standings. Norfolk recovered to win two out of three against Richmond, one when Bender muffed an easy fly. The Tars then traded wins with the Suffolk Rubes, when Buddy Culloton pitched 15 innings to win, 2–1, with "Uncle Ichabod," an occasional sports columnist in Portsmouth, describing the "troubled Tars" as "wallowing in sweet revenge" and wearing the "sublime robes of conquest."[9]

In early July, Portsmouth slipped by its archrival, 1–0, in 11 innings, but Norfolk rallied to take both ends of the July 4 double bill, 3–0 and 3–2. They also won the next encounter, 6–3, to end the first half of the season with 26 wins and 26 losses, just behind Portsmouth (26–25) for third. Petersburg (33–17) carried the first half, followed by surprising Suffolk (28–21). Richmond rated fifth some 11 games below .500, with the Builders placing dead last at 19–32.

Norfolk got away to a quick start in the second half, winning nine of its first twelve contests. Then the Tars dropped five of the next six to Richmond and Newport News, supposedly the two weakest teams. After flirting with .500, the Tars took advantage of an unusually dry, pleasant and sunny August to grab second place, just a game below Richmond, which had suddenly emerged as a contender. Newcomer Rion Mitchell, now leading the Norfolk staff, rarely tried to strike out rival hitters; rather he relied on his fielders. A reporter described him as a "smooth piece of machinery." Mitchell's mix of pitches won several low-scoring contests, but he could not pitch every game, even though he did win both games of a doubleheader on one occasion.[10]

In the middle of July, Bender stopped the "flying Tars," 3–2, in the opener of the series, but Mitchell responded by besting Richmond, 6–0, in the next game. Norfolk then split the next two with the capital club, and looked like it could hold its own against its chief competition for league honors. Again, however, it faded back to about .500, though the league was so competitive that only two games separated first and last place.

In August, Bender beat Portsmouth, 1–0, but then lost to the Tars 5–2, only his second defeat in nineteen decisions. Norfolk still stood at .500, but Richmond had won two more than it lost. Bender then pitched his club to two victories in a doubleheader at Newport News. In the ensuing crucial series, he beat the Tars and Mitchell in Norfolk, 3–0, before some 2,600. One reporter expressed relief that someone else would pitch the next day to give the home club a chance. But Bender pitched that game too and bested Norfolk's other reliable pitcher, Culloton. Finally the Tars won the high-scoring finale without Bender on the mound, but by that point Norfolk's chances of taking the second half of the season were rapidly diminishing. Norfolk and Portsmouth split their traditional Labor Day engagements, with Portsmouth prevailing in the morning in 13 innings, and Mitchell in the afternoon, 4–0.

Behind Bender's amazing season's 29–2 record, Richmond won almost all its games down the home stretch to finish with a record of 40–19, compared to 33–27 for runner-up Norfolk. Portsmouth, Petersburg, Newport News and Suffolk followed in that order. Had the two half-seasons been combined, Petersburg had the best mark at 61–49, with Richmond (60–50), Portsmouth (57–51), Norfolk (59–53), Suffolk (50–58) and Newport News (43–68) trailing, with but three or four games separating the first four teams.

After Norfolk player/manager Bill Schwartz suffered a late-season injury when his spikes caught the third-base bag during a slide, Win Clark, the Director of Athletics at the Naval Base, arranged a benefit game for him between the Base and Air Station. Reporter Tom Jones took the occasion to reassess the player/manager and the season, based to some extent on the comments of the secretary of the Norfolk club, Perry Ruth. After a phase of disposing of several players and sustaining the loss of Harry Kane due to a broken leg, Schwartz got the club moving in the right direction. Even after that, many fans expressed discontent about him for his constant apparent bawling out of the youngsters on the field, but Ruth explained that Schwartz constantly coached to get the best from his people.

Most player discontent disappeared when pitcher Claude Edney departed the team. Before heading to Louisville, shortstop Ballinger told Ruth that he and some other players did not understand Schwartz's methods in getting everyone to work for the team until late in the season. Schwartz demanded a lot, but also gave much, apparently not knowing what the word "quit" meant. Before one of the Richmond games, he had a boil on his left arm lanced. His right arm, hit by a pitch, swelled, but he still played on Labor Day, with two bum arms. He previously played for a week with skin scraped off his left leg, opening himself to blood poisoning. As he recuperated at the Lorraine Hotel from one injury, appreciative fans sent him books and flowers.[11]

In an earlier article, Jones had contended that Schwartz endured all sorts of hard luck and had started the season with only two really good players—Ballinger and Culloton. He found Rion Mitchell and several other capable men as the season progressed. As manager, he had capitalized on the squeeze play to win games, and devised techniques to stop rivals from using double steals.

Not mentioned by Jones but implicit in game accounts from Norfolk and elsewhere was the lack of objectionable behavior by Norfolk players. In the first part of the season, Schwartz persisted in arguing with umpires until Ruth advised him to make his complaint known and then let the matter rest. Eventually the entire team must have followed that advice, because the club experienced fewer ejections and fines than usual. Even the fans modified their usual unruliness.

Such was not the case in Portsmouth, Petersburg or possibly Suffolk. Drunken Portsmouth fans behaved so badly against visiting Suffolk that club management wrote a letter calling for a constant police presence. Even the residents of Suffolk occasionally felt put upon by league umpires in their home park. Despite its small population and sometimes borderline questionable behavior, "the Peanut Capital" came through with sufficient spirit and attendance that the club apparently ended up in the black.

In Norfolk, Schwartz's efforts kept people coming to the park. As a result, the club appeared to have made money. Jones based this assertion on the fact that the War Camp Community Service received $3,000 from the club, based on the agreed-to 25 percent of the receipts at the ballpark. That meant that the club took in at least $12,000, which was certainly more than enough to pay visiting clubs, players' salaries and incidentals. They also likely received some money from the sale of Ballinger to Louisville and outfielder Frank Welsh to the Philadelphia Athletics. The returns also gave the War Camp folks a net of $600, because they only paid the owners of the park $2,400.[12]

Norfolk led the league in hitting with a .249 average, compared to .243 for Suffolk and .239 for Portsmouth. Shortstop/pitcher Ballinger, having returned from war service, hit .325 for the season to lead the league. Although Ballinger needed some "finishing touches," he was "a free, hard swinging batsman with good eyes, and every qualification to become a great hitter." In the field he exhibited quickness, poise and accuracy in his throws, traits that might well put him in the majors. One scout rated him as "the likeliest player he had looked over in minor company."

Hal "Bud" Leathers, the third baseman, led the league in scoring runs. Outfielder Frank Welsh and George Champagne, who started out with Portsmouth, hit over .300 for the Tars. However, Welsh left the team in August, claiming he had to tend to a sick wife in Alabama. The next year it was revealed that Welsh really wanted better pay, so he played for a team near Birmingham which, with extracurricular sources of income, paid him considerably more than Norfolk. The local press expressed the opinion that the loss of Welsh had severely reduced Norfolk's chances of winning the flag. Norfolk had two creditable pitchers, Culloton (15–11) and Mitchell (14–8), although Edney occasionally won. Mitchell had an astoundingly good earned run average — an all-time league-leading 1.09. He also hit around .300.[13]

Richmond did not need much hitting because it had Bender, who went to the New England League the next season. In well over 300 innings, he walked but 22. Years later, folks recalled the "wiley old Indian" deriving "great delight in playing in Norfolk," especially when he faced Tar manager Bill Schwartz. "Time and again Bender would toss Schwartz three balls and then follow with three straight strikes." Such baiting "angered Schwartz, but pleased Bender!"[14]

First-half winner Petersburg should have played Richmond for the title, but when Petersburg management said it would not share postseason gate receipts with the players, they went on strike, thereby aping what many others were doing across the American economy. Ben Wilson, the primary owner of the Richmond club, further complicated negotiations when he demanded that he be able to keep a larger share of his home game receipts.

Tom Jones, the sports editor of the afternoon daily, wrote an article that included comments about the postseason situation from old Ted Sullivan. The old baseball promoter decried the role of "commercialism" behind the decision not to have Virginia League playoffs that year. "Mental sparrows" had replaced eagles among league officials, he thought. The president of the association, according to Sullivan, should have forced the teams to play, or resigned if they failed to do so. Baseball, he intoned, was a sport, not a business. Sullivan, who helped found the Virginia League in 1894 and also took credit for its revival in 1906, praised the major leagues for having found the solution for insuring a proper World Series. Sharing a portion of the gate receipts of the World Series gave the players some financial incentive, but also kept commercialism under control. (Of course, the World Series that year featured the Chicago "Black Sox," making one wonder about the success of the major-league plan.) Jones considered Sullivan a "foster father" of baseball, being exceeded in influence on the national game only by Henry Chadwick, the Englishman who had written extensively on the origins of baseball and its condition during various stages of its early development.[15]

In the fall and winter of 1919–1920, Norfolk and environs experienced drought conditions, continued high prices, striking workers, a possible return of the Spanish flu, assorted other disasters and a much-needed religious revival, led in this case by Billy Sunday, the former major leaguer. When he first appeared at the special tabernacle a couple of blocks from League Park, he prayed for rain. Eventually it started to rain; then it poured. Finally a huge nor'easter swept up the coast, causing a blizzard at sea, sinking ships and sending torrents of rain into the hastily constructed tabernacle, soaking those who came to hear Billy preach against rum (now made illegal by the 19th Amendment) and other sinful things. Sunday then prayed for dry weather as well as a similar condition regarding alcohol, and the storm finally stopped.

The 1920 season brought the good ship Mary Jane into a new era for the city, state, and

9. Stormy Seas, 1919–1923 153

nation—once they cleared the wreckage of a major recession. The "Roaring Twenties" eventually became known for prosperity, Fords, flasks, flivvers (small, inexpensive autos), fads, college football and a phenomenon known as the "live ball" era. A baseball manufacturer, noting the upsurge in hitting, said it could not be attributed to any changes in the balls, as they were the same as before. Some question remains about when Organized Baseball turned to the cork (as opposed to the rubber) core, but few can doubt that hitting averages went up along with earned-run averages. Most importantly, baseball banned the spitball, save for those who already made a living using the technique. Babe Ruth earned his reputation as the "Sultan of Swat" as the New York Yankees won three World Series.

During this new era, the record of the Crew of the Mary Jane proved modest, with nary a pennant, but the Tars also never occupied the cellar. While Tar fans had little to roar about at League Park, at least they had to limit their complaints as the team came ashore with several second- and third-place finishes.

Raising the Anchor for a New Decade (1920)

Near the end of March, the men of the Mary Jane said "Aye, Aye, Sir" as Schwartz "pipes Crew to Training Deck for Long Grind." They came on board to get ready for the season's voyage, as "Skipper Bill Schwartz Drops Anchor in Tarville Harbor." That day a cartoon by

This cartoon by Herman Thomas in the *Virginian-Pilot* on March 28, 1920, shows Norfolk manager Bill Schwartz sailing the Mary Jane in choppy waters as the season approached. Thomas, probably without meaning to, captured the attitude of the American people as they coped with an uncertain post–World War I economy (*Virginian-Pilot* and Norfolk Public Library).

Herman Thomas appeared in *The Virginian-Pilot* depicting a tiny sailing craft called the "good ship Mary Jane," with a sailor contending with waves with labels "Petersburg," "Richmond," etc nearly lapping into the tiny craft. The cartoon carried the title "His Bearings Correct, but Voyage Stormy." A question mark appeared just over the head of the sweating skipper, who had an expression of puzzlement or downright bewilderment. The cartoonist probably did not intend to have manager Schwartz represent Americans as they faced a most puzzling future, but the image presented seemed especially apt.[16]

At the time of the postwar crisis, the nation entered its most difficult phase with the economy either perched on a high wave about to crash on a sandy shore or in a small craft about to be overcome by a surging sea. Prices fell and workers lost jobs in droves. It would take several years for the economy to adjust itself. Warren Harding, the Republican standard-bearer, won the presidency by calling for "Normalcy." Schwartz had no similar slogan and would not survive even into the summer, at least as helmsman of the Tars.

After some dull preliminary contests, among which was a loss to Clark's Naval Base nine, the Tars took a 5–0 victory at Portsmouth before 5,000, lefty "Lou" Stanley getting credit for the win. This was the same Stanley who had pitched for the Crew in 1906. Known as "Buck" in some circles, he had a brief fling with the Philadelphia Phillies in 1911 but had bounced around the minors until returning to Norfolk.

Management in Norfolk's sister city had added 50 feet to the distance from home plate to the shortest points in both right and left field; now a ball had to carry at least 283 feet and 332 feet for a home run in left and right fields, respectively. The Truckers recovered to take the home opener at Norfolk before a mere 1,500. In the next encounter, Portsmouth prevailed, 15–4, in front of 3,000 and exhibited indications that it might be a force to be reckoned with that season. When Norfolk lost, 11–8, to Suffolk, a Portsmouth reporter, noting that the "cats tore big holes in the sides of the Mary Jane," predicted the Tars would have trouble surviving even in "shoal water."

Despite the dire predictions, Norfolk did tolerably well, going 14–7 and winning six straight at one point. Stanley won ten straight early in the season and George Terhune captured a few. Rion Mitchell, while quite erratic and only occasionally displaying the talents of the previous year, won about as many as he lost. Arthur "Bunny" Corcoran, who played professional football in the fall for Canton, Ohio, in a forerunner circuit to the National Football League, led in fielding and wrestling with opponents.

A little over a month into the season, the record stood at 18–10, good for a distant second place behind Richmond. But Norfolk lost its manager when either the club or the league suspended skipper Schwartz for arguing with an umpire at Suffolk. Schwartz resigned and then secured the managerial job with the Newport News Shipbuilders. Catcher Bill Bribeck temporarily took over, not only managing but also hitting at a .368 clip. With lefty Lou Stanley winning a 16-inning game in which he pitched the distance, and with Terhune beating the Builders in a contest, the Tars looked solid, but they would have been stronger had they not let George Champagne go the Builders, where he ended up hitting .350.

On Memorial Day, the Tars and Truckers battled in the traditional morning/afternoon double bill. An umpire ejected Bribeck, who took issue with a decision, eventually forcing the police to intervene. The two teams split, with the Tars winning in the morning at Portsmouth, when Terhune tossed a shutout. The next day, Stanley stuck around for a 10–9 win. At this time, Norfolk's record of 23–15 was only good enough for third.

In June, Norfolk experienced a turn of fortunes—on the negative side. When Suffolk beat the Tars, 3–2, on June 11, they suffered their fifth straight loss and Stanley absorbed his first defeat of the season. With Bribeck losing his touch as a manager, the club signed former Boston Red Sox star Heinie Wagner as the new skipper in the middle of June. Wagner considered finding a new pitcher after the Truckers overwhelmed Terhune with three homers in a contest at Portsmouth, but the Tars recovered with "Wagner at the helm" the next day as Stanley won, 3–0. They won the following day as well and had a nice little streak going for a week or so in June, but overall the team played just below .500 through early July.

In an early July column, "Over the Pan for Fans," Sam Potts praised southpaw Terhune for regaining his form in besting the Truckers. "He had the hooks, good control to find the corners and kept his old buzz wheel working in the pinches to pull out of the holes." Skipper Wagner had a good day hitting against the Truckers, "his first flashy showing on the offensive [he had a single and a double] side of the game since joining the club as leader."[17]

The Truckers had some capable players, including Pie Traynor, who was batting .288 and playing shortstop brilliantly. After the season, Traynor commenced a long major-league career with the Pittsburgh Pirates. When Traynor went 4-for-5 in a Portsmouth win over Newport News, Potts pointed out that he demonstrated "a steady improvement in his work, displaying remarkable headwork for a youngster and a whip that is the envy of all the players." Not only did he field cleanly, he was also quick. Potts considered him "the class of the league in defensive work." Moreover, he was "developing into a hard and timely hitter." A few days later, Pott praised Traynor's running prowess as he scored in the ninth inning on a short fly ball just behind first base when "the shortstop hooked into the plate under the delayed throw with the winning run."[18]

Portsmouth also had Lester Bangs, who played third base before Eddie Goosetree's recovery from an injury. Bangs then switched to center field, where the diminutive, speedy youngster excelled. For several seasons, the New Englander had been trying to play professional baseball, but each time a family emergency or accident prevented him from fulfilling his ambitions. In 1919, he headed to Portsmouth, only to have the ship he was on rammed as it entered between the Capes. Thus he missed that season and subsequently became known as "Shipwreck" Bangs. It seems a pity that he did not sign on with the Tars, as they not only could have used his fleet-footedness on the basepaths and in the field, but also it would have been quite appropriate to have

After playing for the Portsmouth Truckers in 1920, shortstop Harold "Pie" Traynor enjoyed a 19-year career with the Pittsburgh Pirates as player and later as manager. A brilliant fielder for Portsmouth, he continued to receive high marks in the field in his major league career; he also maintained a lifetime batting average of .320 (National Baseball Hall of Fame Library, Cooperstown, New York).

someone named "Shipwreck" as a member of the Crew of the Mary Jane. Although his career in the Virginia League never made him a Tar, he nonetheless eventually moved to Norfolk, where his son later became a multi-sports star at Maury High School.[19]

Suffolk and Newport News were also not without talent. Gabby Street managed and occasionally caught for the Bears (Wildcats). He had major league experience and would eventually go on to manage the St. Louis Cardinals to a couple of pennants. As of late June, he was hitting .286 for his team.[20]

Over on the north side of the Roads, Builders' management under G.S. Barnes started out with boilermaker Joe Wall (a member of Local No. 24 in Brooklyn) as manager. During the Great War, he managed a team in Brooklyn, after spending some time in the majors with the Dodgers, Giants and Braves. Wall put out a call for the "Shipbuilder Clan" in March. He hoped to strike a deal with Clark Griffith for an extra catcher and an outfielder.[21]

In the first game the Suffolk "Sirens" outwalloped "Walls Wallopers," 12–7, before 4,000. Before the game, "Connie Mack," garbed in an evening dress suit of blue denim and a hickory hat (he liked tall hats) led a parade. Before leaving in the fourth inning with an injury, veteran Taylor "Deacon" Joliff gave up far too many hits for the home team to have a chance to win.

Suffolk then took Newport News several more times, one being a 17–6 thrashing at Suffolk's Peanut Park. Such debacles compelled Barnes to fire Wall and hire Bill Schwartz, who had just been released by the Tars. Lefty Cy Fried settled down, and Newport News became somewhat competitive. Fried ended up the season with 11 wins and 10 losses, while Bill Morgan and Bill Coggins came in at 16–10 and 13–8 respectively. The club, however, ended the first half of the season well back in the standings.[22]

Most of what the Tars, Truckers, Builders, Wildcats (Bears or Sirens) and three other teams did in the so-called Virginia League went for naught, because Richmond's mid-point record of 43–14 was good for a commanding lead. Only the Rocky Mount Down Homers and the Petersburg Nuts were above .500—but barely so. At 24–25, Portsmouth proved a bit better than Norfolk's 29–31. Newport News and Suffolk were fighting it out for sixth place. The Wilson Bugs brought up the rear, losing two for every win, despite having former Builder "Rasty" Walters, who led the league with a phenomenal .435. With the Virginia League now having two teams from the Tar Heel state, the Carolinians asked the league to change its name, but the Virginians ignored the request.[23]

The Tars started the second half by losing two to the Truckers, with Stanley absorbing one of the defeats. This doubleheader would prove a good omen for the Truckers, despite a Tars' win the next day with Terhune on the mound. A few days later, Stanley lost again, this time to Petersburg, as the Truckers took Richmond in a 14-inning encounter at the capital city. The Tars, however, recovered to take the next two from the Petersburg Nuts, with Buddy Culloton the winning pitcher in one and Homer Summa showing great speed and ability in the outfield. Toward the end of July, he was hitting at an astounding .407. Shortstop Bunny Corcoran returned and hit a solid .282 at the end of July.

In the middle of July, the Tars signed Jack Warhop, "the famous Indian hurler," who years before pitched for the New York Yankees. Warhop, a close friend of manager Wagner, was ready to help the club immediately. Wagner also acquired a new experienced catcher and several other new players. The "rejuvenated crew of the Mary Jane," returning to Norfolk for a home series, would certainly rise in the standings, or so the press hoped. At this point Summa, Kraemer and Bribeck were all hitting between .320 and .335 for Norfolk, while Traynor raised his average to .327 for Portsmouth.[24]

In the last half of July, Culloton posted three wins by pitching 27 scoreless innings and followed that feat with another win. Warhop did well too, although he only won five of eight decisions before becoming ill and returning to New York to recuperate.

In early August, Portsmouth led in the second-half standings at 16–10, one game above Richmond and two and a half games above Norfolk. A series of losses in Richmond brought out the charge that the Tars enjoyed too much "night life" in the capital. Potts thought the complaint should be investigated, but no additional information surfaced. When Norfolk lost to a second-division team, Potts, mixing metaphors with abandon, opined that the Tars were on "some tough road. There must have been numerous ruts, mud holes and sharp turns when Jack Warhop, Buddy Culloton and Old Man Stanley fail to hurl the Mary Jane into the harbor of game won. Ain't it awful?"[25]

A week into August, the Tars absorbed a doubleheader loss against the Truckers, as the latter increased their league lead. Culloton lost one of the games in thirteen innings before the largest crowd of the season, with no seats unfilled. About the same time the Pittsburgh Pirates promised to pay Portsmouth for the future services of Pie Traynor, even though his hitting had slumped.

Later on, the Tars took a doubleheader from the Richmond Colts with right-hander Bill Schmidt and lefty Stanley receiving credit for the victories, both shutouts. But against the Nuts about a week later, Linwood T. (Lin) Smith, probably a local lad, lost both ends of a twin bill, 3–2 and 1–0. Smith even hit a home run in the first game.[26]

Although sometimes described in the press as the "Wrecking Crew of the Mary Jane," Norfolk's .250 average ended up in the middle of the pack. Overall, batting averages were not as low as in the depths of the Dead Ball Era, but the Tars lacked heavy firepower. Norfolk's top hitter that year turned out to be Homer "Sat" Summa, at .351, but he played only part of the season, and had but one home run and very few runs batted in. Outfielders Henry "Rusty" Henges and Frank Simmons (another late acquisition, from Newport News), batted in the .260s or .270s and hit a homer or two each, but had few runs batted in. Catcher Bill Bribeck finally ended up at .286, with five homers and 60 runs batted in to lead the club in at least one crucial category. Infielders Hal Leathers at .237, second baseman Bill Wagner at .251 and third baseman Bunny Corcoran at .255 also had so-so seasons.

Pitching provided more of a plus. Despite weak hitting on his behalf, Stanley came through with 18 wins against 14 losses, Bernard Culloton stood at 12 and 9, George Terhune took 9 of 18 decisions and Jack Warhop won 5 and lost 3. Rion Mitchell (4 wins and 3 losses) incurred some sort of sickness sometime after the start of the season, went under a doctor's care at team expense, and then went home to go into business with his brother.

Portsmouth won the second half of the season with a record of 39–19, three games better than Petersburg. The Mary Jane came back to its harbor in fourth place at 28–30, almost an exact duplicate of its performance in the first half. Newport News fell well back at 25–34.

The Builders started off the second half of the season winning enough to give them first place — temporarily. Fans were willing to "let bygones be bygones" as their team pushed for the pennant. They attributed the poor showing in the first half to bad luck. One writer thought Schwartz was "doing splendidly and even though he does not hit the old pill as often as he ought to it is certain that by knocking him will not benefit the team at all."[27]

Bad luck must have surfaced again as the Builders dropped in the standings. Despite the humorous efforts of a sports columnist who went by "Office Boy" to have imaginary conversations with owner Barnes and manager Schwartz, resentment rose among fandom. Barnes was practically forced to fire Schwartz, replacing him with catcher Harry Lake. It didn't much matter. The Bears beat the Builders once when Gabby Street won a game by cleverly hitting the fourth pitch of an intentional walk. That defeat typified the season. Once Newport News slipped below .500 it plunged even further into mediocrity.[28]

Portsmouth clearly had superior hitting, pitching and probably fielding. Although Traynor's overall average fell off some, he had one game when he hit two home runs and his fielding continued to be impeccable. (The next year found him a Pirate farmhand in Birmingham burning up the Southern Association in all categories.)

Portsmouth also had Jimmy Viox, the club player/manager at .365 at one point, but he ended up at .298, while center fielder "Shipwreck" Bangs hit .267, right fielder Ben Mallonee hit .270 and second baseman Al Watt hit .301. Others included Ed Goosetree at .251 and first baseman Frank Rooney at .287.

Pitching strength lay with Pat McGloughlin at 22–8 with 32 complete games and 334 innings to his credit. Larry "Rube" Benton posted a 13–10 mark, lefty Sam Post, a local favorite, came in at 14–10. Pat Crockett won 9 of 14 decisions, and Frank (Ed) Fromholtz broke even in 18 decisions.

Playing solid ball, the Truckers not only captured the second-half flag but also beat the Richmond Colts in the seven-game league championship playoffs. The initial game, which ended in a tie, drew some 7,500 fans to the park in Portsmouth. Richmond then won on its home field, and the two teams traded wins at home until Portsmouth, playing without Traynor (who had been elevated at least temporarily to the Pirates in Pittsburgh), captured the finale in the Capital City. One of the Richmond wins came on the same day a bomb exploded in front of the stock exchange in New York, killing more than 30 people and injuring about 200. Baseball was a pleasant diversion for an America that continued to cope with a dangerous postwar world.[29]

A Scandalous Ending (1921)

In Richmond that winter, Jake Wells formed a new corporation and secured the franchise for the Capital City, which league officials had taken from Ben Wilson, who controlled the Colts' park on Boulevard Avenue. Wells moved quickly to construct a new park on Mayo's Island in the middle of the James River, about a five-minute walk from the business section of the city, compared to the 25-minute ride required to get to the old ball field. Wilson sued the league for $50,000, but he apparently did not gain much for his legal efforts.

In January, Jack Warhop promised that the Tars would be on their toes when the 1921 season started. The newspaper in Newport News described the "brave skipper" as a "diminutive Indian who pitched winning baseball [for] seven years" in the majors. Manager Warhop started the process of signing on old and new players, as Sam Potts warmed up his typewriter to prepare to comment on developments. Principal owner C. Moran Barry was determined to bring home a winner. April came and so did the potential players, along with an old picture in the newspaper depicting the 1896 Crew of the Mary Jane.[30]

Skipper Jack piped some twenty hands in the fo'castle at the start of training. Warhop soon released at least seven, but brought in several more under contract or just for tryouts, then dismissed thirteen. A Norfolk fan who ran into Buddy Culloton in Washington D.C., where the athlete was playing basketball, reported that Buddy planned to come back to Norfolk. But he was not among those who signed contracts. Occasional references during the season strongly suggest that Culloton was pitching for Fordham College late in the spring.

Bunny Corcoran also held out, as did Rion Mitchell. Management, feeling that Mitchell's high salary of the previous season had not been warranted, refused to negotiate. Although hundreds of fans greatly admired the pitcher for his remarkable performance in 1919 and also wanted Culloton to return, the press agreed with Warhop and company policy of not sending holdouts money for transportation.

Potts praised this principle, but at the same time condoned Dave Robertson, who refused to report to spring training on the West Coast. Robertson said he was not holding out for money, but preferred to stay in Norfolk, probably because he had a sporting goods store there. He went through his own exercise regimen and on occasion joined Win Clark's Naval Station team along with big Norm Glockson, who ended up catching with Portsmouth. The Cubs traded Robertson to the Pirates after the start of the season. Meanwhile, at League Park, Norfolk management loaded on a foot or two of topsoil and seeded the infield for grass.

In Newport News in January, Barnes bought out Abe Horwitz's interest in the club, a decision that surprised few because Abe had not played a major role for some time. Actually, he sold Barnes the stadium and its fence but not the property itself. Barnes had to have major work performed on the bleachers and the stands, which were "considered unsafe." The grounds needed a hundred loads of dirt. Having arranged for all that, Barnes renamed the place Newport News Athletic Field (formerly Horwitz Park).

Harry Lake, considered by Potts to be the classiest catcher in the league, remained as manager and signed several players from the previous year. Lake spent the winter, appropriately enough given the name of the team, working in a Wilmington, Delaware shipyard.[31]

The new season started off much better for the Builders than the preceding one, as they registered a 6–3 verdict over Gabby Street's Suffolk club before some 5,000. But the team soon reverted to form, lost more than it won, and slowly sank in the standings. Catcher/manager Lake did his part by hitting over .300.

In Portsmouth, President Henry Percy Dawson offered season tickets at $25 for the stands and $30 for box seats. Dawson even played second base in an intra-squad game between the Regulars and the Yannigans (scrubs). Dawson was a Yannigan, and his or someone else's error(s) let the Regulars win. Later, in the regular season, Dawson substituted for one of the regular outfielders and made two hits. In the preseason the Truckers lost two of three games to the Newark Bears, but surprisingly swept the Baltimore Orioles in three games and by fairly wide margins. With the return of several players, except Traynor and Frank Rooney, the latter going AWOL for part of the season, they looked quite formidable.[32]

The Tars edged Toronto, 3–2, in one of the highlights of the preliminaries at League Park after struggling against two local amateur or semi-professional clubs. The press attributed one 9–8 loss to Warhop's argument with an umpire who walked off the field with the Tars at bat in the last of the ninth. Even before the start of the season, many fans believed the aggregation had at least two gaping holes in its defense. Partially as a result of not pursuing holdouts more vigorously, the Tars once again ended up with a lot of "young blood," a fact highlighted in several cartoons that showed up in the April newspapers. On the positive side, the popular "Rusty" Henges looked good at third. "Rabbit" Yoter (spelled Yoder for some time), a youngster from the shipyard leagues in New York City, lived up to his name at shortstop, but the other side of the infield seemed weak.

For the outfield, Joe Kelly, a farmhand from the New York Yankees, exhibited hustle and speed to go along with some power. Ed Burke, a "game youngster," could play both infield and/or outfield. In the absence of Culloton, fans could only hope that Lou Stanley, manager Warhop and possibly Terhune would have good years. They also held out hope that one of the new prospects would have what it took to win at "B" level baseball.

When the league season started, the Tars came up on the short end of a 9–6 score at Portsmouth before 5,600, one of the largest crowds ever in that city. The Portsmouth reporter compared the Tars to Napoleon at Waterloo or the Yankees at Bull Run. Too bad he failed to use the Germans at Jutland or some other naval disaster to describe what happened to the Crew in that first game. That game took place after the Tars surrendered to the Truckers on their own home field, 7–6. In the next contest, Norfolk pummeled the defending league champions, 17–4.

The relatively inexperienced Tars soon ran into trouble with the Wildcats and the Builders, and fell below .500. Warhop came through with a shutout against the league-leading Nuts on May 21, but at mid–May the Tars stood last in the league with a record of 7–14, just the opposite of the previous year. James Kelley and Alexander Peterson joined the pitching staff, Kelley soon departed after more bad than good outings, but "Pete" Peterson stuck. Peterson pitched a three-hitter to shut out Portsmouth in one of his first starts around the middle of June, but the Truckers overpowered Charles "Iron Man" Eckert the next day, 9–6. Connie Mack of the Philadelphia A's had sent Eckert, who pitched for the Suffolk Cats the previous two seasons, for more seasoning.

Overall, the situation looked less than positive. A cartoonist depicted a Tars player sitting chained to a large ball in a cellar with a black cat called "Jinx" sitting on the stairs. Warhop continued to plug the holes in his leaky craft by disposing of slick-fielding first baseman Bob Kelley, who proved to be a totally ineffective batsman. The club replaced him with G. Kelly (the fourth Kelly or Kelley to play that year), who proved equally ineffective.

The manager secured Elmer Bowman to play outfield, but finally used him at the first sack. That left a hole in the outfield, which Warhop tried to cover with players released from Newport News and Petersburg. When neither proved up to the task, the Norfolk club then acquired John Vermilyea, a hard-hitting third baseman from Petersburg. That allowed Warhop to move Henges back to the outfield, but Rusty ended up with another league team. Later, Norfolk acquired Tom (sometimes called Sam) Daughton to replace Henges in left field. The Tars also signed Howard Burkett to cover second base. He didn't even hit his weight for a few games, but Potts urged the club to keep him because he possessed great range and good hands and seemed to have a "good eye." Potts proved to be prescient, for Burkett soon caught up with the pitchers. This acquisition permitted the local lad, Jack Kroger, shaky at best on second, to become a utility man.

For a time, the club used "Dusty" Rhodes, another product of Norfolk's sandlots, to roam the outfield. Early in the season, when two catchers proved inadequate, Norfolk brought on Fred Leahy. On the pitching side, Norfolk came up with southpaw Jim Garton, which gave the club four creditable starters. Management released Terhune.

After losing almost two games for every one they won, the Tars began to improve, encouraging cartoonist Herman Thomas to turn the Mary Jane into an auto, driven by a happy Tar, knocking Richmond and Wilson out of the way, singing "Merrily We Roll Along, Roll Along, Roll Along." A few days later, after some defeats, Thomas turned the Tars into an acrobat, carrying a pole on a high wire and being dragged to one side by a weight in the form of too many loses. But when the record improved and the club pulled out of the cellar, the Tars became a barber, who recently clipped Rocky Mount and planned on doing the same to Petersburg, fearfully waiting its turn.[33]

After hoisting their 1920 pennant, the Truckers did better than the Tars in the early going, holding second for a time. But by mid–June, even the Truckers had fallen below .500. They called on Harry Hartsell, the old Tar and now a collegiate coach, to canvas the South for new talent. New pitchers Ed Lennon and "Slats" Ledbetter did well at times, but all of Hampton Roads seemed destined to come up short in the 1921 race.

Around that time, although the Tars beat the Builders twice, their record fell ten games below .500. As June came to a close, Portsmouth suddenly surged and edged closer to first with Rocky Mount and Wilson. The North Carolina entries both stood 38–25 on the last day of the first half, with Rocky Mount later granted first place. Norfolk remained tied for sixth with Suffolk at 26–36, about one game ahead of last-place Newport News, as the first half came to a close. Portsmouth placed third with a record of 34–28.

Statistics for the first part of the season showed that Elmer Bowman, at .363, had the best average for the Tars and was third among the Virginia League regulars. Catcher Fred Leahy carried the next best average (nearly .350) and part-timer Kroger did surprisingly well at about .325. Kelly, Vermilyea and Burke all hit in the low 300s, with Yoter (Yoder) at .290. The diminutive shortstop started off hitting .354 and stole 28 bases in about the same number of games. Burke acquired quite a reputation as an unusually tough competitor. In preseason, when he somehow dislocated a bone while standing on deck preparing to hit, he allowed his fellow players to move his bone back into place without so much as a whimper and immediately took his turn at the plate. Warhop, in addition to pitching, also played in the field about half the time and hit around .250. In the power department, both Bowman and Kelly each had six home runs and twelve doubles. These numbers reflect the general increase in run production around the Virginia League and throughout professional baseball.

Portsmouth also had some offense, with catcher Norm Glockson walloping the ball at a .350 clip and hitting nine round-trippers. Jim Viox had a slightly higher average but only three homers. Henry Mallonee reported in at about .310 and five home runs. Goosetree also came in above .300. Other Portsmouth players fell well below that level, leaving one with the impression that the Crew had the advantage with the bat, but Portsmouth's defense was superior.

As for the pitchers, Jim Garton, a left-hander who joined Norfolk after the start of the season, had the best won/lost record at 6–4. Eckert won 8 of 15 decisions, while Peterson won seven, the same number as he lost. Warhop appeared to be struggling at 5–7, while several pitchers were released after losing a game or two. Manager Warhop had the best runs-allowed ratio on the staff, with Garton second.

At the outset of the second half of the season, the Truckers and Tars divided their traditional twin bill on July 4 in low-scoring contests. The Tars then took two straight from their sister-city rivals, a result that boded a possible better performance in the second season. Tar pitching yielded but four runs in the four games. After losing a couple to the Builders, Norfolk won five straight and looked like a different team. The Mary Jane sailed at a pretty fair rate, despite one squall when a Rocky Mount pitcher threw a no-hitter at them. After losing to the Wilson Bugs, they took the next two from the same team. Later in the month, they edged Portsmouth 8–7, with Warhop winning in relief. Warhop also gave the ship some extra sail with a 1–0 win over Portsmouth before 6,000, as the Tars held onto first place through much of July.

On the same early August Day that a Chicago jury acquitted those implicated in the Black Sox scandal, the Tars occupied first at 18–7. At that point, cartoonist Thomas drew Norfolk behind the wheel of a racing car. Then the cartoonist put the representative Tar on a bicycle, riding toward a glow in the distance labeled "1921 Pennant Hopes," under the title "Smooth Sailing From Now On."[34]

Portsmouth was performing so poorly that the local press called for an overhaul of the

"Trucker machine." Some pitchers had already been released. After a lopsided loss to the Colts on Mayo Island, *Star* sports editor Arthur Mackie opined that the team was "skating on thin ice" and riding that oft-used but inappropriate vehicle for writers about a summer sport, the "toboggan," on a downward course.

By this time, league officials had met, and planned to meet again, to try to resolve the propensity for some teams to exceed the salary cap. A few days later, league owners and representatives met at the Monticello Hotel, where officials from Rocky Mount and Wilson admitted that they were operating about $500 a month above the salary lid. The league officers then wrote to Secretary J.H. Farrell of the National Association for advice. Much to the dismay of the Portsmouth press, Norfolk voted with the 4–2 majority to give Rocky Mount the title as winner of the first half of the season, despite the lack of resolution about the matter of salaries. Only Portsmouth and Newport News voted in the negative. Wilson was not given an opportunity to finish a game shortened to seven innings that it had originally received credit for in the standings, thus forcing an extra game against Rocky Mount to determine the first-half winner.[35]

Mackie expressed the view that ever since the disclosure of the Black Sox scandal that marred the 1919 World Series, baseball fans kept a more watchful eye on possible signs of cheating. To Mackie, a new age had dawned, one in which "dishonesty in baseball would be obliterated." That dishonesty, to Mackie, included his opinion that the Virginia League constitution was a mere "scrap of paper." By giving Rocky Mount the first-half championship, Wilson, Norfolk, Suffolk and Richmond had turned down a chance to make history, according to Mackie, who also praised Newport News and Portsmouth for sustaining the standard set by Judge Landis. He urged all Portsmouth fandom to rally for its team, both to help it win games and to reinforce its management's high ethical position.[36]

In response to a letter, the National Commission representative Mike Sexton made his way to Norfolk. After an ample meal and doubtless a good bit of cigar smoking, he decided to stay out of the affair, saying it was "family business." Mackie thought it likely that more than two teams broke the rules, thus forcing the teams to resolve the matter themselves. The only thing that could be done was to fine teams, up to $100 a day. Because no teams wanted to drive anyone out of business, fines were an unacceptable solution. The decision of Rocky Mount and Wilson to reduce salaries by 20 percent, approved by the players and attested to by affidavits, seemed to settle the question.[37]

Meanwhile the Tars, picking on hapless Petersburg (18–0 in one contest), looked impressive. But the Nuts were experiencing hard times, starting with a fire at their ballpark and spilling over onto the field. For a time, it looked like new owners might be able to rebuild with league help, but shortly thereafter, the franchise and most of the players went to Tarboro, North Carolina. There they became known as the Tar Babies, as opposed to the Rocky Mount Tar Heels. As such, they inherited a record of 4–22.

Once reorganized, Tarboro gave the Tars fits. In early August, the Tars had the league lead at 19–8, compared to Wilson's 18–10, but Norfolk lost to the Tar Babies, 8–0, and although Warhop came back the next day to post a win against the visitors, keeping Norfolk in first, the club lost two of three in its first visit to the North Carolina city. At that point the Tarboro record was 7–32. Indeed, the only team the Tar Babies beat immediately after their admission to the league was the Mary Jane. When the Tars fell back some, Thomas depicted the fans, standing on a pier and sending out three life preservers (new infield, new outfield and new pitching staff) to the Tars sinking in a pond.[38]

Those losses proved pivotal as Wilson forged ahead of the Tars, posting a 28–12 mark compared to Norfolk's 25–16 with about ten days left in August. At this point, the 1921 trip for the Tars seemed relatively uneventful — almost boring, save for the time Portsmouth police arrested thirteen players for disorderly conduct. They sat around headquarter in their wet uniforms until Frank Lawrence sent surety for them. Burkett, who instigated the dispute by cussing, paid $15 and the others came up with $40 each in bonds, presumably to cover future misdeeds.[39]

Portsmouth sent big Norm Glockson and money to Columbia of the Sally League for catcher Joe Casey. Glockson's hitting, both for average and power, had been trailing off since before midseason. With Casey, management had a solid hitter, but more importantly someone who could really handle pitchers. Ironically, on the day before the news appeared about the trade, Portsmouth police arrested Glockson for interfering in an argument over the arrest of a player from Wilson. The police court assessed Glockson a $5 fine for cursing. If the court ever received the money is unknown, for "Beef" had already left for his new home.[40]

With Casey in camp, Portsmouth markedly improved on its record then at about .500. With Casey's help and Goosetree's home run, "Smiling Rube" Benton upgraded his efforts, beating the Tars, 1–0. McGloughlin followed that with a 3–1 win over the Tars, giving Portsmouth the series, though Warhop brought his team victory in a rain-shortened five-inning affair in the third contest.

A series of victories prompted Earl Wright, the one-time president of the Truckers, to regale the public once again with one of his "poems," a take-off on "Casey at the Bat," which ended "Forget about old Casey, who crabbed poor Mudville's game/And give a cheer for his son Joe, who's winning back the name." Just before those lines, Wright described "a mighty clout that cleared the fence and rolled a country mile/All's happy here in Portsmouth, even old maids dance and smile."[41]

Norfolk's losses to Portsmouth, along with those to Tarboro, contributed to Norfolk's yielding first place to Wilson. They also reflected improved play by Portsmouth, which now moved up in the standings, passing the Tars by the first Sunday in September. When the Truckers swept the Tars that day, their record went to eleven above .500, with one more win and the same number of losses as Norfolk. Wilson ran well ahead, some twenty games above .500. Portsmouth continued the onslaught, pounding Peterson and reliever Eddie Johnson, 11–0, at Norfolk on Labor Day afternoon, while Norfolk slipped by the Truckers, 4–3, in the morning contest at Portsmouth. Another loss to Portsmouth the next day almost sealed Norfolk's fate for the season.

A few days later, Judge Kenesaw Mountain Landis, the Czar of Baseball, delivered an earthshaking edict relating to the complaint sent by Portsmouth management and half-heartedly supported by Norfolk. Based on what the owners from Wilson and Rocky Mount admitted to him, Landis decided that both teams had to forfeit almost all their wins in the first half of the season. Thus, third-place Portsmouth now retroactively had the best record for the first part of the season.

We will likely never know the truth about other clubs exceeding the salary limit. Perry Ruth with Norfolk admitted that his club paid Elmer Bowman $350 a month. This amount exceeded the $200 average players received, but Norfolk possibly offset this amount by paying some players a lot less than the average. Potts of the Norfolk press thought Rocky Mount had clearly violated the rule, but he was less certain about Wilson.

As the second part of the season came to an end, the Tars surged a bit, improving to 39–26, tied with Portsmouth for second but six games behind Wilson. The Tars then took at least two close battles after a lopsided win over the assumed frontrunners, bringing them to within two games of the top and pulling ahead of Portsmouth, which fumbled away a game against the Colts.

At this point, President Bradley, after initially saying he would not change anything in the second part of the season without the approval of league owners, decided that Landis's decision meant that thirteen Wilson wins, credited from the start of the second half of the season and running through July 24, should not be counted. Norfolk, relieved of one loss, assumed first at 42–25. Richmond ranked second, at 39–25, and Portsmouth third, at 40–26. Wilson fell to fourth at 31–23. On the day the paper presented these standings, the Tars added to their lead by disposing of Wilson at home, 2–1, with Warhop on the mound, to sweep the series against the Bugs.

It will never be known whether the Tars could have captured first place without the help of President Bradley. He later gave Wilson back a win against Norfolk, making the whole business quite confusing. Thereafter, the Crew split with Richmond and finally found a way to beat Tarboro, thus ending the second half at 46–27, two games up on Portsmouth and three games above the Colts in the win column. Ending right at .500, Wilson fell to fifth, and should Landis have changed his mind and given Wilson back all of its thirteen games as some people in North Carolina hoped, the Bugs would have had one more win than the Tars, but they also would have exceeded Norfolk's number of losses by five games. Wilson clearly suffered a mortal psychological blow, and lost many of its last games, particularly against archrival Rocky Mount.

The Newport News Builders did not do well in the second half of the season, falling to 17–31 near the end of August. At the end, Roy Stickradt (alias Foley) led the staff at 22–14, but the other pitchers — Carl Ray (before going to Portsmouth), Ken Heatwole and Clarence Phiffer, and reliever George Zinn — lost far more than they won. The Builders lost a lot of games in the late innings. Among the hitters, Harry Lake carried a respectable .320 average, infielder Ray Whitcraft did tolerably well, and outfielders Talbot Riggs and Charlie Allen hit over .300, but no one hit more than three home runs for the entire season.

After losing five straight, the Builders rebounded to sweep Rocky Mount, then the top club, at which time the local press begged fans to come out to support the team, even though the team had played badly all summer. With injuries threatening to end some players' careers, the reporter would not accept that situation as an excuse for not coming to the games. Visiting teams were only receiving an average of $23 in gate receipts for each appearance. If that trend continued, the team would have to go on the road to complete its schedule. Somehow, the Builders finished the season, but future play in Newport News seemed in jeopardy.

Fans in both Norfolk and Portsmouth were agog over the sudden change in the standings. As the "friendly enemies" prepared for combat to determine the pennant winner for 1921, the Norfolk press assessed the two teams, concluding that the Tars hit better but the Vioxmen were better fielders and pitchers. The Tars had won the season series over the Truckers. While both teams had plenty of hitters, the Tars averaged .291, almost twenty points higher than the Truckers. Yet the latter scored more runs, suggesting they had more power, better baserunning, or superior clutch hitting.

Among Norfolk's players, former Colt Tom Daughton, who joined the team well after the season's start, hit .328. John Kroger and Ed Burke, two other outfielders, both hit .298, with Kroger contributing two home runs and Burke six. Regular left fielder Joe Kelly blasted 17 home runs to lead the league to go along with a .306 average. In the infield, third baseman John Vermilyea hit .287 and shortstop Elmer "Rabbit" Yoter hit .314. Catchers Fred Leahy and Bob Fuhrman, who overcame an injury to his eye, reached .327 and .369, respectively.

Herman Thomas provided several cartoons for the *Virginian-Pilot* during the 1921 season, but only a few times did he use nautical metaphors. In this cartoon from August 14, he visualized the troubled Tars (Mary Janes) needing a major rescue effort, especially when first baseman Elmer Bowman experienced a slump (*Virginian-Pilot* and Norfolk Public Library).

Big Elmer "Babe" Bowman came in at .356, including an 18-game hitting streak, and Chap Marable, who replaced Yoter a few weeks before the end of the season, chipped in with a .354 average. Among pitchers, Jack Warhop received credit in one accounting for 20 wins against 7 losses, while Jim Garton stood at 17–13, Alex (John) Peterson at 18–16, Charles Eckert at 17–17 and Eddie Johnson at a lowly 11–17.

For Portsmouth, manager Jimmy Viox hit near .370 as right fielder and catcher Casey attained .364, while outfielder Henry B. "Lefty" Mallonee hit .341 and shortstop William Black .313. Pitchers McGloughlin and Ray excelled at the plate. On the mound, the Truckers had William Morris "Mac" McGloughlin, who won 26 and lost but 8. Ralph "Slats" Ledbetter won 12 of 18 decisions and Lawrence James "Larry" or "Smiling Rube" Benton sported a 17–16 record, according to a Portsmouth reporter. Late in the season lefty Carl Ray, a longtime nemesis for the Tars, became a Trucker.

The Portsmouth press was less impressed with the Tars, maintaining that only first baseman Bowman ranked better in hitting than his counterpart Trucker, who far surpassed him in the field. Otherwise, the city south of the Elizabeth had players at each position that were more than a match for those on the north side. It was like comparing a Chalmers, a high-priced automobile, to a "Lizzie" made by Henry Ford, one car-crazy reporter opined. The Portsmouth reporter may have had a valid point in giving his club an edge in talent, for the New York Giants had already purchased at least three Truckers—pitchers Benton and McGloughlin and shortstop Black—while Philadelphia had already paid for Mallonee. They even called him up, but returned him for the playoffs.[42]

Above and opposite: In illustrating a playoff loss against Portsmouth on October 1, cartoonist Thomas empathizes with pitcher Jack Warhop for his first defeat after 17 straight wins and criticizes the Tars for their lack of effort in the series. (*Virginian-Pilot* and Norfolk Public Library)

With the showdown earning front-page coverage, the Tars easily won the first encounter, 8–2, behind Warhop. The press described the winners as a "Vicious Wrecking Crew" supporting their "Skipper with Pep and Go" before 4,500 at home. Kelly slugged a home run over the right-field fence that supposedly struck the old Standard Oil building on the other side of Church Street. But in subsequent games the Crew lost their lust for destruction. After a tie game that went 10 innings before being terminated by rain, the Truckers took a crucial game at Norfolk, 7–4, knocking out Alex Peterson after just three innings. Peterson then lost 6–1 at Portsmouth to Rube Benton.

With poor field support but also walking several and hitting a batter, Warhop lost his first game after 17 straight wins, 3–0, at Norfolk. The day after this loss, cartoonist Herman Thomas portrayed a sailor on a half-submerged raft in the middle of a river, with a stick in his hand on which appeared a flag labeled "Indifference." A Trucker on shore yelled that one can't row "with an oar like that." On the bottom of a side tablet, the commentary concluded "Too Bad Jack, Too Bad." The Tars lost the finale, 13–4, seemingly giving up before the game even started.

By defeating Norfolk four straight, Portsmouth emerged with its second straight league title, much to the pleasure of its fans and press.[43] An angry Barry, convinced that the players

THE TRUCKERS BROKE WARHOP'S STRING OF VICTORIES BY YESTERDAY'S GAME, BUT IT CAN SAFELY BE SAID THAT THE FAULT WAS NOT HIS. CARELESS, INDIFFERENT BALL PLAYING BEHIND HIM WAS THE CAUSE. "TOO BAD JACK, TOO BAD."

had let down and being familiar with the recent Black Sox scandal, asked Commissioner Landis's office to investigate. Near the end of the series, a frenzied atmosphere swept across the city. Fans accosted players on the streets. Someone even burned down the right-field bleachers. Some fans claimed that the players were not at their usual spot on the corner of Tazewell and Granby at the time of the fire, inferring that they, resenting the club management, might have torched the park. Fans also understood that several players made reservations for travel tickets to leave right after the game in Portsmouth, when Norfolk trailed in the series, 3–1.

Nearly everyone knew the players were angry about Barry's decision not to share a higher proportion of the gate receipts. A great deal of confusion pervaded reports about player payments as the series progressed. Some fans thought the players would receive half of the gates receipts of the first four games, minus money paid out for the war tax (10 percent) and to the league (10 percent). But they would receive nothing for the next games in the series, the lion's share of those receipts going to the owners. Thus, they had no financial incentive to play any more than four games. Secretary-Treasurer Perry Ruth later claimed that the club, abiding by rules of the National Commission, paid $230 for the six games, with higher returns the longer the series went.

Someone in management blamed Warhop for not communicating the terms properly to the players, making it seem as if the ballclub would keep the bulk of the receipts. Warhop implored the men to play their best, but they simply laughed at him. Daughton, just 2-for-19 in the series, complained after teammates voted against giving him a full share. Marable, who played in only a few games, took his half share gratefully and graciously. The team batted only .218 compared to over .280 for Portsmouth. Discontent, if that was the determining factor in the series, went far beyond any one player.

The series was also marred by Percy Dawson's decision not to let newsmen covering the games have access to telephones and telegraphs. Portsmouth management believed that play-by-play reports reduced attendance. Facing this obstacle, Tom Hanes arranged for a phone right next to the grounds. Reporters shouted out what was transpiring on the field to a colleague outside the park, who then called the main office with the results of each play. In contrast, Barry and company in Norfolk allowed full coverage of the contests at League Park.

In February 1922, Dawson sold his interest in the Portsmouth club to Frank D. Lawrence and purchased the majority of shares in the club in Newport News.⁴⁴ Barry said he would soon sell most of his stock in the Norfolk club, ending any role in management. The next year he would come to the games, "sit in the stands, and enjoy myself. If the team is winning, I'll be glad, but if it loses I'll be just as sore as the most rabid fan in the park. But, thank goodness, nobody can blame me with it if the club is not a success because I am through." Ruth followed up that announcement by noting that, "dissatisfied with baseball for several years," and retaining his role in the organization simply to help out Barry, he would also be an "innocent bystander" the next season. The article quoting Barry and Ruth listed thirteen players, headed by Jack Warhop, who would not be returning to the club the next year. The great exodus would include virtually the entire team. Yoter had already been turned over to the Philadelphia A's before season's end.⁴⁵

Jack Warhop, pitcher and manager of the Norfolk Tars in 1921, played for the New York Yankees between 1908 and 1915, winning 69 and losing 91 and posting an earned run average of 3.09. Norfolk management blamed him for the lack of effort on the part of his club in the 1921 playoff series against Portsmouth (National Baseball Hall of Fame Library, Cooperstown, New York).

It turned out that management did reserve several Crewmen (Burke, Leahy, Marable, Rhodes, Peterson, Henges, Johnson, Vermilyea, Garton, Kroger and pitcher Musselman, obtained late in the season). The team sold Burkett to Birmingham for $1,750. Garton also seemed destined for greatness in the big time with the New York Giants. Sometime after the season, Warhop found out he could not keep his share of the sale of Burkett or Garton. Warhop complained to Landis about not receiving his 10 percent cut on the Burkett deal in a timely fashion. After reading documents on the subject and ascertaining the existence of a questionable deal, Landis rejected both the Burkett and Garton arrangements, thus giving the two men the choice of signing on with any professional team save the ones with which they had previous commitments. Thus Warhop, now the manager of the Columbia club in the Sally League, never did receive his cut. Nor were the Tars able to keep the men on their reserve list.

After the regular season, the people of Portsmouth tried to keep the season going by inviting some major leaguers who were not involved in the World Series between the New York Giants and the New York Yankees to come to Tidewater. The All-Stars arrived, minus their Cleveland contingent, and whipped the Truckers 9–5, but surprisingly lost against the same team in Norfolk, 14–7. Unfortunately, attendance was so weak in the community of the Tars that the big timers decided not to play any more games in the area. In North Carolina, Rocky Mount and Wilson played off what they and their fans considered the real championship of the Virginia League.

As the season was coming to an end, the owners of the Norfolk Baseball Association (C. Moran Barry, Perry W. Ruth and G. Serpell) made plans to build a new park, this one in the suburb of Villa Heights. They bought several lots from developers for $37,000 and then convinced the city council to eliminate two streets to give them enough room to erect their new facility, about a block east of Church Street, near where it met up with Granby Street and right next to the trolley line.

In October, residents of the area demanded that the council rescind its action. One woman, through her lawyer, complained that the closure of 29th Street meant she would have to wade at high tide to leave her neighborhood. The commonwealth attorney for the city agreed with the residents that council had no legal right to close the streets. Edward R. Willcox, one of the attorneys for the club, claimed the council had to abide by its original decision. The baseball magnates expressed willingness to drop their plans if the original owners of the property would return their payments in return for the land. Most of those who had sold the land refused the deal. Then the club said it would not fight rescission of the street closures if it received 65 percent of the original price. A little later some of those who said they would buy back the property changed their minds. Then the baseball moguls said they would be satisfied with 50 percent. At this juncture, Teddy Willcox thought the matter should go to court.

The press presented the matter as if the residents of Villa Heights were caught in the middle of two feuding factions, but clearly the residents demanded that council protect their interests. It is exceedingly doubtful that the ball team would have any luck taking either the residents or the former landowners to court. With feelings running high at the meeting, council stuck with rescinding the street closures. How much the baseball men ever retrieved from the deal is not clear, but no baseball park appeared in Villa Heights. This dispute doubtless encouraged Barry and Ruth to hasten their departure from club ownership and management. After leaving baseball ownership and management duties to his brother, J. Carmen Barry became an active stockholder in an auto speedway in Ocean View.[46]

In January 1922, R.A. Jones, R.A. Marshall, and James E. Barry acquired the club. For a time, it looked like the previous owners might sell to outsiders. Clark Griffith, it was rumored, hoped to make Norfolk a farm club, a possibility not well received in a local press that thought civic pride would make such a development impossible. Percy Dawson, then one of the owners of the Portsmouth club, said he would be happy to run the Tars. Local fans had a great deal of respect for Dawson and would likely have accepted this new role. But in the end, the Norfolk Baseball Corporation reorganized, with C.M. Barry and Ruth selling out to James Barry and other businessmen. The company then secured a new lease for League Park.[47]

Rebuilding the Park and the Crew (1922)

Over the winter, officials of the Virginia League got into a spat over electing a new president. At first, Lawrence seemed willing to drop his holdings in Portsmouth and assume the league leadership role, but the banker changed his mind and Portsmouth people backed Jesse Overton, the president of the local organization of retail merchants. Norfolk supported Teddy Willcox, a local lawyer and son of Judge Willcox. Two North Carolina franchises supported

Judge Bramham, president of the Piedmont League. Dawson, now at Newport News, and Lawrence from Portsmouth came out for Overton and hoped for a supporting vote from the Richmond delegation.

The Portsmouth press assumed that after casting its ballot for Norfolk's native son, Tar management would turn to Overton. According to one Portsmouth reporter, Willcox had no chance of winning since he was not known outside Norfolk. Exactly why Overton had a bigger reputation remains unknown. As the voting proceeded, the Norfolk delegates continued to support Willcox while the North Carolina cities turned to W.S. Moye, the current vice president of the league. Finally, Norfolk came out in favor of the Carolinian, and Richmond followed suit. The Portsmouth press attributed Norfolk's behavior to the famous "rivalry" between the Twin Cities and expressed bitterness about the outcome.[48]

In other actions, the league dropped the split-season format, the owners doubtless wary of any more playoffs, given what happened in two of the previous three years. Officials also supported Moye's proposal to ensure that every game had two umpires, at least one with considerable experience.

The Norfolk press wrote off the 1922 season before it started, particularly after learning that Garton would not return. One reporter suggested that those trying out for the team would likely produce the nucleus for a 1923 drive for the title. A bit belatedly, the new management came to terms with manager Win Clark, who ended his work as athletic director at the Navy Base. Clark had a reputation as a hard taskmaster and one who could develop young talent.

About 50 men tried out for the team, but the press hoped, unlike many previous clubs, that Clark's club could develop some stability as it matured. As it turned out, the club started training with a mix of returnees from the previous year, a few other old veterans, and several newcomers, some with prior experience. Left-handed pitchers included Lou Stanley and Zellers; right-handers John Carey, Alex L. (now known as "Old Pete") Peterson, Johnny Bates (a local who played on the Eastern Shore the previous summer), Arthur Johnson, and local lads Linwood Smith and John A. Jones. The Tars signed veteran lefty Bert Garden, who tossed for "Buck" Pressley at Roanoke nine years earlier, but he did not stay long. Norfolk then turned to another experienced southpaw, J.D. Bruner.

Fred Leahy, Thomas Leddy and local Gene Hudgins competed as catchers. In the infield, Abe Routman and Charles Tolson tried out for first, with the other three infield posts picked from Vermilyea, Marable, Kroger and newcomers George Carey, Bob Spencer, Izzy Bandrimer and Lawrence K. Gallagher, a promising shortstop. Burke competed for a backup role.

By early April, Clark was conducting regular drills, using the Naval Station gymnasium on rainy days. A cartoonist depicted several ballplayers exercising on the bowsprit, masts and spars of a two-masted ship labeled the "Mary Jane."[49]

The reorganized company renovated the ballpark by erecting new grandstands that held over 2,000, equipped with opera-style chairs and also adding to the bleachers in left field. The park now had an exit along 20th Street that gave fans easy access to a walkway that covered the "two squares (blocks)" back to Granby Street. Management also pushed back the left-field fence another ten feet closer to the railroad tracks, and raised its height to 18 feet, with three tiers of advertisements. They moved the entire field of play three feet farther away from the stands, thus giving more space for catching foul flies and also eliminating a curve in left field that allowed for fluke home runs hit directly down the line.

When workmen started to repair the right-field bleachers, they discovered that the

Charles Degges replaced Thomas for the 1922 season as cartoonist for the *Virginian-Pilot*. As the season approached, on April 2 he provided an interesting representation of the Mary Jane (a sloop), with the relatively inexperienced Tars engaged in exercises on the ship (*Virginian-Pilot* and Norfolk Public Library).

wooden supports were so rotted that they needed replacement. Management then called for a new and larger set of bleachers to be placed on anchors that allowed for easy moving in 32-foot sections toward center field, to prepare for football. Workers also doubled the height of the fence in right field. Teams would now have concrete dugouts, partially submerged so that fans in the stands could easily look over them onto the field of play. When all the changes were completed, the place could hold 8,000.

With a coating of dark green stain for the stands, storage sheds and other structures, and a good whitewashing elsewhere, the park no longer looked like an "eyesore." Clark, who supervised these changes, apologized because the field lacked the quality of grass he wanted, but he promised to work on that problem. The club also purchased the traditional two sets of uniforms, the home ones being white with blue trim, a solid blue hat, and stockings that were blue except for white near the ankle. Travel attire substituted gray for white.

As the Tars prepared for the season, four major league teams came to League Park in late March. Some 8,000 fans watched the "Mighty Mauler," Babe Ruth, take aim at the short fence in right field when the Yankees took on the Brooklyn "Robins" (aka Dodgers, named for manager Wilbert Robinson). Fans feared that Babe might threaten the very existence of the fence, but Ruth was mired in a slump and managed but a feeble pop up, a strikeout on three pitches, and a foul out in a 2–0 loss.

The New York Giants showed up the next day to beat the Chicago White Sox before a smaller crowd. In neither game did anyone seriously threaten to hit one over the short fence in right or the longer one in left, 320 feet away at its shortest point. Some of the major leaguers remarked that the park was the nicest they had seen coming north from spring training that year.

Although Ruth was the main attraction, reporters expressed interest in seeing ex–Virginia League players such as Burleigh Grimes, who pitched for Richmond, and at least four men who once toiled for Portsmouth. Jesse Haines, with the Giants, went by a different name because when he played for Petersburg, he used an alias to avoid losing his amateur status as a collegian.

The 1922 voyage of the Mary Jane commenced with preliminary losses to Newark, Toronto and Syracuse, all teams in the higher level International League. The young Tars easily beat back the Naval Air Station before a huge throng of 6,000. Realizing that none of the first-base candidates could handle the task, Clark acquired Bebe Roth, who batted .319 for Wilson the year before.

With a spirit of optimism, buoyed by an improving economy symbolized by a drop in unemployed skilled workers in Norfolk from 6,000 to 1,000 over the previous six months, the Mary Jane started its 20th voyage. As more sailors began to find jobs aboard ships in the harbor, relieving the overburdened relief agencies, the Crew of the Mary Jane went to work to return Norfolk to baseball greatness.

Across the river, Viox returned as manager and the Truckers acquired Frank O'Brien from the Texas League to replace Casey. Outfielder Alva Nally and a pitcher came from Columbia of the Sally League when Lawrence traded Les Bangs to Newport News for Charlie Allen and a catcher who were then sent south. The owner of the Columbia club, likely at manager Warhop's request, made every effort to pry Garton, Burke and/or Peterson away from the Tars, but with the Landis ruling, he did not need Norfolk's approval to acquire Garton and he was not willing to pay the amount asked for Alex Peterson. Arthur E. "Buddy" Crump, a Norfolk resident, joined the Truckers, but did not play much. Carl Ray returned but ended up with another team in the league. Pitching relied heavily on Michael Soo and pitchers secured after the season commenced.

In the preseason Portsmouth lost to Chief Bender's Reading team and to McGraw's second-line Giants, who were coming off spring training. Portsmouth tied Syracuse in a wild 18–18 slugfest.

These preliminaries, plus an inspection of the respective rosters, led a Portsmouth reporter to note that the Mary Jane "is not in such good shape as she might be." He observed that "she has barnacles," and while some of her holes had been filled, others had not. As a relatively new ship, some of its seams had yet to be "caulked with experience." On the positive side, the crew seemed to willing to scrap to fight off "pirate boarders."[50]

For the Tars, the regular season got off to a bad start as home-standing Portsmouth, not unexpectedly, plowed Norfolk under before 3,000. Dressed in their new cream-colored uniforms highlighted with vermillion trim, the Truckers overcame the young Tars, attired in "sailor blue," 9–6, with Vermilyea making two errors, one critical to the outcome. The Tars recovered to win in their own park behind Peterson, but then they lost at home, 1–0, with Carl Ray besting J.D. Bruener in front of 8,000. Yoter, now toiling for the Truckers, chipped in with a crucial double in the third encounter.

Peterson went on to win another start and one in relief to even off Norfolk's record at 3–3. A few games into the season the Tars lost catcher Leahy due to a broken bone when the "Hard Luck Mariners," as described in the Portsmouth press, lost to Rocky Mount, 11–5. Although three rookies collaborated for a 9–8 victory over Richmond, the Tars tended to lose far more often than they won, and soon sank well below .500.[51]

In early May, many residents of Lambert's Point, a blue-collar neighborhood next to the Norfolk and Western piers, occupied the right-field stands to watch favorite son Johnny Jones win 8–2, the team's first triumph in seven games. Another "kid pitcher," Charlie Zellers, also won to help keep the "rickety ship Mary Jane" afloat. Linwood Smith started, but needed relief help from Lou Stanley to eke out another win. Around mid–May the club stood in fifth place with a record of 7–11.

In a contest in late May "the passengers of the Mary Jane," coarsely commented on the performance of Captain George Carey, according to the Portsmouth press. Even Norfolk's morning daily chastised the cranks for their vulgar comments. Potts urged fans to give the man, who had a wife and two small children, a chance. In the next game the fans reversed course and gave him an ovation.[52]

On the day before Memorial Day, Portsmouth lefty Michael Soo stopped the "Invading Tars" and Lou Stanley, 1–0. Young Gene Hudgins, another resident of Norfolk, evidenced "super stupidity" by throwing the ball out in the middle of the infield after a strikeout, thinking it was the third out in the inning. A Tar baserunner, George Tice, exhibited considerable "dumbness," according to one report, by being caught off base with what could have been the tying run.

On Memorial Day itself, Ledbetter bested Johnson, 1–0, before some 4,000 in Truckertown, when Vermilyea dropped the ball, as he also had on Opening Day. In the afternoon fray at Norfolk, the Truckers once again prevailed, 2–1. In an encounter a day or two later, Johnny Jones bested Soo, 4–3, at Norfolk, giving the Tars one of the four games in the series.[53]

During one of these losing streaks, one fan suggested to Sam Potts that the people ought to advertise the sale of the leaky Mary Jane, using the method of installment buying that had now become popular. In this case, people would expect only a small down payment and it would be okay if the recipient never came up with an additional funds. Clearly, some members of the press and the people were getting fed up with the poor performance of the Tars.

At the end of May, folks held out some hope for improvement when Talbot Riggs, a Suffolk school teacher, came on board to help cover the outfield, although most accounts praised little Eddie Johnson, who had been filling the position. A capable portsider, Vince Matthews, also joined the crew.[54]

Norfolk improved enough to move into third place with two more wins than losses. But the Tars lost seven straight to bring their total number of losses to 26. A new pitcher, acquired from Newark, lost two starts against Portsmouth, which led the league in early June with a record of 23–17 despite a 27–5 pasting by Wilson. Another new Norfolk pitcher, "Big Arthur" Johnson, then came through with a win against the Truckers to take one game in the series. In the return series, the Tars finally took two out of three from their biggest rivals when their hitters finally woke up.

In early July, with Viox and Rooney back in the Portsmouth lineup, the Tars lost to their "friendly enemies," 7–4, and then split the July 4 contests, winning at Portsmouth in the morning. At the end of the day and at the halfway point of the season, Norfolk ranked fifth in the six-team league (now minus Tarboro and Suffolk), with a record of 29–31. That was ten fewer victories than Wilson but only five back in the loss column. Rocky Mount placed second at 36–30, and Portsmouth came in at a surprisingly weak 33–30, virtually tied with the Builders of Newport News. Only Richmond presented a disastrous record (19–42).

In late July, Clark and company made more moves. First baseman Bebe Roth, who had just returned from a serious injury and recovered his hitting eye, expressed discontent with the city or the club or possibly both, and asked to be transferred back to Wilson. Clark accommodated him, receiving the Bugs' first sacker in return. When the replacement could not hit, Clark bought Mike Kelliher from Greenville. Clark also peddled much-maligned George Carey to Durham. Around the same time, when Vermilyea went into a slump, Clark sold him to Columbia, saying a change of scenery might help him. Norfolk acquired Al Watt, a Washington Senators' farmhand and one-time Trucker (1919), along with shortstop Bill Maitland, found in the camp of Connie Mack. Thus the Tars ended up with three new infielders, with only Larry Gallagher at third base remaining from the group that started the season. With the departure of Vermilyea and the disappearance of Art Johnson, who went AWOL after being criticized by Clark for his poor performance, only three men were left from the team of the previous year — outfielder Burke, pitcher Peterson and utility man Jack Kroger, a resident of Norfolk.

At the halfway point, Wilson and Rocky Mount fought it out for the top, with Portsmouth and Newport News vying for third.

In July and August, the team showed modest improvement and even managed to make a scramble for second, at 41–40, seven games behind Wilson at the time (at one point they trailed by twelve). A Portsmouth reporter thought they had the best hitters in the league at this juncture, as they closed in on the Truckers, finally taking them in a doubleheader in early August, 10–5, behind Matthews and 3–1 with Peterson on the mound. At three games above .500, they were only a few games back of Wilson, Portsmouth and Newport News, all battling for supremacy.

Then the Tars once again fell into a phase where they lacked "vim and vigor." The hitters reached a particular low when they scored but one run for Vince Matthews in an 18-inning loss. As the team appeared ready to plunge, a revitalized crew improved enough to end up two games above .500.

They split the Labor Day contests against Portsmouth, winning at home in the afternoon, with Mathews beating Soo, 4–1, after losing 4–3, at Portsmouth. They then eased by Portsmouth, 12–5, but lost the last game of the season, 8–7, as fans in the sister city learned that two of their men had been sold to the Philadelphia Phillies. Despite a ton of hits and baserunners, the game consumed but one hour and five minutes, considered a club record. Obviously, everyone hurriedly hit grooved pitches and moved quickly after each half inning in order to end the season as quickly as possible.

The season confirmed the original analysis that 1922 would be a year of developing the talent of untried seamen. Johnny Jones from Lambert's Point did well for a time but finally came in at 9–11. Alex "Iron Man" Peterson led the staff with a 21–16 mark, most as a starter. Left-hander Mathews broke even in 16 decisions. Frank Noel, acquired from Richmond during the season, was a disappointment at 8–11, as was Lou Stanley at 7–11.

Eddie "Shag" Burke, in the outfield for most of the season but at second base at its end, proved outstanding for a time but tapered off to .276. Three others — Mickey Kelliher, George Tice and Tolbot Riggs — all hit over .300. First baseman Kelliher led the trio at .331, while Tice came in at .320 and Riggs at .318. Shortstop John Vermilyea posted a .275 average before being sold, and second baseman Allie Watt did nearly the same, at .268. Reporters played up the role of third baseman Lawrence Kirby Gallagher, who along with Matthews, signed on with the Boston Braves at season's end.

Wilson won the title with a record of 68–51. Newport News placed second at 63–57. Rocky Mount, Portsmouth and Richmond comprised the second division in that order. In the second half of the season, the Tars won a few more times than they lost to edge one game above .500, good for third place. After the season, the city of Norfolk hired catcher Gene Hudgins, a local lad, and Lou Stanley as policemen. They eventually became fixtures in law enforcement.

At the start of the season a new league rule said the home team got to keep all the revenue it took in for its own contests, but the North Carolina teams that tended to have smaller gates complained about this idea. They eventually persuaded the league to allow gate sharing, which ironically turned out to be beneficial for Percy Dawson at Newport News as well.

In June, Dawson moved over from Portsmouth, leaving the Truckers in the hands of Frank Lawrence. He temporarily had to allow the Builders to go on the road for all their games because attendance remained so low. Reporters now called them the "Outcasts," "Orphans," or "Gypsies." Before that, the Portsmouth press called them "the Leviathans," in honor of the old troop ship at the Newport News Shipyard at the time. Whatever their name, they led Norfolk in a fight for fourth place in the first half of the season.

To the team in Newport News, Dawson demanded guarantees against any more losses. Then he agreed to absorb half the future losses if the city would just come through with $1,500 of the $3,000 he projected as future necessary expenditures. With residents of Roanoke interested in acquiring the franchise, the Newport News Chamber of Commerce studied the matter. An editorial asked "Shall We Have a Ball Club?" The writer thought that although baseball was an amusement, it was also an asset the city could ill afford to lose. It was bad enough not to have a team in the league, but it was even worse to lose the club for lack of support. Finally the Chamber decided to sell a hundred season tickets (for half a season) at $35 each. If it reached its goal, the amount should be more than enough to carry Dawson. The editor thought that is was "not a begging proposal. It is business."

The plan worked, for the Builders not only returned home, but they also demonstrated steady improvement in the second part of the season. Dawson turned down Richmond management's proposal to allow the Colts to have nearly all weekend games, along with a larger share of the receipts. Richmond management also extended the "offer" to the North Carolina cities, and threatened to end its season unless it had its way. But it finally backed down.

No longer considered "Gypsies," the Builders went to Norfolk to play the Tars in a different state of mind from their previous visit to the city, when they had to move their home games there and the Norfolk press made a big deal about how all the Builders were dissatisfied about their predicament. The Tars enjoyed a sweep in that series. The players denied they ever said anything negative to anyone in Norfolk. The Builders, now led by new manager Roy Whitcraft, had vengeance in mind and gave the Tars considerable trouble the rest of the way.[55]

Despite improved play, fans on the Peninsula often criticized the club. In early August, a reporter lambasted the fans for "unmercifully" razzing Walter Main, who had only given up four runs while his mates did not score a run. "This stuff has got to stop and it should never have started." A team in a slump and playing with crippled men was no excuse for all the "razzing." Such behavior "won't get them anywhere." The reporter hoped Roy Whitcraft could soon recover from his injury.[56]

Among the Builders' hitters around the middle of August, Henry Mallonee, the old Trucker secured from Philadelphia, led the way. He ended up just over .360. Les Bangs, who came over from Portsmouth, came in just over .300 and led the league in triples. But George Champagne fell off to below .250. The Builders' leading pitcher was Ray Stickradt at 19–14. He completed 30 games and led the league in strikeouts.[57]

After the season, the press maintained that the 1922 team was likely the city's best team since 1916. If not for some tough breaks, the team's second-place finish could as easily been good enough for first. As it turned out, it would be the Shipbuilders' last chance to cop their first Virginia League title since 1916.[58]

Jim Barry Fails to Keep His Cool in the Age of Coolidge (1923)

With the rebuilding year over, fans expected an improved Tar aggregation in 1923. Management retained a sizeable nucleus from the previous year and invited a smaller number of possible candidates to try out for the team. It really only needed to replace Gallagher and Matthews, but ended up changing about half the regulars.

Clark invited Bill Pike to cover third, but also added new players like Roy Whitcraft, the former Leviathan, to take over at shortstop from Maitland. Outfielders Harry (Henry) Kraemer and Kenneth (Forrest) Cobb, who played for the College of William and Mary in 1921 and rode the bench for Rochester in 1922, also came on board. In the middle of the season, when Cobb said he wanted to quit the team to get married, Clark brought on Champagne, the former Tar, Trucker and Builder. But Cobb must have had a change of heart, for his name appears in the lineup right to the end of the year.

Kraemer, who had sat out a season after jumping his contract, had to pay a $200 fine to the National Association to be eligible to play professional ball. After watching young fielder Carr Smith for a time, Clark farmed him to Raleigh for further seasoning, where he hit near .400 and received a tryout for the major leagues. Clark also peddled Leahy to Columbia in the Sally League and signed Rhineheart "Jake" Kress, who hit only .213 the previous year at Chattanooga, and infielder/outfielder Tommy Morris from Georgia. After the commencement of the regular season, Clark let Petersburg have the young man on loan. Toots Brandon from Michigan was supposed to carry the heavy catcher load, but Gene Hudgins did most of the catching toward the end of the season, with W. "Sid" Womack, acquired from the International League, joining the Crew for the last few games.

Pitching looked ready for a good season. Vince Matthews came back from the Boston

Braves just as the regular season was about to commence, thus depriving the Norfolk club of the full sale price of $4,000 agreed to the previous August if the major league club kept him past May 1, 1923. Former Trucker pitcher Ken Sedgwick, once in the Philadelphia Phillies system, seemed to be the best prospect of the new slabmen, although quiet rookie Johnny Firth exhibited some talent. Clark wanted him to go to Raleigh for more seasoning, but the Peninsula lad returned home instead, and the club recalled him later in the year. Sometime after the start of preseason, the Tars picked up Red Turk, for whom Griffith had paid $4,000. With "Smiling Pete" Peterson retuning, Johnny Jones one year more mature, and Art Johnson back in the fold after his departure the previous year, the Tars looked loaded in the pitching department.

Across the river, Eddie Goosetree, who first played in the Virginia League in 1910, took over from Viox as Portsmouth manager. Among their new players was a former Blue Ridge leaguer "Babe" Wilson, who impressed Portsmouth fans by hitting two straight foul home runs, followed by the real thing over the left field fence, in one of the preliminary games.

During the offseason, the league switched the Newport News franchise to Petersburg, which called its new team the Trunkmakers (rather than the Goobers). Petersburg got the team even though folks in the Cockade City had trouble putting the $3,000 entry fee together. But once they did, other league owners quickly ratified the arrangement, thus ending an unusually harmonious set of winter meetings. The former owners of the Builders, Percy Dawson and George Barnes, went up the Peninsula to take over the Richmond Colts. They soon hired the famous Dave Robertson, a native of Portsmouth, as their player/manager.

Officials in Norfolk, Portsmouth, and Richmond thought seriously about joining a proposed new association that would have linked these three cities with the northeastern part of the country. Such proposals frequently surfaced, along with other ideas to form a league made up exclusively of teams from the Old Dominion. When these ideas faded, baseball people returned to the idea of keeping the existing but misnamed Virginia League for another season.

Even though Norfolk had a veteran team, the Tars did not dominate in preseason. They did win handily against the Navy Base but barely got by the Naval Air Station, 2–1. They were trailing Reading, 1–0, before some 5,000, including many ladies fashionably attired, when rain ended the affair. They were supposed to play some contests against other professional clubs, but rain intercepted.

The Tars started the 1923 season by defeating traditional rival Portsmouth, 5–3, but the Truckers returned the honor the next day. Norfolk secured the rubber game of the series when Alex Peterson benefited from an explosion of hits to post a 12–1 win. The Crew took nine of their first ten and the 15 of the first 18. The situation looked especially encouraging when "Shag" Burke hit two homers in a 16–6 rout at Rocky Mount.

The middle of May, however, brought several losses and internal disorder for the team. After a game in which Ken Sedgwick pitched a twelve-inning tie, he and Burke got into an altercation, during which Sedgwick broke Burke's jaw. Both soon returned, even though Burke's injury could have kept him out of any games for several weeks. But when replacement Bill Pike broke his leg, Burke left the stands and temporarily filled in there before returning to the outfield. After going several weeks with backups at third (one being Pie Traynor's brother), Clark turned to Jimmie Durkin, who had covered the hot corner for the Builders the previous year. When finally installed in the lineup halfway through the season, Durkin hit around .350 before tailing off.

Although the Tars and Truckers divided their Memorial Day twin bill, with some 6,000 watching Sedgwick win the second game at Norfolk, the Tars temporarily lost their grip on first place to Richmond in early June. Around the time the nation celebrated the fifth anniversary of the heroics of marines and others at Bellau Wood during the Great War, Norfolk lost to Wilson twice, swept Petersburg, and ran about two or three games behind Robertson's men from the capital and a little less behind Wilson.

Just as the Tars surged at the start of the season, they also took off at the onset of July. On July 4 they took two from the Truckers, 5–4 and 7–3, to keep their record ten games above .500 and hold onto second despite losing Sedgwick to Clark Griffith's Senators. Then after losing 3–2, the Tars rebounded to take two from the Colts at Mayo Island. Now, Norfolk pulled back into first at 39–27, a few percentage points up on second-place Wilson.

At this point, Burke had hit in fifteen games straight. But while the outfielder remained hot at the bat, the Tars overall became less torrid. Around the middle of July, the Tars lost two to the Colts but recovered the next day to split with Petersburg and bring their record to 43–32.

In late July, Portsmouth got revenge by taking two from the Tars, but the Truckers also helped out the Tars when they beat the Bugs in an extra-inning classic. The next day, the Truckers split with the Bugs as the Tars took two from the Trunkmakers. Norfolk also helped its own cause when it scored five runs in the top of the 11th inning to beat Wilson ace Cy Fried.

Fortified by new pitchers and better hitting, the Truckers battered their biggest rivals in three straight to force the Tars back into second. Richmond, managed by Dave Robertson, now led the league by a game. Earl Wright, the sometime Portsmouth poet, could not refrain from putting each game and even one rainout into a rhyme of sorts. Called "Current History," the poem recounted how "chesty" the Tars acted with Peterson, their ace, going in the game at Portsmouth on July 23. "So Pete went in but came right out, was walloped hard and put to rout/And thus a chapter now begun, the Tars lost battle number one."

Not able to get revenge the next day because of rain, the Tars awaited the upcoming doubleheader. And soon "The Tars had five the Truckers none, but that's where the row begun/ Sent Johnson to the showers tall, good boy Peter received a call. The stands did rock, the bleachers roar, as Palmer (shortstop) hit for bases four/On every sack there was a man, so it is not hard to understand/The dope don't always run so true, so the Tars lost battle number two." Now perhaps with less confidence the Tars approached the second part of the twin bill. "A lad named Manners (John) pitched his game, upon his shoulders are the blames/For he was there all will agree and the Tars lost ball game number three."[59]

Although nearly derailed by Portsmouth, a sweep of Rocky Mount permitted the Tars to edge closer to the lead. In a 4–3 victory over the Down Homers, Burke got the winning run on a double steal in the ninth. Two more victories over Rocky Mount accompanied a continuation of Burke's hitting streak, which now stood at 35.

As July ended, Peterson sustained a 1–0 loss against the Richmond Colts. The Crew then took a doubleheader, with Johnson and Jones the winning pitchers. Old Trucker "Lanky" or "Slim" McGloughlin temporarily joined the Tars, did fared so poorly in one outing that Clark returned him to Toledo and demanded a refund. Clark claimed to have received damaged goods; that's how badly the pitcher was out of condition.

In an August showdown rightfully overshadowed by the death of President Warren G. Harding from apoplexy, Portsmouth took the Tars, 9–6, before 5,239 at the victor's city. Judge Landis asked the game on August 4 be postponed as a tribute to the deceased president. President Moye's edict that all games be postponed arrived just as the Norfolk club arrived for the contest.

Calvin Coolidge took over the presidency and in time the phrase "keep cool with Coolidge" was heard across the land. After the postponement, the Tars miraculously managed to beat the Truckers in a doubleheader, with Matthews tossing a shutout and Jones eking out a win in relief. Now the Tars' record was at 54–39.

In spite of his team's ups and downs, Burke sustained a pace near .400 and closed in on Willie Keeler's 1897 consecutive-game hitting streak record of 45. His streak finally ended at 42 when Rocky Mount pitcher Mark Webb threw a no-hitter. Toward the middle of August, just after Burke's streak came to an end, the Tars still clung to first at 55–43. But a 2–1 loss to Wilson in 13 innings hurt the cause considerably. Two losses in a row to Richmond at home also hampered the chances of the Crew. Norfolk recovered to win over the Truckers, but the Tars then lost a doubleheader to them. Then they won, 5–4, with another game ending in a tie. The Tars even beat the famed and well-traveled Virginia circuit celebrity Taylor "Deacon" Joliff in the process. In one of these games, Mollie Craft, the one-time Tar who now played for Portsmouth, got into a fight with a Norfolk fan who had been cursing him. Clark convinced the police not to arrest Craft.

After this spell, the Tars placed third in league standings, some eight games above .500, a game behind Wilson and two in back of Richmond. Then they swept Rocky Mount. Now with a record of 60–49, they were tied with both the Colts and the Bugs, with all three teams having identical records. That position, however, proved to be the Crew's high-water mark during the last part of the season.

In the next several encounters, the Bronchos of Rocky Mount secured vengeance for their recent debacle by taking a doubleheader from the Tars, but Norfolk recovered by taking two from Richmond. At this point, Wilson moved into first and took on the Tars in Norfolk. In this crucial series, the Bugs captured three heartbreakers: 3–2 in 11 innings, 4–3, and 3–2 in 10 innings. Though these wins proved pivotal in the North Carolinians' championship, a double loss of 14–2 and 8–2 to archrival Portsmouth on Labor Day dropped Norfolk much further back in the standings. Indeed, the club lost its last nine games, the last three of the season to the hapless last-place Petersburg Trunkmen, who buried them, 3–0, 8–6, and a resounding 11–0. With their collapse, the once-proud Crew finished at the head of the second division of the six-team league with a record of 62–60.

Wilson, at 68–51, eked out the title over the Richmond Colts in disputed final standings. Dawson protested that a loss against Petersburg should be discounted, but President Moye and other owners thought otherwise. Moye, in rendering this verdict, also pointed out that the second game of a doubleheader between the Colts and Trunkmakers, won by the former, should never have been played, as the league had ordered no games that day due to Harding's death.

Moye understood that the first game had likely started by the time word arrived of his decision, but he could not comprehend how the second game had been allowed to proceed. Of course, park managers might well have had to deal with unruly crowds who paid to see a double bill. At any rate, the Bugs got to play the Charlotte Hornets, to whom they lost despite having Al Watt sent over from Norfolk to help them out.

In the first of the losses to Wilson near the end of August at League Park, Norfolk's fans, undoubtedly frustrated, "invaded" the playing area intent on assaulting the umpire for calling a Wilson player safe at the plate with the deciding run. According to an account in *The Pilot* the day after the incident, the Norfolk players prevented bodily harm by hustling the umpire into their dugout, where owner Jim Barry punched him in the face.

A few days later, a staff reporter tried to explain the causes of the incident. Nearly everyone who knew anything about local baseball believed the umpires in the league were the worst in years, with only two really qualified for their jobs. Several times in the season, Portsmouth reporters complained about the inadequacies of the umpire staff. It seemed not necessarily to be a problem of too few officials at each game. Three umpires covered one contest in which all three miscalled critical plays, depriving the Truckers of a victory. Portsmouth people urged fans throughout the league to besiege the league president's office with appeals for better umpires. Needless to say, the umpire Barry assaulted was not one of the two competent officials. Even worse, the president of the league had assigned two of the weakest umpires to the most important series of the season. So, primary blame for the incident fell to the president of the league.

Despite a physical appearance that seemed to resemble a barrel (only 5 feet, 6 inches tall, more than 190 pounds, with size 6 shoes), Portsmouth fans in 1923 knew they were watching a great hitter when Lewis "Babe" Wilson became a Trucker. Providing most of the bat work for Portsmouth, he led the Virginia League in at least four offensive categories: .388 average, 19 home runs, 15 triples and 101 runs batted in. In a 12-year career with four different National League teams, the renamed "Hack" Wilson produced 244 home runs, 67 triples, 266 doubles, and 1,063 runs batted in. His 191 runs batted in for the Cubs in 1930 remain a major league record. A weakness for whiskey doubtless shortened his career (National Baseball Hall of Fame Library, Cooperstown, New York).

What the reporter failed to mention was that umpire Al Orth, who should have been assigned to Norfolk, had but a few days before fell when a weak knee gave way. "Dutch" Revelle, the old Virginia Leaguer and now a resident of Norfolk, came out of the stands to give satisfactory service. Such criticism must have rankled Moye, who made improving umpiring a cornerstone of his program when he took over league leadership in 1922.

The reporter also believed that far too much gambling took place at the park, with a short-handed police force doing nothing about it. Fans ordinarily became excited when an umpire made a controversial call, but betting made these situations even more dangerous. The reporter did not mention Barry's earlier efforts to prevent gambling at all league parks, including his own, which had been the subject of an article in the newspaper that appeared well before the Wilson series.[60]

In describing the umpire–punching incident, sports editor Tom Hanes claimed that most everyone in the stands thought the Tars' catcher tagged out the runner two feet short of home plate, but this error of judgment did not condone what followed. Hanes maintained that the beefy Barry (200 pounds) led the mob of some 500, twenty of whom were so infuriated that they wished to inflict serious injury on the 120-pound umpire, with the others hopeful of watching the assault. Hanes found great irony and inconsistency in Barry's condemnation of Mollie Craft's similar behavior in a game a few days earlier.

The next day, a judge decided that the umpire's word on the matter was insufficient, his face failing to exhibit any noticeable marks from the attack. Only the umpire testified about the incident. Although the umpire might not have exhibited damage to his face, the incident gave the city of Norfolk "a black eye," if the morning newspaper is to be believed. As the season came to an end, the National Association of Minor Leagues suspended both Barry and the Norfolk Baseball Corporation and imposed a hefty fine ($1,000) on Barry, who received notification the same day from President Moye of a fine for half that amount.

Neither decision prevented Norfolk from reserving players, but supposedly management could not participate in league affairs until the matter was resolved. Barry appealed the league president's decision to the body that had just fined him double the original amount, contending that he had not really led the riot. Disgusted with the situation and the recent failings of his team, Barry planned to sell his interest in the club. The Virginia League and the National Association then moderated the penalties.[61]

"Iron Man" Alex Peterson, considered the best Tar pitcher of the era, led the staff with a record of 22–17 (19–8 through July). He also led the league in strikeouts and earned-run average (1.78). Vince Matthews managed to win 12 of 23 (8–3 through July), John Jones split 24 decisions evenly, and three others all fell below .500. The precipitous decline for Peterson suggests the "Iron Man" may have tired out or, more likely, the Tar batters stopped hitting when he was on the mound.[62]

Overall, it was not a particularly good year for Tar batters, who finished fifth in the league with an average of .273, and a league-low 39 homers. Eddie "Shag" Burke led the club at .331, followed by Talbot Riggs, at .305 and Mickey" Kelliher at exactly .300. Harry Kraemer and Paul Kirby shared duties in right field, with the former coming in at .291 and the latter at .266. In the infield, Roy Whitcraft came over from Newport News to anchor the infield at shortstop and hit .258, while second baseman Al Watt registered .289 and Jim Durkin batted .288 after dropping way off toward the end of the year. Kress hit a respectable .285 through July, and Ken Cobb came in at .297, with a long hitting streak earlier in the season. Clearly many hitters slumped in August and September.[63]

In Portsmouth, Lewis "Hack" Wilson won the triplecrown by hitting .388, slugging 19 home runs, and driving in over 100 runs to go along with 174 hits, including 15 triples. Years later, as a Chicago Cub, he set the still-existing major-league record for runs batted in for a season. With Wilson, Portsmouth did not need many other hitters to back Abe Applegate, who led the club at 12–6, and well-traveled Taylor Joliff (15–17), who joined a little after mid–season.

10

Final Voyages, 1924–1928

The mid–1920s brought great prosperity to the American economy — and a lot more hitting to the Virginia League. The Tars, however, somewhat like the country's shipbuilding industry, did less than a booming business, either at the box office or in the standings. The team survived with the help of a local celebrity, and even captured a pennant in a season cut short in 1928 by the demise of the league.

Davis Robertson Joins the Crew (1924)

As usual, the Virginia hot-stove league simmered over the winter of 1923–24. Oddly, the banned Jim Barry represented the team at Virginia League meetings in Wilson and at the Southland Hotel in Norfolk. Just after the start of the regular season, Thomas Willcox, a onetime judge and sometime lawyer for the Tars, assumed the presidency of the club. His son E.R. "Teddy" Willcox, vice president, also acquired shares in the organization.

Backers in Petersburg finally raised $5,000 to pay the franchise fee and repay debt that included the player paychecks from the previous September and payments to other clubs for new players.

In Richmond, owner H.P. Dawson feuded with the owners of the Mayo Island Park when, after a fire that destroyed the grandstand and part of the bleachers, they rebuilt stands with only half the former capacity. Jake Wells and his cohorts insisted on the same rent, but Dawson balked. Wells talked about taking over the team and proposed that the Virginia League drop its Class B status to something between Class C and D, relying extensively on amateurs. Reporters in Norfolk rejected the idea, arguing that the league actually deserved a higher classification. Ultimately, Dawson worked out a deal and retained control of the franchise.

In other winter decisions, the league modified and accepted a schedule produced by sports editor Tom Hanes. Delegates unanimously agreed with Frank Lawrence that visiting teams be required to use hotels and other facilities located in the city in which the games were played. Portsmouth had long complained about losing such business to Norfolk. The league emphasized the need for owners to prevent gambling at the parks, a practice they maintained endangered the core values of professional baseball.[1]

Around the Ides of March, players started on their way to Norfolk to work under Win Clark. Third baseman Bill Pike, his broken leg mended, and pitcher C.L. Gillenwater came from Flint, Michigan, where they worked in an auto plant over the winter. Possessed with skills as mechanics, they drove sometimes nonexistent roads to Tidewater. They made it in a little over a week, with fans more concerned about their fate than that of the corrupt officials of the Harding administration, whose misdeeds now blared from the headlines.

Clark assembled the usual mix of veterans and newcomers to see if he could improve on the fourth-place finish of the previous year. Key "Parson" Perryman, an old-time Virginia Leaguer, sent word that he would like to return to Virginia, as the Texas League where he had been playing had started to allow baseball on Sunday. Clark figured he had enough pitchers with Johnny Jones, Gillenwater (once a Detroit farmhand), Norman Garrison, Johnny Firth, Frank Watt (Al's brother), a youngster named Benson Brillheart (a Virginian affiliated with the Senators), H.F. "Tiney" Owens and others.

In the field positions, fans soon became impressed with the speed and batting acumen of first baseman Dick Attreau, the replacement for Mike Kelliher. Catching duties fell to either Tom Hipple, who had played for the Naval Station and worked for the Tars the previous year, H.R. Funk or Sid "Tex" Womack. It appeared the outfield might have a big hole despite the presence of Olin Parrett and F. Scott, until Shag Burke unexpectedly showed up.

In the preseason, the Tars played at least twice on Sunday, with some 6,000 showing up for a contest easily won against the receiver ship. A 4–3 weekday win over the local police drew far fewer people, but fans enjoyed watching the great but aging Lou Stanley baffle the Tars with his tantalizing hooks. Several other ex–Tars, including Dusty Rhodes and George Champagne, also worked for the police department.

Against professional teams, the Tars were unimpressive, losing two of three at Raleigh, barely edging Durham and succumbing to Syracuse, 10–2, before a massive Sunday crowd of over 8,000 at League Park. Fans sat in the outfield, which forced the team to use the rule that a ball a hit into the crowd was only good for a double, not a home run, unless the ball sailed over the fence on the fly. The Tars secured a more respectable 10–7 loss in their next encounter with Syracuse, managed by Frank Shaughnessy, the old Roanoke player/manager that Happy Chandler had his encounter with 26 years before. Buffalo also beat them, 3–0.

These seemed like acceptable defeats, given that International League clubs ranked higher in the minor-league system. But Portsmouth, still under Eddie Goosetree, split with Buffalo and took three of four visiting York. In their losing effort against the Bisons, Portsmouth played the game on Sunday at the Naval Base before a huge congregation.

The Tars helped Portsmouth christen its new ballpark on Upper High Street, located west of the Belt Line just beyond the Norfolk County line, by obligingly losing 3–2, before some 3,000. In the next day's opener for the Tars, Brillheart pitched brilliantly in tossing a shutout, and even chipped in with a homer.

Norfolk carried a record just above .500 a week or two into May, but Portsmouth took off like a rocket. With Eddie Goosetree still managing and Norfolk native Buddy Crump showing that he had learned something about hitting after being farmed out the previous year, the Truckers rolled to a ten-game lead.

The Tars had some occasional bright spots. Brillheart often pitched brilliantly, even in losing, as he did to Taylor "Deacon" Joliff of the Truckers, 2–0, in early May. The next day, however, catcher Funk and outfielder Scott homered as Norfolk scored five times in the top of the 12th to subdue the Truckers.

Ever tinkering with his roster, Clark released pitcher Frank Watt and brought back Charlie Zellers from Tampa in the Florida State League. Zellers had a reputation of being erratic on the mound. Curiously, the press kept describing him as a young and inexperienced pitcher, even though he had pitched for Clark at the Navy Base during the Great War. When captain

Pike proved not to be his old reliable self, Clark released him to Rocky Mount. Early in May, Attreau left town to tend to a sick wife and did not return to Norfolk until the next year. His hitting had trailed off some, with only one hit in ten at-bats just before he left, but that hit was a home run that helped win against Rocky Mount. In his last game he made a spectacular catch of a foul fly, falling over an obstruction and landing in the right field bleachers. When a Portsmouth reject failed to do the job as Attreau's replacement, Clark had backup catcher Sid Womack fill the hole in the infield.

Early in the season, the Tars farmed Johnny Firth to Raleigh and carried on with a rotation of Jones, Brillheart, Gillenwater and Owens. The club soon sold outfielder Ezra Scott and Owens to Topeka to play for Red Cleveland, the old Tar third sacker, and acquired catcher Fred "Red" Fisher, shortstop Johnny Carlin and Mollie Craft, the latter from the Southern League. Carlin could not make the grade and Fisher, after helping out as catcher and at first base, disappeared from the lineup. Clark considered using Craft as a pitcher, then tried him in the outfield, but soon shifted him to first base, thereby finally covering the gap opened when Attreau left.

Craft, who hailed from Portsmouth where he starred for his high school in several sports, started his professional career as a pitcher with the Tars before the Great War. After a brief major-league experience with the Senators, he played for several upper-level minor league clubs before returning to his hometown. Craft spent winters playing basketball for one of the local area's independent teams, and was known for his aggressiveness. On one occasion while playing at center, he slugged an opposing player who ran into him. Later in the 1924 baseball season, he became so irritated with an umpire's strike call that police arrested both him and the umpire for their uncivil language.

In June, Clark secured Raymond Joyce from the Senators, but he proved a dud. After the Truckers feasted on his offerings, Joyce was described by a Portsmouth reporter as having a "quivering frame." After two less than mediocre performances, he disappeared from the roster. Temporary third baseman Bill Maitland, who substituted in the outfield when Parrett sustained an injury, moved over to Petersburg. To bolster the infield, Clark traded the slumping Shag Burke to Rochester for Elliott "Pea Head" Walker, at first mistakenly called "P.D." and "Pee Wee" by the Norfolk press. Acquiring a new shortstop allowed the manager to move Bert "Half-Pint" Hewell to third base.[2]

In late May and most of June, the Tars continued downward. They lost three straight to ex-major leaguer Ed Konectchy and his Petersburg Goobers. Against Portsmouth over Memorial Day weekend, they managed to win the afternoon contest at home behind Brillheart, 6–0, then lost not only the morning part of the holiday doubleheader but also succumbed the day before and in two home games on the Saturday after the holiday, 5–4 and 6–4. That brought their record to 15–21, putting them in the cellar, while Portsmouth soared in first at 26–9.

Only a few incidents relating to Norfolk's mistreatment of umpires surfaced during the season. The record was clearly better than in earlier years, but between the two games of the Memorial Day doubleheader, two Tars accosted the umpires. When one of the umpires was safely in Rocky Mount, he complained to President Moye that Al Watt had struck him and Win Clark had "roundly abused" him. Somehow, the other umpire came under arrest. In an account of the story in the Monday daily, the reporter took pains to note that the two arbiters were, like many of the umpires in the league, borderline incompetent. Unlike an umpire named Fred Westervelt, they lacked the ability to control players.[3]

In June, Davis "Dave" Robertson, another native of Portsmouth, came to the club from

Richmond, where he had missed winning the pennant by one percentage point the previous year. At season's end, when owner Percy Dawson sold him to Atlanta, Robertson refused to go, but he was quite happy to return to his old stomping grounds in Hampton Roads. Dawson struck an arrangement with the Tars whereby the Colts received young Johnny Jones for Minnie Manning, who had seemingly lost his stuff after a brilliant campaign in 1923. As part of that arrangement, the left-handed hitting Robertson and his big bat came to Norfolk.

Robertson, a standout at Portsmouth High School and a multi-sports star at North Carolina A&M (N.C. State), played for the Elizabeth City club in the Albemarle League in 1910. The next season he returned there to play in the Tidewater League, supposedly for no pay. That fall, he continued his football career for A&M and returned to old Lafayette Field in Norfolk in a contest against Virginia Tech. Thinking he had played baseball as a professional, the Virginians reluctantly agreed to play against Robertson, but said they would thereafter end relations with the North Carolina school. Afterwards, John McGraw offered Robertson a contract, which he did not sign until he completed college. A shoulder injury sustained playing football ended his chances as a pitcher, but his athletic prowess made him an excellent major-league prospect. After adjusting, he emerged seemingly as another Ty Cobb. Although he never reached such a high station, he did become a solid player for a few years, even hitting .500 in the 1917 World Series.

Shortly before Robertson arrived, fans called for Clark to confine himself to duty as a scout. They wanted Robertson to take over, contending that league rules allowed the team to have one extra player if the manager also played. The team could then hire a fifth pitcher. Clark let it be known that he would quit only after he had the Mary Jane headed in the right direction and not resting in last place. Clark's ownership of stock in the corporation and excellent record of securing money via player sales discouraged any effort to fire him. Robertson let it be known that he came to Norfolk with the understanding that he would not replace his good friend as manager. That disclosure muted Clark's critics.

The presence of Robertson and Craft gave the Tars a creditable one-two punch in their lineup, although it took some time for them to

Born in Portsmouth, Davis "Dave" Robertson, the highly-respected player/manager for the Tars from 1925 through 1927, pitched for Elizabeth City in the Tidewater League in 1911. He then played outfield for John McGraw and the New York Giants. After batting .500 in the 1917 World Series, he managed a local military club in 1918 before returning to the Giants in 1919. He also played with the Chicago Cubs and Pittsburgh Pirates in a career that spanned a decade, during which he averaged .287. In 1923, he played for and managed Percy Dawson's Richmond Colts, batting .334 and hitting 9 triples, though only 7 home runs. The Colts narrowly missed the Virginia League title that year. In 1924, he joined the Tars for a little more than half the season, batting .304 and hitting 11 homers. Over the next two years, "Demon Dave" caught up with Virginia League pitching, hitting .388 (24 home runs) and .382 (31 home runs). An injury cut short his playing time in 1927, though he still batted .350 with 16 homers. After completing his baseball career, he became a game warden in the Norfolk area (Norfolk Public Library).

find a groove. Fans figured that given time, the Crew would move toward the top of the league. With Robertson in the fold, they hoped that president Moye might call for a telegraph vote on creating a split season. Moye decided otherwise. Because the team continued to tread water well into July, it seemed to have little chance of winning the pennant even had the season been split.

Not that the team and its fans had no pleasurable moments. The day after Portsmouth blasted Joyce, Brillheart won his sixth decision, this one over Portsmouth, 4–2. Two days earlier, the Tars got to Abe Applegate at Portsmouth for a win during which Robertson appeared at the plate as a pinch-hitter, to thunderous applause from residents of his native city. Although he flied out, the Tars took a series from the Truckers for the first time that season. In other games, Gillenwater beat the popular Bunny Hearn of Wilson, and Lou Stanley came back from the semipro ranks with the police to shut down the Bugs and Cy Fried, 6–2, in the battle for last place.

After beating up on the Tars at the end of May, Portsmouth leveled off. At one point, the Truckers had at least three regulars hitting between .356 and .391. A few days later, the New York Giants purchased Buddy Crump, hitting .375, and John Manners, and ordered them to report after the Virginia League season ended. Then the Truckers experienced a noticeable drop among their hitters. Crump held up well at .376, but first baseman Jim Keesey, who had been hitting home runs at a pace of one every two days, fell to .303 and rarely hit a home run.

When the infielders slumped in early July and attendance weakened despite the overall excellent record, Lawrence purchased one-time Tar Chap Marable to fortify his infield. Early on, the team lost the services of backup catcher Warren Perry, who contracted tuberculosis and was sent to a sanitarium, after which $275 was raised for him at a benefit game.

In the last week of June Richmond, at one point far back in the standings, pressed hard on the league leaders. When Petersburg captured a doubleheader from the Truckers, the Colts moved into first by percentage points. In a showdown series in Portsmouth, the Colts won the first contest. The next day the Truckers took vengeance, shutting out the visitors behind John Manners. But on a day made noteworthy by the Democrats for carrying out another 49th ballot in their failed attempt to pick a presidential candidate, the Colts prevailed in the finale to increase their lead. Johnny Jones, the former Tar, won one of these contests for the Colts.

The Truckers now faced the Tars in their traditional battles of early July. On July 3, Portsmouth prevailed, 5–3, to close the gap with Richmond to one-half game, Manners besting Gillenwater. The clubs split their July 4 doubleheader with Zellers winning in the morning, 8–0, at Portsmouth and Applegate carrying the afternoon contest at Norfolk, 2–1. The Tars then earned a split of the four-game series, as Manning beat Manners. At this point, Richmond, at 41–27, led the Truckers by one game, with Norfolk virtually tied with Wilson for last, both ten games under .500. Rocky Mount stood a game or two above .500 and Petersburg held fourth, seven games below that mark.

Around mid-July, the Tars reached their low point, falling 14 games below .500. Hitting improved, but pitching failed to hold up, although Minnie Manning bested the Truckers early in the month and later managed to shut out Rocky Mount. When the Wilson Bugs released Art "Cy" Fried, Clark signed him. He soon won several times, including stopping a 13-game winning streak of his old mates, 6–3. Around the same time, Clark gave up on Brillheart, who, after leading the staff, had temporarily lost his talent. The Colts later acquired him and with another ex-Tar, Johnny Jones, had enough to win the pennant. At the time of these deals, the Tars were fighting the Goobers for last place.

The Tars showed improvement through the rest of July, as the hitters wracked Trucker pitchers for nineteen hits in one game, giving them a 12–7 win. Abraham Lincoln Applegate, the ace of the Portsmouth staff, took a beating (victimized by ten errors), while lefty Gillenwater for Norfolk hung around to take the win. Norfolk also took the next encounter, 8–6, before Applegate recovered to win the finale with a shutout, with Gillenwater absorbing the defeat.

In the next series, Manning and Zellers yielded 16 runs to the Goobers while the Tars scored 10. Lefty Cy Fried, however, won the ensuing contest.

With criticism mounting, Tar management purchased right-hander Frank Loftus from New Haven. On the day it sustained a 12–6 loss to Richmond, the club announced the acquisition of Bill Clarkson, another right-hander, from Galveston. The team released submariner Gillenwater, who became a Goober and Manning, who became a Trucker. One wonders what Pike and Gillenwater did about the car they drove from Michigan, one now being at Rocky Mount and the other in Petersburg. Secretary Marshall told a reporter that if the current crop of pitchers could not do the job, they would all be replaced. When catchers Funk and Womack sustained injuries, the club secured Ed Spellman, who was headed to Greenville when diverted to Tidewater.

Starting at the end of July, the Tars asserted themselves. They beat Richmond, 11–2, behind Fried. They took two of three from Rocky Mount, with Clarkson winning the opener and Fried the second game with solid performances. But the Tars lost two of three at Wilson and were still some twelve games below .500.

Returning to Tidewater in early August, however, they swept the Truckers, winning the first 7–5, behind Clarkson. In the second fray, Craft hit three home runs and Zellers pitched well to win, 11–2. The Tars followed the double win with a 9–2 triumph with Fried receiving the verdict. The losses seriously jeopardized the Truckers' position in the standings and served as a turning point for the Tars, who finally looked like they might be able to reach .500.

During one of these August games, Craft hit two homers against his hometown team, the second the longest blasted to that point at the new Trucker Park on High Street. Craft and Robertson, the two men from Portsmouth, provided numerous exciting moments. On one occasion, the headline read "Demon Dave Again Leads Tars." A reporter described one of his round trippers as a "roaring, snarling" hit over the fence in right-center field, certainly something befitting the "Roaring Twenties."[4]

Following the sweep of the Truckers, Norfolk feasted on the Goobers with another nineteen hits, then after a tie, won the final game of the series. Bernie Cleveland put in an appearance in right field to help out when Parrett and Riggs were both injured. When the team he had been managing disbanded, Cleveland ended the year at Rocky Mount and returned to Norfolk the next year as the regular third baseman.[5]

The club then swept the league-leading Colts, with Clarkson besting Jones 2–1 and "Demon" Dave supplying a crucial hit in a 5–4 cliffhanger. Now just four games below .500, the Tars took to the road and slipped, losing two of three to the Bronchos. Cy Fried prevailed 3–2 in the finale, yielding only two hits — both homers — to the great Frank Walker. As principal owner of the Rocky Mount club, Walker sold himself to the Yankees later that year.

Norfolk came close to losing its ballpark late in August when someone left a lighted cigar in the padding on the fence near the entrance. The resulting fire damaged part of the stands, including four box seats. In a day or two workmen had repaired the damage.[6]

In the ensuing series against Wilson, then a few games ahead of Norfolk, Parrett's game-saving catch highlighted a 2–0 win enjoyed by 2,000. The second game of the double bill ended in a tie caused by darkness at the end of nine innings. Wilson won the next day, 4–3, with another nightcap ending in a 6–6 tie because of darkness after seven innings. In the third doubleheader, the Tars took two to win the series three games to one. Fried shut out his old club, exacting revenge for not having been given a fair chance, and expressed considerable pleasure afterward.

During the streak, Fried won five out of six contests and Clarkson tossed nearly eight innings before yielding a hit. In another game, he edged Richmond, 2–1, to defeat former Tar Johnny Jones. Within a month, Clarkson defeated every team in the league at least once. Frank "Hay" Loftus also proved successful for a time. Johnny Firth returned to help out near season's end. Zellers pitched off and on most of the season, his wildness keeping him from being an outstanding thrower.

A nasty incident marred the usually good relations between the Colts and Tars that season. In a 5–2 win over Richmond, manager Jack Onslow ordered ex-Tar "Bugs" Brillheart to hit Robertson with a pitch. Two Norfolk businessmen, both of whom signed affidavits, overheard Onslow tell his pitcher to throw at Robertson's head. They told Dave what they heard. Two Richmond players, who played for Robertson when he managed the Colts the previous year, corroborated the story. In his first at-bat, the Tar outfielder dodged two balls thrown near him. Because two previous batters had walked, the gentlemanly "Demon Dave" attributed the close pitches to the pitcher's wildness. In his second at-bat, Robertson swatted the ball over the right-field fence. In the sixth inning, Brillheart threw a hard, high one that suddenly broke and beaned Big Dave. As Robertson fell to the ground, Al Watt and Mollie Craft ran from the dugout and, ignoring the pitcher, went after manager Onslow, an action that puzzled the fans who had not heard about Onslow's instructions.

A reporter speculated that the Richmond manager had several reasons to hurt Robertson. Although Richmond had an excellent shot to win the title, many Colts contrasted Onslow's bombastic style with Robertson's gentlemanly demeanor. Onslow also might have been angry over his failure as a catcher to prevent seven Tars from stealing bases in one game, or his recent weak hitting. But the most likely cause, the reporter believed, was that in a recent series in Richmond, Dave hit three home runs and a double in eight at-bats. Robertson recovered from the blow. The main Richmond daily had nothing to say about the affair.[7]

On another occasion, a Richmond fan hit long-time league umpire Fred Westervelt with a bottle. In the same game, Richmond outfielder Al Maloneee, upset at fouling out, threw his bat over the stands. In the next game umpire H. Herbert Hirtzel, banished the Colt from the game and shoved him, for which Maloneee brought charges. After being arrested, both men had to come up with $100 in bail.[8]

Perhaps because of the debacle at the end of the previous year, Norfolk fans behaved better, with an exception or two. In a win against Rocky Mount, they let Westervelt know they were displeased with his calls by throwing rental cushions onto the field, despite the umpire's threat to forfeit the game should they persist. The press maintained Norfolk fans had not done that particular stunt for some time, but the same thing had occurred earlier that season, with the same umpire the object of this gentler form of abuse.

A few days after the Onslow incident in Norfolk, the Tars went to Richmond, where the Colts clubbed the Crew in three straight games. Robertson managed three hits in eight trips, none for extra bases. That sweep ended any realistic chance the Tars had for a pennant run, with their record standing at 54–59.

Norfolk remained below .500 as September started. The Tars and Truckers split the traditional Labor Day doubleheader, with Rube Zellers overcoming John Manners in the morning at Portsmouth, and Deacon Joliff cruising past Clarkson that afternoon at Norfolk. The Truckers then won the rubber game in the series.

In the next series, Norfolk once again swept the Colts at home. In the last game, Johnny Firth clung to a 5–4 lead at the end to beat Richmond ace Joe Maley, recently sold to the New York Yankees. Norfolk fans sailed numerous cushions at the Richmond players after the game, as the police stood idly by. The young Colts took the abuse with good humor. Despite losing shortstop Pea Head Walker, forcing Riggs to move to the infield and bringing policeman George Champagne back into the lineup, the Tars took two of three at Wilson, winning one in 13 innings and another by the score of 16–10.

In a three-way race for the top, Portsmouth pulled within three games of the lead, as Rocky Mount briefly jumped into first place. Richmond quickly resumed the lead, but when Portsmouth beat Petersburg and Rocky Mount bested the Colts, the Truckers closed the gap with the Colts to one and a half games. Then, in a series crucial to its hopes, Portsmouth took three of four from the Tars, splitting in Norfolk and taking both contests across the river with scores of 11–7 and 9–4 to clinch the season series by a healthy margin.

But the Colts captured their clashes with the Goobers, so Portsmouth's victories allowed it to only keep pace with Richmond, while Rocky Mount faded. Richmond fans accused the Crew, which had recently been dominating everyone else in the league, of purposely lying down on the job. Many Norfolk fans openly favored Portsmouth, despite the natural animosity between the sister cities, because of Richmond manager Onslow's behavior in the Robertson affair.

As the Colts moved into Portsmouth, Mother Nature intervened by moving a huge tropical storm along the coast, forcing a cancellation of all three games. On the third day, Frank Lawrence insisted on making up the contests by playing one in the morning followed by a doubleheader the same afternoon. Dawson balked at the idea. President Moye refused to say whether a tripleheader could be allowed under league rules. But the whole thing proved moot, as the storm continued for one more day, forcing Lawrence to demand makeup games at the end of the season. When that proved impossible, he asked for a postseason series with the Colts. That did not happen either.

In the last series of the season, Norfolk swept cellar-dwelling Petersburg at home with Clarkson, Loftus and Fried doing the honors. Portsmouth took two straight from Rocky Mount at home. Richmond split with Wilson. With Portsmouth trailing Richmond by one-half game as the last Saturday of the season arrived, Lawrence persuaded Norfolk to play a makeup game at 10 A.M. Most people presumed Portsmouth would win.

Owner Dawson in Richmond registered a protest, but when the headline read "Tars Squelch Truckers" he, of course, withdrew his protest, as Zellers had an outstanding outing to defeat the Truckers, 2–1, a "cruel jab" in the estimation of a local reporter. The Truckers then lost the regularly scheduled game that afternoon to Rocky Mount, 8–7, as Richmond also lost. Richmond ended up with a record of 76–59, one game over Portsmouth.

The Crew won their last game to end up three games above .500. Because the club stood some eleven games below .500 at the halfway point in the season, Norfolk might well have challenged for the second-half title, had there been a split season. Certainly, Norfolk had the best team in the last month.

Most of the Norfolk players soon left town, with Parrett headed back to California. Shortstop Walker left a few days earlier to reach the high school in Georgia that hired him as athletic director and educator. Al Watt accepted an invitation to do office work for the Norfolk police and play for its ballclub. The press expected to see many of the men the next year and openly expressed confidence about the future of the Crew on its next voyage.

Among the Crew hitters, Craft came in at .333 and 15 homers, while Robertson posted a .304 (11 homers). Center fielder Parrett batted .282 (13 home runs), and Talbot "Totie" (aka "Professor") Riggs in left field finished at .285. Reporters particularly liked Riggs, the Suffolk High School teacher who hit above .300 in prior seasons. Shag Burke fell off to .226 before being dismissed. Popular and talented third baseman Pea Head Walker led the infielders besides Craft in hitting at .311. Al Watt, considered the best second baseman in the league, hit above .290 and shortstop "Half-Pint" Hewell averaged around .270. At one point Eddie Spellman, the late-season catcher, posted numbers well up in the .300s, but ended up below .280. The other catcher, Chuck Funk, proved adept at catching pop flies in dugouts.

Although the Crew had plenty of capable hitters and pretty fair fielding, the Tars had only a couple of consistent pitchers. Every season brought great changes in the pitching staff of the Crew, but 1924 seemed unusually active. Fried was 12–3 for the Tars (18–8 overall) and Clarkson, at 9–6, did pretty well. Zellers was erratic and inexperienced, despite having played professional ball for at least five years.

The Truckers had first baseman Jim Keesey at .326 (17 homers), left fielder Art Crump at .302 (16 home runs), third baseman Chap Marable at .299 (6 home runs) and reliable Les Bangs in center at .291. Joe Ritz led the Trucker pitching at 21–12, with help from Applegate (16–12), Deacon Joliffe (14–14) and John Manners (13–13).

Plenty of Hitting But No Pennant (1925)

In 1925, the batting average for the entire Norfolk club was just over .300, a first for Norfolk. The number of home runs also broke preceding records. But prolific as Tar hitting was, the club finished third in both categories. Portsmouth led the league in hitting at .311 and Richmond placed first in homers at 123, compared to but 87 for Norfolk and 109 for Portsmouth.

During the winter, the Virginia League meetings produced a new president and a new team. Delegates representing five teams finally settled on Judge William Bramham to replace Moye as president. Richmond interests presented a candidate, but the majority supported the judge who already held down two other baseball presidencies — the Piedmont League and the Sally League (South Atlantic League).

In return for his $2,500 in compensation, Bramham said he would stop rowdy behavior at the parks. The Virginia League also admitted the small city of Kinston, North Carolina, transferring the old Petersburg franchise for $3,000. It also looked like Raleigh would join, but the capital of North Carolina belonged to the territory of the Piedmont League (Class C). Technically there would be no violation of National Association rules should a higher class league establish a franchise there, but Bramham did not want to cause ill will. Virginians probably preferred clubs from Lynchburg or even Roanoke, but Kinston got the nod for having a concrete plan and coming up with the entry fee.

Folks in Kinston debated what to call their team. They could have called the team the Highwaymen or the "Bandits," names used when the city belonged to the East Carolina League, but they finally came to call themselves the "Eagles." As contenders in the Virginia League, the Eagles failed to soar, but, as might be expected, they occasionally stuck their talons in the Tars.

In 1925, Tars fans thought things looked promising after Robertson took over as manager and several experienced players returned. Arrangements were made with Memphis to permit Craft to remain with the Crew, so it seemed simply a question of adding quality pitchers and a replacement or two in the infield. Third baseman "Red" Cleveland returned to the fold.

The Tars acquired Elton Slayback from Morristown in the Appalachian League. Norfolk won a dispute with another club over the services of Cy Fried. Clarkson held back in sending in his contract, but he eventually appeared on deck. Frank Hummer, who threw in the Eastern Shore League the previous year, joined up. Pol Parrett left California to meet Harold Funk in Kansas City, and both arrived at the City by the Sea.

As usual, the entourage assembled for the next voyage in mid–March. *The Pilot*, referring to the maritime metaphor for the first time in a while, had Robertson "Pipe All Hands on Deck," as the club prepared to sail into the "bounding deep." Management arranged for all the players to stay at Hotel Norfolk and eat at a nearby restaurant.

Meanwhile, in Portsmouth, Shipwreck Bangs took over as manager and put together a capable aggregation to battle the Tars.[9]

In the preseason, the Tars lost several games to higher-level clubs. Jersey City beat them, 10–5, but they also triumphed, 9–4, in a second encounter, with left fielder John W. Mundy leading the hitters. Once the season started, Mundy became a pinch-hitter and soon disappeared from the roster.

With the press labeling Ty Cobb as the greatest player ever, the Detroit Tigers came to town. Cobb gave a speech, tantalizingly ironic for historians, at a luncheon, during which he emphasized the virtues of baseball in developing character. Directly addressing Maury High School athletes, he pointed out how one learned to lose with grace. He advised young athletes never to argue with umpires, saying he had never been thrown out of a game. After this sterling speech, Cobb and the Tigers submerged the Tars, 13–5, with Ty going 0-for-1 and Harry Heilman clubbing two homers before some 1,500 on a somewhat damp day. Although the Norfolk press ballyhooed the contest and believed that hundreds of Norfolk fans liked Detroit, this small attendance suggests that Cobb was nowhere near as popular as Ruth.

Around the same time the Philadelphia Athletics, with several young players such as Jimmie Foxx, Al Simmons and Mickey Cochrane, appeared in Portsmouth for an easy win over the Truckers. In subsequent preliminaries, Durham edged the Tars and Raleigh, also from a lower classification, shut them out, but the Crew got by Toronto, while the Truckers lost to the same club, 2–1.

Despite comparative scores seemingly giving the Tars an edge, Norfolk lost the opener to Portsmouth, 10–7. That result hinted at the possibility that pitching might be a problem, but the Crew rebounded the next day at Portsmouth, 4–2. Even though his club won, Robertson became so annoyed with the umpire that he fired off a note to Bramham asking for his removal. The press agreed that the man simply did not know how to move a game along and allowed too much bickering. The contest required two hours and fifty minutes, an unheard of amount of time for a ball game in the fast-moving 1920s.

After the third game in the series resulted in an 8–8 tie, Richmond blasted the Tars, 8–2 and 10–6. The Tars managed to clip the wings of the Kinston Eagles 14–5, when Craft hit three homers and his mates clubbed four more. So many balls hit the fence that the reporter joked about the amount of damage the groundskeeper needed to repair. Then the Crew lost two to the same club, only securing five runs against Parson Perryman while yielding nine in one of these losses.

Meanwhile, the Truckers posted a 14–10 win over the visiting Bugs. Sid Womack, secured from the Tars, irritated with an umpire for uttering a "vile epithet," that he made the arbiter "kiss the sod." Judge Duke assessed a fine and Bramham suspended him. Because Womack did not show up in the Portsmouth box scores for some time, we may surmise that, at long last, the league punished players for striking umpires, no matter the reason.[10]

Early that year, the Tars and Wilson Bugs split a doubleheader in which the two teams amassed 46 runs. In a four-game stretch, the Tars produced 45 runs but only won twice. In early May, Portsmouth swept the Tars by scores of 11–9, 15–12 (19 hits by the Tars) and 13–6. Tars management sent out a "Cry for Help" that brought a "Quick Reply" in the person of Cecil Duff (the press at the time called him John), who rushed to the "Rescue of a Riddled Scow" on option from Columbus, Ohio. But scoring was so prolific that although Duff promised before his first game, presumably in jest, to allow the Truckers no more than ten runs, he failed to live up to his pledge. The Tars did subdue the Colts, 13–9 and 9–5, and split two low-scoring contests with Kinston. Around this time, Red Cleveland, who had returned to the fold, led the Tars in hitting, at .480, but the record stood at 8–13, miring the team in fifth place.

Although Duff's efforts further endangered the Mary Jane, other pitchers were equally responsible for the condition of the vessel. Cy Fried injured his arm and lost his stuff. Zellers failed to show even his occasional brilliance, and disappeared from the box scores, as did newcomer Norman Garrison, who won a few early but had obvious deficiencies. The club signed on Noel "Red" Proctor, the one-time Trucker from Williamsburg.

Among the fielders, Hewell dislocated an arm, which a nationally renowned Ohio chiropractor put right. By the time "Half Pint" completed the train ride back to Norfolk, the swelling had disappeared and he resumed his place in the infield. That necessitated farming out Elton Slayback to the Blue Ridge League for a time, but when Hewell failed to exhibit his usual talents (his two errors helped lose a game), Slayback replaced him.

Meanwhile, the people of Portsmouth became so excited about their team's prospects that they began to go to a building on High Street to listen to telegraphed reports from away games. In late April, Lawrence and company staged a game seen by some 5,000 people on a Sunday. The county sheriff hesitated to act against this encroachment of the Sabbath because no tickets were sold. The Truckers beat the Colts, 7–5, so things seemingly were looking good across the river.[11]

Then the fickle fans of the sister city almost completely lost interest in their team despite its winning ways. An average attendance of less than 400 further encouraged Lawrence to pursue having games on the Sabbath, but it also caused the people of Wilmington, North Carolina, to try to convince Lawrence to move his team there. The owner of the Truckers made sure that the press knew he was seriously considering the offer. Presumably, fans might respond to this threat by developing some civic pride.

Even though Crew's batting average far exceeded .300, it was good enough only for fourth place among the teams in the league early on. Cleveland dropped off to a mere .397, but the rest of the league hitters dropped even more, leaving Norfolk with the best average in the circuit well into May, after which the team settled into third for most of the season. In early June, the Truckers had four youngsters averaging well above .300. An infielder out of Norfolk, Abe "Abbie" Hood, who led everyone with .398, would soon be sold to the New York Giants for immediate service. Late in the season, the Giants returned him. Harry Collenberger, Jim Keesey and Paul Kirby carried .361, .357, and .355 averages, respectively.

The Philadelphia Athletics made an acceptable bid for Keesey, but he stayed most of the season, despite Connie Mack occasionally expressing the need to bring him up. Later in the season, when Hood and Keesey slumped, the Portsmouth press attributed the decline to their swelled heads caused by having major-league clubs seek their services.

All of this made little difference to the Tars, for they continued to lose more than they won, posting a record of 11–18 with about a week left in May. They did take two of three from Jimmy Viox's Rocky Mount club, with Frank "Horse" Hummer besting Jake Hehl in one victory. They also overcame the Colts, 12–11, in a barnburner, but then lost three straight to the Colts, including both games of a doubleheader by identical scores of 9–4.

After splitting with Wilson, the Tars played the Truckers in their usual series at the end of May. The league-leading Truckers took the first contest, but by the comparatively low score of 4–3. During that game at Norfolk the fans, doubtless frustrated by the recent performances of what they had assumed would be a great team under Robertson, unmercifully yelled at the once-popular Red Cleveland for making two errors in the late innings, one of them essentially sealing the Crew's fate. Mollie Craft became so upset about the insulting language ("insulting" and "filthy" as described by the press) by the "two-bit bettors" in the bleachers that he threw a ball at a fan. Police arrested the fan, but released him after removing him from the premises. Craft later explained that he had not thrown the ball into the bleachers; rather, he aimed it at several blacks sitting atop the nearby brick factory. Under no conditions, he argued, would he have thrown a baseball at white spectators, who generally did not use such language. Craft's racist actions and words hint at possible tension between black fans and at least some players.[12]

It also suggested other problems on Craft's part. After a hot start, his hitting and fielding began to drop off as he adjusted to a move from first base to left field necessitated by the return of Attreau, the clever and hard-hitting first baseman. On the day before the above incident, management decided to trade Craft to the Truckers for one of their fleet fielders. The deal struck the press and the fans like "a thunderbolt from the sky," but the reporter noted that Craft had become *persona non grata* for many of the locals who had recently subjected him to "severe roastings." Craft heartily approved the change, but the Portsmouth player who originally approved the switch nixed the deal by not reporting. Restored to the Tars lineup, Craft started to play better, and then endured a series of injuries (a minor leg fracture) and sicknesses.[13] Despite winning one of the Memorial Day contests, the Tars slowly rolled down hill, their record bottoming out at eleven games below .500, their position the cellar. The Tars acquired lefty Gus Lindberg, who led Washington and Lee to a state collegiate title, to fortify the pitching. As Robertson continuously worked to settle on a rotation from among Clarkson, Duff, Fried, Proctor and occasionally Linberg or the Eastern Shore's Frank Hummer, the team slowly began to rise in the standings.

In the last few weeks of June, the Tars staged a comeback despite losing two of three to the Truckers. One of their home victories took place before the commissioner of baseball, Kenesaw Mountain Landis. In his first trip to the City by the Sea, the "Czar of Baseball" spoke at a luncheon at the Monticello Hotel, where he said his primary purpose was to insure that professional baseball players served as good models for the nation's youngsters. The press published a picture of three judges — Landis, Bramham and Willcox. After the festivities, the three watched the Tars nip Kinston, 9–8, in a typical game for that season.

With another victory over Kinston, part of a seven-game win streak, the Tars improved to 25–31 and rose to fourth. With Lindberg showing improvement, they continued to win most of the next encounters, including four from the Colts. They even beat Deacon Joliff, an event comparable to the fall of the walls of Jericho. In one of these, they blasted Percy Dawson's Capital City boys, 21–6, a league record for runs witnessed by 2,500 fans, few of whom remained through the entire debacle. Black fans celebrated by dancing to music on Church and Queen. A 5–3 win over Wilson finally brought the Tars to .500 at 32–32.

The Tars' streak continued, including three wins over the Bugs at Wilson, where Lindberg gave up only one run and Fried another run in a second encounter. That brought the

Crew back into contention, just one game back of third place, as preparations were made to play the traditional July 4 doubleheader with Portsmouth. As usual, the two cross-river rivals split the morning/afternoon session before a combined audience of some 7,000. The Truckers took the morning contest, 16–0, to end the Crew's winning streak and put themselves twelve games above .500. But the Tars rebounded at home to take the afternoon affair. Portsmouth then captured the rubber game of the series.

During one of the games, the usually calm Robertson tore some wire netting and otherwise behaved like a monkey (it was the time of the famous "Monkey Trial" regarding the teaching of evolution in public schools) in an argument with an umpire. The official first ejected Robby and then banished him from the park. Lawrence filed a report, not meaning, he later said, to cause trouble since Robertson had agreed to pay for the damaged net. After reading the umpire's report, Bramham suspended the Tar manager indefinitely. With the players incensed and reporters questioning the decision, Bramham later lifted the suspension, but not until Norfolk had lost a game in Kinston. Bramham made it clear that umpires could not have their authority undermined.

Although Robby never swore, the right fielder/manager ridiculed the umpire by walking off with his whisk broom, returning it only when the umpire threatened to forfeit the game to the Truckers, who won anyway, 7–0. The league simply could not allow Robertson to carry out his Alphonse and Gaston routine. Bramham believed that excessive hero worship caused players to think they could behave "monstrously." We can only wonder what Bramham did, if anything, about Onslow instructing his pitcher to hit Robertson the previous year. On his return to the park on 20th Street (the Norfolk press still insisted on putting it on 18th Street), Norfolk's fans gave Robertson a royal welcome and roared its disapproval of the umpire in question.[14]

When the Tars were going well, they could be overwhelming. After taking two of three from the Colts, Clarkson shut out Wilson, after which the Crew beat Wilson 27–3, with southpaw Fried the beneficiary. In this contest, they drew eight walks and hit three homers, nine doubles, and 15 singles in a game that took all of 2 hours and 15 minutes. After beating the Tars the next day, 7–6, Wilson went across the river to shut out the Truckers.

Disaster struck League Park in July, when a lit cigarette fell through the planking of the grandstand just after a game in which Portsmouth and Norfolk tied. It combusted a pile of peanut shells and caused a huge fire. Norfolk firemen had trouble reaching the scene because cars blocked the roads, so they arrived about the same time that the roof fell. The owners, covered by insurance for at least part of the $10,000 in damages, set about to build even better stands, sufficient to hold some 3,500.[15]

In early August, with Bill Clarkson's record at 13–6, Robertson arranged for his sale to the Giants for $10,000, the deal taking effect at the end of the season. At that time, the Tars received right-hander Alex "Iron Man" Peterson, who had been the best pitcher in 1923.

The pitching stabilized, the team's record improved to 53–46, as Norfolk beat Portsmouth twice behind Peterson and Proctor. With no team in the league doing spectacularly well, Norfolk closed to within one-half game of the league leaders — only to lose every game they played for one disastrous week in August. The Tars also had a victory taken away when league officials called a previous game with Richmond a tie, even though an umpire publicly admitted that he misinterpreted the rules in calling a Tar out at the plate. The bad spell dropped the club into fourth place, for and a half games behind Richmond and Portsmouth.

Over in Portsmouth, Joe Poetz bested Richmond's ace as the Truckers took two of three from the Colts. The Tars ended the losses with two victories over Portsmouth by identical scores (3–2), which left Portsmouth in first place but only four games above the Wilson Bugs. Norfolk subsequently defeated the Truckers twice more, 5–0 and 3–1. Clearly, pitching had finally caught up to the hitters and Wilson, now less than three games back, was closing in on the Truckers. In the second week in August, the Bugs swept the Truckers and moved into first place by half a game. Norfolk held at about four off the pace, with Richmond one game behind that. Wilson and Portsmouth then traded places several times.

In a curious twist, Wilson began to exhibit considerable weakness and Richmond astounding strength, despite a no-hitter tossed at the Colts by Trucker Joe Poetz. On Labor Day, Norfolk knocked Portsmouth out of the race by beating them twice, 5–3 and 18–6, to knot the season series between the two, as Peterson won his tenth in a row in the morning. But the Truckers rebounded to triumph twice against their biggest rivals the next day. Norfolk went on to sweep Wilson to end the season.

On the last day of the season, with the score tied in the top of the ninth, Robertson, at the insistence of the fans, sauntered to the mound to pitch for the first time in ten years. He first gave up a bloop Texas Leaguer. Then, fastball blazing, he struck out three straight Bugs. In the last of the ninth, he unloaded a home run to win the game in dramatic fashion.

Norfolk posted a 72–61 final record, good for third place. Richmond, under owner/manager Percy Dawson, led the pack at 79–54, and Portsmouth placed second at 75–58. The three North Carolina teams — the Wilson Bugs, the Rocky Mount Bronchos and the Kinston Eagles — occupied the second division in that order.

Percy Dawson had to his credit four pennant winners in six years, two at Richmond and two with Portsmouth in 1920 and 1921. Second-place finishes with Newport News in 1922 and Richmond in 1923 also indicated that the man knew something about putting out first-class baseball teams.

Statistically that year, Robertson posted gargantuan numbers, batting .388 while slugging 24 homers. Craft came in 50 points below that average with 10 home runs. Pea Head Walker hit .328 and Elton "Scotty" Slayback ended up at .323, with 16 round-trippers. He returned to the New York Giants at season's end. Slick-fielding Dick Attreau, later one of the most prolific hitters ever to wear a Tar uniform, hit .312. Bernie "Red" Cleveland, after a blazing start, fell off to .309, while Olin Parrett posted a .283 average. Cecil Duff crafted a .313 as a reserve outfielder, although he was primarily a pitcher. After the season, management traded him to the Bronchos for catcher Sam Hamby. In 1925, catcher Funk hit a creditable .289, raising his output from the year before in all the crucial categories.

As in the entire era, Crew pitching remained suspect, even though the staff included Alex "Iron Man" Peterson, who posted the best earned-run average in the league at 1.58. Peterson won every one of his 11 decisions, coming on board well past half way through the season. Bill Clarkson led the club with 16 wins, and soon joined the New York Giants. Cecil Duff came in at 14–15 by one account. Red Proctor lost three more than he won. Season-ending data gave several wins to Frank Dodson as a member of the Crew, but newspaper accounts have him pitching but once as a Tar and driven from the mound in the second inning. The Tars recovered in that contest to win handily. A reporter intimated at the time that this one-time ace pitcher had already lost his stuff. Cy Fried broke even in 18 decisions. Frank Hummer stood at 4–6.

Second-place Portsmouth, which led the league for most of the season, also put up some pretty fair numbers in hitting, with seven regulars, a backup right fielder and a reserve infielder all hitting above .300. Roy Buckalew anchored the Trucker staff at 18–12, while submariner Joe Poetz came in at 15–13 and Carl "Doc" Dunnegan at 14–9. Frank Lawrence constantly complained about poor attendance in Portsmouth. After selling his ace pitcher, Al Reitz, early in the season, he threatened to dismantle the club unless the situation improved.

In league business that winter, the owners took the franchise away from Rocky Mount and gave it to Petersburg. Some North Carolinians protested the action at a league meeting. Despite their complaints the Virginia club now became known as the Petersburg Bronchos.

A Repeat Scenario (1926)

In the spring of 1926, Tar management totally rebuilt the bleachers. It made a special effort to improve the seating for blacks who occupied the area behind first base by elevating the seats on platforms to prevent people's knees from jamming the backs of those seated in front of them. The bleachers angled toward the field of play in deep right field, allowing fans to have a better view of the proceedings. But doing so meant that only a few inches separated the fans in the extreme right corner and a right fielder trying to catch a fly ball in that location. Groundskeeper Sam Childress also put down grass in the infield, which apparently had not been done for a year or two.

Robertson had a pretty fair idea of the composition of his club long before practice commenced in mid–March. Even though a league rule supposedly required that no more than six of 13 players have B level experience or higher, all the clubs contained more than that number, suggesting that teams must have had some latitude about their own holdovers. The purpose for the rule was to keep costs down and also compel clubs to bring in young talent. Both Robertson and Bangs abided by the spirit of the rule by taking in several farmhands, the former using his connection with John McGraw.

Over the winter Norfolk management traded Craft for Chap Marable and Jack Sauter, but Marable stayed on board only early in the voyage despite telling Robby in the preseason that he had not come to Norfolk just to play croquet. Outfielder Joe Klinger, who played for a team in West Virginia the previous year, looked like a keeper from the start of training. Facing the season without an experienced shortstop, Robby asked McGraw for help, which came one day after the season started in the form of Walter Novak. That filled the hole created by the transfer of Pea Head Walker. Pea Head refused to report to Buffalo, going instead to the Eastern Shore to be under Win Clark, who had recently been scouting for the New York Yankees. The shortstop later joined the Wilson Bugs.

Another McGraw recruit, Sam Hanby, who caught for Rocky Mount for most of the previous season, came on deck, as did backup catcher Souter, with Tommy Hipple, a local military man, on call. Larry Boerner, who pitched briefly the year before, looked good for a brief time. As usual, Robby could pick only a few of those who tried out as pitchers. Red Proctor, Frank Hummer and finally Alex Peterson showed up, with the first and last sticking with the team for a good part of the season. The press talked about Cy Fried, now residing in Suffolk, as a possible prospect, but his days as a Tar were over. Missourian Frank J. Riel, who previously pitched for Kinston, made the club. After the season got underway, Vance Page and Harry Moger joined the rotation.

Across the river, Lawrence brought in Ducky Smith to cover first base. Toots Brandon, the one-time Tar, soon replaced another catcher in the starting lineup. Another ex–Tar, Mollie Craft, cavorted in the outfield. Jim "Red" Rollings roved the short field. Bangs and Craft, at age 31, were the oldest members; all the others ranged in age from 22 to 27.

Lefty Roy Buckalew won the team pool championship and continued to be one of the best pitchers. Everyone expected Joe "Holy Cow" Poetz to win the most games. John Dempster, a reliable lefty, gave Portsmouth at least three returning twirlers. As they watched the 1926 team prepare for the upcoming season, fans in Portsmouth got a big lift from reading about the exploits of former Truckers such as Rube Benton (Braves), Hack Wilson (Cubs), Pie Traynor (Pirates) and Kent Greenfield (Giants).

As usual, the Crew started off slowly, losing nearly every preseason game against representatives from the International League and other minor leagues. Elmer Bowman, who now toiled for New Haven after having played as a Tar on the celebrated, if infamous, 1921 team, appeared on the scene, with a newspaper displaying his picture under the title "Remember this Bozo." Bowman had added considerable girth since 1921 and the Portsmouth paper wrote about how his movements around first base were a study in the "economy of motion." Former Tar pitcher Pat Loftus also worked for New Haven that year. The Watchmakers easily won a Sunday game against the Tars and edged them at the New Haven training grounds at Suffolk before 500 spectators, 3–2. The scores by which the Tars lost to Syracuse — 10–4, 8–2 and 8–4, the last one at Elizabeth City with Pepper Martin, future member of the "Gas House Gang" in St. Louis starring for the winners — hinted at the presence of pitching problems.

The Truckers looked a bit better than the Tars based on preseason performance. New Haven split high-scoring contests with Portsmouth. In major-league competition at Norfolk, as teams headed home from spring training, the Giants eased by the Senators before some 7,000 one day in April.

In the season opener, a Robertson homer and pitching by Peterson propelled the Tars to a home win over the Truckers and Poetz. John Mundy substituted for Parrett, who had been called back to California because of illness in his family. Marable covered shortstop in the absence of the expected newcomer Novak. Some 5,000 watched, providing pretty fair attendance in the face of a competing circus in town.

Portsmouth recovered the next day to smear its biggest rival, 14–6, and followed that with another lopsided win, 9–1. Peterson got the Tars back on track against Petersburg 8–4. The two teams then split the next two. Against Richmond, the Tars posted a 17–9 triumph, but the Colts dominated the next game, 13–3, and then took a twin bill by 12–11 and 10–9. Riel took a pounding from the Truckers, but excellent fielding allowed Peterson to return the favor. Boerner lost the rubber game, 5–4. A 4–3 win over Wilson brought April to an end, with Portsmouth and Richmond battling for first place and the Tars well back.

Norfolk started May with a win over the Bugs, but Wilson recovered to take a doubleheader the next day, during which the Tars' "growling and spitting" at each other prompted Robertson and other club management to rake four or five "over the coals." The club soon lost three in a row to the Kinston Eagles, two by routs. In the finale Peterson found himself on the small end of an 8–0 score. Finally, two homers by Attreau and one by Sauter brought about a win over the Petersburg Bronchos in the opener of a series that produced three wins out of four. Two homers by Robertson helped the cause.

On May 10, the Tars and the Colts fought to a 7–7 draw. Later in the series, the two clubs split a doubleheader, with the Colts prevailing 12–9, and then losing 12–8, as good pitching continued to be at a premium. To address this problem, the Crew hired George Quinn, once a craftsman among Virginia League pitchers. In a prolonged series with Richmond, Quinn mastered the Colts 9–0, giving fans hope that the pitching woes might be over. Although Moger gave up five runs in the top of the ninth inning to put an end to a tight duel the next day against the Truckers, the Tars recovered to carry the next three close encounters, 5–3, 6–5 and 4–3.

With the situation seemingly improved, the Crew went on the road to lose two of three in Wilson. Quinn got a win, despite pitching poorly at Kinston. After losing the next battle, 8–7, the Tars recovered to take a doubleheader in the Eagles' nest, thus winning three of four and finally bringing their record to 19–19. The team, however, quickly fell back when, with Robertson incapacitated by an ailment, they incurred two losses in close games at Richmond. Proctor then fought through for a 10–7 win in the Capital City. Splits in doubleheaders against Petersburg and Portsmouth, the latter on Memorial Day (9–8 in the morning in favor of the Truckers and 10–4 at Norfolk in the afternoon) left Norfolk at one game below .500 at the end of May.

In the third match at Portsmouth on June 1, young Vance Page hung on for a 12–7 win as Poetz faltered. Norfolk tried out another youngster, Bill Poyner of the University of North Carolina, with less positive results the next day, leaving Norfolk still one game below .500. Tommy Hipple got a game-winning hit in the 10th inning of the next game to allow the Crew once again to reach the hallowed level, but his presence behind the plate meant that a split finger had sidelined Hamby.

And so the Tars muddled along, playing just under .500 before Novak left and flirting with last place after his departure. Novak fielded well and hit well over .300, but in May, McGraw re-assigned him to Waco. Novak, who had not wanted to come to Tidewater, now did not want to leave it. His mates prevailed upon him to obey, so that he would not have to quit playing the game. His leaving left a gap on the left side of the Tars infield. After losing one game due to poor work at shortstop, Robertson borrowed shortstop "Sailor" Harris from the Norfolk Air Station. Harris not only fielded adequately but also went 4-for-7 at the plate in helping the Tars win a doubleheader. The next day Shorty Bauchand arrived to cover the short field. A few weeks later Novak returned to resume his position with the Crew, having been acquired from the Texas team.

The Tars fell back in early June, doing especially abysmally on the road, when they won only one of nine in one stretch. After falling to 26–31 to occupy fifth place in the standings, they bested Petersburg in three of four, with Peterson and Page pitching well. The Tars then took two of three against the Eagles. Norfolk had won five out of seven against teams that rested in the lower half of the league standings. These wins allowed Norfolk to aspire to a higher level in the standings.

Battles against the Wilson Bugs, one of the better clubs in the league, sometimes provided excitement as the two teams struggled for third place. They once played for 14 innings, with fans once again assaulting umpire Westervelt with seat cushions and four or five bottles (fortunately they all missed). Also in this game, Kid Sterling, a local wrestler of some repute who also served the Tars as the designated ball retriever, went into the left-field bleachers to locate a baseball, only to have two fans attack him. Police arrested the culprits.[16]

By the end of June, the Tars being around .500, management voted with the majority of owners against having a split season. Showing measurable improvement during this time, the club ran all over the Colts for four straight wins, three by healthy margins, with a variety of heroes on the mound and at the plate. After this series the record stood at 36–36. But the Capital City still rested in first place at 47–30, with Portsmouth in second just a game ahead of the Tars. In the next few weeks, the Tars split their traditional July 4 double bill with the Truckers and then took two from the Truckers to climb into second place in the league at 43–38, one of several teams bunched together three or four games below Richmond.

If the Tars thought they had troubles, they paled in comparison to those of the Truckers. Lawrence had so few fans attending games that he agreed to play the holiday morning game in Norfolk on July 5 (July 4 was a Sunday, so the games were played on Monday) as well as the afternoon game. The first attracted 3,000, the second about twice that number. The Truckers also played at least two series in Norfolk, with Lawrence saying he wanted his team to be called the "Norfolk Truckers." In one series, the new Norfolk team split with Petersburg, with ex–Tar Cecil Duff winning for the Bronchos. Rain reduced attendance and forced postponement of the last game in the series. The Monday matinee, even though called "Blue Monday" because of its traditional weak attendance, drew about twice as many as showed up in Portsmouth on the same day of the previous week. After a couple of weeks, Lawrence turned down a firm offer from Wilmington for his club in the belief that it was too late in the season to change locales, and moved back to the Portsmouth park on Upper High Street.

During this time, it looked like the Tars might make a run for the pennant. Norfolk beat Kinston twice by lopsided scores; the Crew then educated Wilson in the art of hitting in winning three out of four. In a doubleheader at Wilson, Robertson poled three homers in one game, and clubbed another in the second game, giving him 23, nearly his entire previous year's output, as the league reached the middle of July. At that point, Robertson had also hit safely in 21 straight games. Norfolk held onto second place, five games above .500.

At this juncture, the Truckers broke through the Crew defenses, taking a double bill, 3–2 and 8–3. The Tars retaliated by capturing a doubleheader the next day, 4–3 and 7–6. Norfolk remained in second, still five games above .500, trailing Richmond by five games in the win column but with only one more loss.

In ensuing battles after the middle of July, Cecil Duff put the clamps on the Crew and the Bronchos swept three at the City on the Appomattox, despite which the Tars still clung to second. Norfolk rebounded to corral the Colts for two, 8–6 and 11–4 at Richmond, followed by a split in a doubleheader by the same two clubs, with Frank Riel shutting out Richmond in the finale. But losses to Kinston and Wilson dropped the Tars from second to fourth, at 53–51. Eagle pitchers blanked Robby in one of these encounters to end his hitting streak at 31.

Pea Head Walker and Bunny Hearn carried the day for the Bugs, with the Norfolk press wondering how the old Tar shortstop could be so "mean and unfriendly" to his old mates. The Tars recovered to win two the next day, with new third baseman Frank McCue in a starring role.

Early in August, with Robertson away in New York and Novak suffering a broken nose, the Tars submitted to the Truckers. The injury forced Robby to bring on board another one-time Naval Station man, Pat Doss. Like Harris, he held down the temporary post quite admirably. Portsmouth also won the next day to ensconce the suddenly hot Truckers in second and bring them within three games of league-leading Richmond. Two homers by Robertson and a gutsy performance by new lefty Luther Barnes permitted the Tars to hold on to the last game in the series, despite three runs by the Truckers in the ninth inning. The Colts then beat the Tars three out of four, to maintain a narrow lead.

Just two games above .500, the Tars made a run of five straight wins at the expense of the Bronchos and Bugs at home, after which Norfolk and Wilson split a double bill, with Bunny Hearn finally halting Norfolk's streak. The wins that week allowed the Tars to retake second place.

Norfolk and Portsmouth planned to play a series at the same time that Norfolk put on a giant water carnival. The event included King Neptune crowning a queen at The Hague. As the gods of ocean and sky fought it out, with the latter prevailing, the Tars, better in ocean storms than the Truckers, triumphed 7–3, with Peterson delivering in relief. On the same day, thousands lined the banks of the eastern branch of the Elizabeth River to watch a motorboat regatta.[17]

After that storm system passed through the area, Norfolk bounced Richmond for two straight, 5–0 and 11–1. It looked like the Tars were about ready to make a run at the Colts, despite still trailing them by four games. The next day, however, rain again washed out the game. And in the last two days of August and the first of September, the Tars lost three games at Wilson, allowing the Bugs to move ahead of them in the standings by one and a half games. Then at Kinston, the Crew won the first, but lost two low-scoring affairs. Once again, the club lost all but one game on a week-long road trip. The two losses to Kinston likely deprived the Tars of any possibility of catching Richmond. That result left Norfolk in third place at 72–68. A Norfolk sweep of the Truckers on Labor Day improved Norfolk's chances of catching Wilson in the struggle for second place.

Through the second half of the season, the press suspected that the team needed to buttress its pitching. Frank Riel, Bill Sawyer, Harry Moger and later Luther Barnes did very well on occasion but they lacked consistency — at least the kind that Peterson and even Red Proctor provided. Living up to his label as "Iron Man," Peterson once won both ends of a doubleheader. The problem with pitching was pervasive throughout the league, due mostly to the expanded schedule that included a lot of doubleheaders, especially on Saturdays.

Whatever the cause for the weak pitching, every time it looked like the Tars were gaining traction, they would take a road trip and suffer a sweep, such as happened against last-place Petersburg near the end of July. On the other hand, when it looked like traveling would lead to their final downfall, Robby's men braced, like they did at Richmond to win three out of four, and closed the gap between themselves and the league leaders. Then just as it looked like the club might make a run at Richmond, the Crew lost three of four in the capital toward the middle of August.

Near the end of the season Bramham received a complaint from the Norfolk club that Richmond had exceeded its limit of first-class players. When Dawson sent in a counter complaint, charging the Tars with the same violation, Norfolk management hastily withdrew its petition. At this time, any pitcher with 75 or more at-bats, or any hitter with 150 or more at-bats for a team above Class B level counted as a class player. Judge Bramham paid scant attention to the Norfolk complaint, but he did review an earlier one from Wilson, when the replacement for Richmond's injured Rube Oldring rated too high a level of experience. As a result of this decision against Richmond, the Colts, instead of having a four-game lead over the Wilson Bugs, now trailed them by one-half game.

The folks in Wilson believed this decision made up for the one when Landis deprived their team of the pennant in 1921, but the Bugs failed to take advantage. On the day of the Bramham pronouncement, the Bugs shut out the Tars, but Norfolk then beat the Bugs twice, giving Richmond a one-half game lead. As Norfolk took two out of three from Petersburg to finish off the year with a record of 79–73, Richmond defeated the Kinston Eagles the same number of times as the Bugs beat the Truckers. Those outcomes allowed Richmond to claim the championship by one-half game. Portsmouth nestled in fourth place, one game over .500. Kinston and Petersburg fought for the bottom, with the Bronchos winning that dubious distinction.

Richmond went on to lose the postseason series, four out of five, against the South Atlantic League's Greenville Spinners, now under the command of Frank Walker. The year before the Colts lost to Spartanburg, also of the Sally League, again winning but one contest.

As the season wound down, Judge Bramham, after studying reports from umpires and other witnesses sent to watch the games between the Bugs and Truckers, exonerated Bangs and his men from the charge of letting Wilson win the final series. Dawson initially wanted the matter to go before Judge Landis, with participants being compelled to go to Chicago to testify, but with Richmond's narrow win, such an exercise seemed moot.[18]

Despite not doing any better in the standings than they had the previous year, the Tars led the league in hitting, amassing their highest level ever, at .313. As for the individual numbers, Robertson once again led the league with .382 and drilled 35 homers (second in the league). Left-handed hitting Dick Attreau hit his stride with a .371 average, producing a league-record 225 hits. With a game or two left in the season, Attreau, his contract purchased for some $11,000, headed off to Philadelphia to join the Phillies.

Other .300 hitters included Scotty Slayback, Frank McCue, Walter Novak, Olin "Pol" Parrett, Joe Klinger and catcher Sam Hamby, who was sent back to the New York Giants toward the end of the year, and made good on the opportunity. Novak became the property of the Chicago Cubs. Only one regular fielder failed to hit at least .300, that being Jack Sauter at .282. Late in the season, Norfolk could put eight .300 hitters on the field in any game.

In slugging 143 home runs, the Tars broke the previous season's record output by 56 and also nearly exceeded the total number of home runs hit by the Norfolk club from 1906 through 1918. High as that total was, it paled in comparison to the Richmond club, which was credited with 183, most of them in cozy Mayo Park.

Once again, the heaviest weight of the pitching fell to Alex "Iron Man" Peterson, at 22–16. Red Proctor came in at 18–12. Frank Riel ended up with Wilson where he proved something of a jinx for his former mates, though he returned to the Crew at the start of the next season. Other victories and losses were distributed among several participants. Harry Moger won a few. George Quinn, once an ace for the Bugs and purchased from Wilson for $1,000, helped out for a time, but was finally released. By season's end, Luther "Lethal" Barnes and Bill Sawyer pitched a lot.

Across the river, Portsmouth hit about as well as the Tars for average, but slugged nowhere near as many homers. Among the regulars, the Truckers were led by Ducky Smith at .340, second baseman Harry Collenberger at .335, with 15 home runs, shortstop Jimmy Rollins at .332, third baseman John Rice at .326, and Mollie Craft, finally playing for his hometown and batting .325, with 17 homers. Norfolk resident Les Bangs in the center garden hit a consistent .302, with 10 home runs. Catcher Hilton "Toots" Brandon, missing .300 by .001, slugged 16 homers and headed off for a tryout with the Senators. Joe Poetz anchored the pitchers at 21–13 while four others flirted with .500.[19]

As was their custom, newsmen assessed the situation at the end of the season. A reporter summarized the views of many when he pondered why the "greatest ball club assembled in Norfolk in ten years could finish no better than third place." He also believed, as doubtless did many others, that the Tars, with much of their nucleus still available, would be an excellent contender in the 1927 voyage. That proved to be an overly optimistic prediction.[20]

Truckers Triumphant, Tars Troubled (1927)

Over the winter, it looked like Kinston would not be able to renew its franchise. The 1926 season cost investors there some $55,000 with only $42,000 in receipts. Its citizens reluctantly returned their franchise to the league. Faced with the withdrawal of Kinston, its natural Carolina rival Wilson threatened to pull out as well. A reporter, possibly recalling the nautical background of the Norfolk club, warned of "Breakers Ahead," and described this episode as the "severest gale in the history of the sloop," which threatened to sweep the league into the "breakers."[21]

While rumors circulated in the media that the Piedmont League might pick more cities in North Carolina, Bramham encouraged businessmen in Lynchburg and Roanoke to enter the Virginia League. Lynchburg had a new football facility about two blocks from downtown, which could, with a little effort, be converted for baseball. Some 200 Roanoke residents listened to the judge as he estimated that it would only cost about $30,000 to run a team for a year, a little more than half the amount Kinston had spent the year before. Unfortunately, the Norfolk and Western Company owned and utilized the only real ballpark every afternoon but Sunday. Plans to have the city build such a facility started too late to have any chance at completion for the season.

When it looked like the Virginia League might field fewer clubs, Kinston came up with $10,000, sought readmission to the league, and changed its name to the Bluebirds. Thus, after much discussion, the stormy waters calmed and the league ended up with the same configuration it had in 1926. Bramham and company, however, expected to continue their "missionary work" to create franchises in other Virginia towns.

Despite the league's decision in a fall meeting in Norfolk not to play doubleheaders routinely on Saturdays, skipper Robertson knew that he needed better pitching. Eighteen hurlers showed up at the initial practice or shortly thereafter. Robertson brought back Peterson, Proctor, Boerner, Sawyer and Poyner, all pitchers from the previous season, while big lefty Art Johnson came at the recommendation of new catcher Charles Rowland. Southpaw Jack Arthur also looked like a great prospect.

Over the winter, the club let go Parrett. Although he had been the best defensive outfielder in the league the previous three years, he did not hit for power (22 home runs, though in former times that would have been the output for an entire team). Besides, fans often wanted to see a new face. Parrett joined Funk, former Tar catcher and now manager of a team in Missouri.

In a seemingly contradictory move, management moved the left-field fence back another 12 feet to allow outstanding fielders to exhibit their talents.

Former Trucker and Norfolk resident Buddy Crump looked like a likely replacement for Attreau at first base. The manager held out hope that shortstop Novak, who had failed to stick with the Giants, might rejoin the Crew. When that hope failed to materialize, the team purchased Walter White from Petersburg. The original roster also listed former Broncho manager and catcher Tommy Abbott. Backup catcher Jack Sauter went across the Capes to manage a team in Northampton County on Virginia's Eastern Shore.

Across the river, Lawrence bubbled with optimism, as he always did at the beginning of a season. Paving the extension of High Street might help the attendance problem, as more residents now had automobiles. Even though the park was not close to downtown, few folks had used the bus service Lawrence offered the previous year. As a further inducement, he offered 60 tickets for $40, which the recipients could use for any games and distribute as they saw fit. If daylight savings time returned that summer, Lawrence said he would start games at 5 P.M. and provide free transportation from the Navy Yard.

The Truckers carried over only a few men. They brought in Zinn Beck, a third baseman and former St. Louis Cardinal, to play and manage. The club tried Craft at the first sack, but soon acquired someone else for that position, leaving the celebrated Craft in the outfield. Jose Ramos, "a stocky and flashy Cuban" brought over from Richmond via a trade, would certainly help. Other prospects included Red Thomas, Izzy Bandrimer, Norfolk lawyer Bill Dietrick, plus pitchers Bill Coggins, Chuck Warden and Ben Weaver, the latter recommended by Kent Greenfield. With Craft, Thomas and Ramos in the outfield, the Truckers had three players who had hit at least .300 for three straight years.

The preseason offered few clues to the comparative abilities of the Tars and Truckers. The Tars narrowly lost to the New York Giants' second team whereas the Truckers beat them, 4–0. The Truckers beat the New Haven "Professors," 2–1 in the initial exhibition and then lost, 1–0, to the same team. Crump hit a homer and a triple, as Norfolk downed the Eastern League champs, the Providence Grays, 8–5. Norfolk overwhelmed the Air Station while Portsmouth bested Lou Stanley and the Norfolk police, 5–1. The Grays beat the Truckers, 7–0. Portsmouth fans saw Jersey City Skeeters, including Harry Collenberger, Toots Brandon and Roy Buckalew lose to the locals, 4–1. Just as the regular season was about to start, the New Jersey club sent Brandon back to Portsmouth, but held onto the other two.

The Tars and Truckers opened the season, as they usually did, by splitting the first two games. Three errors by substitute shortstop Pat Doss, another Air Station player, helped give the Truckers a 9–8 win on their home turf, after mayor Vernon Brooks opened up the festivities. Zinn Beck, a bat manufacturer by trade, gave away miniature missiles to all paying customers. Fortunately, no one felt the need to use them against an umpire, opponent, or their own players. In the second encounter, the Truckers reciprocated by making errors to allow the Tars to take the opening game 5–4 at League Park, with Larry Boerner getting credit for the win in relief of Jack Arthur. Then Norfolk took the third game in the series, 17–12, with a flood of long hits, including four home runs. Portsmouth, however, recovered to triumph, 10–1.

For some time, the Crew followed its usual early-season pattern of losing a few more than they won. The Tars lost two of three to the Bluebirds in Kinston, winning the one game, 9–3, when four of their balls went on "shore leave." They also lost three games by one run each to Wilson. Returning home, they lost 2–0, a hard-luck loss for Peterson, but the team recovered to beat the Truckers twice by the same score, 8–7, as Johnson and Boerner got credit for wins in relief. Peterson and Johnson victories against Petersburg brought the Crew back to .500 as April ended.

In an early-May game in Richmond, the Colts won by registering eight runs in the last of the ninth, the last three coming when a backup player slugged a three-run homer. Even though such a debacle might ordinarily ruin a team for the next day, the Crew triumphed 9–5, with Alex Peterson getting credit for the victory. A few days later, clever base running by John Rice, who had been acquired from Portsmouth when Craft resumed his post in the outfield there, brought another victory over the league-leading Colts in the tenth inning. Larry Boerner won in relief of Cecil Duff, who had been traded back to the Tars.

As a Trucker, Rice almost ran through a fence near the right-field bleachers and knocked himself out in a vain attempt to catch a foul fly. For Norfolk, Rice made a game-saving catch in a win at Kinston. He ran through the outfield fence, demolishing two planks, and held onto the ball despite being unconscious. Rice injured his back on the play and had to be hospitalized. Despite these heroics, after he recovered he found himself traded to the Bluebirds.

In May, the Tars, with local Raleigh "Mullett" Saunders in his only start on the mound, lost to Chuck Warden and Portsmouth, 6–1. Soon thereafter, the Truckers let the Tars have Warden. The next day Klinger and Robertson hit homers to win one against their archrivals. Even so, the Tars' record remained five or six games below .500 during all of May and into June. Back home, the Tars lost two to the Bugs but Peterson, according to the press, won his

100th game (the records only give him 93) as a member of the Crew one Wednesday afternoon after trailing 7–0 in the first inning. Robertson refused to have him relieved, and the "Iron Man" settled down to win, 11–7. (On that same day, two semipro teams played at League Park to raise money to cover hospital costs for Dutch Revelle, who had been umpiring in the local semipro league. Harry Mace organized the benefit.)

After losing more games to the Truckers, the Tars compounded their problems by dropping two of three to Petersburg at Norfolk. The club signed up Jimmy Duffy, originally with Kinston, to buttress the staff, which gave up 12 runs in each of the losses to the Bronchos. In its one win, the Crew scored 14 runs. Norfolk then bested the Colts in two, winning the second in 10 innings, 6–5.

The next day, Art Johnson lost, 3–2, to the visitors from the capital, before one of the largest crowds of the season. A poor road trip then ensued, with a win, a loss, and a tie in Kinston, and three straight defeats on the Appomattox, when the team scored but two runs in three games.

That disaster set the stage for the traditional Memorial Day doubleheader, when some 5,000 sailors "invaded" the area, coming off some 80 ships. Whatever they were doing on shore, they weren't watching baseball. Before 1,500 fans, the Crew of the Mary Jane got by the Truckers in Portsmouth, 6–3, with Larry Boerner receiving credit for the win. But that afternoon, Doc Dunnegan beat the Tars in their home park, 5–3. Portsmouth followed with another win, as Bill Coggins beat former Trucker Chuck Warden, leaving Norfolk in last place in the league, at 17–24. Portsmouth, at 23–18, was vying for the league lead with Richmond at the end of May. To make matters worse, the Truckers plowed under the Tars on June 1, 9–3.

On the road, Duffy managed to beat Wilson on the same day that Calvin Coolidge came in the presidential yacht to watch the Atlantic Fleet, spaced out over 15 miles, head out to sea. Norfolk then split with Richmond at Mayo Park. At home, the club lost to Kinston, but won 9–2, behind Peterson. Despite this win, the Tars remained in the cellar, but by winning the rubber game, 7–0, the Crew exited the basement with a record of 21–30.

The team remained in peril, however, as it split with Petersburg and lost again at Portsmouth. Johnson held on in relief to attain a victory as fans, players and an umpire exchanged nasty words. Lawrence went into the stands with a megaphone to restore order. The umpire later apologized for saying that Portsmouth players were not gentlemen. Peterson and Johnson then won easily over the Bugs to allow the Tars to hold off Kinston.[22]

In the last week of June, the Tars swept the Colts, with Boerner, Peterson and Johnson registering wins by fairly wide margins. The Tars continued flirting with .500, a 12-inning win at Wilson improving their record to 31–34. Unfortunately, Robertson suffered an apparent broken angle hook-sliding into second base, and the team's chances for success pretty much disappeared. With several players lifting him up and the batboy holding his hanging ankle, Robertson left the field. At Sarah Leigh Hospital, doctors, using an X-ray, verified the fateful news.

In searching for a replacement, management first thought it might acquire Mike Smith, a farmhand and the greatest athlete in the history of South Norfolk, from the New York Giants. When that could not be arranged, they acquired Jack Smith from Toledo. Although Smith helped beat the Truckers a couple of times late in August, once with a homer, and hit for a high average, he was no Dave Robertson.

Even without Robby, the club again mastered the Bugs, 5–4, again in 12 innings, with Johnson securing credit. In an ensuing series against the league leading Truckers over July 4,

Norfolk was conquered twice. Portsmouth won the morning home game, 8–2, before 2,500, and the afternoon game 4–3, before 3,500 at Norfolk. After the double loss, Norfolk's record stood at 32–37, a game or so above Kinston, which was mired in last place. The Truckers followed up with three more wins in a row.

The Tars finally stemmed the downward flow by stopping Kinston, with Boerner in the box. Jimmy Hines, recently purchased from the Bronchos, followed with an easy win against the former Eagles, but the Colts then swept the Tars. A defeat at Petersburg brought the losing streak to four before Johnson went the distance in winning, 8–7, at the Cockade City. The Tars also carried the rubber game, but then lost two of three at Wilson.

Back at home against the Bronchos, Boerner bested Vince Matthews, a one-time Tar who had recently been seen wandering the streets of Norfolk in search of a berth. Hines then overcame his former mates for the Tars, but after this excellent start to the home stand, Peterson and company lost two to the visitors. They then took the Kinston Bluebirds for two of three but lost two of three to Richmond as July came to an end. That left the Tars in fifth place at 42–52, while Portsmouth remained well ahead of the second-place Colts.

Just after "Iron Man" Alex supposedly won his hundredth game in a Tar uniform, he began to exhibit signs of discontent. Robertson fined him $25 for failing to show up for the morning game he was supposed to pitch on July 4. Some of his mates said he was sick, but because he had previously failed to catch a train in time for a start in Kinston, it looked like something more serious might be the case. In many of his starts, rival hitters got to him in the first inning, but even when he survived that inning, poor support prevented him from winning games. Robertson ultimately dismissed him and he headed to Harrisburg, Pennsylvania, where Win Clark oversaw his resurgence. The loss of Peterson only partially explains the weak performance by the Tars that season.

The biggest news in local ball in 1927 occurred when a tornado touched down on Portsmouth Stadium, tearing the roof off the stands in right field, killing at least two and injuring many more. The 300-foot-wide twister caused considerable havoc and could have done even worse had not an eerie yellow light and a "giant black curtain" off to the west convinced reporters to leave the press box atop the stands, thus saving their lives. Stunned fans and reporters made their way to the only nearby phone, located at Judge Duke's office, to call for help. Judge Kenesaw Mountain Landis, watching the ballgame at the time, escaped injury, and applauded the rescue efforts of the players from the Portsmouth and Petersburg teams.[23]

The Portsmouth paper editorialized that the rising popularity and progress of the national pastime made it too strong to be ended by a "squall," however powerful that act of nature might be. With their grandstand on High Street in ruins, Lawrence and the Truckers accepted the Sewanee Athletic Association offer to let them use the old Washington Street Park. Its bleachers, however, seated only 600, so Portsmouth fans would be inconvenienced no matter where the games were held. But because so few showed up for the games, it actually made little difference where they were played.

Lawrence offered to raise $5,000 by having Norfolk and Portsmouth play a Sunday game, the receipts to go to the victims of the disaster. But Norfolk County authorities said, in no uncertain terms, they would arrest anyone who dared to start such a contest. A storm might not kill pro ball in the sister city, but the absence of Sunday ball and lack of home attendance just might do the job.[24]

A few days after a new grandstand was erected, it burned to the ground, once again compelling Lawrence to seek an alternative venue for home games. At first, he went to Norfolk, but people in Portsmouth complained so much that he brought the team back to Washington Street.

In early August, the Truckers retained their dominance over their neighbors as Craft led them in an easy romp, 9–0. But the Crew performed an admirable job of bailing, as they recovered the next day to take a doubleheader 4–0 and 3–1, avoiding the league basement. Two losses to Kinston, however, dropped them into last place, but a subsequent win against the Bluebirds revived their chances. Then solid performances from Hines and Boerner allowed them to win two of three from the Bugs. An Art Johnson 4–3 win over Wilson permitted the Tars to exit the cellar. Even though the Crew lost the finale with the Bugs and two of three to Petersburg, they captured two of three from the Colts to close the week at 49–62, still good for fifth place.

A Smith home run and Boerner's pitching brought a surprising win over the league leaders. Alexandria High School student Leon Riley, a new Tar, beat June Green of Portsmouth, 2–1, the next day as Robertson went north to see if he could sell some of his players. In the third game, Hines beat Joe Heving as the Tars took their third straight from the formerly dominant Truckers. Three losses out of five to Kinston and a split with Richmond, with Johnson shutting out the Colts, brought August to an end, with Norfolk still fixed in fifth.

The season for the Truckers must go down as one of the most remarkable in the annals of the Virginia League. Halfway through, Portsmouth led the league with a record of 40–29, despite not being able to use its home field for some of that time. The Truckers continued their solid work the rest of the way despite the tornado and fire.

Under third baseman/manager Zinn Beck, the "Orphans" clinched the race before the Labor Day contests with the Tars, which the two teams split, both games being played at Norfolk's League Park. Leon Riley won the morning tilt 5–1, but Portsmouth prevailed in the afternoon, 8–7. The two teams then split the next two contests, bringing the season to a close with the Truckers, 76–52, holding a commanding six-plus game lead over the second-place Petersburg Bronchos. Third-place Richmond played exactly .500, while Wilson, in fourth, fell just below that mark. Norfolk, at 58–72, had fifth place all to itself, its worst showing since 1918, with only last-place Kinston in pursuit.

The Truckers also led the league in hitting, averaging .306, as league numbers in that category dropped far below the 1926 peak. They had at least seven batters over .300. The Tars, averaging but .285, had five over .300, with Robertson, who missed about half the season, leading at .350. John Mundy and Buddy Crump did almost as well as Robertson. Home run output fell way off, as Robertson only slugged 16, the same number as Buddy Crump, both three more than Joe Klinger. Overall, the Tars managed but 67 round-trippers, less than half the number of the preceding year. The Truckers, while not setting any records in home runs, ran ahead of their neighbors.

Without Peterson enjoying his usual season, having fallen off to 9–16 late in August, the Tars relied extensively on lefty Art Johnson, at 19–10, as their ace. After the season, Johnson joined former Tar Bill Clarkson with the New York Giants. Chuck Warden split 10 decisions working for both Norfolk and Portsmouth. Lefty Larry Boerner won 13 of 27 decisions for Norfolk, while Jimmy Hines won 12 of 26, mostly for Petersburg. Except for Warden and particularly Johnson, other pitchers were below .500, some by quite a lot.

Despite a record of 3–4, another lefty, Leon Riley, showed promise. He appeared on the deck after management resolved a dispute with Clark Griffith. The Tars signed him as a rising senior at his high school in Alexandria late the previous year, but the lad's outstanding spring caught Griffith's attention. The baseball commissioner's office demanded the original contract be upheld.

In addition to reporting on the doings of the members of the Crew playing for Norfolk, the afternoon daily also highlighted the opening of the season for the Eastern Shore League. Norfolk people were especially interested in the Northampton Red Sox because they were managed by Jack Sauter, a one-time Tar, and lefty Jack Arthur (who started the season with Norfolk), toiled for that club. Sauter soon returned to the Tars and his former team promptly fell into last place. Someone going by "Deshong" (an alias for collegiate purposes) supposedly played part of the season, but Deshong's true name was Jack Arthur — and Jack Arthur played for the Tars that year. Deshong's story, which appeared in 1931 when he was playing for Allentown, must be fiction.[25]

Having triumphed during the season, the Beckmen, as Portsmouth was occasionally called, took on gray-haired Win Clark's Harrisburg Senators. All three games were played in Norfolk, with 3,500 coming out for the first contest. At least half the fans supported the Pennsylvanians because of the presence of three former Tars — Alex Peterson, Larry Gallagher and Shag Burke. Peterson recovered his form late in the season and won three straight for the Senators to give them the Pennsylvania League pennant. The "visitors," or surrogate Tars, took two of three from the Truckers, even though the losers imported Petersburg's ace pitcher and one of Richmond's best hitters. The Truckers then went on to lose four of five to South Atlantic League champion Greenville, with three games played in Greenville and two in Charlotte.

The Sunday Baseball Imbroglio

During most of the 1920s, the issue of Sunday baseball would not go away. Many states had either already permitted professional sporting teams to play on Sunday, or soon would do so. But Virginia, ever a conservative enclave, held out. Despite herculean efforts, particularly by Frank Lawrence, the movement to persuade the state legislature or the courts failed to achieve its objective.

In 1922, Lawrence persuaded the Virginia League to let him reschedule a contest between Portsmouth and Newport News on Sunday. A Newport News sports columnist praised the idea because should the authorities allow the game, it would help the two cities involved and potentially all the cities in the circuit. But in Portsmouth, the authorities arrested 18 players, along with the umpire and the groundskeeper, much to the disappointment of the 3,000 that watched the one inning they managed to play. The fans did not directly pay admission, but turned in a complimentary ticket given when they paid 50 cents for a scorecard available in several outlets.[26]

The Newport News editor, expressing a view almost directly opposite to the paper's sports columnist, noted that under the law "no one should labor at any trade or calling, or employ his apprentices or servants in labor or other business except in household or other work of necessity." Financial penalties could be severe for violations of at least three versions of the Virginia Code. The law, if we are to believe the editor, clearly considered professional baseball a business because management charged admission and paid players who belonged to a trade. The editor hoped to hear nothing more about any attempt to subvert the law. A few days later, the local press followed up this editorial with a more general comment, arguing strenuously against allowing Newport News to have an open Sunday.[27]

The editor of the Portsmouth paper also thought the local authorities had to uphold the law, even though a good many citizens had doubts about the obvious inconsistencies in its application. "Many good men" saw "nothing wrong in a game of baseball, whether it is played on Sunday or Monday. They hold that such recreation is better than visits to crowded seaside resorts at which temptation of various sorts is frequently met." But the local writer detected a "decided sentiment against anything that will break down the respect for the Sabbath." Many people felt that "we have gone too far already in the direction of the Continental Sunday. To go further will be to abolish Sunday in the real meaning of the day, which is one of rest and not necessarily of recreation." For those who wanted to attend a baseball game after church, they could "still find the game in progress on government reservations in and near the city."[28]

The Norfolk Council of Churches asked Norfolk's owners not to cooperate with Portsmouth baseball men on the subject of Sabbath games. At least one Norfolk editor opposed any change from the status quo because he believed professional baseball came under the heading of "entertainment" rather than "recreation." Whether the owners or anyone else understood the distinction is not known, but Lawrence agreed not to play games on Sundays in the immediate future. The police justice in Portsmouth cut fines in half when Lawrence's lawyer agreed not to appeal his decision to the circuit court.[29]

Lawrence and his lawyer maintained that they simply wanted to test the law. They argued that the participants received no pay and that contracts did not force them to play on Sunday. Recent court decisions allowed professionals to play on the Sabbath in Maryland and a boy to sell candy on Sunday in Virginia. The defense attorney thought it highly unfair that someone with an automobile could drive to a country club and play golf on Sunday, but those without such transport could not go to a professional game.

Manager Viox, the only Trucker to show up for the case because the team was playing in Rocky Mount, testified that the game was not on the regular schedule and no one *had* to participate. The Commonwealth's Attorney contended that no matter the prevailing public view, state law mandated against professional ball on Sunday because the work involved was certainly not a necessity. The proper recourse for the club was to work to change state law.[30]

When rain postponed the second game of the 1924 season in both Norfolk and Portsmouth, Lawrence and Percy Trotman, who had recently acquired half the stock in the Portsmouth club, again tested the waters for Sunday baseball by rescheduling the contest for the next day — Easter Sunday. Predictably this decision, made late Saturday evening, outraged many ministers and parishioners.

In their Easter sermons, ministers called for parishioners to return season tickets and boycott all future games should Lawrence persist. Several days before the rescheduled game, an Oklahoma congressman who faced sharp criticism for a social indiscretion, stated that the House and Senate office buildings in Washington, D.C., were rife with illicit liquor, making the nation's capital no better than Sodom and Gomorrah. Referring to Lawrence's efforts to have Portsmouth play on the Sabbath, the pastor of the First Presbyterian Church said "if Sunday baseball does come to Portsmouth, I would not think that Portsmouth had been given over entirely to the devil, but if Sunday baseball comes with the sanction and consent of the Christian people of the city, then Sodom and Gomorrah have nothing on us."[31]

Facing the wrath of the clergy, as well as the sheriff of Norfolk County who called for police to stop the game before the start of the second inning, Lawrence cancelled the contest at 11:30 Easter morning. Not having heard this pronouncement, some 5,000 (7,000 by one estimate, with 500 autos) soon-to-be disappointed fans assembled at the new park for the anticipated game.

In the aftermath of this affair, the Portsmouth newspaper conducted a poll. Although the results were never announced, the paper carried an equal number of brief pro and con comments, plus two longer commentaries, one on each side of the issue. Several people expressed the view that professional baseball on Sunday defied the laws of God and man and that everyone needed to rest on the Sabbath. The editor stood with the opponents of Sunday ball, saying people should go to church that day. The writer never responded to numerous points raised by other commentators about being able to play golf, sometimes at municipal courses, on Sunday afternoons. He simply believed that, like movies, professional ballgames should be off limits, even though the editor admitted resorts like Ocean View and Virginia Beach usually had a full range of entertainment.[32]

Lawrence resumed his campaign in late August. He issued "invitations" in the form of scorecards for a Sunday afternoon exhibition against Rocky Mount, the results of which would not count in the standings. Only about 2,000 fans showed up, the number kept low because of the last-minute decision to play and the likelihood that management would back down or that authorities would stop the game. The players received no extra compensation nor did the fans pay anything for entering the park, except to show scorecards they had already bought. County authorities let the game proceed, but handed out summonses with $25 fines after the first inning, with an additional $5 fee levied at the end of each inning. Everyone involved was supposed to appear in court the next Wednesday, when the Bronchos were still in town, but the sheriff asked for a continuance because the prosecuting attorney was out of town.[33]

In September 1924, 80-plus-year-old Confederate veteran Judge J.T. Duke listened to arguments and testimony from both sides for two hours. Commonwealth Attorney B. Carney and sometime city councilman J. Alden Oast, representing the Portsmouth Ministerial Association, presented the case for the prosecution. T.E. Gilman carried the cause of the defendants, Frank Lawrence and one player from each of the two teams: Taylor "Deacon" Joliff of the Truckers and Jake Hehl of the Bronchos.

County authorities testified that, indeed, a ballgame had transpired on the Sunday in question. Oast argued that the defendants obviously violated the Sunday labor law in that they received a monthly salary, the sale of scorecards being a subterfuge. Using cases recently decided by the State Court of Appeals, the defense attorney contended that the statute in question could not be a religious law, but was designed only to provide working people with a day of rest and recreation. He also sharply criticized all the ministers and church people who, even before the trial, deluged Duke with demands that the defendants be severely punished. Carney contended that that the State Court of Appeals did not have professional baseball players in mind when it recently allowed "necessary" jobs on Sundays. After hearing the evidence, Duke decided that none of the players violated the law because they had not directly received compensation. He did, however, fine the scorecard distributors for selling on Sunday.[34]

Feeling vindicated, Lawrence next planned a Sunday contest, a makeup game between the Tars and Truckers in early September. When Saturday newspapers announced that such a game would take place, the local ministers' union sent a telegram to Governor E. Lee Trinkle to stop the violation. The state assistant attorney general soon met with representatives on both sides of the issue behind closed doors. Lawrence wanted an injunction barring any interference with his scheduled game, as his agents took to the streets on Saturday to sell scorecards for the game for 50 cents apiece. To enter the park for "free," one showed the gatekeeper the previously purchased scorecards. Sales of these cards ceased at midnight on Saturday in order to be in compliance with Duke's decision concerning the Rocky Mount game.

After the meeting, the sheriff of Norfolk County announced that there would be no game. The recent decision of Judge Duke, it seems, had set no precedent. Even though the game would doubtless have drawn thousands, Lawrence cancelled it to stave off an unpleasant conflict between the authorities and management.[35] But he continued to insist that Sunday baseball did not violate the laws of God or the State of Virginia any more than several other forms of amusement in which the public participated and which were tolerated by authorities.

In 1925, both the Tars and the Truckers played to sizeable Sunday crowds during the preseason, Norfolk losing to the New Haven Watchmakers and Portsmouth taking on Frank Shaughnessy's Toronto club of the International League. The clergy's lack of reaction encouraged Lawrence to play a Virginia League regular-season game in late April against the Colts. The Truckers prevailed over the visitors before 5,000, with fans spilling out of the stands and bleachers. Parking lots were filled with cars, in addition to lining both sides of High Street and several neighboring streets. The results counted, and it looked like Lawrence was about to get his way regarding Sunday baseball.[36]

Following up, Lawrence arranged for the Pittsburgh Pirates to play another major league team or the Truckers on a Sunday in May. Such a contest would bring the great Pie Traynor back to Portsmouth, where thousands admired his work. Learning of this new assault on the Sabbath, dozens of Portsmouth Baptist and Methodist clergy besieged Governor Trinkle. Representatives from 17 Bible-study groups met with Portsmouth's city manager, who said afterwards that he concurred with their desire to stop professional games on Sundays. Because Norfolk County was outside his jurisdiction, this official was vague about any specific action on his part. The ministerial association also sent dozens of telegrams to Pirate management, which backed out of the contest. Lawrence demanded to see the telegrams, believing they could be evidence of slander he could use in a civil suit.

In an official letter that appeared in the press, the Attorney General informed the Commonwealth Attorney that it was "not illegal *per se* to play baseball on Sunday." However, if the game were played in such manner as to "interrupt the repose and religious liberty of the community," or should the pubic pay admission "directly or indirectly," the activity became illegal. The statute would not be violated if no admission were taken in any form. Having written all that and more, the Attorney General also strongly advised that his "only solution of the matter is to institute a prosecution" and have "the courts determine the question."

He really did not want to put undue pressure on the local authorities, but urged the case be taken into the circuit court to avoid letting it be handled by a local justice (like Duke). The Commonwealth Attorney stressed using a grand jury to bring an indictment. Appearing before Duke, who was suspected of harboring a liberal agenda, or another police justice might leave "the matter in worse shape than it is at present."[37]

With the major-league game no longer possible, Lawrence next arranged a game between the Truckers and a team of marines from the Navy Yard. A few hundred showed up for this contest and, as expected, the sheriff arrested the professionals after the first inning. After the completion of the paperwork in the clubhouse, he let the game proceed. But because Lawrence simply wanted a test case before a jury, the players voluntarily left the park and two amateur or semipro clubs carried on. Duke initially fined the players $5 each, but when the defendants asked for a rehearing, he dismissed the case, an action that inadvertently deprived Lawrence of his test case. Duke did fine two men for selling scorecards on Sunday. Neither the state's Attorney General nor Lawrence got what they wanted.[38]

Foiled again, Lawrence arranged for the Truckers to play the Colts on the next available Sunday. He organized the distribution of "invitations" using several outlets. Those who accepted these pieces of paper had to sign a statement that no money, either "directly or indirectly," had been given for them. As soon as the game was underway, the county sheriff arrested 18 players and two umpires. When the assembly reached the county courthouse in Portsmouth, the men made bail for $25 each and agreed to appear before the court on the following Thursday. The cooperative bail commissioner, noting that no one was deliberately violating the law, refused his usual fee. Despite what the Attorney General wanted, the case went to a county justice, but that worthy turned out not be Duke, who was vacationing in Texas. The new justice fined everyone $5 and when they appealed, set a bond of $50 each, thus sending the case on to the circuit court, which, after a continuance, tried the case.[39]

More than 200 fascinated spectators packed the courtroom near the end of July. The judge quickly turned down the defense call for a dismissal on the grounds that police justices had allowed games on two previous occasions. After two state prohibition enforcement officials (why they should have been involved is a mystery) and a county policeman testified about seeing the cited individuals playing a game on Sunday, the Commonwealth Attorney asked Lawrence whether he staged the contest to make money. Lawrence, of course, replied in the negative, which drew loud guffaws from members of the clergy. Banker and Baptist Lawrence responded by asking for the judge's protection from this negative reaction. Looking at the clerics, Lawrence vowed to give to charity any money obtained from such ballgames, which was more than "a great many people in Portsmouth would do."

The Commonwealth Attorney then wanted to know if Lawrence built the ballpark in Norfolk County to avoid effective law enforcement. Claiming that he was solely interested in letting some 5,000 people have some pleasure on the Sabbath, Lawrence maintained that he did not think so doing broke any laws. The Portsmouth owner then introduced examples of contracts players signed. Although most of them were in the offices of the secretary of the National Association of Baseball Clubs, Lawrence was nevertheless able to locate a few in his nearby office. While not divulging any individual salaries, Lawrence maintained that the contracts proved that players did not receive any income for participating in the Sunday game.

The defense attorney then asked Lawrence to talk about the occupations of the players. Jim Keesey, the skilled first baseman, worked for the Pennsylvania Railway. The Nashville Telephone Company employed Paul Kirby, and Harry Collenberger was a machinist. These three men, and by implication, all the members of the team, worked for seven months of the year at some skill or in a profession. In truth, they played baseball from mid–March to mid–September, six months any way you slice it. Based on this evidence, the defense contended that playing professional baseball was really a sideline.

Lawrence finished by maintaining that all he wanted to do was provide entertainment for laboring people, most of whom did not own automobiles. Over 5,000 folks came to one of the completed Sunday games. Most of them were laborers, as determined by the fact that the same number of cars could be seen on the streets near the ballpark whether the game was played on a weekday or the Sabbath. Although this assertion contradicted what had been reported earlier, the prosecution did not respond.

The defense then called upon several members of the community. When one local government official maintained that the sheriff never allowed games of professional ball in his county, several boisterous clergymen called him a liar and reminded him of an exhibition against Syracuse. The official merely noted that he had no awareness of any such game.

A physician, testifying about the benefits of athletic activity, criticized the prosecutor for calling him a "sport," noting that he had been a constant supporter of "sports" for 30 years. The doctor also pointed out that many Portsmouth people played golf, a very beneficial activity, on Sunday. His not-so-veiled inference was to municipal employees who collected greens fees and provided course maintenance on Sundays without restriction. In response, the Commonwealth Attorney muttered, "We'll have to look into that."

Judge Duke, magistrate of the Western Branch part of Norfolk County and whose office stood near the ballpark, believed all the contests at the facility were orderly. He also believed that preventing some 15,000 wage earners in the area under his jurisdiction from seeing games on Sunday interfered with their religious liberty.

Manager-turned-witness Les Bangs reiterated that the players received no compensation for playing on the Sabbath, and noted that his primary job was as a box cutter in a New England mill. The prosecutor wanted to know whether baseball or box-cutting paid better, to which Bangs replied that he had to eat in the winter as well as the summer. "Shipwreck" said that he had no chance of ever playing ball in the major leagues and played the game because he loved it.

The judge turned the case over to the jury, with the instruction that they were not to decide the legitimacy of the law in question, but rather to determine whether the players were fulfilling their contracts by playing on Sunday. After the better part of an hour in deliberations, the jury decided such was the case. Lawrence paid $5 per person plus court costs and the matter went to the State Court of Appeals.[40]

While waiting for action from the Court of Appeals, Lawrence went to Richmond to argue for a change in the law. Senator Alfred Smith of Norfolk County proposed local-option legislation, which received the backing of nearly all the delegates from the sister cities. Portsmouth poet and legislative delegate Earl H. Wright thought Smith's amended bill stood a good chance.

This assessment proved overly optimistic. Among other problems, Smith came under attack for a totally unrelated matter, for which he would be removed from the Senate. Even though he received a pardon from Governor Harry Byrd, he lost his law license when members of the Ku Klux Klan claimed he had been cheating them in handling their accounts.

During the Senate hearing on the issue, Lawrence got into a debate with several ministers. In an overheated hearing (physically and emotionally), Lawrence and a Baptist minister claimed each was lying about the attitude of local citizens regarding Sunday ball. During the fray, the Portsmouth owner contended that a church in one ward only had 10 percent of the population of that district, not a much larger number claimed by its minister. That minister said that his congregation was overwhelmingly against a change in the laws despite Lawrence's claim that almost all of Portsmouth wanted it. In a curious twist, the minister resigned from his church, with a Baltimore newspaper reporting that he left because of criticism of his behavior in confronting Lawrence.

A Portsmouth newspaper editor, without mentioning the minister's name and despite formerly being opposed to changes in the Sabbath laws, sharply criticized the unseemliness of having ministers participate in political debates. Whatever his reasons for departing, the Baptist minister delivered his last sermon at the Park View Church (a building Frank Lawrence had raised money to construct) to an audience heavily laced with hooded members of the Ku Klux Klan who had marched to the service en masse to support the minister.

The Speaker of the House of Delegates became so upset by the behavior of the clergy in the Senate session that he banned all such lobbyists in future meetings. Lawrence, however, received rave reviews from members of the legislature. Newspaper accounts gave the impression that the reform stood a good chance of passage.[41]

Arguments for the proposed change ranged widely. A Richmond delegate argued that the proposal would allow those unable to afford memberships in exclusive clubs to attend professional ballgames as a form of recreation and relaxation. The absence of professional sports on Sunday likely kept residents of other states from moving into Virginia, he contended. A Portsmouth delegate said if the workers could not have wine and beer during prohibition, at least let them have some Sunday recreation. An official from Norfolk County pointed out that the sheriff of his county always acted swiftly to suppress Sunday baseball in Portsmouth. A Portsmouth minister cried out "Tell the truth."

Virginia League President William G. Bramham, a deacon and Sunday school teacher in his Presbyterian church in Durham, begged for tolerance, saying no conflict existed between religion and recreation. Bramham said a businessman told him that strikes could be averted if workmen had a chance to unwind on the Sabbath. Someone on the other side of the issue contended that this particular Presbyterian had a financial interest in his league having Sunday ball.

Chap Marable, a former Trucker and the only professional ball player to attend the session, testified that almost all players would rather play ball on Sunday than loaf. Such an assertion offset a minister's comments that great ballplayers like Christy Mathewson had clauses in their contracts exempting them from participating on Sunday.

Tom Hanes, sports editor of *The Ledger-Dispatch* and now a witness, simply could not understand how anyone could be against having ballgames on Sunday.

On the other side, another Portsmouth banker said sentiment in his city opposed change. Virginia, he thought, clung to the Sabbath observance despite the fact that most of the country outside the South and parts of New England had turned to the continental Sabbath. That was the case, he averred, because foreigners were more prevalent in other places.

Another said that should Norfolk and Portsmouth get the right to have a referendum on the issue, youth from the countryside for 50 miles around would go to these cities to desecrate the Sabbath. Civilization simply could not survive the loss of a day of rest. Critics called the proposed legislation mere camouflage to allow Norfolk and Portsmouth baseball clubs to make money.

Lawrence, his face flushed and sweating, angrily charged that his opponents persecuted him, comparing him to Judas Iscariot. Raised in the Baptist Church, he supported that denomination his entire life until he was "driven out by the intolerable persecutions heaped upon him," as he tried to give working people innocent recreation on the Sabbath. To prove that God was on his side, Lawrence noted that his club lost $4,000 in 1922, but rain insurance and the sale of players allowed him to keep going. He urged the Senate committee to forward the bill so that Virginia would no longer be one of but four states that prohibited professional ball on Sundays.[42]

Although many likely said "Amen" to that sentiment, the proposed legislation failed, as made clear in the headline: "Norfolk Sunday Baseball Bill Dies on Third Base as Senate Fails to Act." The Smith bill was removed from the calendar in the final reading when religious forces mounted a powerful campaign. One Norfolk realtor, who was also an officer in the Anti-Saloon League, sent word that he had a petition signed by 15 prominent Norfolk people against the measure. The press pointed out that seven of the 15 said they had not signed any petition. The realtor later admitted that at least three of the assumed signers had not authorized the use of their names. Despite such questionable tactics, the Senate dropped the matter, using the excuse that it was too late in the session to have the House of Delegates act on the measure.[43]

One editor for *The Pilot* came down hard on the "vulgarized" practice of passing out petitions and persuading the uninformed to sign. On the major issue, the editor saw "but a slender distinction" between Sunday golf and Sabbath baseball, but that small distinction was sufficient under current law. On the one hand, neither Virginia nor the Norfolk-Portsmouth community seemed ready to accept the continental Sabbath. On the other hand, if a majority of Virginians really wanted such contests, they were certainly entitled to them. Such an ambivalent attitude toward the issue of Sunday ball did little to help Lawrence's cause.[44]

A Portsmouth editor did not take a stand on the issue itself, but in "Back to St. Paul," while supporting the separation of church and state as a fundamental and permanent policy, he lamented the breach between the clergy "and the hundreds, if not thousands, in the community who favor said sports, and who are placed beyond the influence of the clergy—as to spiritual betterment—by reason of the militant attitude of the latter on the subject." Appeals for punishment seemed to run against a basic principle of Christianity—forgiveness. The editor urged the ministers to use "moral suasion" rather than a rigorous enforcement of laws to attain their ends.[45]

Despite this defeat, the Sunday baseball issue would not go away. In late August 1926, 250 petitioners begged Norfolk's city manager to allow Sunday ball in his city. On advice from the city's assistant attorney, he turned down the request, noting that the police would continue to prevent any professional games on the Sabbath. Norfolk owners failed to persuade a substitute judge in the Court of Law and Chancery to issue an injunction to prevent city authorities from interfering with a possible game between Norfolk and Portsmouth. The city manager had no objection to making a test case, but the game could not proceed in defiance of the law.[46]

Around the same time, the press predicted that a member of the House of Delegates from Norfolk would bid for re-election the next year using a modification of the "state Blue Sunday law" in his campaign. This unnamed potential candidate confided to the reporter that he had nothing to lose, as he did not receive the church vote in the last election anyway. The candidate, believing that Norfolk was becoming ever more liberal toward playing baseball on Sundays, pointed to the recent opening of a municipal golf course on the Sabbath. "Successful resorts and Blue Laws don't go together," he opined, and most business people thought tourism would play a major role in the city's chances for prosperity. The unnamed candidate was probably A.L. Jordan, who served as lawyer to both Frank Lawrence and R.A. Jones, business manager of the Tars. Jordan also testified at the legislative hearing.[47]

In 1926, Norfolk's afternoon daily assumed that most of the residents of Norfolk and the surrounding area favored changing the blue laws. But such legislation would "have a hard row to hoe in the legislature," where rural districts dominated and were "almost solidly" against any change.[48]

In January 1927, Virginia's Supreme Court finally ruled in the case that had become known as *T.A. Crook et al. versus the Commonwealth*. The reformers lost, 3–2. Writing the majority position, Judge Jesse F. West argued that the statute clearly called for Sunday as a day of rest from every kind of mental and physical labor, excepting for household chores or charity. Every businessman working at his desk, farmer plowing his field, or even a teacher grading tests broke the law if they did their regular work on Sunday. West and the two other judges dismissed the Portsmouth club's argument that their players received no pay for the particular game in question and noted that the men received higher pay than in other vocations. Their participation permitted the owners of the club to receive a return at some point even if they charged no admission on any particular Sunday. Whether the club turned a profit did not matter one iota. West and company found no error on the part of the judge or his circuit court. They also pointed out that the recent failure of the bill introduced by Senator Smith underscored the position of the Assembly against easing restrictions.

Two judges, taking issue with the majority, agreed that Section 4570 made plying a trade on Sunday a misdemeanor. They, however, disputed the notion that one could not play for sport on Sunday what one did for pay other six days of the week. They contended that baseball, as played in Portsmouth on the day in question, was a sport and not really a business since the players received no compensation.

Lawrence's tactics had convinced two of the five members of the court. Yet even this minority stated unequivocally that had the players received remuneration or admission been charged, they would have been guilty of violating the statute.[49]

In its coverage of the court decision, the Portsmouth paper concluded that the verdict "spells the end of organized ball in this city." Professional baseball would likely survive in Virginia only in Norfolk and Richmond, with their greater populations.[50] In order to avoid this inevitable end, Frank Lawrence took his case to the people of Portsmouth in an attempt to be elected to the State Senate. One headline called the team the "Senators — nee Truckers," possibly a reference to Lawrence's political aspirations, although the unaware might have thought that Clark Griffith had purchased a farm team. The Norfolk press later attributed Lawrence's defeat in the election to his stance on Sunday baseball.[51]

The Pilot editors continued to stew about the issue. Just after the end of the 1927 season, one editor sharply criticized Norfolk's municipal government for letting golfers play for free on Sunday at all three city-owned golf courses because city authorities did not want to come into conflict with Sabbath rules. Yet no one seriously considered closing down the private clubs in the area, which remained open on Sundays and whose clientele paid membership fees on a seasonal or yearly basis. Such private clubs, however, now labored under a serious disadvantage in competing against free public links. Moreover, the city was losing substantial revenues. As late as 1931, the newspaper agreed with a federal circuit court decision to prevent municipal authorities from stopping privately owned golf clubs from operating on Sunday.

Despite the attitude in the editorial offices of many of the area's newspapers, most of the sports reporters through the 1920s solidly and consistently backed the owners' efforts to play baseball professional baseball on Sundays.[52]

The Last Voyage in the Virginia League (1928)

At the end of the 1927 season, the financial condition of the teams looked desperate. In summing up the situation, a reporter thought "interest in local baseball both professional and amateur during 1927 dropped to the lowest ebb recorded in two generations." Attendance fell to its lowest level. Every team, even the Mary Jane, was sinking in a sea of red ink.

Norfolk had "distressingly small" numbers at its games, but people came to Portsmouth in "mere handfuls, despite the fact that the Trucker team was the class of the season and finished in first place." Once, Lawrence even gave away tickets and had Vaudeville skits before the game with a band entertaining between innings. Nothing seemed to attract fans.

After the 1927 season, Portsmouth was one of four teams not to pay association dues. That failure signaled the presumed demise of the league. One newsman reported that the Virginia League disbanded after 21 years of continuous operation except for the World War period, when all organized leagues suspended. The reporter proved just a bit premature in announcing the demise of the association, but given the situation, the real demise of the league could not be far off.[53]

That winter, Kinston and Wilson gave up their franchises, and the owner of the Petersburg franchise, a North Carolina judge, pulled out of the baseball business. Efforts to persuade Lynchburg and Roanoke to resume relationships with the Virginia League failed, doubtless due in some measure to the ability of their residents to recall the complaints about travel costs in earlier times.

With the supposed death of the Virginia League, Judge Bramham tried to convince the Carolina clubs in the Class C Piedmont League, over which he also presided, to extend franchise offers to Norfolk and Richmond. But those clubs insisted on special consideration in covering train travel in the Old Dominion. Bramham then tried to create a North Atlantic League which would include Richmond, Norfolk and teams from Pennsylvania and New Jersey. That effort also died, when only three northern communities expressed any interest.

In November, Dave Robertson approached his old ally John McGraw about purchasing stock in Norfolk's club. Because McGraw already had a working relationship with the Tars, especially when Robertson managed them, he might have been thinking of establishing a farm system similar to what Branch Rickey had done with the St. Louis Cardinals. McGraw and his brother came to Norfolk, but negotiations came to naught. When the current owners failed to consummate a deal with the McGraws, Lawrence, now known as the "Pollyanna of the Virginia League" to some members of the press, acquired many of the shares of Norfolk's corporation.

Lawrence bought into Norfolk baseball in order to ride the good ship Mary Jane into the Piedmont League, but when Bramham failed to find homes for the Colts and the Tars, his only option was to reorganize the Virginia League. As Lawrence concluded, "I tried every way I knew to get Norfolk into a real league, but playing in the Virginia League was at least better than having no professional baseball at all."[54]

The press assumed that Petersburg had turned in its franchise, but later the Cockade City agreed to field a team. Bramham, representing owners in Richmond and Norfolk who realized they could not acquire franchises in any other league, sweetened the deal so that the new Petersburg owners were nearly guaranteed protection from any financial losses. All visiting teams would receive at least 50 percent of the gate for admissions to both the bleachers and stands. The other clubs would also share the pool of baseball talent available. In return for these concessions, the Petersburg club agreed to a league-appointed business manager. Reporters initially had the idea that the league actually owned the team, but such was not the case. Petersburg stockholders owned the enterprise, and could keep any profits, although everyone knew that would be an unlikely prospect.[55]

In Portsmouth in February, Sol Fass, a long-time rabid Trucker fan and Kiwanis leader, reorganized the company. He took over as president, secured a franchise, and arranged to play at Washington Park. Fass hired Texan Sam "Stump" Eddinger to manage.

The Virginia League now consisted of Richmond, Norfolk, Petersburg and Portsmouth. Although the absence of North Carolina clubs might satisfy purists who liked to have league names that reflected reality, it meant that professional baseball was susceptible to destruction by even a mild storm.

When Lawrence crossed the river to Norfolk, he brought Portsmouth talent with him. Harry Collenberger and manager/third baseman Zinn Beck now joined the Crew. Beck spent the preceding winter in Norfolk running a roller polo operation on Boush Street. He organized five-man teams from Portsmouth and Norfolk to engage in highly exciting contests. Unlike in New England, however, where this sport had quite a following, crowds did not knock down the doors, except when Beck offered free admission. Former Tars manager Dave Robertson moved on to the Pennsylvania League, where he joined Win Clark at York.

And so, despite dire predictions at the end of the previous season, the four teams prepared for the preseason as usual. In Norfolk, many fans hoped young shortstop George Loder,

Jr., who starred for Maury High in its successful drive for the public school state title and whose father played for the local independent Red Men, might make the club. As the preseason progressed, Loder proved his ability in the field and played regularly once the season commenced, although weak hitting forced manager Beck to move him from leadoff to eighth place in the batting order. They were also interested in Bill Dietrick, a sports star at the University of Virginia and now a local lawyer. Over in Portsmouth, Mike Smith from South Norfolk looked good in right field.

Overall, the Tars did well in the preliminary contests, twice beating the team from Harrisburg, which now not only had Peterson, Burke and Gallagher but Attreau as well. In the preliminaries, the semipro Sewanees overcame the Truckers, 6–4, as did Harrisburg, 7–4, while Norfolk edged New Haven, 3–2. The Tars whipped Williamsport and the Norfolk police, with Champagne still in the lineup for the semipros. A 7–1 defeat at the hands of the Buffalo Bisons brought preseason to a close.

The Crew lost their home opener against the Truckers, 8–0. Despite "Little" Loder's single-handed brilliance in the field and a cacophony created by the pounding of souvenir bats given to the fans, the Truckers submerged the Mary Jane in a pile of runs. Lanky Joe Heving returned to his winning ways of the previous season and brought great "sadness to the 2,000 local customers and gladness to the 500 Portsmouth clients who clinked the turnstiles at League Park."

Hanes thought "mercy had no place in Joe's makeup. He mowed down the Tars with the kind of brutality that would cheer the soul of the most cold-blooded machine gunner. He tantalized and tortured them. He laughed at their misery, jeered at their feeble efforts and taunted them as they welted in the sweat of homeless desperation." In other words, "Joe beat the tar out of the Tars."[56]

A week or so later, the Truckers pounded out another 8–0 triumph, this one over Ken Yeisley. A few weeks later they again beat Yeisley, 11–1, on the day they raised the 1927 pennant in Portsmouth. Within a matter of days, Norfolk released Yeisley. But in between, the Tars also took it to the Truckers, and both picked on the other two teams in the association. In mid–May, the Crew edged ahead of the team from the sister city and held onto a one and a half game lead early in June. Once the season started, Lawrence sent Red Proctor from Norfolk to the Truckers in an obvious effort to keep Portsmouth competitive.

Throughout May the press frequently mentioned the weak attendance, especially at Portsmouth. Lack of fan interest received most of the blame, but a cold, damp spring did not help matters. After a postponement, the league occasionally went nearly a week before resuming play. The press talked about needing to play nine games over six days, then the need for three doubleheaders in a row, as more games fell to Mother Nature. But even when the weather improved, attendance did not.

Portsmouth moved a home game with Norfolk to Elizabeth City, where about 1,000 saw the Tars triumph, 10–5. In another contest, the Crew edged out a 9–8 win before 600 near the Pasquotank River, but back in Portsmouth the average crowd to see the Truckers numbered about 100. One day only 49 paying customers congregated and the team disbanded. Petersburg quickly followed.

Even Norfolk was not breaking any records in attendance. A 12-inning tie brought some 1,500, the second largest crowd of the season, in the waning days of May. The Tars lost the last game of the season on June 3 to the Colts, in a game played at Newport News, where a little over 1,000 viewed a contest terminated after the fifth inning because of rain. That loss left Norfolk in first place at 26–13, followed by Portsmouth at 25–14. Petersburg and Richmond ended up with identical records of 15–27.

When Bramham's renewed efforts to convince the teams in the Piedmont League to admit Norfolk and Richmond failed, Lawrence and George Barnes, a resident of Newport News who now presided over the Richmond club, tried to extend the season by having the Colts compete against the Crew in a lengthy postseason series. The Colts had just brought back the great Chief Bender. After playing one game under his guidance, won by Richmond as might be expected given Bender's history of dominance over the Tars, the "series" ended.[57]

The demise of the league at a time when the entire country, including Hampton Roads, enjoyed considerable prosperity suggests that more than a good economy determines the fate of professional sports. It is possible that full employment, with an average work week approaching 50 hours, meant that many workmen simply could not find time to attend ballgames. It is likely that middle-class interests were now shifting toward golf and tennis. Boxing continued to attract audiences about once a week. Movies, radio and other forms of entertainment competed for discretionary dollars. Allowing the league to play Sunday ball likely would have allowed it to survive, but the popularity of low-level professional baseball had declined in the 1920s, even as major-league ball ascended into a golden age.

In addition to lacking Sunday ball, the Virginia League had many small cities. Kinston and Suffolk had but 10,000 residents, while Wilson and Rocky Mount were only somewhat bigger. That Suffolk and Kinston could carry on for two or three years and Wilson and Rocky Mount for even longer, given the costs involved, is certainly a testimony to the civic pride of these communities. Such pride was proportionately less visible the larger the community. It is unlikely that the small population losses that Portsmouth and Newport News sustained after the Great War could be responsible for the failure of professional baseball, given that both communities were considerably larger than they had been before the war started.

It seems strange that the game lost popularity in Virginia, just when increased hitting should have made it more attractive. Some of those who watched the professional Tars during the Dead Ball Era had complained that it was much more exciting to watch semipros or amateurs play because of the more prolific hitting. But the increased scoring may have been a detriment, because games now required almost two hours rather than a hour and forty-five minutes in former times. Most people attended weekday games right after work, just before suppertime, and the greater lengths of these contests might have posed a hardship. It is also possible that fans missed the rowdy behavior of earlier times that Bramham worked so hard to eliminate.

It's a preposterous notion that the failure of the Norfolk press to keep alive the image of the Mary Jane in the mid–1920s had anything to do with reduced attendance. But for those who appreciate metaphors, it may be appropriate that professional baseball was scuttled just about the time the Mary Jane sank from the scene, never to return.

Epilogue

With the demise of the Virginia League, Norfolk and Portsmouth baseball fans had to depend on semipro athletic clubs like the Orioles or the Police, who sometimes played on Sundays, for their baseball entertainment. The latter had lefty Lou Stanley, the old Tar, on the mound, and folks would turn out at old League Park to watch him beat most of the local talent and even the police squads out of Baltimore or D.C.

A major league team or two, moving north after spring training, played another professional club in 1929 and 1930. Black professionals affiliated with one of the two black major leagues, especially the Black Sox and the Backarah Giants, sometimes played at League Park. In 1930, the Black Sox went up against the Cuban Stars.[1]

In 1929, after Norfolk failed to join a professional league, a committee for the local Chamber of Commerce tried to revive the old Virginia League. They convinced delegates from Richmond, Petersburg, Newport News, Suffolk, Norfolk and Portsmouth to meet at Norfolk's Southland Hotel. These representatives wanted to re-create the league, but following some deliberation they also unanimously agreed that it could not be done unless Virginia liberalized its rules about the Sabbath. A delegate from Petersburg contended that by not allowing "innocent Sunday recreation" Virginia was retarding its industrial development, for manufacturers simply did not want to set up shop where their workers could not watch professional baseball or see a movie on the Sabbath.

The Southland Hotel gathering proposed that the state Chamber of Commerce have its industrial committee take up the topic. Representatives included, among others, Abe Horwitz and George Barnes from Newport News, Percy E. Trotman from Portsmouth, several from Richmond, Petersburg and Suffolk as well as many Norfolk residents, including sporting goods store owners Lou Northrop and Dave Robertson and sports reporters Tom Hanes and Sam Potts. Frank Lawrence was conspicuously absent, but one may safely assume he fully agreed with the findings of the delegates.[2]

Despite the postulating, no Virginia League emerged. In 1930, the Norfolk ballpark burned and the peanut company that owned the field rebuilt it, in the process renaming it Bain Field in honor of the family that owned and managed the company. The next year, Win Clark spearheaded a drive to follow Richmond into the Eastern League.

As one of the owners of the new Tars, he brought back Davis Robertson, but the great man's numerous injuries made that season his last hurrah. In 1923, Robertson had been appointed to the new Virginia Commission on Game and Inland Fisheries, a progressive agency devoted to conserving natural resources. At the time, Robertson was still capable of playing professional baseball and received no pay as a "special game warden." After ending his career in baseball and reducing or ending his connection to the sporting goods industry in Norfolk, he started a new career as an official game warden. He remained in that status until 1960, noting the progress made in reducing those who hunted and fished without a license but worried about the practice of exceeding legal limits.[3]

When he died in 1970 at age 81, obituaries and sports columnists mostly focused on Dave's relationship with John McGraw. Turner Dozier of *The Ledger Star* reiterated the old story about how in 1917 (it actually may have been 1915) McGraw had fined Dave $100 when he ignored a bunt signal and hit a homer. Supposedly, McGraw never collected the penalty because Davey got a double as a pinch-hitter after "Little Napoleon" promised to call off the fine. Another anecdote concerned a spring-training game at San Antonio. Robertson impressed the manager with a solid hit over the fence, but McGraw supposedly tried to collect money from the hitter when the ball struck the rear of a mule, which crashed into a nearby plate-glass window. Dozier pointed out that although young Dave liked to spend money for fancy clothes, he became more conservative with age. As a hunter, he only used shotguns that would kill, not cripple, a bird.[4]

George McClelland of *The Virginian-Pilot* also stressed the connection with the Giants' McGraw, pointing out that when McGraw learned that Dave had injured his shoulder playing football, he "reacted with Vesuvian rage." McGraw was doubtless pleased with Dave's .500 batting (11-for-22, a record at the time) in the 1917 World Series, but certainly had the opposite reaction when Robertson dropped a fly at a critical juncture to help the White Sox become champions. McClelland affirmed that the big outfielder never liked New York City and couldn't wait to come home and that by becoming a major leaguer he had given up his goal of becoming a physician. Robertson, a lover of the outdoors, had often been less than a happy camper in his dealings with the businessmen of baseball. In these obituaries and columns, no one mentioned his 1911 pitching in the Tidewater League or his managerial record with Norfolk in the mid–1920s.[5]

Although Norfolk resided in the second division for its two years in the eight-club Eastern League, attendance proved steady, suggesting that what Norfolk needed all along was a higher level of baseball to appeal to a greater number of potential spectators. But the weight of the Depression, especially as it affected northern industrial cities, forced the closure of the Eastern League, after which Norfolk endured another year (1933) without professional baseball.

When Percy Dawson became the general manager of Norfolk's franchise in the Piedmont League in 1934, the Tars' legacy resumed. As a farm club of the New York Yankees, Norfolk saw a steady parade of talent at B level ball. The club placed first and won the playoffs in 1934 and 1936, carried the playoffs in 1937 after finishing second in the standings, and placed first in 1938. These Tars won about as many championships in five years as it had taken the Virginia League Crew of the Mary Jane to achieve in over 25 seasons. Attendance proved strong as the economy improved a bit, and the Virginia courts (the legislature still failing to approve) decided that professionals could play baseball on Sunday. That change resulted from a liberal trend sweeping across the land.

After struggling through World War II, with only one really good season but with attendance surprisingly strong, the Norfolk Tars resumed their dominance in the Piedmont by taking four straight first-place finishes and two pennants in the early 1950s. Then the popularity of minor-league ball waned nationally, despite a strong economy and frequent night games (which the Yankees resisted for several years), and attendance dropped. Despite having dominant teams the four previous years, in the middle of the 1955 season Norfolk yielded a franchise for the first time since 1901.

When professional ball returned several years later, the team became known as the Tides, probably because too few people knew the definition of a "Tar." By that point, the public memory of the Crew of the Mary Jane had almost been lost in the mists of time.

In the 1931–32 seasons, when Norfolk had a club in the Eastern League, fans found a great deal to criticize about Win Clark's management, but because he was one of the principal owners he remained in charge. With the failure of the league, Clark devoted time to encouraging amateur baseball in the area along with a variety of other activities. The local amateur association was even named for him. In 1937, he moved to Los Angeles to become

Win Clark from Circleville, Ohio, first came to Norfolk in 1894 as a player for the Staunton club in the Virginia League. In 1900 and 1901, he captained and later managed Portsmouth. In 1906, he took the helm of the Mary Jane, leading the league in hitting (.303) and guiding the Crew to a second-place finish. Although he moved around in the minor leagues over the ensuing decades, he tended to gravitate toward either Portsmouth or Norfolk, with a stop to manage Hopewell in 1915. During World War I, he supervised athletics at the Norfolk Navy Base (Naval Station Norfolk), coaching its baseball team and guiding the construction of McClure Field. From 1922 through 1924, with an ownership stake in the club, he managed the Tars in Norfolk. The late 1920s found him managing in different places and scouting for talent for the majors. In 1931 and 1932 he spearheaded the revival of professional baseball in Norfolk as an investor and manager in the Eastern League. In this photograph published in the *Virginian-Pilot* on June 26, 1931, he received a button with the initials "P.A." on it (for Personal Appearance), from Catherine Henley. The awards, given by *the Virginian Pilot*, went to businessmen and government officials who exhibited qualities that raised morale among employees, which was considered a worthy endeavor in the midst of the Great Depression (*Virginian-Pilot* and Norfolk Public Library).

the secretary of the National Association of Professional Baseball Players of America. But nearly every year in October, during the time of the World Series, he would return to Norfolk, which he always considered his home.

The local press marked these annual pilgrimages with photographs and commentary. Even though diabetes forced the amputation of both his legs in 1951, he continued his secretarial duties for the association until his death in the spring of 1959 from heart failure. Among those assignments was making sure indigent former players received financial assistance.

In December 1950, Clark returned for the last time to the City by the Sea. Former players like Red Cleveland and Dave Robertson trouped to his room at the Monticello to see "Uncle Win." After a postponement because he did not feel well, he made his way to a grand dinner sponsored by the Norfolk Sports Club, where 450 guests honored him. Nearly all the former players who still lived in the area showed up: Mike Smith, Les Bangs, Dutch Kroger, Tommy Hipple, Allie Watt, Harry Lake, Rasty Walters, Gene Hudgins and Jimmy Jobson, all of Virginia League fame. As might be expected, several former players had died. John "Lou" Stanley passed away in 1940 from a heart attack, while he was still serving as a detective on the Norfolk police force.

Other guests included Tars of the Piedmont League, including Ray White, who served as president of the Win Clark Chapter of the Hot Stove League of America and also emceed the banquet festivities. "Bubba" Staylor, future Norfolk police chief who had played both for and against the Tars in the Piedmont League showed up, as did famous ex-major-leaguers like Lefty Gomez. Percy Dawson, Frank Lawrence and others represented the business side of baseball. Norfolk mayor W. Fred Duckworth presented Clark with a small replica of the city mace. As an aside, Duckworth noted that although the guest of honor lived in Los Angeles, more Norfolk people knew Clark than they did the mayor of Norfolk.

With tears in his eyes as he sat in his wheelchair, Clark told everyone, "The happiest years of my life were spent in Norfolk. I consider it my second home. I played my first professional game of baseball with the Staunton club right here in Norfolk. And when I decided to settle down, I picked Norfolk as the city I wanted to make my home." Clark noted how impressed he was with the improved transportation in the area and urged the city to work hard to reestablish minor-league baseball in the city. Later in December, the *Los Angeles Times* honored Clark with one of its national sports awards at the Coconut Grove of the Ambassador Hotel. Yankee manager Casey Stengel served on the committee that selected Clark for the award.[6]

Several local columnists commented on Clark. Tom Fergusson repeated the story Clark told about being hauled off a baseball field by a mounted policeman at Wilkes-Barre, Pennsylvania, in 1927 when he managed the Harrisburg club, after he threw 33 bats out of the dugout (each incurring a $5 fine). Fergusson recalled Clark during the Depression "spreading uniforms out on a table" as he told municipal leaders about all the positive publicity the city would get with its new club in the Eastern League. When that league folded in 1932, Clark organized a benefit game at Bain Field to give the players enough money to return home. The old manager was also known to treat fired players with the biggest steak at a restaurant. The columnist, recalling some of the well-known major leaguers who played for the Navy Base team (he mistakenly called them the Minesweepers), thought McClure Field at the Navy Base should be renamed Clark Stadium, because Win had been the one to supervise its construction.[7]

Writing for *The Ledger Dispatch and Portsmouth Star*, Norfolk's afternoon daily, Turner Dozier recalled watching one former player after another come see the old man at the Monticello. Although "their hands are wrinkled and soft, their arms too weak to throw a baseball across the street," they treasured the memories of their experiences under Clark's tutelage. Win showed off his own arms, made muscular from the constant need to lift himself. That reminded him of his old friend Jim Jeffries and another boxer named John L. Sullivan and led to the story about the 1900 season, when Clark captained Portsmouth.[8]

The death of William Winfield Clark in Los Angeles on April 15, 1959, brought an era of Hampton Roads baseball to an end. Reporters referred to him as Norfolk's "Mr. Baseball," but he could as well have been considered the symbolic captain of the Mary Jane.

Appendix: Leagues and Standings*

Eastern League 1885	W	L	W	L
Washington Nationals	70	25	70	25
Richmond Virginians	67	26	67	26
Trenton Trentonians	43	49	43	49
Newark Domestics	41	51	42	49
Norfolk Norfolks	33	42	32	44
Lancaster Maroons	28	39	28	39
Bridgeport Giants	12	17	12	17
Jersey City Skeeters	9	27	9	27
Waterbury	8	9	8	9
Atlantic City/Wilmington Blue Hens	5	31	5	31

Encyclopedia, p. 109

	DC	R	T	Ne	No	L	B	JC	W	AC	W
Washington	X	10	12	11	13	8	6	3	1	6	70
Richmond	8	X	16	9	11	10	2	1		10	67
Trenton	6	1	X	11	7	4	4	6	2	2	43
Newark	6	6	7	X	3	6	3	6	2	2	41
Norfolk	1	3	4	8	X	7		2		8	33
Lancaster	3	2	5	3	5	X		8		2	28
Bridgeport		3	1	4			X		4		12
Jersey City		1	2	1	1	3		X		1	9
Waterbury	1		2	3			2		X		8
Atlantic City				1	2	1		1		X	5
L	25	26	49	51	42	39	17	27	9	31	

7 October 1885 *Sporting Life*

Virginia League 1894	W	L	W	L
Petersburg Farmers	71	44	72	44
Norfolk Clams	66	44	66	45
Richmond Crows	65	48	67	48
Staunton Hayseeds (Newport News-Hampton)	51	67	50	64
Roanoke Magicians	45	67	45	71
Lynchburg Hill Climbers	41	72	43	71

Virginian Encyclopedia, p. 119

---

*Sources: *The Encyclopedia of Minor League Baseball*; Norfolk *Landmark, Public Ledger, Virginian*, and *Virginian-Pilot*; Portsmouth *Star*; *Reach's Guide*; *Sporting Life*; *Sporting News*. Team standings and other seasonal data often appear in parallel columns because of inconsistencies in the sources. The sources cited appear below each column.

Virginia League 1895

	W	L	W	L
Richmond Blue Birds	77	45	78	45
Lynchburg Hilltoppers	67	48	67	52
Norfolk Clams (Crows)	59	66	56	61
Portsmouth Truckers	60	67	57	68
Petersburg Farmers	54	65	55	69
Roanoke Magicians	49	72	52	70

Virginian Encyclopedia, p. 120

Batting	Pct.
Lynchburg	.273
Norfolk	.263
Richmond	.261
Roanoke	.245
Portsmouth	.238
Petersburg	.237

3 October 1895 *Public Ledger*

Virginia League 1896

	W	L	W	L
	First Half		**Whole Season**	
Richmond Bluebirds	35	29	71	55
Lynchburg Hill Climbers	44	22	68	37
Roanoke Magicians	27	28	49	56
Norfolk Gulls	31	33	70	60
Portsmouth Grangers	34	31	65	64
Peters/Hampton	24	42	39	90

1 July *Virginian Encyclopedia*

Second Half	W	L
Richmond	26	14
Lynchburg	24	15
Roanoke	23	16
Norfolk	22	21
Portsmouth	16	25
Newport News/Hampton	8	25

21 August *Virginian*

	L	No	NN	P	Ri	Ro	W	Pct.
Lynchburg	X	5	4	5	5	6	24	.615
Norfolk	4	X	10	16	8	2	40	.597
Newport News/Hampton	5	2	X	1	5	2	15	.238
Portsmouth	1	10	11	X	7	2	31	.477
Richmond	3	7	15	5	X	6	36	.581
Roanoke	2	3	8	7	2	X	22	.550
L	15	27	48	34	26	18	168	

	N	P	Ri	NN	W
Norfolk	x	5	5	5	15
Portsmouth	5	x	4	5	14
Richmond	1	2	x	6	9
Newport News/Hampton	1	1	4	x	6
L	7	8	13	16	44

29 September 1896 *Sporting Life*

Supplemental	W	L
Norfolk Mary Janes	17	7
Portsmouth	14	9
Richmond	9	13
Peters/Hampton	7	16

Virginian; *Reach's Guide*, pp. 75–76
Norfolk loses playoff to Richmond, 4 games to 1

Atlantic League 1897

	W	L	W	L	Pct.
Lancaster Maroons	90	45	90	45	.667
Newark "Thugs"	88	54	89	52	.631
Hartford	78	55	78	55	.546
Richmond Bluebirds	73	58	71	59	.546
Paterson Silk Weavers	68	74	68	79	.463
Norfolk Brooms	62	73	66	72	.478
Philadelphia Athletics	49	86	49	88	.355
Reading Coal Heavers	40	100	40	100	.286
	548	545	551	550	

19 September *Landmark Encyclopedia*, p. 122

Atlantic League 1898

	W	L	W	L	Pct.
Richmond	78	43	77	44	.685
Lancaster	82	48	82	50	.644
Reading	72	57	72	56	.559
Paterson	64	71	65	70	.481
Allentown	55	67	55	67	.451
Newark	57	72	58	71	.450
Hartford	56	75	57	76	.427
Norfolk	47	78	47	79	.373

Landmark Encyclopedia, p. 123

Virginia League 1900

	W	L	Pct.
Norfolk Mary Janes	43	15	.741
Portsmouth Pirates	29	29	.500
Hopewell (Hopewell did not exist then)	29	29	.500
N News Shipbuilders	23	39	.371
Richmond Colts	21	15	.583
Petersburg	8	26	.235

Encyclopedia, p. 126

Supplemental Season	W	L
Portsmouth	23	20
Norfolk	20	23

N. Carolina–Virginia League 1901

	Split Season			
	First Half		Second Half	
1901	W	L	W	L
Wilmington Giants	34	24	8	5
Norfolk Skippers	33	25	9	4
Newport News (Tarboro)	32	26	2	11
Raleigh Senators	29	28	8	5
Portsmouth (Charlotte)	24	30	4	8
Richmond Grays	19	38	7	5

	W	N	NN	Ra	P	Ri	Wins
Wilmington	X	6	6	8	6	8	34
Norfolk	6	X	3	9	6	9	33
Newport News	7	7	X	3	9	6	32
Raleigh	4	3	9	X	4	9	29
Portsmouth	4	7	3	4	X	6	24
Richmond	3	2	5	4	5	X	19
Losses	24	25	26	28	30	38	

24 June 1901 *Portsmouth Star*

Virginia League 1906	W	L
Lynchburg Shoemakers	72	36
Norfolk Tars	62	44
Richmond Lawmakers	57	54
Danville Tobacconists	50	58
Portsmouth Truckers	44	63
Roanoke Highlanders	42	72

Encyclopedia, pp. 150–151

Virginia League 1907	W	L	Pct
Norfolk Tars	67	48	.583
Danville Red Sox	67	58	.536
Lynchburg Shoemakers	65	62	.512
Richmond Colts	62	62	.500
Roanoke Tigers	62	62	.500
Portsmouth Truckers	46	77	.374

Encyclopedia, p. 154

Team Batting	AB	R	H	2b	3b	HR	SB	Pct.
Danville	4242	450	989	126	44	24	220	.233
Norfolk	3633	394	820	100	35	9	275	.223
Richmond	4355	433	967	96	42	6	252	.222
Roanoke	4308	396	896	76	29	6	162	.208
Lynchburg	4167	398	853	86	38	15	149	.205
Portsmouth	4067	324	831	88	31	6	246	.204

Team Fielding	PO	A	E	Pct.
Norfolk	3222	1526	180	.963
Danville	3490	1663	227	.958
Roanoke	3461	1707	251	.954
Richmond	3604	1742	270	.952
Portsmouth	3375	1625	259	.951
Lynchburg	3569	1770	274	.951

Reach's Guide (1908), p. 259

Virginia League 1908	W	L	Pct.
Richmond Colts	87	41	.680
Danville	74	52	.587
Roanoke Tigers	63	67	.485
Portsmouth Truckers	57	71	.445
Lynchburg Shoemakers	52	76	.406
Norfolk Tars	52	78	.400

Encyclopedia, p. 159

Team Batting	AB	R	H	SB	Pct.
Richmond	4228	459	984	217	.233
Danville	4231	477	970	178	.229
Portsmouth	4406	413	985	252	.224
Lynchburg	4327	358	948	175	.219
Norfolk	4156	365	900	196	.217
Roanoke	4182	371	903	228	.216

Team Fielding	PO	A	E	Pct.
Richmond	3659	1596	196	.964
Danville	3562	1783	215	.961
Roanoke	3552	1748	236	.957
Norfolk	3495	1762	250	.955
Portsmouth	3726	1775	268	.954
Lynchburg	3569	1770	274	.951

Reach's Guide (1909), pp. 297–299

Virginia League 1909	W	L	Pct.
Roanoke	73	49	.593
Norfolk	72	49	.595
Richmond	63	51	.508
Danville	60	62	.496
Portsmouth	49	72	.406
Lynchburg	50	74	.403

Team Batting	G	AB	R	H	2b	3b	HR	SB	Pct.
Norfolk	127	3948	441	985	120	33	6	271	.249
Roanoke	126	3973	436	958	127	48	10	166	.241
Richmond	129	3951	373	893	100	31	3	180	.226
Lynchburg	126	3980	333	884	119	42	2	125	.222
Danville	126	3854	388	813	126	39	14	183	.211
Portsmouth	126	3937	324	802	119	22	8	141	.204

Club Fielding	PO	A	E	Pct.
Danville	3299	1802	180	.966
Roanoke	3380	1649	178	.966
Richmond	3305	1514	177	.965
Portsmouth	3258	1580	224	.956
Lynchburg	3314	1694	262	.950
Norfolk	3363	1641	263	.950

Reach's Guide (1910), pp. 345–347

Virginia League 1910	W	L	W	L
Danville	69	45	69	45
Roanoke	68	52	68	52
Norfolk	59	56	58	56
Lynchburg	56	61	47	60
Richmond	50	67	49	67
Petersburg (Portsmouth)	47	68	47	68

Reach's Guide, p. 403 *Encyclopedia*, p. 169

Club Batting	G	AB	R	H	SB	Pct
Roanoke	123	3842	436	971	223	.253
Danville	117	3663	392	831	238	.228
Lynchburg	127	4091	360	931	150	.228
Norfolk	123	4130	437	925	229	.224
Petersburg	122	3837	377	860	186	.224
Richmond	123	3773	300	801	152	.212

Club Fielding	PO	A	E	Pct.
Richmond	3287	1626	182	.964
Roanoke	2202	1685	195	.962
Danville	3139	1566	186	.962
Lynchburg	3366	1756	203	.957
Petersburg	3210	1592	254	.956
Norfolk	3401	1776	255	.953

Reach's Guide, pp. 403–405

Virginia League 1911	W	L	W	L
Petersburg Hustlers	68	51	68	51
Norfolk	67	54	67	54
Roanoke	63	56	63	56
Richmond	56	62	55	63
Lynchburg	56	65	56	65
Danville	49	71	50	70

Reach's Guide, p. 391 *Encyclopedia*, p. 177

Club Batting	G	AB	R	H	Pct.
Richmond	118	4107	610	1106	.269
Roanoke	119	4146	549	1099	.266
Norfolk	121	4121	559	1074	.261
Danville	120	4081	504	1060	.260
Petersburg	119	4058	509	1027	.253
Lynchburg	121	3998	467	399	.250

Virginia League 1912	W	L	W	L
Petersburg	81	55	81	55
Roanoke	79	54	79	54
Richmond	77	56	77	55
Norfolk	68	65	67	65
Portsmouth	65	63	65	53
Newport News	46	84	46	84
Danville Red Sox	16	32	16	32
Lynchburg	11	34	11	34

Reach's Guide (1913), p. 359 *Encyclopedia*, p. 182
Virginian-Pilot has Norfolk record at 66–67

Virginia League 1913	W	L	Pct.
Petersburg	89	46	.659
Roanoke	82	57	.590
Richmond	74	60	.552
Portsmouth	57	77	.425
Newport News	53	83	.390
Norfolk	51	83	.381

Club Batting	G	AB	R	H	2b	3b	HR	SB	Pct.
Roanoke	139	4619	604	1172	152	57	10	234	.254
Richmond	134	4501	556	1135	149	63	25	328	.252
Portsmouth	134	4413	495	1072	148	45	31	248	.244
Norfolk	134	4441	486	1074	170	27	21	231	.242
Petersburg	135	4605	516	1068	202	61	32	224	.232
Newport News	136	4442	439	996	140	43	18	204	.224

Club Fielding	PO	A	E	Pct
Roanoke	3890	1692	253	.957
Newport News	4010	1865	320	.948
Richmond	3738	1588	289	.948
Norfolk	3623	1857	298	.948
Portsmouth	3993	1615	321	.946
Petersburg	3784	1860	465	.924

Reach's Guide (1914), pp. 347–349

Virginia League 1914	W	L	W	L	W	L	W	L
			Split Season					
Norfolk	44	21	49	27	93	48	93	48
Richmond	38	24	40	32	78	56	78	56
Newport News	38	28	30	40	68	68	70	69
Roanoke	33	34	32	38	65	72	65	72
Petersburg	22	40	41	34	63	74	63	74
Portsmouth	20	48	26	48	46	96	46	96
	195	195	218	219	413	414	415	415

Reach's Guide (1915), p. 249 *Encyclopedia*, p. 196

Club Batting	G	AB	R	H	2b	3b	HR	SB	Pct.
Richmond	140	4583	638	1184	160	83	16	229	.258
Norfolk	147	4635	649	1140	224	55	15	341	.246
Portsmouth	144	4842	482	1191	163	39	31	144	.246
Newport News	145	4889	632	1191	174	84	22	291	.244
Roanoke	142	4597	531	1101	156	38	21	183	.240
Petersburg	148	1813	512	1147	169	46	14	260	.238

Club Fielding	PO	A	E	Pct.
Norfolk	2916	1939	220	.957
Richmond	3583	1499	243	.955
Petersburg	3586	1920	264	.954
Newport News	3941	1985	298	.952
Roanoke	3669	1540	309	.944
Portsmouth	3688	1876	372	.937

Reach's Guide (1915), pp. 249–251

Virginia League 1915	W	L	W	L	W	L	W	L
Rocky Mount Tar Heels	35	23	39	25	74	48	74	48
Newport News Builders	34	24	29	37	63	61	63	62
Norfolk Tars	30	28	36	28	66	56	66	56
Portsmouth Truckers	27	32	41	25	68	57	68	58
Petersburg Orphans	25	31	16	52	41	x82	40	84
Suffolk Tigers	24	36	34	27	58	63	59	62
	175	174	195	194	370	367	370	370

Neither *V-P* nor *Reach's Guide* can be correct *Encyclopedia*, p. 202 x *V-P* 83 losses
Rocky Mount over Portsmouth in playoffs

Club Batting	G	AB	R	H	2b	3b	HR	SB	Pct.
Rocky Mount	130	4142	523	1079	174	18	35	106	.261
Newport News	128	4022	476	970	173	43	29	219	.241
Portsmouth	133	4393	491	1048	155	19	67	128	.239
Norfolk	129	4185	462	958	153	21	25	209	.229
Suffolk	125	4105	435	918	152	12	44	225	.224
Petersburg	129	4085	342	904	128	18	26	157	.221

Club Fielding	PO	A	E	Pct.
Norfolk	3485	1742	228	.958
Rocky Mount	3409	1516	225	.956
Suffolk	3387	1609	240	.954
Petersburg	3346	1616	245	.953
Newport News	3317	1517	239	.953
Portsmouth	3559	1823	299	.947

Reach's Guide (1916), pp. 269–271

Virginia League 1916

	W	L	W	L	W	L	W	L
Portsmouth Truckers	41	19	36	20	77	39	76	42
Newport News Builders	38	25	41	13	79	38	79	39
Rocky Mount Tar Heels	31	31	30	29	61	60	61	60
Norfolk Tars	25	34	9	43	34	77	38	77
Hopewell Powder Puffs	25	37	4	16	29	53	30	52
Petersburg Goobers	24	28	30	30	54	58	54	68
	189	174	150	151	344	325	338	338

(Split Season)

Virginian-Pilot Encyclopedia, p. 206
Newport News won playoff against Portsmouth 4 games to 3

Virginia League 1917	W	L	Pct.
Newport News	10	5	.667
Portsmouth	9	7	.563
Lynchburg	7	7	.500
Norfolk	7	9	.438
Petersburg	6	8	.429
Rocky Mount	6	9	.400

Encyclopedia, p. 210

Virginia League 1918	W	L	Pct.
Richmond	29	21	.580
Newport News	28	21	.571
Petersburg	27	22	.551
Norfolk	13	33	.239

Club Batting	G	AB	R	H	SB	Pct.
Newport News	50	1657	199	409	59	.247
Richmond	50	1605	189	391	71	.244
Petersburg	49	1585	159	368	87	.232
Norfolk	46	1455	114	294	48	.203

Club Fielding	PO	A	E	Pct.
Petersburg	1305	616	89	.955
Norfolk	1241	647	97	.951
Newport News	1355	681	89	.951
Richmond	1316	694	100	.951

Reach's Guide (1919), pp. 321–322

Virginia League 1919

	W	L	Split Season W	L	W	L	W	L
Petersburg	32	16	28	32	60	48	62	47
Suffolk	28	21	22	37	50	58	49	58
Portsmouth	26	24	31	27	57	51	57	51
Norfolk	25	26	33	27	58	53	58	53
Richmond	19	30	40	19	59	49	60	50
Newport News	19	32	24	36	43	68	42	69
					327	327	328	328

Reach's Guide, p. 341 *Encyclopedia*, p. 216

Team Batting	G	AB	R	H	SB	Pct.
Norfolk	114	3587	433	894	169	249
Suffolk	110	3475	356	844	112	243
Petersburg	111	3496	370	848	121	242
Portsmouth	110	3484	411	835	141	239
Richmond	111	3551	397	841	171	237
Newport News	112	3468	317	806	166	232

Team Fielding	PO	A	E	Pct.
Petersburg	2851	1332	169	961
Newport News	2717	1300	197	953
Richmond	2969	1370	217	952
Portsmouth	2884	1415	218	952
Suffolk	2605	1260	206	949
Norfolk	2889	1475	241	948

Reach's Guide, pp. 341–343

Virginia League 1920

	W	L	Split Season W	L	W	L
Richmond	43	13	33	25	76	38
Portsmouth	34	26	39	19	73	45
Rocky Mount	32	28	21	38	53	66
Petersburg	29	28	39	22	68	50
Norfolk	28	30	26	29	54	59
Newport News	26	34	25	34	51	68
Suffolk	22	36	25	33	47	69
Wilson	19	38	25	33	44	71

Virginian-Pilot Encyclopedia, p. 221
Portsmouth over Richmond, 4 games to 3 in playoffs

Team Batting	G	AB	R	H	SB	Pct.
Richmond	121	4194	586	1085	149	.259
Portsmouth	121	4012	495	1037	185	.258
Petersburg	120	3991	501	1023	190	.256
Wilson	118	4128	451	1053	118	.255
Norfolk	117	4010	447	1001	176	.250
Suffolk	120	3905	397	956	127	.245
Rocky Mount	123	4016	385	930	116	.231
Newport News	126	4062	384	936	172	.230

Team Fielding	PO	A	E	Pct.
Portsmouth	3197	1535	194	.961
Richmond	3344	1650	216	.959
Norfolk	3241	1574	206	.959
Petersburg	3225	1476	218	.956
Newport News	3364	1647	233	.956
Wilson	3210	1509	223	.955
Rocky Mount	3261	1660	249	.852
Suffolk	3167	1797	252	.851

Reach's Guide, pp. 285–289

Virginia League 1921

	Split Season					
	W	L	W	L	W	L
Rocky Mount	38	25	39	32	77	57
Wilson Bugs	38	25	34	26	72	51
Portsmouth	34	28	44	28	78	56
Richmond	30	30	44	28	74	58
Peters./Tarboro	29	35	17	53	46	88
Suffolk Cats	28	36	31	42	59	78
Norfolk	28	36	46	28	74	64
Newport News	26	36	26	45	52	81

Portsmouth won playoff against Norfolk, 4 games to 1

Batting	G	AB	R	H	Pct.
Norfolk	138	4779	725	1381	.291
Rocky Mount	137	4702	805	1364	.290
Wilson	139	4721	745	1368	.290
Richmond	137	4775	722	1318	.276
Portsmouth	138	4336	740	1179	.272
Newport News	137	4446	513	1173	.264
Peters./Tarboro	139	4629	550	1205	.260
Suffolk	142	4605	558	1122	.217

Club Fielding	PO	A	E	Pct.
Suffolk	3650	1946	187	968
Richmond	3539	1875	224	960
Wilson	3694	1760	229	960
Portsmouth	3673	1694	257	955
Rocky Mount	3645	1701	253	955
Norfolk	3633	1880	281	952
Peters./Tarboro	3494	1781	271	951
Newport News	3487	1596	277	948

Reach's Guide, pp. 339–344

Virginia League 1922	W	L	W	L	Pct.
Wilson Bugs	68	51	68	52	.567
Newport News Builders	63	57	63	56	.529
Norfolk Tars	58	56	58	57	.504
Rocky Mount Tar Heels	59	61	60	61	.496
Portsmouth Truckers	58	61	57	61	.483
Richmond Colts	48	68	49	68	.419

Virginian-Pilot Encyclopedia, p. 228
Box scores show Norfolk record at 59 and 56
All games accounted for in box scores

Virginia League 1923	W	L	Pct.
Wilson	70	52	774
Richmond	71	53	773
Rocky Mount	63	59	516
Norfolk	62	60	508
Portsmouth	58	62	483
Petersburg	43	81	347

Team Batting	G	AB	R	H	2b	3b	HR	SB	Pct.
Wilson	126	4225	606	1198	182	73	44	98	.281
Rocky Mount	126	4238	635	1182	199	48	64	155	.279
Richmond	129	4323	606	1204	226	49	55	94	.278
Portsmouth	125	4304	633	1185	178	48	82	95	.275
Norfolk	128	4339	550	1185	192	26	39	134	.273
Petersburg	129	4367	535	1149	168	40	56	98	.261

Club Fielding	PO	A	E	Pct.
Wilson	3313	1594	199	.980
Norfolk	3455	1862	191	.965
Petersburg	3409	1716	194	.964
Richmond	3352	1555	200	.961
Portsmouth	3302	1507	233	.954
Rocky Mount	3359	1516	241	.953

Reach's Guide, pp. 403–410

Virginia League 1924	W	L	Pct.
Richmond	76	59	.563
Portsmouth	75	60	.555
Rocky Mount	74	62	.544
Norfolk	69	66	.511
Wilson	66	70	.485
Petersburg	46	89	.340

Encyclopedia, p. 236

Team Batting	G	AB	R	H	2b	3b	HR	SB	Pct.
Richmond	136	4605	726	1346	224	34	67	136	.292
Norfolk	142	4712	620	1262	217	28	70	145	.268
Portsmouth	137	4593	670	1226	200	33	106	87	.267
Wilson	142	4651	617	1229	166	42	28	132	.264
Rocky Mount	138	4574	619	1198	203	21	66	137	.260
Petersburg	135	4489	500	1130	168	27	50	105	.252

Club Fielding	PO	A	E	Pct.
Wilson	3716	1762	193	.966
Rocky Mount	3700	1790	205	.964
Petersburg	3557	1712	196	.964
Portsmouth	3648	1583	203	.963
Norfolk	3694	1738	221	.961
Richmond	3709	1785	225	.961

18 December 1924 *Sporting News*

Virginia League 1925	W	L	W	L
Richmond Colts	79	54	78	54
Portsmouth Truckers	75	58	73	59
Norfolk Tars	72	61	72	60
Wilson Bugs	68	65	68	64
Rocky Mount Tar Heels	53	80	53	79
Kinston Eagles	52	81	52	80

Virginian-Pilot Encyclopedia, p. 240

Batting	G	AB	R	H	2b	3b	HR	SB	Pct.
Portsmouth	135	4627	764	1440	240	47	109	131	.311
Richmond	135	4611	832	1428	226	49	123	121	.310
Norfolk	136	4611	789	1392	220	36	87	141	.301
Kinston	135	4645	642	1356	253	33	52	80	.293
Wilson	134	4422	658	1243	207	47	70	156	.281
Rocky Mount	133	4428	649	1157	121	33	43	105	.261

22 October 1925 *Sporting News*

Virginia League 1926	W	L	W	L
Richmond	85	68	85	68
Wilson	85	69	85	69
Norfolk	70	72	79	73
Portsmouth	74	78	74	78
Kinston	69	82	69	83
Petersburg Nuts	65	87	66	87
	448	456		

Virginian-Pilot Encyclopedia, p. 244

Batting	G	AB	R	H	2b	3b	HR	SB	Pct.
Norfolk	157	5265	921	1650	243	28	100?	213	.313
Richmond	156	5191	917	1621	259	42	183	123	.312
Portsmouth	154	5260	834	1636	281	44	104	108	.311
Wilson	157	5112	725	1492	249	55	56	125	.292
Kinston	156	5184	693	1488	211	47	51	96	.287
Petersburg	154	5019	622	1342	223	52	83	106	.267

4 November 1926 *Sporting News*

Virginia League 1927	W	L	Pct.
Portsmouth	76	52	594
Petersburg	72	61	541
Richmond	65	65	500
Wilson	65	67	492
Norfolk	58	72	446
Kinston	56	75	427

Encyclopedia, p. 249

Batting	G	AB	R	H	2b	3b	HR	SB	Pct.
Portsmouth	123	X	837	1334	254	45	97	147	.306
Richmond	131	X	651	X	211	33	99	81	.298
Petersburg	135	X	644	1279	X	42	56	138	.288
Norfolk	133	4472	651	1365	180	30	79	97	.285
Wilson	132	4351	594	1206	190	61	39	116	.278
Kinston	132	4406	580	1202	182	33	42	81	.273

13 October 1927 *Sporting News*

Virginia League 1928	W	L
Norfolk	26	13
Portsmouth	25	14
Petersburg	15	27
Richmond	15	27

Encyclopedia, p. 254

Chapter Notes

Chapter 1

1. 25 November 1865 *Norfolk Post*.
2. 9 December 1865 *Norfolk Post*; 26 February 1866 *Virginian*.
3. 23 May 1867 *Norfolk Journal*; 5 and 17 September 1867 *Virginian*.
4. 28 September 1868; 7 June 1871 *Virginian*.

Chapter 2

1. 26 April 1884 *Virginian*; 11 June 1884 *Public Ledger*; 13 June 1884 *Landmark*.
2. 13 June 1884 *Home Bulletin*; 12–13 June 1884 *Public Ledger*; 13–18 June 1884 *Landmark*.
3. 11 July 1884 *Virginian*.
4. 26–27 July 1884 *Landmark*.
5. 29–31 July 84 *Virginian*; 21 August 1884 *Landmark*.
6. 23 August 1884 *Landmark*; 23 July 1884 *Virginian*.
7. 31 August 1884 *Virginian*; 2 September 1884 *Landmark*.
8. 18 September 84 *Virginian*.
9. 23 September 1884 *Landmark*.
10. 30 September 1884 *Virginian*; 8 October 1884 *Sporting Life*.
11. 30 September 1884 *Virginian*.
12. 11 October 1884 *Virginian*.
13. 17, 22 and 23 October 84 *Virginian*.
14. 23 June 1884 *Virginian*.
15. 29 and 30 August 1884 *Virginian*.
16. 5 September 1884 *Virginian*.
17. 30–31 August 1884 *Virginian*.
18. 11 September 1884 *Virginian*.
19. 13 August and 5–6 September 1884 *Virginian*.
20. 28 October 1884 *Landmark*.
21. 17 February 1885 *Virginian*.
22. 17 February and 31 March 1923 *Norfolk Journal and Guide*.
23. 1 and 22 February and 12 and 29 March 1885 *Virginian*; 29 June 1885 *Public Ledger*.
24. 3–10 April 1885 *Virginian*.
25. 25 April 1885 *Landmark*; 2, 9, and 17–30 April 1885 *Virginian*.
26. 3 May 1885 *Virginian*; 3 May 1885 *Public Ledger*.
27. 27 May 1885 *Public Ledger*.
28. 20 June 1885 *Landmark*.
29. 17 June and 4 July 1885 *Landmark*.
30. 2 August 1885 *Landmark*.
31. 19 August 1885 *Public Ledger*.
32. 28 August 1885 *Virginian*.
33. 26 July and 30 August 1885 *Virginian*.
34. Robert H. Gudmestad, "Baseball, the Lost Cause, and the New South in Richmond, Virginia 1883–1890," *Virginia Magazine of History and Biography* 106 (Summer 1998): 267–300.
35. 17 April 1886 *Public Ledger*.
36. 25 June 1886 *Virginian* and *Landmark*.
37. 24 June 1885 *Public Ledger*; 11–21 July 1886 *Landmark*; 11 August 1886 *Sporting Life*.
38. 24 July 1886 *Home Bulletin*; 25 August 1886 *Sporting Life*.
39. 11 August 1886 *Sporting Life*.
40. 3 April and 10 May 1889 *Landmark*.
41. 31 May 1889 *Virginian* or *Landmark*.
42. 17 June 1889 *Public Ledger*; 31 March 1889 *Virginian*.
43. 12 June 1890 *Virginian*; 16 July 1890 *Landmark*.
44. 7 March 1890 *Public Ledger*.
45. 6 April 1895 *Sporting Life*.

Chapter 3

1. 11 November 1893 *Sporting Life*; 14 March 1894 *Virginian*.
2. 13 September 1894 *Virginian*.
3. 24 April 1894 *Sporting Life*; 8 March 1894 *Virginian*.
4. 15–24 March 1894 *Landmark*.
5. 12 April 1894 *Virginian*.
6. 22 April 1894 *Virginian*.
7. 25–28 April and 6 May 1894 *Virginian*; 12 May 1894 *Sporting Life*; and 15 June 1894 Petersburg *Index-Appeal*.
8. 12 and 13 June and 26 July 1894 *Virginian*.
9. 26 May 1894 Petersburg *Index-Appeal*.
10. 6 June 1894 *Virginian*.

11. 2 and 23 June 1894 *Sporting Life*.
12. 10 July 1894 *Virginian*; 14 July 1894 *Sporting Life*.
13. 12 May, 1 and 8 September 1894 *Sporting Life*; 7 July 1894 *Virginian*.
14. 26 June and 7 July 1894 *Sporting Life*.
15. 9 June 1894 *Sporting Life*; 6 June 1897 *Daily Pilot*.
16. 7–11 July 1894 *Virginian*.
17. 1 September 1894 *Sporting News*.
18. 21 July Petersburg *Index-Appeal*; 24–25 July and 4 August 94 *Virginian*.
19. 25 August and 1 September 1894 *Sporting Life*.
20. 27 August 1894 *Landmark*.
21. 18 August 94 *Virginian*.
22. 31 August and 1–3 September 1894 *Landmark* and *Virginian*.
23. 4 September 1894 *Landmark*.
24. 6 September 1894 *Landmark*.
25. 4 September 1894 *Lynchburg News*.
26. 6 September 1894 *Lynchburg News*.
27. 7 September 1894 Petersburg *Index-Appeal*.
28. 8–9 1894 September *Landmark* and *Virginian*; 15 and 22 September 1894 *Sporting Life*.
29. 8 September 1894 Petersburg *Index-Appeal*.
30. 8–9 September 1894 *Virginian* and *Landmark*; 9 September Petersburg *Index-Appeal*.
31. 9–10 September 1894 *Virginian* and *Landmark*.
32. 10–13 September 1894 *Virginian*.
33. 14–16 September 1894 and 18 March 1898 *Virginian-Pilot*.
34. 15 September Petersburg *Index-Appeal*.
35. 28 June 1940 *Virginian-Pilot*.
36. 18 May 1894 *Virginian*; 16 September 1894 *Landmark*.
37. 2 January, 19–20 February 1895 *Virginian*; 5, 10 and 21 March 1895 *Landmark*.
38. 20 March 1895 *Virginian*; 6 April 1895 *Sporting News*; 9 April 1895 *Landmark*.
39. 22 December 1894, 9 February, and 2 March 1895 *Sporting Life*; 23 February 1895 *Portsmouth Star*.
40. 23 February and 14 March 1895 *Portsmouth Star*.
41. 8 and 14 May 1895 *Virginian* and *Landmark*; 15 June 1895 *Sporting Life*.
42. 7–9 June 1895 *Virginian*.
43. 5 May 1895 *Richmond Dispatch*.
44. 24 and 30 May 1895 *Virginian*; 1 and 22 June 1895 *Sporting Life*.
45. 2 August 1895 *Sporting Life*.
46. 5 July 1895 *Virginian*.
47. 5–6 July 1895 *Virginian*; 5 July 1895 *Public Ledger*.
48. 19 June 1895 *Virginian*.
49. 13 and 20 August 1895 *Daily Pilot*.
50. 30 June and 15 August 1895 *Virginian*.
51. 27 July and 24 August 1895 *Virginian*.
52. 4 and 6 September 1895 *Virginian*; 10 and 13 September *Portsmouth Star*.
53. 12–16 September 1895 *Virginian* and *Public Ledger*.
54. 15 September 1895 *Daily Pilot*.
55. 19 October 1895 *Sporting Life*.
56. 23 September 1895 *Public Ledger*; 16 October 1895 *Portsmouth Star*.
57. 22 September, 3 October 1896 and 6 January 1897 *Public Ledger*.
58. 18 July 1895 *Richmond Dispatch*.
59. 1 September 1895 *Richmond Dispatch*.
60. 22 August 1896 *Sporting Life*; 18 August 1896 *Portsmouth Star*.
61. 3 March 1896 *Portsmouth Star*.
62. 1 and 29 January and 10 March 1896 *Virginian*.
63. 19 February and 15 March 1896 *Virginian*.
64. 28 March 1896 *Virginian*.
65. 29 May 1896 *Virginian*.
66. 7 August 1896 *Daily Pilot*.
67. 26 July 1896 *Virginian*.
68. 17 and 26 July 1896 *Virginian*.
69. 10 and 17 July 1896 *Virginian*.
70. 15, 19, and 20 August 1896 *Portsmouth Star*; 23 August 1896 *Landmark*.
71. 16–17 May 1896 *Virginian-Pilot*; 28 May 1896 *Sporting News*.
72. 23 May 1896 *Sporting News*; 18 May 1896 *Sporting Life*; and 15 July and 4 August 1896 *Lynchburg News*.
73. 7 August 1896 *Landmark*.
74. 16–18 August 1896 *Portsmouth Star*.
75. 6 August 1896 *Portsmouth Star*.
76. 13 May 1900 *Virginian-Pilot*.
77. 29 July and 12 August 1896 *Portsmouth Star*; 10 July 1896 *Landmark*; and 5 September 1896 *Sporting Life*.
78. 28 August 1896 *Virginian*; 6 September 1896 *Sporting Life*.
79. 26 September 1896 *Sporting News*; 1 and 13 December 1896 *Virginian*.
80. 1 December 1896 *Public Ledger*; 10 January and 26 February 1897 *Virginian*.

Chapter 4

1. 26 and 28 September 1896 *Virginian*.
2. 19 September 1896 *Sporting Life*; 21 October 1921 *Virginian*; 14 July 1895 and 22 April 1896 *Lynchburg News*.
3. 2 April 1897 *Virginian*.
4. 11, 15, 16, and 22 April 1897 *Virginian*; 9 April 1897 *Philadelphia Inquirer*.
5. 4 May 1897 *Virginian*.
6. 4–22 May 1897 *Virginian*.
7. 6 April 1897 *Virginian*.
8. 5 June 1897 *Sporting Life*.
9. 18 and 24 June 1897 *Virginian*.
10. 22 June 1897 and 13–14 July 1897 *Virginian*.
11. 1 July 1897 *Virginian*.
12. 29 July and 7–9 August 1897 *Virginian*.
13. 23 July 1897 Newark *Daily Advertiser*.
14. 20–31 July 1897 *Virginian*; 28 June 1940 *Virginian-Pilot*.
15. 29 July, 7–9 and 16–17 August 1897 *Virginian*.
16. 25 June 1897 *Virginian*.
17. 12 December 1927 *Virginian-Pilot*.
18. 8 January 1904 *Virginian-Pilot*.
19. 1 June 1897 Lancaster *Daily Intelligencer*; 1–6 and 24 July 1897 Newark *Daily Advertiser* and *Richmond Dispatch*.

20. 25 and 26 August 1897 *Virginian*, Newark *Daily Advertiser*, *Philadelphia Inquirer*, and Lancaster *Daily Intelligencer*.
21. 28 August 1897 *Sporting Life*.
22. 7 September 1897 *Richmond Dispatch*.
23. 11 September 1897 *Sporting Life*.
24. 6 August 1897 *Virginian* and *Philadelphia Inquirer*.
25. 5 September and 14 October 1897 *Virginian*.
26. 5 September 1897 *Virginian*; 11 September 1897 *Sporting News*; 27 March 1898 *Landmark*.
27. 16 April, 7 May 1897 *Virginian*; 27 December 1897 *Public Ledger*.
28. "Poor Old Norfolk," 16 May 1898 *Landmark*; 14 and 22 July 1898 Newark *Daily Advertiser*.
29. 15 May 1898 *Landmark*.
30. 31 August 1898 Lancaster *Daily Intelligencer*.
31. 9 August 1898 *Landmark*; 21 June 1898 Lancaster *Daily Intelligencer*.
32. 13 June 1898 *Landmark*.
33. 1 June 1898 *Richmond Dispatch*; 15 July 1898 *Landmark*.
34. 13 August 1898 *Landmark*; 15 June 1898 Lancaster *Daily Intelligencer*.
35. 28 July 1898 Lancaster *Daily Intelligencer*.
36. 6 and 9 August 1898 Newark *Daily Advertiser*.
37. 13 August 1898 *Landmark*; 8 September 1898 Lancaster *Daily Intelligencer*.
38. 7 June 1898 *Hartford Times*; 17 July 1898 *Landmark*.
39. 22–24 and 28 July 1898 Lancaster *Daily Intelligencer*.
40. 24–25 August 1898 Allentown *Morning Call*.
41. 22 August 1898 Lancaster *Daily Intelligencer*.
42. 31 August and 1 September 1898 *Landmark*.
43. 10–13 September 1898 *Richmond Dispatch*; 11 September 1898 *Landmark*.
44. 26 November 1898 *Sporting Life*.
45. 1 August 1898 Lancaster *Daily Intelligencer*.
46. 28 November 1898 *Landmark*.

Chapter 5

1. 25 August 1899 *Daily Press*; 15 September and 20 November 1899 *Virginian-Pilot*.
2. 30, 31 March and 2 April 1900 *Virginian-Pilot*.
3. 1 April 1900 *Virginian-Pilot*; 20 January and 3 March 1900 *Sporting News*.
4. 7 June 1900 *Morning Herald*.
5. 1 May 1900 *Virginian-Pilot*.
6. 17 April 1959 *Virginian-Pilot*; Clay Shampoe and Thomas R. Garrett, *Baseball in Norfolk, Virginia* (Charleston: Arcadia, 2003), p. 21.
7. 27 June 1900 *Morning Herald*.
8. 5, 8, 13, and July 1900 *Virginian-Pilot*.
9. 8 and 15 June 1901 *Sporting News*.
10. 24 July 1900 *Virginian Pilot*.
11. 9 August 1900 *Virginian-Pilot*.
12. 2 August 1900 *Portsmouth Star*.
13. 29 August 1900 *Virginian-Pilot*.
14. 9 December 1900 *Ledger-dispatch* and *Portsmouth Star*.
15. 5 September 1900 *Virginian-Pilot*.
16. 12 March 1901 *Virginian-Pilot*.
17. 19 February 1901 *Virginian-Pilot*.
18. 16–17 March 1901 *Virginian-Pilot*.
19. 31 March and 12 April 1901 *Virginian-Pilot*.
20. 3 and 31 May 1901 *Virginian-Pilot*.
21. 1 May 1901 *Virginian-Pilot*; 3 May 1901 *Richmond Dispatch*; 2 May 1901 *Morning Star*.
22. 14 and 17 June 1901 *Portsmouth Star*.
23. 8 May 1901 *News and Observer*; 8 June 1901 *Morning Star*.
24. 23, 28 June 1901 *Virginian-Pilot*.
25. 22 June and 7, 9 July 1901 *Virginian Pilot*.
26. 18 and 25 August 1901 *News and Observer*.
27. 26 May and 1 June 1904 *Virginian-Pilot*.

Chapter 6

1. 5 September 1905 *Public Ledger*.
2. 28 June 1940 *Virginian-Pilot*.
3. 27 April 1906 *Portsmouth Star*; 25 April 1906 *Virginian-Pilot*.
4. 26–30 April 1906 *Portsmouth Star*.
5. 13 and 17 July 1906 *Virginian-Pilot*; 28 July 1906 *Sporting Life*.
6. 11 and 22 May and 17 June 1906 *Times-Dispatch*.
7. 29 July 1906 *Virginian-Pilot*.
8. 5, 11 and 27 August 1906 *Times-Dispatch*.
9. 21 August 1906 *Times-Dispatch*; 30 July 1908 *Landmark*.
10. 23 August 1906 and 12 April 1907 *Virginian-Pilot*.
11. 14 April 1907 *Times-Dispatch* and *Virginian-Pilot*.
12. 13–14 April and 1 August 1907 *Virginian-Pilot*.
13. 2 April 1907 *Virginian-Pilot*.
14. 31 March and 7 April 1907 *Virginian-Pilot*; 13 April 1907 *Sporting Life*.
15. 14 April 1907 *Virginian Pilot*.
16. 2 April 1907 *Ledger-Dispatch*; 18 April 1907 *Landmark*.
17. 2 February, 13 and 20 April, and 8 June 1907 *Sporting Life*.
18. 9 May 1907 *Landmark*; 19–26 April 1907 *Virginian-Pilot*; 26 and 27 April and 12 May 1907 *Times-Dispatch*.
19. 7 September 1907 *Sporting Life*.
20. 22 May 1907 *Virginian-Pilot*.
21. 31 May 1907 *Virginian-Pilot*.
22. 5 June 1907 *Virginian-Pilot*.
23. 18–19 June 1907 *Times-Dispatch*.
24. 7 July 1907 *Virginian-Pilot* and *Landmark*.
25. 27 April 1907 *Ledger-Dispatch*; 9 August 1907 *Virginian-Pilot*.
26. 5 August 1907 *Portsmouth Star*.
27. 5 August 1907 *Portsmouth Star*.
28. 6 September 1907 *Portsmouth Star*.
29. 16 August 1907 *Virginian-Pilot*.
30. 17 August and 21 September 1907 *Sporting Life*.
31. 8–15 September 1907 *Virginian-Pilot*.
32. 10 March 1932 *Virginian-Pilot*.
33. 28 November 1907 *Sporting News*.

34. 31 March, 17 April and 26 May 1907 *Virginian-Pilot*.
35. 16 July 1907 *Virginian-Pilot*.
36. 16 July 1907 *Portsmouth Star* and *Virginian-Pilot*; 27 June 1908 *Ledger-Dispatch*.
37. 4 June 1912 *Virginian-Pilot*.
38. 24 March 1913 *Virginian-Pilot*.
39. 4 April 1908 *Sporting Life;* 13 March 1908 *Portsmouth Star*.
40. 16 February 1908 *Virginian-Pilot*.
41. 20 February and 8 March 1908 *Virginian-Pilot*.
42. 24–29 March, 3 April, and 21 June 1908 *Virginian-Pilot*.
43. 31 May 1908 *Times-Dispatch*.
44. 1 July 1908 *Landmark*.
45. 19 June 1908 *Virginian-Pilot*.
46. 5 August 1908 *Portsmouth Star*.
47. 6–8 August 1908 *Landmark*.
48. 8 August 1908 *Ledger-Dispatch*.
49. 23 July 1908 *Portsmouth Star*.
50. 20 May 1908 *Portsmouth Star*.
51. 9 August 1908 *Virginian-Pilot*.
52. William Simpson, "1908: The Year Richmond Went Baseball Wild," *Virginia Cavalcade* 26 (Spring 1977): 184–92.
53. 21 July 1908 *Portsmouth Star*; 10 August 1908 *Ledger-Dispatch*; 16 January 1909 and 28 June 1940 *Virginian-Pilot*.
54. 9 October 1911 *Virginian-Pilot*.
55. 16 January and 5 February 1909 *Virginian-Pilot*; 1 March 1909 *Portsmouth Star*.
56. 26 February and 20 March 1909 *Virginian-Pilot*; 24 July 1909 *Sporting Life*.
57. 17 and 29 March 1909 *Virginian-Pilot*; 21 April 1909 *Ledger-Dispatch* (photograph).
58. 19 April 1909 *Virginian-Pilot*.
59. 6 May 1909 *Virginian-Pilot*; 8 May 1909 *Sporting Life*.
60. 24 June 1909 *Virginian-Pilot*.
61. 2–6 July 1909 *Virginian-Pilot*.
62. 5 June 1909 *Sporting Life*.
63. 10 September 1909 *Portsmouth Star*.
64. 12 September 1909 *Virginian-Pilot*.
65. 14 September 1909 *Virginian-Pilot*.
66. 21 August 1909 *Ledger-Dispatch*.
67. 22 September and 16 November 1909 *Virginian-Pilot*; 9 December 1958 *Ledger-Dispatch*.
68. 17–19 March 1910 *Virginian-Pilot*.
69. 5 April 1911 *Ledger-Dispatch*.
70. 26 April 1910 *Times-Dispatch*.
71. 31 May 1910 *Ledger-Dispatch*.
72. 7 May 1910 *Sporting Life*.
73. 9 and 10 June 1910 *Ledger-Dispatch* and *Virginian-Pilot*.
74. 4 July 1910 *Ledger-Dispatch;* 4–5 July *Portsmouth Star*.
75. 5 July 1910 *Virginian-Pilot*.
76. Clay Shampoe and Thomas R. Garrett, *Baseball in Norfolk, Virginia* (Charleston: Arcadia, 2003), p. 21; 9 July 1910 and *Ledger-Dispatch* 7 January 1911 *Virginian-Pilot*.
77. 12 September 1910 and *Virginian-Pilot*.
78. 11 September 1910 *Virginian-Pilot*.
79. 10 November 1910 *Virginian-Pilot*.

Chapter 7

1. 29 August, 4 and 21 September 1910 *Virginian-Pilot*.
2. 9–10 October 1910 *Virginian-Pilot*.
3. 21 and 27 September 1910 *Virginian-Pilot*.
4. 10 April 1911 *Virginian-Pilot*.
5. 10 and 15 October 1910 *Virginian-Pilot*; 16 October 1910 *Ledger-Dispatch*; 7 and 24 June 1911 *Sporting Life*.
6. 12 and 17 March and 16 April 1911 *Virginian-Pilot*.
7. 12 and 17 March and 16 April 1911 *Virginian-Pilot*.
8. 2 April 1911 *Virginian-Pilot*.
9. 17 February 1911 *Ledger-Dispatch*; 26 March and 6, 10, and 11 April 1911 *Virginian-Pilot*.
10. 9 March 1911 *Virginian-Pilot*.
11. 19 April and 15 May 1911 *Virginian-Pilot*.
12. 24 May 1911 *Virginian-Pilot;* 19 May 1911 *Daily Press*.
13. 25 May 1911 *Virginian-Pilot*.
14. 11 and 25 June and 1 and 5 July 1911 *Virginian-Pilot*.
15. 5, 6, and 18 July 1911 *Virginian-Pilot*.
16. 2 August 1911 *Virginian-Pilot*.
17. 5 July 1911 *Virginian-Pilot*.
18. 16 July 1911 *Virginian-Pilot*.
19. 19 July 1911 *Virginian-Pilot* and Norfolk *Ledger-Dispatch*.
20. 31 July and 5 August 1911 *Virginian-Pilot*; 12 August 1911 *Sporting Life*.
21. 30 March 1915 *Ledger-Dispatch*.
22. 9 October 1911 *Virginian-Pilot*.
23. 20 September 1911 *Virginian-Pilot*.
24. 16 January 1912 *Virginian-Pilot*.
25. 27 January 1912 *Virginian-Pilot;* 17 February 1912 *Sporting Life*.
26. 31 January 1912 and 10 and 24 February 1912 *Virginian-Pilot*.
27. 16 February 1912 *Virginian-Pilot*.
28. 2 March 1912 *Sporting Life*.
29. 3 and 11–13 June 1912 *Virginian-Pilot;* 12 June 1912 *Ledger-Dispatch*.
30. 16 February 1912 *Virginian-Pilot*.
31. 1 April 1912 *Virginian-Pilot*.
32. 21 March 1913 *Virginian-Pilot*.
33. 6 April 1912 *Ledger-Dispatch*.
34. 6 April 1912 *Sporting Life;* 19 April 1912 *Virginian-Pilot*.
35. 13 January 1912 *Virginian-Pilot*.
36. 23 March 1912 *Ledger-Dispatch*.
37. 14 April, 17 July, and 13 August 1912 *Virginian-Pilot*; 9 March 1912 *Sporting Life*.
38. 28 March 1912 *Ledger-Dispatch*.
39. 18 and 25 May 1912 *Virginian-Pilot*.
40. 25 August 1912 *Virginian-Pilot*.
41. 3 September 1912 *Virginian-Pilot;* 14 September 1912 *Sporting Life*.

42. 3 August 1912 *Ledger-Dispatch*.
43. 28 December 1912 *Virginian-Pilot*.
44. 30 June 1912 *Virginian-Pilot*.
45. 22 March 1913 *Sporting Life*.
46. 4–7 April 1913 *Virginian-Pilot*.
47. 8 May 1913 *Virginian-Pilot*.
48. 6 May 1913 *Portsmouth Star*.
49. 8 May and 7 July 1913 *Virginian-Pilot*.
50. 31 May and 2 June 1913 *Virginian-Pilot*.
51. 5 April 1913 *Virginian-Pilot*.
52. 9 April 1913 *Virginian-Pilot*.
53. 11 April 1913 *Ledger-Dispatch*.
54. 23 April 1913 *Ledger-Dispatch*.
55. 14 May 1913 *Ledger-Dispatch*.
56. 11–12 June *Virginian-Pilot*.
57. 11 June 1913 *Times-Dispatch*.
58. 7 July 1913 *Virginian-Pilot*.
59. 10 July 1913 *Virginian-Pilot*.
60. 13 July 1913 *Virginian-Pilot*.
61. 21 July 1913 *Virginian-Pilot*.
62. 14–15 September 1913 *Virginian-Pilot*.
63. 15 March, 9 May, and 8 June 1914 *Virginian-Pilot*.
64. 16 and 25 January and 1 March 1914 *Virginian-Pilot*.
65. 7 May 1914 *Virginian-Pilot*.
66. 2 May 1914 *Sporting Life*.
67. 12–17 June 1914 *Daily Press*.
68. 13 and 17 June 1914 *Virginian-Pilot*.
69. 26 August 1914 *Ledger-Dispatch*; 9 September 1914 *Virginian-Pilot*.
70. 10 and 30 August 1914 *Virginian-Pilot*; 19 June 1914 *Ledger-Dispatch*.
71. 4 August 1914 *Virginian-Pilot*.
72. 28 July 1914 *Virginian-Pilot*.
73. 28–30 July, 4 September 1914 *Virginian-Pilot*.
74. 25 May 1915 *Daily Press*.
75. 17 September 1914 *Virginian-Pilot*; 7 November 1914 *Sporting Life*.
76. 30 August 1914 *Virginian-Pilot*.

Chapter 8

1. 22 May 1915 *Sporting Life*.
2. 13 March 1915 *Sporting Life*.
3. 8 May 1915 *Sporting Life*.
4. 6 May 1915 *Virginian-Pilot*.
5. 5 July 1915 *Virginian-Pilot*.
6. 23 and 24 June 1915 *Virginian-Pilot*.
7. 23 April 1915 *Daily Press*.
8. 24 June 1915 *Daily Press*.
9. 19 June 1915 *Sporting Life*.
10. 29 June 1915 *Daily Press*.
11. 5 July 1915 *Virginian-Pilot* and *Daily Press*.
12. 25 July 1915 *Virginian-Pilot*.
13. 29 July to 1 August 1915 *Virginian-Pilot*.
14. 31 July 1915 *Sporting Life*.
15. 19 August 1915 *Virginian-Pilot*.
16. 7 September 1915 *Daily Press*.
17. 23 July 1915 *Virginian-Pilot*.
18. 6–10 July 1915 *Virginian-Pilot*.
19. 1 August 1915 *Virginian-Pilot*.
20. 2 September 1915 *Virginian-Pilot*.
21. 2 September 1915 *Virginian-Pilot*.
22. 7 September 1915 *Ledger-Dispatch*.
23. 6 January 1916 *Daily Press*.
24. 13 March and 12 June 1916 *Virginian-Pilot*.
25. 19 April 1916 *Virginian-Pilot*.
26. 15 May 1916 *Virginian-Pilot*.
27. 11 March 1916 *Portsmouth Star*.
28. 14 March 1916 *Portsmouth Star*.
29. 11–14 March 1916 *Portsmouth Star*.
30. 22 and 25 March 1916 *Ledger-Star*.
31. 25 April 1916 *Portsmouth Star*.
32. 26 April 1916 *Ledger-Dispatch*; 26 April and 11 May 1916 *Portsmouth Star*.
33. 9 May 1916 *Virginian-Pilot*.
34. 12 May 1916 *Ledger-Dispatch*, *Virginian-Pilot* and *Portsmouth Star*; 27 May 1916 *Sporting Life*.
35. 9 May 1916 *Portsmouth Star*.
36. 3 June 1916 *Portsmouth Star*.
37. 26 June 1916 *Portsmouth Star*.
38. 24 July 1916 *Virginian-Pilot*.
39. 5–6 August 1916 *Virginian-Pilot*.
40. 18 August 1916 *Portsmouth Star*.
41. 5 September 1916 *Virginian-Pilot*.
42. 5 February and 12 March 1916 *Daily Press*.
43. 28 April 1916 *Daily Press*.
44. 12 September 1916 *Daily Press*.
45. 19–20 August 1916 *Portsmouth Star*.
46. 21 August 1916 *Portsmouth Star*.
47. 21 August 1916 *Portsmouth Star*.
48. 18 July 1916 *Daily Press*.
49. 22 September 1916 *Daily Press*.
50. 29 January 1917 *Virginian-Pilot*.
51. 28 June 1940 *Virginian-Pilot*.
52. 15 February 1917 *Virginian-Pilot*; 20 February 1917 *Sporting Life*.
53. 20, 26 May 1918 *Virginian-Pilot*.
54. 17 February 1917 *Sporting Life*.
55. 6 June 1926 *Virginian-Pilot*.
56. 28 April 1917 *Sporting Life*.
57. 25 April 1917 *Ledger-Dispatch*.
58. 27 April 1917 *Ledger-Dispatch*.
59. 16–17 May 1917 *Virginian-Pilot*.
60. 6 June 1926 *Virginian-Pilot*.
61. 15 June 1917 *Daily Press*.
62. 4 May 1918 *Virginian-Pilot*.
63. 26 May 1918 *Virginian-Pilot*.
64. 5 July 1918 *Virginian-Pilot*.
65. 19 July 1918 *Virginian-Pilot*.
66. 20 July 1918 *Virginian-Pilot*.
67. 20 August 1918 *Daily Press*.
68. 25 April and a May 1918 issue of *Virginian-Pilot*.
69. 4–5 May 1918 *Virginian-Pilot*.
70. 24 June and 2 July 1918 *Virginian-Pilot*.
71. 11 and 20 July 1918 *Virginian-Pilot*.
72. 5 August and 17 September 1918 *Virginian-Pilot*.

Chapter 9

1. 5, 20, and 22 March and 2, 4, 11, 17, and 27 April 1919 *Portsmouth Star*.
2. 27 March and 9 April 1919 *Virginian-Pilot*.

3. 17 May 1919 *Virginian-Pilot*.
4. 5 April 1919 *Ledger-Dispatch*.
5. 11 May 1919 *Virginian-Pilot*.
6. 30 and 31 May 1919 *Portsmouth Star*.
7. 27 May 1919 *Portsmouth Star*.
8. 17–18 June 1919 *Portsmouth Star*.
9. 23–28 June 1919 *Portsmouth Star*.
10. 27 August and 2 September 1919 *Ledger-Dispatch*.
11. 9 September 1919 *Virginian-Pilot*; 11 September 1919 *Ledger-Dispatch*.
12. 6 September 1919 *Ledger-Dispatch*.
13. 10 August 1919, 7 September 1919 and 11 February 1920 *Virginian-Pilot*.
14. 10 January 1937 *Virginian-Pilot*.
15. 9 September 1919 *Ledger-Dispatch*.
16. 28–29 March 1920 *Virginian-Pilot*.
17. 7 July 1920 *Virginian-Pilot*.
18. 7 and 15 July 1920 *Virginian-Pilot*.
19. 2 April 1920 *Portsmouth Star*.
20. 28 June 1920 *Virginian-Pilot*.
21. 28 March 1920 *Daily Press*.
22. 23 April and 7 May 1920 *Daily Press*.
23. 6 July 1920 *Virginian-Pilot*.
24. 15 July 1920 *Virginian-Pilot*.
25. 3 August 1920 *Virginian-Pilot*.
26. 25 August 1920 *Virginian-Pilot*.
27. 31 July 1920 *Daily Press*.
28. 14 August 1920 *Daily Press*.
29. 17 September 1920 *Virginian-Pilot*.
30. 9 January and 10 April 1921 *Virginian-Pilot*; 9 April 1921 *Daily Press*.
31. 10 January and 20 March 1921 *Daily Press*.
32. 17 March and 1 April 1921 *Portsmouth Star*.
33. 29 May and 3 June 1921 *Virginian-Pilot*.
34. 31 July and 7 August 1921 *Virginian-Pilot*.
35. 8–10 July 1921 *Portsmouth Star*.
36. 26 July 1921 *Portsmouth Star*.
37. 24 July 1921 *Portsmouth Star*.
38. 14 August 1921 *Virginian-Pilot*.
39. 12 August 1921 *Virginian-Pilot*.
40. 7–8 August 1921 *Portsmouth Star*.
41. 12–17 August 1921 *Portsmouth Star*.
42. 13 September 1921 *Portsmouth Star*.
43. 1 October 1921 *Virginian-Pilot*.
44. 28 September 1921 *Ledger-Dispatch*; 10 February 1922 *Virginian-Pilot*.
45. 3 October 1921 *Ledger-Dispatch*.
46. 5 and 19 October 1921 *Virginian-Pilot*.
47. 31 January 1922 *Virginian-Pilot*.
48. 1 March 1922 *Portsmouth Star*.
49. 2 April and 12 March 1922 *Virginian-Pilot*.
50. 10 April 1922 *Portsmouth Star*.
51. 5 May 1922 *Portsmouth Star*.
52. 24–25 May 1922 *Portsmouth Star* and *Virginian-Pilot*.
53. 30 May 1922 *Ledger-Dispatch*.
54. 17 June 1922 *Virginian-Pilot*.
55. 24 June 1922 *Daily Press*.
56. 3 August 1922 *Daily Press*.
57. 20 August 1922 *Daily Press*.
58. 31 December 1922 *Daily Press*.
59. 24 July 1923 *Portsmouth Star*.
60. 29 July 1923 *Virginian-Pilot*.
61. September 1923 issue of *Virginian-Pilot*.
62. 29 July 1923 *Virginian-Pilot*.
63. 29 July 1923 *Virginian-Pilot*.

Chapter 10

1. 20 January 1924 *Portsmouth Star*; 18 April 1924 *Virginian-Pilot*.
2. 18 June 1924 *Portsmouth Star*.
3. 2 June 1924 *Virginian-Pilot*.
4. 9 August 1924 *Ledger-Star* and *Virginian-Pilot*.
5. 13–14 August 1924 *Ledger-Dispatch*.
6. 21 August 1924 *Virginian-Pilot*.
7. 18 August 1924 *Ledger-Dispatch*.
8. 12 August 1924 *Virginian-Pilot* and *Ledger-Dispatch*.
9. 16 March 1925 *Virginian-Pilot*.
10. 26 April 1925 *Virginian-Pilot* and *Portsmouth Star*.
11. 1, 5 May 1925 *Virginian-Pilot*; 27 April 1925 *Ledger-Dispatch*.
12. 29–30 May 1925 *Virginian-Pilot*.
13. 29–31 May 1925 *Virginian-Pilot*.
14. 5–8 July 1925 *Virginian-Pilot*.
15. 22–24 July 1925 *Virginian-Pilot*.
16. 25 June 1926 *Virginian-Pilot*.
17. 22 August 1926 *Virginian-Pilot*.
18. 17 September 1926 *Virginian-Pilot*.
19. 4 November 1926 *Sporting News*.
20. 10 September 1926 *Virginian-Pilot*.
21. 24 January 1927 *Virginian-Pilot*.
22. 17 June 1927 *Virginian-Pilot*.
23. 26 May 1927 *Virginian-Pilot*.
24. 26 May 1927 *Ledger-Dispatch*.
25. 29 April 1931 *Ledger-Dispatch*.
26. 25 June 1922 *Daily Press*.
27. 27 June and 12 July 1922 *Daily Press*.
28. 27 June 1922 *Portsmouth Star*.
29. 27 June 1922 *Virginian-Pilot*.
30. 26–27 June 1922 *Virginian-Pilot* and *Ledger-Dispatch*.
31. 20–21 April 1924 *Virginian-Pilot*.
32. 21 April 1924 *Portsmouth Star*.
33. 25 August 1924 *Virginian-Pilot*.
34. 6 September 1924 *Virginian-Pilot*.
35. 8 September 1924 *Virginian-Pilot* and *Ledger-Star*.
36. 27 April 1925 *Virginian-Pilot* and *Portsmouth Star*.
37. 7 May 1925 *Ledger-Dispatch*.
38. 10 May 1925 *Virginian-Pilot*.
39. 18 May 1925 *Ledger-Dispatch*.
40. 30–31 July 1925 *Portsmouth Star*.
41. 26 February and 2, 4, 9, 7, and 14 March 1926 *Virginian-Pilot*; 21 February 1926 *Ledger-Dispatch*.
42. 20–26 February 1925 *Virginian-Pilot* and *Ledger-Star*.
43. 9 March 1926 *Virginian-Pilot*.
44. 20 February and 9 March 1925 *Virginian-Pilot*.
45. 3 March 1926 *Portsmouth Star*.

46. 29 August 1926 *Virginian-Pilot.*
47. 30 August 1926 *Ledger-Dispatch.*
48. 30 August 1926 *Ledger-Dispatch.*
49. 21 January 1927 *Virginian-Pilot.*
50. 20 January 1927 *Portsmouth Star.*
51. 12 January 1941 *Virginian-Pilot.*
52. 20 February 1926, 9 March 1926, 11 September 1927 and 2 December 1931 *Virginian-Pilot.*
53. 3 January 1928 *Virginian-Pilot.*
54. 6 May 1928 *Virginian-Pilot.*
55. 31 March 1928 *Virginian-Pilot.*
56. 19 April 1928 *Ledger-Dispatch.*
57. 4 June 1928 *Virginian-Pilot.*

Epilogue

1. 19 April and 1 September 1930 *Virginian-Pilot.*
2. 10 May 1929 *Virginian-Pilot.*
3. 24 June 1960 *Virginian-Pilot.*
4. 6 November 1970 *Ledger-Star.*
5. 9 November 1970 *Virginian-Pilot.*
6. 3 September 1940, 9 December 1958 and 17 April 1959 *Virginian-Pilot.*
7. Ibid.
8. 9 December 1958 *Ledger-Dispatch and Portsmouth Star.*

Bibliography

Books and Articles

Chambers, Lenoir. *Salt Water & Printer's Ink*. Chapel Hill: University of North Carolina Press, 1967.
Chrisman, David F. *The History of the Virginia League (1900–1928; 1939–1951)*. Bend, OR: Maverick Publications, 1988.
Daniel, W. Harrison, and Scott P. Mayer. *Baseball and Richmond: A History of the Professional Game, 1884–2000*. Jefferson, NC: McFarland, 2003.
The Encyclopedia of Minor League Baseball. 2d ed. Durham: Baseball America, 1997.
Gudmestad, Robert H. "Baseball, the Lost Cause, and the New South in Richmond Virginia, 1883–1890." *Virginian Magazine of History and Biography* 106 (Summer 1998): 267–300.
Jones, David, ed. *Deadball Stars of the American League*. Society for American Baseball Research. Dulles, VA: Potomac Books, 2006.
McGraw, John. *My Thirty Years in Baseball*. New York: Arno Press, 1974.
Neft, David S., and Richard M. Cohen. *The Sports Encyclopedia: Baseball 1997*. 17th ed. New York: St. Martin's Griffin, 1997.
Reach's Official Base Ball Guide. 1886, 1894–1928.
Robinson, Ray. *Matty, An American Hero: Christy Mathewson of the New York Giants*. New York: Oxford University Press, 1993.
Seymour, Harold, and Dorothy Seymour Mills. *Baseball the Early Years*. New York: Oxford University Press, 1960.
_____. *Baseball: The Golden Age*. New York: Oxford University Press, 1971.
Shampoe, Clay, and Thomas R. Garrett. *Baseball in Norfolk, Virginia*. Charleston: Arcadia, 2003.
_____. *Baseball in Portsmouth, Virginia*. Charleston: Arcadia, 2004.
Simpson, William. "1908: The Year Richmond Went Baseball Wild." *Virginia Cavalcade* 26 (Spring 1977): 184–92.
Wright, Marshall D. *The Southern Association in Baseball, 1895–1961*. Jefferson: McFarland, 2002.

Newspapers

Daily Advertiser (Newark, NJ) 1897–1898
Daily Intelligencer (Lancaster, PA) 1897–1898
Daily Pilot (Norfolk, VA) 1895
Daily Press (Newport News, VA) 1900–1928
Hartford Times 1898
Home Bulletin (Soldiers Home, Hampton, VA) 1884–1900
Index-Appeal (Petersburg, VA) 1894–1896
Landmark (Norfolk, VA) 1883–1907
Ledger-Dispatch (Norfolk, VA) 1905–1928
Ledger-Dispatch and Portsmouth Star (Norfolk) 1958–1959
Lynchburg News 1894–1896
Morning Call (Allentown, PA) 1898
Morning Herald (Newport News, VA) 1900–1901
Morning Star (Wilmington, NC) 1901
News and Observer (Raleigh, NC) 1901
Norfolk Journal 1867
Norfolk Journal and Guide 1923
Norfolk Post 1865
Paterson Call 1897–1898
Philadelphia Inquirer 1897
Portsmouth Star 1895–1928
Public Ledger (Norfolk, VA) 1876–1905
Richmond Dispatch 1894–1898
Roanoke Times 1894–1896
Sporting Life 1884–1919
Sporting News 1886–1928
Times-Dispatch (Richmond, VA) 1906–1916
Virginian (Norfolk, VA) 1865–1899
Virginian-Pilot (Norfolk, VA) 1899–1928

Index

Numbers in ***bold italics*** indicate pages with photographs.

Abbott, Tommy (c) 202
Albemarle League NC 103, 185
alcohol: drinking by players/umpires 27, 36, 89, 91, 111; selling/consuming during games 21, 90
Alexander, "Slim" (rf) 119, 124
Allen, Charlie (of) 119, 128, 164, 172
Allen "Old Tacks" (p) 65
Allentown club (Eastern L) 9, 12, 51, 53–56, 207
Alton, "Lefty" "Rube" (p) 136, 141
Altoona club (Pennsylvania L) 21, 79, 91, 102
Altrock, Nick 139
amateur baseball (sandlots) 49, 86, 106, 215, 221; clubs 6, 7, 9, 12, 31, 41, 59, 71, 137, 138, 142, 159, 210, 219; league 76, 113; players 10, 14, 19, 29, 37, 53, 74, 79, 99, 137, 172, 182
American Association (major league) 8, 10–14, 21; reserve clause 12; rules 15
Anti-Saloon League 213
Appalachian League 107, 119, 191
Applegate, Abraham Lincoln "Abe" (p) 181, 186, 187, 190
Ariel Club (boxing) 24
Arlington, Lizzie (female p) 54
Armory Hall (Norfolk) 21
Armstrong, Frank B. ("Red," "Reddy," "Mate") (1b/c) 36, 38, 40, 59, 63, 65, 68
Army and Navy Field (Phoebus) 101
Arthur, Jack (p) 202, 203, 207; alias Deshong 207
Artillery School (Fort Monroe team) 18
Ashenback, Edward M. "Jolly" (mgr/of) 59, 65, 67, 76
Athletic Field Association (Lafayette Field Norfolk) 77
Atlanta club 22, 40, 47, 93, 111, 119, 185
Atlantic Hotel (Norfolk) 30
Atlantic League 36, 43, 44–57, 58, 59, 65, 73, 77
attendance 13, 16–18, 20, 22, 32, 44, 51, 54, 57, 64, 66, 68, 69, 71, 73, 77, 82, 85, 86, 87, 90, 97, 100, 102–105, 108, 112, 122, 127, 132, 133, 137, 141, 144, 148, 151, 167, 169, 175, 186, 191, 192, 196, 197, 199, 202, 205, 215, 217, 218, 220
Attreau, Dick (1b) 183, 184, 193, 195, 197, 201, 202, 217
Ayers, Yancey Wyatt ("Doc," "Hillsville Hurrah") (p) 116

Babb, Charlie (ss/mgr) 102, 103, 105, 106, 108
Backarach Giants (black professionals) 219
Bain Field (Norfolk) 219, 222
Ballentyne, Jim (c) 39
Ballinger, Pelham "Jack" (ss) 144, 150, 151; sale to Louisville 151
Baltimore (Union A) 13
Baltimore Actives 10, 13
Baltimore All-Americans 21, 59
Baltimore Black Sox (black professionals) 219
Baltimore Monumentals 8, 9, 10 14
Baltimore Orioles 10, 11, 13, 14, 29, 30, 35, 38, 40, 45, 47, 50, 73, 88, 117, 119, 123, 159, 219
Bandrimer, Izzy (p) 170, 203
Bangs, Lester "Shipwreck" (of) 155, 158, 172, 176, 190, 191, 196, 200, 201, 202, 212
Barnes, George S. (Newport News owner) 149, 156, 157, 159, 177, 218, 219
Barnes, Luther "Lethal" (p) 199–201
Barrow, Ed (Atlantic L president) 46, 51, 55
Barry, C. Moran (Norfolk owner) 141, 143, 144, 147, 148, 158, 166–169
Barry, James E. (Norfolk owner) 71, 106, 141, 142, 149, 169, 176, 179–182
Barton, Carroll R. "Buck" (p) 124, 130
baseball: origin in Virginia 5; rules and rule changes 5, 14, 15, 16, 19, 32, 41, 59, 68, 76, 92, 183, 194

Bates, Johnny (p) 170
Bauchand, Shorty (ss) 198
Beaumont, Ben (1b) 63, 64, 65
Beck, Zinn (mgr/3b) 202, 203, 206, 216, 217
Becker, Jesse (of) 112
"Beer and Whisky League" (American Association) 21
Benbow, D.C. (1b) 75
Bender, Albert "Chief" (p) 90, 118, 149, 150, 152, 173, 218
Bender, John C. 90
benefit games 48, 66, 84, 151, 186, 204, 222
Bennett, Jack (p) 134
Benton, Lawrence James ("Larry," "Smiling Rube") (p) 158, 163, 165, 166, 197
Berger, Clarence (of) 124
Berger, Jack (c) 52, 53
Bernhardt, "Big" "Shoulders" (p) 117
Bertrand (Bertram), Hal (p) 82, 83, 84
Bigbie, Stan (if) 109
Binghamton, New York (club) 59
Birmingham, Alabama (team) 152, 158, 168
Bishop, John (p) 47, 48, 52–54, 56
Black, William (ss) 165
black players 14, 19, 23, 71, 219
Black Sox (black professionals) 219
blacklisting 12, 34
Bland, Charles T. 30, 37, 43, 68, 74, 80, 85, 91, 108, 109, 111, 112, 118
Bland Park (Portsmouth) 110, 125, 134
Blankenship (p) 39
Block, George "Bruno" (c) 102, 103, 105, 106
Blogg, Wesley Collins (mgr/1b) 11, 12
"Blue Grass Battery" 102
blue laws 2, 85, 214
Blue Ridge League 177, 192
Boatwright, Jacob O. 107, 108, 110, 119, 122, 127, 132
Boehling, Joe (p) 146
Boerner, Larry (p) 196, 197, 202–206

249

Bonner, Jack (2b) 90–92, 99
Bonno, Gus (p) 76, 86
Booker, G.B.A. (Newport News owner) 58, 77, 102
Boschen, Henry (mgr/p) 9, 18
Boston clubs (National L) 9, 11, 17, 30, 42, 52, 68, 73, 102, 141, 145, 156, 175, 176, 197
Boston Red Sox (American L) 112, 113, 117, 155
Boulevard Avenue (Richmond park) 158
Bowerman, Frank (c) 38, 40
Bowman, Elmer "Babe" (of) 160, 161, 163, 165, 197
boycott: by fans 104; by police 74, 96; by teams 106; due to Sunday games 84, 85, 208
Bradley, William B. (Richmond owner/Virginia L president) 33, 36, 42, 43, 56, 97, 100, 106–108, 147, 164
Brady, John T. (Portsmouth owner) 23, 24, 29–35, 37, 59, 61, 62, 64, 65; death of 68
"Brady's Bunch of Boers" (Portsmouth 1900) *see* Portsmouth clubs
Bramham, William (judge/Virginia L president) 170, 190, 191, 193, 194, 200, 202, 213, 216–218
Brandon, Hilton "Toots" (c) 176, 196, 201, 203
Brandt, William "Willie" (p) 31, 33, 42, 47
Bribeck, Bill (c) 154–157
Brillheart, Benson (p) 183, 184, 186, 188
Brodie, Walter (of) 30 38, 88
Brooklyn Atlantics (American A) 14
Brooklyn clubs (National L) 38, 45, 49, 68, 118, 156, 172
Brooks, Harvey (p) 74, 75, 117
Brooks, Vernon (Portsmouth owner/politician) 97, 118, 127, 203
Broome, C.H. (Norfolk owner) 45, 47, 48, **50**
Brown, Mordecai "Three Finger" (p) 104
Bruce, Fisher (of) 132, 134–137, 142
Bruner, J. D. (p) 170, 173
Brush, John T. (Cincinnati owner) 64
Buckalew, Roy (p) 195, 196, 203
Bucknell College 59, 60
Buffalo (National L) 13
Buffalo Bisons (International L) 132, 138, 142, 183, 196, 217
Burden, Charles "Sheriff" (p) 117–119
Burke, Eddie "Shag" (in/of) 159, 161, 164, 168, 170, 172, 174, 175, 177–179, 181, 183, 184, 190, 207, 217
Burke, Joe (3b) 37, 42, 96
Burkett, Howard (2b) 160, 163, 168
Busch, Heinie ("Heine," "Herr Heinrich") (ss/mgr) 91, 94, 98, 102, 103, 111, 114, 121, 128
Byrd, Harry (governor) 212

Callan, W.J. (Norfolk cartoonist) 114, 116
Cardoza, Hugh L (Richmond reporter) 58
Carey, George (if) 173, 174
Carey, John (p) 170
Carl, Fred (ss) 16
Carlin, Buck (ump) 47
Carlin, Johnny (ss) 184
Carnes, Carl (mgr) 126–128
Carney, B. (commonwealth attorney) 209
Carolina Day (1907) 82
Carolina League 122, 125
Carraway, Harry E. (of) 141–143
Carson, F.R. (National Board official) 107
cartoons (cartoonists) 2, 79, 80, 86, 114, 116, 117, 145, 153, 154, 159–161, 165, 166, 170, 171
Casey, Joe (c) 163, 165, 172
Casino Park (Newport News) 102, 103
Cassell, Norman (Portsmouth Gymnasium president) 12
Castro, Lou "Count" (mgr) 108, 109, 111–113
Centennial Regatta (Philadelphia) 4
Chadwick, Henry ("Father of Baseball") 152
Champagne, George (of) 152, 154, 176, 183, 189, 217
Chandler, R.H. "Happy" (1b) 91, 92, 94, 96, 99, 183
Chapman and Jakeman cup 35
Charleston, South Carolina (team) 78, 79, 82, 84
Charleston, West Virginia (team) 20
Charlotte Hornets 70, 71, 179
Chattanooga (team) 176
Chenauult (p) 88
Chesbro, Jake (p) 54, 56
Cheshire, Ned (Norfolk owner) 90
Chicago (National League) 13
Chicago club (National L) 13, 88, 104, 137, 159, 180, 181, 185, 197, 201
Chicago Unions (Union A) 13
Chicago White Sox (American L) 137, 139, 172, 220; "Black Sox" 152, 161, 162, 167
Childress, Sam (groundskeeper) 196
Chisnell, Fred (reporter/ ump) 42, 45, 46
Chowder, Sam 36
Church Street (Norfolk) 7, 11, 15, 21, 22, 37, 72, 87, 92, 110, 115, 116, 143, 166, 169, 193
Cincinnati (Union A) 13
Cincinnati Reds (National L) 64, 112, 116, 117, 120, 129, 130, 139, 140
Clark, Ed (ump) 26, 27, 69
Clark, William Winfield (Win, Winn, Winsome) 1, 22, 29, 48, 58, 61, 64–72, 74–76, 78–81, 84, 90–92, 94–96, 98, 100, 101, 106, 119, 123, 130–132, 141, 145, 172, 174, 176–179, 182–186, 196, 205, 207, 216, 219, 221, 222, 223; death 223; at Naval Base 151, 154, 159, 170
Clarkson, Bill (p) 187–192, 194, 195, 206
Class B baseball 143, 159, 182, 200, 220
Class C 101, 118, 126, 141, 182, 190, 216
Class D 182
Clausen, Fred (p) 40, 47, 56
Cleary, Dennis "Denny" (of) 24, 31
Cleland, Robert (p) 8, 11, 14
Cleve, George (if) 36, 40
Cleveland (American L) 98, 112, 116, 168, 192
Cleveland (National L) 14, 15, 26
Cleveland, Bernard ("Bernie," "Red") (3b) 126, 129, 130, 132, 184, 187, 190, 192, 193 195, 222
Clifton Club (Baltimore) 10
Cline, Ed (ump) 41, 46
Cobb, Kenneth (Forrest) 176, 181
Cobb, Ty (Detroit of) 185, 191
Cochrane, Mickey (Phil. c) 191
Cockran, Alvah J. ("Gunboat," "Steamer," "Red") (p) 118, 121, 122, 124–126, 128–130, 132, 134, 136, 137
Cogan, Dick (p) 24
Coggins, Bill (p) 156, 203, 204
College Inn Billiard and Pool Association (College Inn) 60, 91, 106
"College Tigers" (Roanoke) 93
Collenberger, Harry (if) 192, 201, 203, 211, 216
Colliflower, Harry (p/of/ump) 21, 22, 24, 26, 27, 29, 30, 73
Columbia, South Carolina (team) 163, 168, 172, 174, 176
Columbus Ohio (American A) 11, 12, 192
"Connie Mack" (Newport News cheerleader) 126, 138
Consolvo, Charles H. (Norfolk owner, hotel man) 90, 91, 93, 94, 96, 100, 101
Conway, Patrick J. (1b) 59
Coolidge, Calvin (president) 179, 204
Cooper, Guy "Rebel" (p) 113, 117, 132
Corbett, "Gentleman Jim" (boxer/player) 38, 51
Corbett, Joe (p) 38, 40
Corcoran, Arthur "Bunny" (3b) 154, 156–158
Corcoran, Jack "Corkie" (ss) 24, 29–31, 35
Corprew, Burrus (Norfolk realtor/Virginia L president) 132, 139
cost of admission 7, 9, 36, 43, 67, 100, 145, 207, 209, 210, 214–216
Cote, Henry J. (c) 33, 47
Cotton States League 88

Cowan, George "Scrap Iron" (c) 75, 88, 109
Cox, W.N. "Bill" (Norfolk columnist) 61, 82–84
Craft, Maurice ("Molly," "Mollie") (p/1b/of) 129, 130, 134, 136, 137, 146, 179, 180, 184, 187, 188, 190, 191, 193, 195, 196, 201–203, 206
Creightons (Norfolk) 5, 6
"Crew of the Mary Jane" 3, 36, 38, 39, 43, 48, 51, 52, 54, 55, 60, 70, 73, 75–77, 89–96, 99, 103–106, 108, 109, 111–114, 118–120, 121, 124, 125, 129–132, 136–138, 141–145, 148, 153, 156, 158, 160, 163, 166, 172, 176–179, 186, 188–195, 197–204, 206, 216–218, 220, 221
Crist, Brooke "Old Mud Hoss" (mgr) 128, 134, 138
Crockett, David (2b) 58
Crockett, Pat (p) 158
Crump, Arthur E. "Buddy" (1b) 172, 183, 186, 190 202, 203, 206
Cuban Stars 219
Cueto, Manuel (Manny) (cf) 131, 134–136, 139, 140
Cullen (c) 18
Culloton, Buddy (p) 143, 144, 149–152, 156–159
Cummings, Roscoe ("Cy," "Big Boy") (p/of) 80, 82, 83, 84, 88
Cunningham, E. Harvey (Norfolk owner) 47, 48, 51–57, 58, 62, **63**, 64, 66–70
Curtis, Charlie (if) 109

Dallas Steers (Southern L) 30, 31
Damrau, Harry (if) 114, 129, 131
Dannehower, Harry (p) 61, 62, 63, 65–68, 70
Danville (1886) 17, 18, 20
Danville (possible team) 20 58
Danville clubs (Virginia L) 72, 75, 78–82, 84, 87, 90, 92, 93, 95, 96, 98–101, 103–108, 111, 112
Danville Mutuals (1884) 8, 9
Darling, Frank D. (Hampton owner/businessman) 41, 42
Daughton Tom (of) 145, 160, 164, 167
Davis, Harry "Slates" (1b) 36, 40
Dawson, Henry Percy (Portsmouth, Newport News, Richmond owner) 147, 159, 167, 169, 170, 175, 177, 179, 182, 185, 189, 193, 195, 200, 201, 220, 222
Dayton (team) 15
Dead Ball Era 72–99, 106, 157, 218
Degges, Charles (cartoonist) 171
Delahanty, Ed (Philadelphia Phillie) 30
USS *Delaware* 124
Dempsey, Jack (c) 131
Dempster, John (p) 196
Denver (club) 82
Depression "The Gay Nineties" 20, 22, 44
Depression, Great 220, 221, 222
Derby, Eugene (c/rf) 16

Detroit (National L) 13
Detroit Tigers (American L) 139, 140, 183, 191
Devlin, Arthur (mgr/1b) 141, 142, 144
Dewey, George (admiral) 52
Diehm, C.W. (Norfolk owner) 48
Dietrick, Bill (Norfolk lawyer/possible player) 203, 217
Dingle, R. F. Lester "Jack" (cf) 74, 76 79, 83
Dixie Adonis Company (theater) 18
Doane, Walter (p) 93
Dodge, Johnny (if) 102, 103, 105, 109, 112
Dodson, Frank (p) 195
Donahue, Charles (3b) 88
Donnell, C.H. (p) 53
Doss, Pat (ss) 199, 203
Douglass, Bill 108
Dozier, Emmett (p) 138, 142
Dozier, Turner (Norfolk columnist) 220, 222
Driscoll (p) 17
Duckworth, W. Fred (Norfolk mayor) 222
Duff, Cecil (p) 192, 193, 195, 199, 203
Duffy, Jimmy (p) 204
Duke, J.T. (Norfolk County magistrate) 191, 205, 209–211
Dunn, Jack (Baltimore owner) 123
Dunnegan, Carl "Doc" (p) 195, 204
DuPont Company Plant (Hopewell) 127, 128, 132, 133
Durham (club) 100, 132, 174, 183, 191
Durkin, Jimmie (3b) 177, 181
Dye, R.E. (p) 117

Eastern League 2, 8–10, 12, 14, 16, 30, 47, 114, 203, 219, 220, 221, 222; Norfolk joins 13; rules 15
Eastern Shore League 191, 207
Eastern Shore of Virginia 170, 196, 202
Eckert, Charles "Iron Man" (p) 160, 161, 165
economy, impact of 7, 20, 153–154, 172, 182, 218, 220
Eddinger, Sam "Stump" (mgr) 216
Edney, Claude (p) 149–152
Edwards, George "Dippy" (c) 74, 75, 79, 81, **83**, 88
Efird, Jack "Jap" 128, 136
18th Street (Norfolk ballpark) 86, 87, 92, 110, 115, 116, 143, 194
Elberfield, Norman "the Tobacco Kid" (if) 48, 49
Elizabeth City, NC (club) 53, 185
Elizabeth City NC Tar Heels 101, 103, 104, 125
Elizabeth River 3, 13, 30, 38, 94, 113, 125, 131; regatta 200
Ellinger, Paul (p) 91
Elliott, H.C. (Roanoke and Norfolk owner) 101, 108, 118 122
Elmira NY (club) 79, 91
Elsey, Charles (1b) 21, 24

Emslie, Bob (p) 10
Epworth Methodist Church 39
Ettinger (lf) 17
Eubanks, Carl (c) 130, 131
Evans, Arthur (of/c) 74, 75, 79, 88
Evansville, Indiana (team) 34

Farming players 2, 25, 38, 41, 45, 158, 159, 169, 174, 176, 183, 184, 192, 196, 204, 215, 216, 220
Farrell, John N. (National A secretary) 102, 107, 108, 116, 162
Fass, Sol (Portsmouth owner) 216
Federal League 123
Fergusson, Tom (Norfolk reporter) 94, 222
Fetzer, William (of) 82
Fields, Jocko (c) 40
Fifth Naval District Athletic Association 145, 146, 147
fights (assaults and other poor behavior) 26, 27, 28, 31, 27, 28, 33, 35, 38, 40, 48, 49, 57, 69, 81, 92, 97, 103, 105, 122, 126–127, 128–129, 134, 154, 177, 179–180, 188, 193
fines 15, 33, 46, 47, 55, 69, 94, 105, 112, 122, 128, 134, 135, 176, 181, 205, 208, 220, 222; for Sunday baseball 209–211
Finneran, Joe (p) 102, 103, 105, 109, 111, 112
fires at ballparks: Mayo Island Park 182; Norfolk 167, 187, 194, 219; Petersburg 162; Portsmouth 205–206
Firth, John (1b) 18
Firth, Johnny (p) 177, 183, 184, 188, 189
Fisher, Fred "Red" (p) 184
Flannagan, Tom ("Cross Fire," "Turkey") (p) 59, 61, 62, **63**, 64–67
Fletcher, "Jim Jeffries" (p) 97, 223
Florida State League 183
Flynn, Don "Broncho" (of) 129, 130
Foiles, Henry "Henery" (1b) 105, 124, 129, 130
Forbes Field Pittsburgh 91
Foreman, Johnny "Brownie" (p) 23, 25, 26, 34, 52, 53
forfeits 26, 32, 34, 35, 39, 41, 42, 44, 46, 55, 67, 70, 71, 81, 84, 96, 108, 138, 139, 163, 188, 194; franchise 127, 137; year of forfeits (1896) 43
Fort Wayne, Indiana 11
Foster, Clarence "Dad" (c) 129, 131
Foster, Oscar "Red" (c) 75; suicide 75
Fourth Ward Social and Athletic Club (Portsmouth) 127, 136
Fox, George (c) 52, 53, 56
Fox, J.A. (Newport News columnist) 140
Fox, Jim (mgr) 134, 136, 140
Fox, John ("Long," "Big Lanky," "Tanglelegs") (p) 80, 82, 83, 92–94, 96, 98

Index

Foxen, Bill (p) 121
Foxen, Tom (p) 92, 93
Foxx, Jimmie (Philadelphia Athletic) 191
USRS *Franklin* 74, 86, 112, 113, 116, 134
Freedman, Andrew (NY owner) 64
Fried, Art "Cy" (p) 156, 178, 186–196
Friend, Dan (p) 88
Frisch, Frankie "Fordham Flash" (if) 142
Fromholtz, Frank "Ed" (p) 158
Fry, Joe "Foxey" (p) 21–25, 27, 29
Fuhrman, Bob (c) 164
Fultz, David (player/ lawyer) 22, 23, 141
Funk, Harold R. "Chuck" (c) 183, 187, 190, 191 195, 202

Gale, Frank H. (prize cup giver) 35
Gale-Greenwood Company Cup 94
Gallagher, Lawrence "Larry" (3b) 170, 174–176, 207, 217
Galveston (club) 187
Galvin, Harry (c) 91
gambling 4, 22, 23, 25, 33, 35, 90, 122, 126, 180, 182
Gannon, William (of) 88
Garden, Bert (p) 170
Gardinier, Roy (p) 126, 128, 138–140
Garrison, Norman (p) 183, 192
Garton, Jim 160, 161, 165, 168, 170, 172
Garvin, Lee "Captain Kidd" 108, 113, 122, 127
Gaston, Steve (p) 111, 112, 116–118, 121, 122, 124, 125, 128, 134, 137, 140
gate receipts 12, 18, 35, 38, 51, 54, 66, 69, 70, 100, 108, 144, 148, 152, 164, 167, 175, 216
George, Bill (of) 52, 53
Georgetown College (team) 68
Gibson, "Whitey" 18
Gillenwater, C.L. (p) 182–184, 186, 187
Gillespie, Jack "Rabbit" (if) 141, 144
Gilligan, Ed (2b/captain) 68–70
Gilligan, T. Red (of) 66, 68, 70
Gilman, T.E. (Portsmouth lawyer) 209
Gilmerton Car Line Portsmouth 101
Gilroy, Jake "Happy Jack" (p/of) 38, 40, 41, 44–46; death from kidney ailment 46
Glass, Carter (newsman/US senator) 27
Glockson, Norm "Beef" (c) 120, 145, 146, 159, 161, 163
"Golden Age" (professional baseball) 147
Gomez, Lefty (NY Yankee p) 222
Goosetree, Eddie (if) 155, 158, 161, 163, 177, 183
Gordon, Frank (p) 111, 112
Graham, Bert "Lefty" (p) 128, 134

Granby Street (Norfolk) 22, 87, 91, 92, 94, 169, 170
grandstands 15, 16, 22, 30, 37, 43, 52, 66, 72, 87, 91, 101, 110, 115, 141, 170, 182, 194, 205
Gray, Carl "Dolly" (of) 124, 131
Gray "Dolly" (ss) 117
Green, June (p) 206
Greenfield, Kent 197, 203
Greenville Spinners 174, 187, 200, 207
Gregory, E.N. (Virginia L secretary) 75
Griffin, Steven (2b) 82, 83, 88, 98, 101, 102, 103, 112
Griffith, Clark (NY mgr/Senator owner) 76, 113, 137, 139, 156, 169, 177, 178, 206, 215
Grim, Jack (mgr/owner) 75, 77, 78, 82, 90, 97, 110, 112
Grimes, Burleigh (p) 121, 172
Guiheen, Tom (if) 92
Gymnasium and Athletic Association 15
Gymnasium Park 7, 8, 10, 13, 14, 17, 18, 21, 52

Haas, Bert (1b) 79, 83, 88
Hager, Fred (c/of) 24
Haines, Jesse (p) 172
Hall, Pete (mgr) 42
Hall, Sam (p) 119
Hamby, Sam (c) 195–201
Hamilton, Earl (p) 128
Hampton Crabs (Virginia L) 42, 58–65, 72
Hampton Nationals 11, 12; *see also* Nationals of the Soldiers Home
Hampton Y (team) 18
Handiboe, Willie (ump) 81
Hanes, Tom (reporter/ columnist) 145, 167, 180, 182, 213, 217, 219
Hannan, William H. "Billy" 60, 72, 77, 84, 86, 87, 90, 91, 94, 101–104, 106, 113, 131
Hardesty, Scott (rf) 53, 55, 56
Harding, Warren G. (president) 1 54, 178, 179
Hardy (c) 10
Hargrove, William ("Will," "Hargy") (Norfolk detective-Portsmouth/Richmond rf) 31, 35, 36, 49, 131
Harris, "Sailor" (ss) 198
Harris, Stanley "Bucky" (ss) 141, 143
Harrisburg Senators (New York-Pennsylvania L) 205, 207, 217, 222
Harrison (Petersburg owner) 25, 27, 28
Hartford Cooperatives (Atlantic L) 47, 48, 51, 53–56, 59
Hartman, Sam (p) 91
Hartsell, Harry (if/mgr) 135, 138, 142, 143, 160
Harvey, Hunter (Newport News owner) 62, 67, 68
Hauptman, Harry "Handsome" (of/3b) 21, 24, 27, 30, 68

Healy, Tom (p) 15, 16
Hearn, Bunny (mgr) 186, 199
Heatwole, Ken (p) 164
Hedgepeth, Harry (p) 117, 121
Hehl, Jake (p) 193, 209
Heilman, Harry (Detroit) 191
Henderson NC (club) 9
Henges, Henry "Rusty" (of) 157, 159, 160, 168
Henry (Portsmouth Athletics gen mgr) 12
Henry, Frede "Snake" (1b) 128
Henry, John (p) 15, 16
Henshaw, Jack (ump) 103
Herbert, Emie (p) 117
Herr, "Big" Ed (p) 24, 30–33; contracts typhoid 24
Heving, Joe (p) 206, 217
Hewell, Bert "Half-Pint" (ss) 184, 190, 192
Heydon, Jack (c) 47
High Street (Portsmouth) 80, 125, 192, 199, 202, 210; new park 183, 187, 205
Hines, Jimmy (p) 205, 206
Hinton, Jack aka Summers (if) 109
Hinton, Phil (c) 75
Hipple, Tom (c) 183, 196, 198, 222
Hirtzel, H. Herbert (ump) 188
Hodge, Ernie A. "Tiny" (c) 21, 25, 26 27, 29, 30, 44
Hoffheimer, Norman (pool room mgr) 106
Hoggins, W.S. (ump) 32
Holland, Joe (Roanoke) 93
Holland, William (ump) 16
Hood, Abe "Abbie" (if) 192
Hoofnagle, Jesse (of) 14
Hooker, Buck (mgr) 103, 112
Hopewell clubs (Virginia L) 132–137, 142, 221
Hopkins, J.W. "Sis" (of) 92, 119
Horner (p) 11, 13, 17
Horwitz, Abe (Newport News owner) 108, 112, 126, 131, 132, 138, 149, 159, 219
Horwitz Park 113, 145, 159
Hotel Norfolk 45, 191
Howell, Clem (p) 117
Hudgins, Harold "Gene" (c) 113, 170, 173, 175, 176, 222
Hughes (p/rf) 15, 16
Hummer, Frank "Horse" (p) 191, 193, 195, 196
Humphries, Charles E. "Rube" (p) 119, 121, 122, 124, 126, 128–130
Hunt, H.H. "Paderewski" (p) 26, 27, 29
Hunt, "Middy" (minstrel entertainer) 134
Huntersville (Norfolk) 85
Huntington, Fred (p) 75
Hutchins (c) 18

Independent Order of Knockers 23
International League 94, 117, 123, 127, 132, 138, 143, 172, 176, 183, 197, 210
USS *Iowa* 145
Isaacs, E.M. (reporter/columnist) 45

Index

Jackson, Jimmy (of) 79, 83, 88, 91, 99
Jefferson, Thomas (president) 74
Jefferson Hotel (Richmond, Virginia) 58
Jeffries, James J. "Great White Hope" (boxer/ump) 67, 97, 223
Jenkins, M.W. (Portsmouth club secretary) 30
Jennings, Hugh (Baltimore player/Detroit mgr) 30, 73, 141
Jersey City Skeeters (International L) 117, 191, 203
Jewell, W. A. (mgr) 52, 56
Joanes, Ralph "Old Soldier" (1b) 24, 31
Jobson, Jimmy (p) 222
Johnson, Arthur "Big" (p) 170, 173, 174, 177, 178, 202–206
Johnson, Eddie (3b/1b) 21, 22; death from typhoid 24
Johnson, Eddie (p) 163, 165, 168
Johnson, Eddie (of) 174
Johnson, Jack (boxer) 67, 97
Johnson, L.E. (Norfolk and Western RR president) 104
Johnson, Walter (Washington Senators) 94
Johnston, C. Brooks (Norfolk mayor) 60
Joliff, Taylor Deacon (p) 156, 179, 181, 183, 189, 190 193, 209
Jones, John A. Johnny (p) 170, 173, 175, 176, 178, 179, 181, 183–186, 188
Jones, R.A. (Norfolk owner) 169, 214
Jones, Tom (reporter/ columnist) 148, 151, 152
Jordan, A.L. (lawyer/politician) 214
Jordan, Ray "Kid" (p) 80, 82, *83*, 84
Joyce, Raymond (p) 184, 186
Juniper Base Ball Club (Norfolk) 5

Kain, Charles "Barley" (of) 36, 53, 63, 74, 75; problem with drinking 36
Kane, Harry (of) 151
Kansas City Unions (Union A) 13
Katzenstein, P. (Norfolk storeowner) 45
Keeler, Willie "Hit-em Where They Ain't" (Baltimore Oriole) 30, 179
Keesey, Jim (1b) 186, 190, 192, 211
Keller, "Wee" (if) 114
Kelley, Bob (1b) 160
Kelley, James (p) 160
Kelliher, Mike (Mickey) 174, 175, 181, 183
Kelly, G. (if) 160
Kelly, George "King" (mgr/of) 25, 47, 48, 65, 68, 128
Kelly, Joe (of) 159, 161, 164, 166
Kemmer, "Big Bill" ("Little Willie") (1b) 65, 70
Kennedy (ump) 135, 140
Kennedy, "Snapper" (of) 53
Kentucky State League 38
Kilroy (p) 18

Kinston (NC) clubs 190–206, 215, 218
Kirby, Paul (of) 181, 192, 211
Kircher, George (of) 102, 103, 109, 114, 117
Kissinger, William F. ("Bill," "Long Boy," "Rube") (p) 22, 23, 24, 26, 27, 29, 30
Klinger, Joe (of) 196, 201, 203, 206
Klusman, Bill (1b) 52, 53, 55
Knowles, Jim (1b) 47
Knox, "Dickie" (of) 31, 53, 131
Konectchy, Ed (mgr) 184
Kraemer, Harry (Henry) (of) 156, 176, 181
Kress, Rhineheart "Jake" 176, 181
Kroger, John (Jack) (utility) 160, 161, 164, 168, 170, 174, 222
Kronprinz Wilhelm (German cruiser) 126
Ku Klux Klan 212

Lafayette Field 71, 72, 75, 77, 80, 84, 86, 87, 102, 110, 113–115, 116, 185
Lafayette Field Corporation 115
Lake, Harry (c/mgr) 138, 139, 157, 159, 164, 222
Lambert's Point 64, 72, 115, 173, 175
Lamont, E. (ss) 39, 40
Lancaster (Pa.) club (Eastern L) 14, 15, 30
Lancaster Maroons (Interstate L) 47, 49–51, 53–57
Land, Gus "Turkey" (c) 24
Landis, Kenesaw Mountain (judge/baseball commissioner) 162–164, 167, 168, 172, 178, 193, 200, 201, 205
Landrum, John (p) 66
Langraf, Ernest C. (mgr) 74
Langsford, Bob "Lily" (ss) 39
Lanser, "Pop" (utility) 24, 27
LaRocque, Sam (Lancaster) 49
Latouche, Paul (p) 9–11, 13
Law, Jack "Jake" (1b) 102–105, 108
Lawrence, Andy (mgr) 88
Lawrence, Frank D. (Portsmouth owner/banker) 118, 148, 163, 167, 169, 170, 172, 175, 182, 186, 189, 192, 194–196, 198, 199, 202, 204, 205, 215–218, 222; run for Senate 215; supporter of Sunday games 207–214, 219
Leach, Edgar ("Eddie," "Adonis") (p) 31, 32, 40, 54, 131
League Park (Norfolk) 21, 23, 30, 31, 45, 51, 60–62, 64, 70, 85, 87, 102, 104, 110, 119, 134, 138, 140, 141, 143, 145, 148, 149, 152, 153, 159, 167, 169, 172, 179, 194, 203, 204, 206, 217, 219; Sunday game 183
Leahy, Danny (ss) 46, 49, 50, 51; death in Texas saloon 49
Leahy, Fred, (c) 160, 161, 164, 168, 170, 173, 176
Leathers, Hal "Bud" (3b) 152, 157
LeBraun, Alvie (c) 109, 111

Ledbetter, Ralph "Slats" (p) 161, 165, 173
Leddy, Thomas (c) 170
Lee, Charlie (Norfolk cheerleader) 68
Leever, Sam (p) 45
Lennon, Ed (p) 161
Leonard, John ("Jack," "Dutch") (p) 74, 75
Lesner's Park 21
Lindberg, Gus (p) 193
Lindsay, Bill (ss) 135
Lipe, Perry (Richmond mgr) 90
"live ball" era 153
Loder, "Little" George, Jr. (ss) 216, 217
Loftus, Frank ("Hay," "Pat") (p) 187–189, 197
Long, Denny (mgr) 55, 56
Loos, Ivan "Pete" (p) 81
Lorraine Hotel 118, 151
Loucks, Sylvester D. (p) 81, 82, *83*
USS *Louisiana* 118
Louisville Colonels 30, 34, 37, 42 151
Luitich, "Big Chief" ("Injun," "Baldo") (p) 58, 61, 63, 66, 68
Lusky, Charley "Silent" 109
Lynchburg Baseball Association 44
Lynchburg clubs (Virginia L) 17, 20, 22, 23, 24, 26, 27, 32–37, 39, 42, 44, 47, 72, 74–80, 82, 84, 87–90, 96–98, 100, 105–108, 111, 112, 116, 142

Mace, Harry "India Rubber" (ump) 41, 46, 204
Mace, Johnny (c) 124, 131
Mack, Connie 113, 156, 160, 174, 192
Mackie, Arthur (Portsmouth columnist) 162
Macon (club) 24
Magalis, Louis Lefty (p) 142, 144
Magic City (Roanoke) 18, 80, 92, 94, 108
Main, Walter (p) 176
Main Street (Norfolk) 87, 94, 105
USS *Maine* 52
Maitland, Bill (ss) 174, 176, 184
Maley, Joe (p) 189
Mallonee, Henry B. ("Lefty," "Ben") (rf) 158 161, 165, 176
Malonee, Al (of) 188
Manchester Virginia (Tri-City League team) 20, 68
Manhattan NY 5
Manila, "Chico" (p) 142
Manion, George "Heinie" (ss) 79, 81, 83, 84
Manners, John (p) 186, 188, 190
Manning, Minnie (p) 185–187
Mansion House (Norfolk hotel) 30, 31
Marable, S.A. "Chap" (if) 141 165, 167, 168, 170, 186, 190, 196, 197, 213
Maranville, Rabbit (ss) 145
Markle, Clifford (p) 119, 120, 121, 122, 129

Marr, Charlie "Lefty" (of) 37, 41, 53
Marshall, R.A. (owner) 169, 187
Marshall, Richard Coke (Norfolk Co. Commonwealth Attorney) 85
Martin, "Brownie" (p) 65–68
Martin, Pepper (if) 197
Martin, Thomas Stapes (U.S. senator) 126
Mary Jane (sloop) 2, 3, 36, 171
Mathewson, Christy (Chris Matthews) (p) 59, 60, 61, 62, 63, 64, 65, 79, 91, 95, 113, 121, 139, 213
Matney, F.B. (p) 79, 82
Matthews, Harry (mgr) 120, 122
Matthews, Vince (p) 174, 175, 176, 179, 181, 205
Maury High School 142, 156, 191, 217
Mayer, Erskine (p) 109, 111, 112
Maynard, Henry Lee (Portsmouth owner/politician) 37
Mayo, W.R. (Norfolk mayor) 45
Mayo Island Park (Richmond) 158, 162, 178, 182, 201, 204
McCarrick, James W. (Captain) 11–13
McClelland, George (columnist) 220
McCloskey, John (of) 25, 27, 34, 43
McCloud, Harry (p) 59, 61, 62, 65
McClure Field (Navy Base) 221, 222
McCrary, Burl (p) 111
McCrary, J.R. (owner) 106, 108, 111, 114, 115, 117–119, 122
McCreary (of) 25
McCue, Frank (3b) 199, 201
McDermott, Sandy (ump) 26, 41
McElroy, George (p) 16
McFarlan, Al (of) 39, 40
McFarlan, Claude "Little Mac" (mgr/of) 37–41, 43–45, 48, 50, 51–53
McFarland, W.T. (p) 47, 48
McGann, Ambrose (2b) 34
McGloughlin, William Morris ("Mac," "Lanky," "Slim") (p) 163, 165, 178
McGraw, John "Mugsy" 30, 38, 45, 59, 63, 94, 95, 121, 142, 146, 173, 185, 196, 198, 216, 220
McKenna, Kit (p) 27
McKevitt, James (Danville mgr) 78, 82
McLaughlin (ump) 26, 27, 36; drinking 27, 36
McLaughlin, James (league president) 41
McLoughlin, Pat (p) 158
McMahon, Morrison ("Molly," "Red") (if) 120, 122, 124, 125, 128, 130, 132, 135, 140
McMahon, William ("Red," "Red Head") (3b) 74, 75, 79, 84
McManus, Joe (p) 129, 130
McMenamin, James (Hampton businessman) 42

McNamara, Tom (ump) 46
McPartlin, Frank (p) 33, 34
Meade, Phil (3b) 70, 71
Memphis (club) 26, 190
Meredith, C.F. "Frog Eye" 38
Meyers, "Smiley" 144
military baseball (World War I) 123, 145, 148
Miller, Lefty (p) 112
Mills, Sam (2b) 34
Minesweepers (military team) 145, 146, 222
Mission College (school for blacks) 14
USS *Mississippi* 145
Mitchell, Charlie (ump) 32–34, 37, 43
Mitchell, Rion (p) 150–152, 154, 157, 158
Moger, Harry (p) 196, 197, 200, 201
Montague (p) 18
Monticello Hotel (Norfolk) 49, 58, 92, 95, 107, 143, 162, 193, 222
Montreal (club) 52, 102
Moody, Dwight (evangelist) 21
Moore, Richard "Al" (3b) 140
Moore, Sheff (p) 82
Morgan, Bill (p) 156
Morgan, Scanlon (c) 88
Morpeth, Casper (1b) 135–138
Morris, Tommy (in/of) 176
Morrison, Morrison "Molly" (ss) 118
Morrissey, Frank (Deacon) (p) 62, 63, 70
Morristown (club) 191
Moss, Charley (mgr) 78, 81, 85
Mt. St. Joseph College (Baltimore) 99
Moye, W.S. (Virginia L official) 170, 178–181, 184, 186, 189, 190
Mullane, Tony "Count of Macaroni" (p) 11
Mullaney, Ed (of) 91, 92, 94, 96, 101, 105
Mullins, George "Dutch" (p) 126, 128
Mundy, John W. (of) 191, 197, 206
Mundy, William E. ("Bill," "Swat") (of) 112, 113, 117, 118
Munson, C.H. "Red" (c) 91, 94, 99
Murdock, Wilbur E. (of) 98, 99
Murphy's Hotel (Richmond) 93
Murray, Jim (of) 58, 65
Musselman (p) 168
Myers (Norfolk reporter) 22
Myers, Charles "Sham" (1b) 58

Nally, Alva (of) 172
Nashville (team) 36
Nashville Telephone Company 211
National Agreement 12, 13
National Association Agreement 107
National Association of Baseball Clubs 101, 102, 162, 176, 190, 211
National Association of Minor Leagues 181

National Association of Professional Baseball Players of America 222
National Board (baseball) 107, 108, 118
National Brewing Company 20
National Commission 108, 130, 137, 139, 162, 167
National League 9, 13–15, 17, 21, 23, 28, 30, 34, 38, 45, 54, 88, 102, 141, 180; pennant 113; reserve clause 12
National Park (DC) 45
Nationals of the Soldiers Home 8, 9, 11, 12, 16
Naval Air Station 145, 151, 172, 177, 198, 199, 203
Naval Hospital "Surgeons" 86, 112, 145
Navy Base (place and team) "Admirals" 145, 151, 154, 159, 177, 221, 222; Sunday game 183
Navy shipyard (US) 3, 4, 74, 76, 101, 113, 124, 125, 145, 146, 202; team of marines 210
Nelson, Harry (c) 61, 63, 65, 68
New England League 39, 40, 59, 68, 72, 75, 125, 152
USS *New Hampshire* 86
New Haven clubs (Eastern L) 38, 187, 197, 203, 210, 217
New Orleans Pelicans (Southern A) 70
New York clubs (American L) 54, 75, 98, 102, 109, 113, 120, 121, 130, 153, 156, 159, *168*, 172, 187, 189, 196, 220
New York Giants (National L) 30, 31, 49, 59, 60, 64, 91, 94, 95, 106, 113, 130, 141, 145, 146, 156, 165, 168, 172, 173, 185, 186, 192, 194, 195, 197, 201–204, 206, 220
New York Metropolitans (American A) 11–13
New York State League (New York League) 17, 79, 88 138
Newark Bears (International L) 159, 172, 174
Newark "Mosquitoes" (Atlantic L) 44, 46, 49–53, 56, 61, 63–65
Newark "Thugs" (Atlantic L) 44, 46, 49–53, 56, 61, 63–65
Newark NJ (Eastern L) 15, 16
Newhouse, Frank (ump) 75
Newport News (team) 20, 25, 29, 30, 40, 43; to Petersburg 177
Newport News Athletic Field 159; *see also* Horwitz Park
Newport News Chamber of Commerce 175
Newport News Independents 102
Newport News clubs 62, 64, 70, 72, 85, 95, 101–103, 107–113, 117, 119–128, 134–136, 138–143, 145, 146, 149, 150, 154–162, 164, 174–176, 181, 195, 207
Newport News Shipbuilding and Drydock Co. 4, 124
Newsome, Frank (ump) 74
Newton, Eugene "Doc" (if) 131, 135, 136, 138

Newton, Eustace J. "Lefty" (p) 45–47, 53–55
Nichols, Kid (Boston p) 38
Nicks, E.A. "Pop Pistol" (p) 132
Nicks, Ira "Shot Gun" (p) 128–130, 132, 136, 137, 142
Noel, Frank (p) 175
Norcum, Frank (ump) 122
Norfolk (team): playing on Sunday 209, 210
Norfolk Air Station "Fliers" 145
Norfolk and Portsmouth Traction Company 92
Norfolk and Western Railroad 32, 44, 72, 104, 115, 202; piers 173
Norfolk Athletic Association 96, 100
Norfolk Athletics (baseball club) 7–10; *see also* Norfolk Gymnastics
Norfolk Base Ball Association 15, 48
Norfolk Baseball Association 110, 169
Norfolk Baseball Corporation 114–116, 144, 169, 181
Norfolk "Brooms" 23, 26, 27, 29–33, 45–47, 52
Norfolk "Clam Diggers" 23, 26, 27, 29–33, 45–47, 52
Norfolk "Clams" 23, 26, 27, 29–33, 45–47, 52
Norfolk Collegians (Norfolk College) 72, 73, 79
Norfolk Council of Churches 208
Norfolk County 23, 37, 84, 85, 183, 208–213
Norfolk (clubs) 2, 3, 8, 22, 23, 26, 27, 29–37, 38, 41, 42, 45–48, 51–53, 55–56, 59, 61–63, 65, 68–71, 73, 76–80, 82–94, 96–98, 101–107, 109, 110, 112–114, 116–126, 128–132, 134–138, 140, 142, 143, 145, 148–150, 152–165, 166, 168, 169–184, 185, 186–201, 203–207, 214–222
Norfolk Gymnasium Baseball Club 7, 13
Norfolk Gymnastic Club 11, 14
Norfolk International Terminals 145
Norfolk Light Artillery Blues 141, 149
Norfolk Railway and Light Company 75
Norfolk "Rookies" (Tidewater L, 1911) 101–103, 110; move to Hampton 104
Norfolk Sports Club 222
Norfolk "Stevedores" 62
Norfolk Street Railway Company 52
Norfolk War Camp Community Service (World War I) 143, 145, 147, 148, 151
Norfolk YMCA (team) 21
Norris (club secretary) 63
North Atlantic League (proposed) 216
North Carolina A&M (North Carolina State) 103, 185
North Carolina League 66, 71
Northampton (Eastern Shore L) Red Sox 207
Northrop, Lou (Norfolk sports store owner) 219
Novak, Walter (ss) 196–199, 201, 202
Nowlan Cup 36, 42, 43

Oast, J. Alden (Portsmouth councilman) 209
O'Brien (p) 66
O'Brien, Frank (1b) 172
Ocean View (Norfolk) 87, 92, 108, 209; amusement park 77; Ocean View Hotel 97; speedway 169
O'Hagen, Harry "Stonewall" (3b) 24–27, 29, 30, 33, 38, 44, 49, 51
Old Dominion Peanut Corporation 143, 147
Old Point (club) 6, 59, 73, 101, 103
Oldring, Reuben "Rube" (of/mgr) 148, 149, 200
Omohondro, Alan C. (Norfolk owner/politician) 96
O'Neil, Jimmy (ss) 88
O'Neill, Arthur A. (Norfolk owner/bicyclist) 32–35, 37–40, 42–44, 48
O'Neill-Barry Company (Sporting goods store) 106
Onslow, Jack (mgr/c) 188, 189, 194
Opdyke (p) 17, 19
O'Rourke (3b) 18
Orr, Jack (p) 140, 142
Orth, Al (p/ump) 33, 90, 110, 180
Otey, "Steamboat" Bill ("Big Bill") (p) 72, 74, 75, 79–82, 83, 84, 86, 91–94, 96–98; death from syphilis 98
Overton, Jesse (Portsmouth businessman) 169, 170
Owens, H.F. "Tiney" (p) 183, 184
Oxford NC club 9

Page, Vance (p) 196, 198
Paige, George (p) 82, 84
Park View Church (Portsmouth) 212
Parrett, Eli ("Olin," "Pol") 183, 184, 187, 189, 190, 195, 197, 201, 202
Parrish, George R (Portsmouth club president) 100
Paterson Silk Weavers 24, 46, 47, 49, 51–53, 55, 56, 73, 77
Pautot, Ed (of) 65
Pawtucket (club) 59, 65
Payne, Fred (mgr) 134, 138
Peanut Park (Suffolk) 111, 156
Pearson, Archie (p) 140
Pender, Robert ("Dad," "Doc," "Old Sea Dog") (mgr/if) 36, 78–82, 86, 88–90, 92, 104
The Peninsula 5, 21, 43, 59, 62, 77, 91, 132
Pennsylvania League (State) 21, 141, 207, 216
People's Tabernacle (Norfolk) 22
Perry, Warren (c) 186
Perryman, Key "Parson" (p) 120, 183, 191

Personal Liberty Club (anti-prohibition) 149
Petersburg, Virginia 6, 20, 28, 38, 97, 132, 133
Petersburg clubs (Virginia L) 10, 17, 20–29, 31, 32, 34, 36, 38–40, 42, 47, 52, 54, 58, 61, 62, 64, 78, 95, 98, 99, 102, 103, 105–107, 111–114, 117, 121–123, 126–130, 134, 138, 139, 142, 144–145, 150, 152, 156, 157, 160, 162, 172, 176–184, 186, 187, 189–190, 196–200, 202, 204–207, 209, 215, 216, 217
Peterson, Alexander ("Iron Man," "Old Pete," "Smiling Pete") (p) 160, 161, 163, 165, 166, 168, 170, 172–175, 177, 178, 181, 194–207, 217
Petty, Charles "Big" (p) 26–29
Pfanmiller, George (p) 37, 38, 40, 44, 45, 46, 48, 50, 51, 53–57, 73
Phelan, Tommy (ump) 55
Phiffer, Clarence (p) 164
Philadelphia (National L) 13, 15
Philadelphia Athletics (American L) 106, 113, 118, 130, 140, 149, 151, 160, 165, 168, 191, 192
Philadelphia Giants (black club) 71
Philadelphia clubs (Atlantic L) 51, 52
Philadelphia Phillies (National L) 13, 15, 30, 45, 49, 51, 111, 112, 124, 154, 175–177, 201
Philadelphia Whartons 11
Phoebus Virginia (team) 18, 19, 119
Pickwick Club (pool/wrestling) 105, 106
Piedmont League 2, 170, 190, 202, 216, 218, 220, 222
Pierce, George (2b) 15
Pierce, Joseph "Cy" (p) 105
Pike, Bill (3b) 176, 177, 182, 184, 187
Pittsburgh Pirates (National L) 36, 52 91, 111, 117, 124, 129, 132, 143, **155**, 157–159, 185, 197, 210
Players Protective Fraternity 141
poems (rhymes) 89, 133, 135
Poetz, Joe "Holy Cow" (p) 194–198, 201
Poole, James "Jimmie" (p) 102, 103, 109, 112, 128
Pooray, Eddie (p) 136, 137
Portland Maine Phenoms (New England L) 59
Portsmouth Athletic Base Ball Club Athletics Association 7, 10, 11, 12
Portsmouth Athletic Park 74, 80, 100, 125
Portsmouth Baseball and Athletic Corporation 111
Portsmouth Cardinals (amateur club) 9
Portsmouth club (Virginia L) 30–35, 37, 40, 42, 43, 48, 59–62, 65–66, 68, 72–75, 79–81, 87, 88, 90, 92–94, 96, 97, 101, 103, 108, 109, 111–114, 117–119, 121, 122–127, 130–136, 138, 140, 142, 149–151, 152, 154, 155, 156–160,

162–166, 169, 172–179, *180*, 183, 184, 186, 187, 189–195, 197–199, 201–208, 217
Portsmouth Exhibition Company 118
Portsmouth Field Sports Association 143
Portsmouth Gymnasium 12
Portsmouth High School 103, 134, 185
Portsmouth "Marines" (Tidewater L) 101–103, 107, 108
Portsmouth "Recruits" (Tidewater L) 101–103, 107, 108
Portsmouth Naval Hospital (team) 145
Portsmouth Stadium 205
Portsmouth Sunday baseball 207–215
Portsmouth War Camp Community Service 147
Post, Sam (p) 158
Potts, Sam (columnist) 155, 157–160, 163, 173, 219
Powell, Jim (1b/mgr) 14, 15, 16
Poyner, Bill (p) 198, 202
Pressley (Pressly), William Lowry "Buck" (1b/mgr/physician) 93, 118–122, 124, 126, 135–137, 144, 170
Price, Jessie (c) 9
Princess Anne Road (Norfolk) 7, 8, 14, 24, 52
Prinz Eitel Frederich (German cruiser) 125
Proctor, Noel "Red" (p) 192–196, 198, 200–202, 217
Prohibition (temperance) 21, 22, 45, 149, 123, 152, 211, 212
Providence Grays (National L) 11, 13, 14, 203
Pulsifer, Nathan (of) 59, 63, 65, 70, 71
Purcell, "Scrapper" (c) 31, 32
Purcell House (Norfolk hotel) 30

Quartermaster Terminal (team) 145
Quinn (of) 38
Quinn, George (p) 90, 197, 198, 201

race relations 6, 23, 33, 87, 104, 105, 109, 110, 115, 118, 131, 148, 193, 196
Radbourne, Hoss (Providence p) 14
railroads 3; expansion of 4; special rates 67
Raleigh NC Capitals (Piedmont L) 176, 177, 183, 184, 190, 191
Raleigh Senators (Red Birds) 68–70, 75
Raleigh Swiftfoots 9, 10, 12, 13
Ramos, Jose (lf) 202, 203
Ramp, "Monk" (3b) 38
Ransome, Will (ss) 24
Ray, Carl (p) 135, 140, 141, 164, 165, 172, 173
Raymond, Arthur "Bugs" (p) 96, 97

Reading (club) 173, 177
Reading clubs (Atlantic League) 45, 47, 49, 51, 53–57
Recession of 1920 (post–World War I) 153, 154
Red Circle Park (Norfolk) 143–146
Red Stockings (Norfolk black club) 19, 23, 71
Redding, Frank (ss/of) 38
Reitz, Al (p) 196
Revelle, Robert ("Smiling Dutch," "Sunny Jim") (p) 76, 80, 90, 109, 111, 180, 204
Reynolds, Tom "Rainbow" (ump) 121, 122
Rhodes, "Dusty" 160, 168, 183
Rhynders, William (Howard) (1b) 88, 91
Rice, John (3b) 201, 203
Rice, Sammy (p) 129
Richmond (club): merger with Manchester 20; thievery by treasurer 17; Tri-City League 20
Richmond clubs 8–12, 14–18, 22, 24–29, 31–36, 38–51, 53–57, 61, 62, 65, 67, 72, 74–83, 88, 90, 92, 93, 96, 97–99, 100, 105–107, 109, 111, 112, 115, 116, 118, 119, 121, 123, 124, 127, 128, 132, 137, 143–145, 148–152, 154, 156–158, 160, 162, 164, 170, 172, 173, 175, 177–179, 182, 185, 186–189, 191–194, 197, 198, 200, 201, 203–207, 210, 216–218
Richmond Dispatch 48
Richmond Grays (amateur) 132
Richmond Manhattans (black club) 23
Rickey, Branch 216
Riel, Frank J. (p) 196, 199–201
Rifle Range (team) 145
Riggs, Talbot ("Totie," "Professor") (of) 164, 173, 175, 181, 187, 189, 190
Riley, Leon (p) 206
"ring rule" (Norfolk political bosses) 21, 22
Rinn, Frank (mgr) 50, 56
Ritz, Joe (p) 190
Riverside (River View) Park Newport News 61, 67
Riverview Line (Newport News/Hampton) 87
Rixey, Eppa Jeptha (p) 124
Roanoke, Virginia 20, 43, 80, 190
Roanoke clubs (Virginia L) 18, 20, 22–25, 31–35, 38, 42, 44, 58, 72, 75, 76, 78–81, 86–88, 92–101, 104–108, 112, 116, 118–122, 125, 128, 136, 170
Roanoke Rapids NC (club) 137
Roanoke "Tigers" 18, 20, 22–25, 31–35, 38, 42, 44, 58, 72, 75, 76, 78–81, 86–88, 92–101, 104–108, 112, 116, 118–122, 125, 128, 136, 170
Robertson, Davis ("Demon Dave") (of/1b/mgr) 103, 145, 146, 159, 177, 178, 182, 184, 185, 186–191, 193–206, 216, 219, 220, 222

Robinson, Wilbert (Brooklyn Dodger mgr) 172
Rochester (team) 17, 33, 176, 184
Rocky Mount Bronchos (Virginia L) 179, 195, 196, 209, 218
Rocky Mount Down Homers 82, 122, 123, 125–131, 137–139, 142, 156, 160–162, 164, 169, 173–175, 177–179, 184, 186–189, 193
Rollings, Jim "Red" (ss) 196
Rollins, Jimmy (ss) 201
Rollins, Pat (c) 17, 37, 42, 75
Rooney, Frank (1b) 158, 159, 174
Roselands Hampton (team) 18
Rosenthal, Ed (of) 18, 19
Rossano, Joe (ump) 135
Roth, Bebe (1b) 172, 174
Routman, Abe (if) 170
Rowland, Charles (c) 202
Rugby Street Norfolk (paper street) 115
Ruhland, Gus (3b) 79, 80, *83*, 88, 125
Rusie, Amos (NY Giant) 31
Ruth, Babe 153, 172, 191
Ruth, Perry W. (Norfolk owner) 151, 163, 167–169
Ryan, "Phenom" (alias for Schaub, William) (p) 98, 99
Ryan, Ray (mgr) 117, 119, 120

St. Helena Saints (military club) 112, 116, 132, 142, 145, 146
St. Louis Cardinals (National L) 95, 139, 156, 202, 216
St. Martin, Vic (of) 131, 140
St. Paul's Catholic Church (Portsmouth) 66
St. Vincent's Hospital (Norfolk) 9, 24, 46, 52
salaries 13, 14, 16, 19, 20, 29, 32, 77, 96, 100–102, 132, 140, 141, 162, 163
Salomonsky, H. (reporter) 41
Samuels, Lewis (p) 150
Sankey, Ira (evangelist) 21
Saracino, Carl (of) 125
Sarah Leigh Hospital (Norfolk) 204
Saunders, Raleigh "Mullett" (p) 203
Sauter, Jack (3b) 196, 197, 201, 202, 207
Savage, William (p) 88, 91
Savannah (club) 112
"Sawbones" (Portsmouth Naval Hospital) 145
Sawyer, Bill (p) 200–202
Saxe, Charlie (p) 117
Schaub, William (alias Ryan) (p) 99
Schmidt, Bill (p) 157
Schmidt, Fred (p) 39, 41, 56
Schrader, Gus "Germany" (1b) 113, 114, 117, 122
Schwartz, Bill (mgr/if) 148, 149, 151, 152, 153, 154, 156, 157
Scott, F. Ezra (of) 183, 184
Scranton (Baltimore's minor league team) 38, 40
Seaboard RR Line 80, 125, 127

season tickets 14, 30, 74, 133, 134, 138, 159, 175, 208
Sechrist, Joe "Doc" (p) 40
Sedgwick, Ken (p) 177, 178
Seiglie, Armando (ss) 126–128
Seitz, Charlie "Dutch" (if/of) 74, 75, 79, 83, 88, 91, 92
Seltz, Charlie (black cheerleader) 87
Serpell, G. (Norfolk owner) 169
Sewanee Athletic Association (Portsmouth) Sewanees 205, 217
Sexton, Mike (National Commission negotiator) 162
Shaffer, Charles ("Big Chief," "Pop") (1b/mgr) 45, 47, 77, 79–81, 106, 108, 109, 111, 113–115, 145
Shaughnessy, Frank (Roanoke player/mgr) 92, 94, 105, 183, 210
Shaw, Johnny (if) 105
Shenn, "Big Jack" (p) 112, 117
shipyard leagues (New York City) 159
Shooting Park, Newark NJ 49
Shuman, R.E. (p) 76
Sicking, Ed (if) 136–138
Simmons, Al (Philadelphia Athletic) 191
Simmons, Frank (of) 157
Slagle, William (p) 70, 71
Slayback, Elton "Scotty" (if) 191, 192, 195, 201
Small (or Smalley), James "Waggy" (Norfolk cheerleader) 68, 73
Small, Sam (evangelist) 22, 24
Smith, Alfred (state senator) 212–214
Smith, Carr (of) 176
Smith, Ducky (1b) 196, 201
Smith, Herb (c) 83, 88
Smith, Jack (of) 204, 206
Smith, Jim (Jimmie, Jimmy) (ss) 59, 62, 63, 68
Smith, John "Phenomenal" 59, 60, 62, 63, 67, 68
Smith, Linwood T. Lin (p) 157, 170, 173
Smith, Mike (of) 204, 217, 222
Smith, William "Billy" 44–46, 50, 51, 52
Smith, Williamson (Portsmouth owner) 68
Snodgrass, Fred (NY Giant cf) 113
Snyder, Barney (c) 50, 52
Snyder, Charley (ump) 49
Soldiers Home (Hampton) 8, 9, 17, 18, 58, 62
Sommers, Camden "Doc" (owner/mgr) 20, 21, 23–32, 36, 54
Soo, Michael (p) 172–174
Souter, Jack (c) 196
South Atlantic League (Sally L) 75, 78, 82, 84, 108, 127, 163, 168 172, 176 190, 200, 207
South Side Park (Portsmouth) 101
Southampton County 148
Southeastern League, Virginia 43
Southern Association 158
Southern League 19, 24–26, 36, 40, 53, 70, 78, 108, 109, 119, 184

Southern Railway 147
Southland Hotel (Norfolk) 182, 219
Southside Park Corporation 101
Spaine, Thomas (reporter) 22, 24, 27, 36, 41, 44, 46, 50, 51
Spanish-American War 52–54
Spartanburg (club) 200
Spellman, Ed (c) 187, 190
Spencer, Bob (of) 170
spitball 76, 81, 94, 96, 121, 122; banned 153
"Sporting Fraternity" 4
Sporting Life 3, **83**, 86
Spratt, William A. (2b) 59, 65, 69
Spratt, William B. (if) 63, 70
Staley, Harry (p/ump) 52, 68, 69
Stanley, John Leonard ("Lou," "Buck") (p) 74, 75, 86 154–157, 159, 170, 173, 175, 183, 186, 203, 219, 222
Stanley, W.E. (Portsmouth owner) 127, 139
Stanton, Andy (ump) 80
Star Baseball Club of D.C. 12
Staub, Joe (of) 103, 106, 109
Staunton (club) 100, 141, 221
Staunton Mountaineers 18, 20–23, 25, 29
Staylor, Claude "Bubba" (if/Norfolk chief of police) 222
Steelman, Morris "Farmer" (c) 53, 55, 57
Steinbrenner, Eugene (if) 117, 118, 128, 130
Stengel, Casey 222
Stephenson, Reuben Carl (of) 39
Sterling, Kid (wrestler) 198
Stewart, B.C. "Red" (of) 124, 125, 128, 144
Stewart, J. (of) 138
Stewart, Mark "Colossus" (c) 116–118, 121, 122, 124, 128, 130
Stickradt (Foley), Roy (p) 164, 176
Stockdale, Otis (p) 40
Stonewalls (Richmond club) 9
Stratton, Edward (rf) 14
Street, Charles Evard "Gabby" (c) 94, **95**, 156, 157, 159
strikes by players 56, 112, 124, 137, 141, 152
Stuart, Chauncey (if) 48, 49
Suffolk (team) 39, 43, 47, 94, 95, 148, 218; to Petersburg 133
Suffolk clubs (Virginia L) 107, 108, 123, 124–130, 132, 136, 148–151, 154, 156, 158–162, 174
Suffolk "Nancies" (Tidewater L, 1911) 101–105
Sullivan, John L. (boxer/ump) 67, 223
Sullivan, Mike J. (3b) 63
Sullivan, Ted (promoter) 19, 20, 29, 30, 44, 152
Summa, Homer "Sat" (of) 156, 157
Sumter, South Carolina (club) 79
Sunday, Billy (player/evangelist) 152
Sunday games 51, 54, 72, 84–86, 192, 197, 205, 207–215, 219; Court of Law and Chancery 214;

demise of Virginia League 218; Idlewood (Wells) case 85; Law and Order League 85; Portsmouth Ministerial Association 209; State Court of Appeals 209, 212; Tars pre-season 183; Texas League 183; Tidewater Ministerial Union 84, 86; Virginia Code 207; Virginia courts approve 220; Virginia Supreme Court *T.A. Crook et al. versus the Commonwealth* 214
Swan, Andy (mgr/of) 14, 15
Swanson, Claude (governor) 73
Syracuse (team) 172, 173, 183, 197, 211

Taft, William Howard (president) 86, 111
Tampa (club) 183
Tannehill, Jesse (p) 36, 40, 118
Tanner, Jack D. (Norfolk reporter) 31
Tarboro, North Carolina (club) 70, 71, 74, 75, 163, 164, 174
Tarboro "Tar Babies" 162
Tate, Edward C. "Pop" (c/1b/mgr) 9, 10, 11, 17, 29, 31–36, 47, 131
Tee (c) 131
Temple, W.T. "Jack" (p) 91–93
Tennant, Jimmy (of) 119
Terhune, George (p) 154–157, 159, 160
Texas League 47, 58, 59, 172, 183, 195
Thomas, B. Red (of) 203
Thomas, Herman (Norfolk cartoonist) 153, 154, 160–162, **165**, **166**
Thompson, Shirley 38
Thornton, Jack (2b) 24, 30
Thornton, John Patrick (cf) 35, 40, 65
Thrasher, Frank "Buck" (of) 119, 124, 125, 128, 130
Thurston, Earl (of) 40
Tice, George (of) 173, 175
Tidewater League (1911) 43, 72, 101, 102, 104–106, 109, 110, **185**, 220
Tierney, James (Norfolk news store owner) 18
Tierney, Mark (p) 61–66
Tinin, Stanley (3b) 141
Titman, Guy (of) 109
Toledo (team) 11–13, 116, 178, 204
Tolson, Charles (1b) 170
Toner, Tommy (3b) 88
Topeka (club) 184
Toronto (team) 159, 172, 191, 210
Tracy, James (reporter) 145
transportation costs 13, 82, 108, 114, 142, 159
Traynor, Harold "Pie" (ss) 155, 156–159, 177, 197, 210
Treakle, George "Beef" 142
Trenton, New Jersey (team) 15, 16, 21, 44, 102
Tri-City League, Virginia 20
Trinkle, E. Lee (governor) 209, 210
Tri-State League 79
trolley car lines 74, 87, 110, 132, 169

Trotman, Percy (Portsmouth owner) 208, 219
Trower (p) 18
Truby, Harry (2b/ ump) 25–27, 81
Trucker Park 187
Turk, Red (p) 177
Turner, Tommy (1b) 39
Twin City League 86, 112, 113

Ulrich, Dick "Bull Durham" (c) 118, 131
Underwood, Ben (p) 8–11
uniforms 14, 17, 22, 30, 32, 37, 45, 58, 68, 73, 79, 91, 109, 124, 138, 148, 172, 173
Union League (Unions) 11–13, 87; demise of 13
United States League 110
University of North Carolina 73, 106, 125, 198
University of Virginia 19, 91, 93, 94, 96, 99, 101, 106, 107, 118, 124, 217

Vail, Bobby (p) 93
Vance, Jim "Subway" (p) 97, 98, 105
Van Patten, Isaac T. (Portsmouth owner) 11–13, 41, 43, 100, 101, 127
vaudeville 112; skits at ball game 215
Verbout, John (p) 117
Vermilyea, John (3b) 160, 161, 164, 168, 170, 173–175
Vetter, Phil(c) 31, 131
Villa Heights (Norfolk) 169
Viox, Jimmy (mgr) 158, 161, 165, 172, 174, 177, 193, 208
Virginia and North Carolina Baseball Association 9
Virginia-Carolina League (1901) 141
Virginia League (State L) 1, 2, 3, 9, 44, 47, 54, 59, 65, 67–71, 77, 78, 82, 83, 87, 91, 94, 98, 99, 101; cartoons about 117; configuration 100–104, 106, 107, 110–112, 116, 118, 120, 121, 123, 125, 128, 130–132, 136, 137, 139, 141, 142, 144, 145, 147, 148, 152, 156, 161, 162, 169, 172, 176, 177, 180, 181–183, 185, 186, 190, 197, 202, 206, 207, 210, 213, 219, 220, 221, 222; demise 219; formation 17, 19; last voyage of the Tars in 215–218; new 20–43; reorganization 58; revival 72; rowdy behavior 37
Virginia–North Carolina Association (1884) 10
Virginia Polytechnic Institute 132, 185
Virginia Railway and Power Company 110, 115
Volz, Jackie "Jake" (p) 68, 91–93
Voss, John (p) 140, 146

Wagner, Bill (2b) 157
Wagner, Heinie (mgr/if) 155, 156
Waite, Richard (p) 38
Walker, Carl (p) 94, 96, 97
Walker, Elliott ("Pea Head," "P.D.," "Pee Wee") (ss) 184, 189, 190, 195, 196, 199, 200
Walker, Flavius B. (Norfolk owner) 122, 125, 127, 129, 130, 137, 143
Walker, Frank (of) 138–141, 187
Wall, Joe (mgr) 118, 156
Walsh, Martin (p) 81, 90, 94, 97–99, 102–106, 108, 109
Walters, "Rasty" (3b) 120, 128, 156, 222
Warden, Chuck (p) 203, 204, 206
Warhop, Jack (p) 102, 156–165, 166, 167, 168, 172
Warner (c) 11
Warner, Jake (ss) 88
Washington & Lee 110, 116, 193
Washing & Lee Generals 116
Washington DC YMCA (club) 21
Washington Monument 94, 95
Washington Nationals 13, 16, 17, 26, 30, 38, 44
Washington Senators (American L) 94, 98, 113, 129, 137, 139, 143, 174, 183, 184, 197, 201
Washington Street Park (Portsmouth) 74, 101. 110, 125, 131, 147, 205, 216
Wasserman, Sam (fan) 98
Watson, John L. (Portsmouth owner) 35, 37
Watt, Al (Allie) 158, 174, 175, 179, 181, 183, 188–190, 222
Watt, Frank (if) 183
Waverlys (D.C. club) 8, 14
Weaver, Ben (p) 203
Weaver, Buck (if) 68
Webb, Mark (p) 79
Weckbecker, Pete (c/mgr) 58
Weddige, Al (3b) 47, 50, 51–53, 55, 57, 70
Weeder, Lefty (p) 117
Weeks, George (p) 34, 37, 40, 68
Weidensaul, Yenter (cf) 65
Weihl, Jake (of) 47, 50, 51, 52
Welcher, Harry (mgr) 125, 132, 136
Weller, George (p) 112, 116, 124, 129
Wells, Jacob "Jake" (Richmond owner/mgr) 33, 35, 36, 40, 45, 48, 58, 72, 77, 87, 91, 93, 94, 97, 100, 101, 131, 158, 182
Wells, Otto (Norfolk owner) 36, 72, 77, 79, 82, 84–87, 89–91
Wells case (Sunday closing) 85
Welsh, Frank (of) 151, 152
Wentz, Jack (2b) 37–39, 44, **50**, 51–53, 57
West Virginia (team) 21, 99
Western Association 52
Westervelt, Fred (ump) 184, 188, 198
Wheeling, West Virginia (club) 117
Wheelock, Bobby (ss) 52, 53
Whitcraft, Roy (ss) 114, 149, 164, 176, 181
White, Ray (p) 222

White, Walter (ss) 202
Whitted, Hugh (of) 130, 136
Wiley, John "Telephone Pole" (1b) 75
Willcox, Edward R. (Teddy) (Norfolk owner) 169, 170, 182, 193
Willcox, Thomas (judge/Norfolk owner) 169, 182
Williams, Gus (Roanoke owner/Virginia L president) 97, 101, 104–108
Williamsport Pa (club) 217
Wilmington (NC) Giants (Virginia-North Carolina L) 15, 59, 69, 70, 79
Wilson, Ben (Richmond owner) 152, 158
Wilson, Lewis ("Babe," "Hack") (of) 177, 180, 181, 197
Wilson Bugs 156, 160–164, 169, 172, 174, 175, 178, 179, 186–189, 191–201, 203–206, 215, 218
Win Clark Chapter of the Hot Stove League of America 222
Winston-Salem Twins 117, 122, 135, 140
Witt, Samuel B., Jr. (judge/Virginia L president) 30
Womack, W. ("Sid," "Tex") (c) 176, 183, 184, 187, 191
women at games 6, 7, 10, 11, 15, 17, 21, 22, 30, 31, 68, 75, 87, 118, 177
Wood, Bob "Smokey Joe" (p) 134, 136, 140
Woods, Lewis, Sidna Allen "Outlaw" (p) 109, 111
World Series 11, 95, 106, 113, 124, 143, 145, 152, 153, 162, 168, 185, 220, 222
World War I 123–149
Wright, Earl H. (Portsmouth owner, politician/poet) 89, 135, 147, 163, 178, 212
Wright, George (mgr, black player) 19, 71
Wyatt, Ida (high school student) 134
Wynne, Billie (ss) 74, 79
Wynne, Willie (if) 32

Yale University 79, 91, 102, 116
Yeisley, Ken (p) 217
York (club) 183, 216
Yoter (Yoder), Elmer "Rabbit" (if) 159, 161, 164, 165, 168, 173
Young, Cy (p) 72
Young, Nick (National L president) 28, 34, 54
Young, W.A. (Norfolk mgr/owner/politician) 17, 18
Young Men's Christian Association 7, 80

Zellers, Rube (p) 145, 170, 173, 183, 186–190, 192
Zinn, George (p) 164

www.ingramcontent.com/pod-product-compliance
Lightning Source LLC
Chambersburg PA
CBHW081547300426
44116CB00015B/2790